Empire State Railway Museum's

Tourist Trains

38th Annual Guide to
Tourist Railroads and Museums

W9-CNM-043

KALMBACH
BOOKS

Front cover: Little River Railroad, White Pigeon, Michigan. Kevin Keefe photo.
Back cover: Durango & Silverton Narrow Gauge Railroad, Durango, Colorado. Mike
Danneman photo.

Cover Design: Lisa Zehner   ISSN: 0081-542X

To the Museums and Tourist Railroads

Listings: We would like to consider for inclusion every tourist railroad, trolley operation, railroad museum, live-steam railroad, and toy train exhibit in the United States
and Canada that is open to the public and has regular hours and about which reliable
information is available.

2004 Directory: To be published in February 2004. A packet that includes all pertinent
information needed for inclusion in *Tourist Trains 2004* will be mailed to all organizations listed in this book. New listings are welcomed. For information, please write to:

>   Editor—Tourist Trains 2004
>   Books Division
>   Kalmbach Publishing Co.
>   P.O. Box 1612
>   Waukesha, WI 53187–1612

On the web go to www.kalmbach.com/books/touristguide.html

Photos: We're always looking for cover images; if you have any high-quality images
that might be available for a cover, please send it to the above address.

Advertising: Advertising space for *Tourist Trains 2004* must be reserved by
November 15, 2003. Please contact Mike Yuhas at 1-888-558-1544, extension 625, or
Lori Schneider at 1-888-558-1544, extension 654.

Publisher's Cataloging in Publication

Empire State Railway Museum's Tourist Trains 2003 : 38th
   annual guide to tourist railroads and museums.
      p. cm
      Includes index.
      ISBN: 0-89024-429-4

   1. Railroad museums—United States—
Directories. 2. Railroad museums—Canada—
Directories. I. Empire State Railway Museum.
II. Title: Tourist Trains 2003.

TF6.U5S75 2003   385'.22'02573

Contents

Advertising Contents

Electric City Trolley Station & Museum

Track the history of the American trolley system at the Electric City Trolley Station & Museum. An impressive collection of antique trolley cars, interactive exhibits, photographs and artifacts preserve the history of the electric trolley system. Hop aboard a vintage trolley for a short ride to the Historic Scranton Iron Furnaces & through the Laurel Line Tunnel.

Lackawanna Ave. downtown
Scranton on the grounds of
Steamtown National Historic Site.
570-963-6590

ALL ABOARD THE HAWAIIAN RAILWAY!

Come ride with us along an historic stretch of track west of old Ewa and listen to stories about the history of railroading in Hawaii.

Rides are Sunday at 1:00 and 3:00   Fares are $8.00 for adults, $5.00 for children ages 2-12, $5.00 for seniors ages 62 and up. Children under 2 ride free. Charters Available

Mention this ad when purchasing tickets and get a free gift.

For more information call (808) 681-5461 or visit our website at www.hawaiianrailway.com

A-4

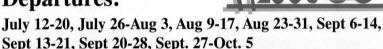
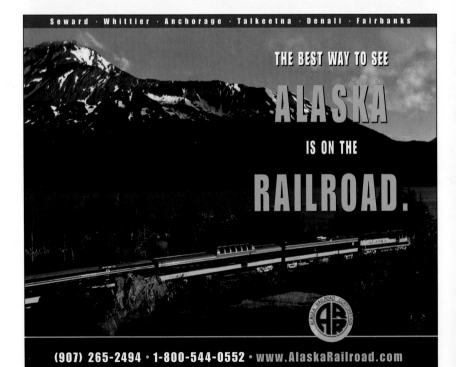

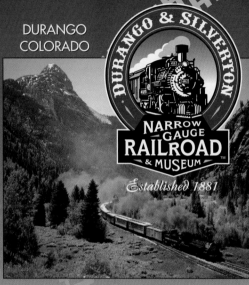

McCLOUD RAILWAY OPEN-AIR TRAIN RIDES

Bring the whole family for a delightful, inexpensive, excursion trip featuring either diesel locomotives or historic steam locomotive No.25. Try our new "double deck" car for incomparable views of unspoiled northern California.

———

Hear the "clickety clack" as your trains winds its way around the base of Mt. Shasta. Open Air Excursion Trains depart McCloud, California, May through September 30th, with trips Thursday through Saturday in mid-summer. Call for schedule details.

ALL ABOARD! SHASTA SUNSET DINNER TRAIN

A nostalgic train ride through spectacular scenery in the shadow of Mt. Shasta featuring elegant four-course dining aboard restored vintage rail cars. A memorable evening riding the rails into yesterday!

———

Experience true luxury in our 1916-vintage rail cars amid surroundings of mahogany and brass. Shasta Sunset Dinner Train departs McCloud, California, weekends year round, Thursday through Saturday June through September. Reservations are required.

To reach McCloud from I-5, take the McCloud/Reno exit and travel ten miles east turning left on Columbero Drive. Follow Columbero into town turning right after the railroad tracks.

———

For schedules & reservations call the

Shasta Sunset Excursions
P.O.Box 1199 McCloud, CA 96057
(800) 733-2141 (530) 964-2142
www.shastasunset.com

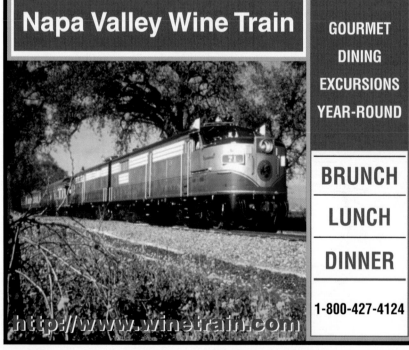
A-13

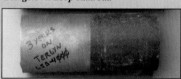

2nd Annual Model Railroad Festival
Saturday July 5, 2003
9am-5pm

A celebration of model railroading featuring music, food, and train vendors. Model railroad layouts on display throughout the town. Children can ride on Little Sykes Railway, a 1949 12-gauge model train. Free parking at the Warfield Complex and shuttle service.

Mark your calendar - 3rd Annual Railroad Festival, June 5, 2004

On Main Street in Historic Sykesville • Exit 80 off I-70
410.795.8959   Sykesville.net

COME RIDE THE TRAIN
ALL ABOARD!

Climb aboard the new Southwest Georgia Excursion Train to discover the real Georgia! Riding in air-conditioned, 1949 vintage cars, you'll enjoy a mix of romantic yesteryear with the excitement of today's South. While the SAM Shortline travels past pecan groves and scenic country farms, it stops in four towns filled with fun attractions, restaurants and shopping. You can step off the train at any of these depots, catching it back on the return trip. Or better yet, spend the night in a charming hotel to resume your excursion the next day.

SAM SHORTLINE TOWNS
Cordele • Leslie • Americus • Plains

1-800-864-7275
or 770-389-7275

See website for Schedule.
www.SamShortline.com

Leadership in Creative Railroading

TRAIN, Inc., the Tourist Railway Association, Inc. was formed in 1972 to foster the development and operation of tourist railways and museums.   Membership is open to all railway museums, tourist railroads, excursion operators, private car owners, railroad publishers, industry suppliers and other interested persons and organizations. **TRAIN, Inc.** is the only trade association created to represent the broad spectrum of what is called "creative railroading".

Our members included in the Guide to Tourist Railroads and Museums may be identified by the **TRAIN** logo on their listing page. Members receive our newsletter, **TrainLine**, which contains articles on creative railroading and railroad preservation, as well as information on upcoming special events. In addition, members receive time sensitive bulletins as needed. Our annual convention provides educational seminars, speakers of national import, updates on federal regulations along with product and supplier displays.

TRAIN, Inc. is a leader on issues such as insurance, safety and legislation affecting the operation and display of vintage and historic railway equipment. **TRAIN, Inc.** serves as a voice for the total industry and keeps members informed on laws , regulations and actions that affect us all.

For More Information Contact:

Tourist Railway Association, Inc.

P.O. Box 1245
Chama, NM 87520-1245
1-800-67TRAIN
(505) 756-1240
FAX (505) 756-1238
Email address: train@cvn.com
Visit our website at *http://www.traininc.org*

19th Year 2003 RAILROAD TOURS

**SACRAMENTO RAIL & RIVERBOAT CRUISE - April 19 * May 3 * June 7. Train and steamboat excursion in the Sacramento area. Great for the family.

**McCLOUD STEAM SPECTACULAR - May 10-11. Two day steam excursion on the McCloud Railroad deep into the backwoods of Northern California.

**GREAT CANADIAN RAIL ADVENTURE - May 17-25. By train through British Columbia and Alberta. Includes the Canadian Rockies.

**ALASKAN RAILFAN ADVENTURE - June 4-14. A railfans adventure riding and photographing the White Pass & Yukon and Alaska Railroads. This is a detailed photo study of both railroads including steam charters.

**WHITE PASS STEAM SPECTACULAR - June 5-8. Four charter trains on the remote White Pass & Yukon Railroad, with steam and diesel.

**ROCKY MOUNTAIN TRAIN SPLENDORS - July 12-27. Spectacular train journeys and sightseeing in Colorado, Utah, Wyoming, Montana, Idaho, Washington and Oregon.

**STEAM IN THE ANDES - July 20-27. Railfans photo study of the famous Guayaquil & Quito Railroad in Ecuador with steam, diesel and railcars.

**GREAT BRAZILIAN RAILFAN ADVENTURE - Aug 16- Sept 3. Railfans photo study of 19 railroads using steam-diesel-electric-railcars-street cars and interurbans. Tour includes 16 charters.

**NEW ENGLAND FALL COLORS RAIL ADVENTURE - Oct 5-11. Grand tour during the fall colors in Vermont, New Hampshire, New York, Massachusetts and Connecticut.

**RIO GRANDE PHOTO FREIGHT - Oct 7-8. Charter railfans photo freight with steam over Cumbres Pass in New Mexico & Colorado.

**DURANGO PHOTO FREIGHT - Oct 9. Charter railfans photo freight with steam on the Durango & Silverton Railroad.

**FALL COLORS EXPRESS - Oct 11-14. Private rail car charter LA-Oakland-Reno and return using the Silver Lariat, Plaza Santa Fe and Tamalpais.

**CHINA STEAM SPECTACULAR - Oct 18- Nov 2. Railfans photo study of the last of the World's big mainline steam.

**RUSSIAN TRAIN TOURS - Several departures in 2003 with steam and diesel.

Please call for our 2003 all-color brochure
1-800-359-4870 USA   1-800-752-1836 Canada   (530) 836-1745   Fax (530) 836-1748

TRAINS UNLIMITED, TOURS

email: tut@PSLN.com
P.O. Box 1997 • Portola, California 96122 USA
Visit our website
http://www.trainsunlimitedtours.com

Empire State Railway Museum's

Tourist Trains

2003

38ᵗʰ Annual Guide to Tourist Railroads and Museums

Symbols

 Handicapped accessible

 Parking

 Bus/RV parking

 Gift, book, or museum shop

 Refreshments

 Restaurant

 Dinner train/dining car

 Guided tours

 Picnic area

 Excursions

Arts and crafts

 National Register of Historic Places

 Brochure available; send SASE

M Memberships available

 arm Association of Railway Museums, member

TRAIN Tourist Railway Association, Inc., member

 Amtrak service to nearby city

VIA VIA service to nearby city

 Credit cards accepted

For our foreign visitors: This year Memorial Day is Monday, May 26; Labor Day is Monday, September 1; and Thanksgiving is Thursday, November 27.

To the Reader

In 1966, railroad enthusiasts Marvin Cohen and Steve Bogen produced, and the Empire State Railway Museum published, the first *Steam Passenger Service Directory* (now titled *Tourist Trains: Empire State Railway Museum's Annual Guide to Tourist Railroads and Museums*). At that time, tourist railroading was in its infancy, and the book featured 62 tourist railroads and steam excursion operations. Four years later, in 1970, the Museum and *Directory* sponsored a tourist railroad conference, and the Tourist Railroad Association, Inc. (TRAIN), was founded.

The tourist railroad industry has flourished over the past three decades, with local groups of rail enthusiasts and preservationists banding together to return to service locomotives and rolling stock that have sat dormant and neglected for too many years. The mission of these organizations includes educating and entertaining the general public. That's where the Empire State Railway Museum and this book fit in. Through the foresight and perseverance of the Museum, this book continues to be published so that rail enthusiasts, as well as those who are only casually interested in trains, can become aware of the hundreds of wonderful tourist railroads and railroad attractions available for them to enjoy and learn from. Kalmbach Publishing Co. is pleased and proud to be able to produce this book on behalf of the Empire State Railway Museum.

Guest Coupons: The reduced-rate coupons provided by many operations in this edition of *Tourist Trains* will be honored by the museums. Be sure to present them when purchasing tickets.

Brochures: Many operations offer brochures and/or timetables. Please see the symbol sections in the listings for those operations that provide brochures.

Every effort has been made to ensure the accuracy of the contents. However, we depend on the information supplied by each operation. Internet addresses, business office locations, and phone and Fax numbers are subject to change. We cannot assume responsibility for errors, omissions, or fare and schedule changes. Be sure to write or phone ahead to confirm hours and prices.

Finally, if you don't see a full listing in the book for a railroad or museum you know exists, check the abbreviated listings at the back of this book. These are organizations that did not respond to our mailings, but which we felt would be of interest to our customers. Again, in all cases, be sure to write or phone ahead.

If you know of an operation that is not included in the book, please send information to the publisher. See page ii.

Alabama, Calera

**HEART OF DIXIE
RAILROAD MUSEUM**
*Train rides, museum
Standard and 24" gauge*

NEIL SMART, JR.

Description: Twelve-acre museum site displays two 100-plus-year-old depots, large shop, yard, and many pieces of equipment and memorabilia. Rides include 8-mile round trip on standard gauge 1910-54 vintage train and shorter trip on narrow gauge former Birmingham Zoo steam train.

Schedule: Museum–Monday through Saturday, 10 a.m. to 4 p.m., year-round, except major holidays. Train rides–Saturdays, April 5 to December 20, and on specially requested dates.

Admission/Fare: Museum–admission free. Donations appreciated. Train rides–adults, $8; children, $6. $3 for narrow gauge.

Locomotives/Rolling Stock: Two 1951 EMD SW-8 locomotives; one 1953 Fairbanks-Morse H12-44 locomotive; one Whitcomb 25-tonner; and four steamers from 0-4-0 to 2-8-0; 65 freight, passenger, and special cars.

Special Events: Cottontail Express, April 19. Museum's 40th Anniversary, May 17. Pumpkin Patch Special, October weekends. Polar Express, November 28, December 6, 7, 13, 14, 20 nights. Santa Claus Express, November 29, December 6, 7, 13, 14, 20 days.

Nearby Attractions: American Village, Oak Mountain State Park; Birmingham, 30 miles, has numerous museums, parks, etc.

Directions: Take exit 228 off I-65, go ⅘ mile on State Route 25 south, turn left on Ninth St., drive to the museum.

Radio frequency: 160.920, 154.54

Site Address: 1919 Ninth St., Calera, AL
Mailing Address: PO Box 727, Calera, AL 35040
Telephone: (205) 668-3435 and (800) 943-4490
Fax: (205) 668-9900
E-mail: csrr_gm@bellsouth.net
Website: www.heartofdixierrmuseum.org

**FOLEY RAILWAY MUSEUM
CITY OF FOLEY MUSEUM
ARCHIVES**
Museum

Description: Museum houses L&N Railroad artifacts, as well as artifacts representing the history of Foley and Baldwin County.

Schedule: Monday through Friday, 10 a.m. to 4 p.m.

Admission/Fare: Free.

Locomotives/Rolling Stock: 1941 L&N diesel switch engine; two boxcars; one caboose.

Special Events: Art in the Park, Mother's Day weekend; 16th Annual Mullet Festival, September 2; 31st Annual Shrimp Festival, October 10-13; German Sausage Festival, October 26.

Nearby Attractions: Foley is 10 miles from the white sandy beaches on the Gulf of Mexico; the Riviera Centre is one of the largest outlet malls in the Southeast; all types of of restaurants and several antique stores are also nearby.

Directions: From I-10, take the Gulf Shores Parkway (Highway 59) south to Foley. The Depot Museum is one block east of the intersection of Highway 59 and Highway 98.

Site Address: 125 E. Laurel Avenue, Foley, AL
Mailing Address: 125 E. Laurel Avenue, Foley, AL 36535
Telephone: (251) 943-1818
Fax: (251) 971-1819
E-mail: foleymuseum@gulftel.com

Description: The depot is one of the nation's oldest remaining railroad structures. A tour includes a one-hour guided experience of the three-story building, including a glimpse into the depot's Civil War era.

Schedule: Tuesday through Saturday, 9 a.m. to 5 p.m. Closed Thanksgiving, Christmas, and New Year's Day. Call ahead for summer hours.

Admission/Fare: Depot–adults, $7; seniors, $6; children, 4-17, $6. Age 3 and under free.

Nearby Attractions: The depot is part of the EarlyWorks History Complex, which includes the Alabama Constitution Village and a large hands-on history museum.

Directions: I-565 east, exit 19-C. The depot is directly on your right.

Site Address: 320 Church St., Huntsville, AL
Mailing Address: 404 Madison St., Huntsville, AL 35801
Telephone: (256) 564-8100 and (800) 678-1819
Fax: (256) 564-8151
Website: www.earlyworks.com

Alabama, Huntsville

NORTH ALABAMA
RAILROAD MUSEUM, INC.
Train ride, museum, display
Standard gauge

HUGH DUDLEY

Description: The Chase Depot offers exhibits, a display passenger train, and a self-guided walking tour. A guided tour, "All Aboard Railroading," is available. Ride on a 10-mile round-trip excursion on the museum's Mercury and Chase Railroad.

Schedule: Museum–April through October: Wednesdays and Saturdays. Train–usually third Saturday of the month. Contact us for information.

Admission/Fare: Museum, parking, and self-guided walking tour–free. Guided tour–adults, $4; children 6-11, $2. Train–adults, $10; children under 12, $5.

Locomotives/Rolling Stock: Excursion train–Alco S-2 no. 484; coach no. 6082; baggage no. 139; and dining car no. 1000. Display train–boxcab no. 11; refrigerator car; RPO car; coach; 6-10 Pullman sleeper; more.

Special Events: North Alabama Railroad History Festival; Goblin Train; Santa Train; call for dates.

Nearby Attractions: Alabama Space and Rocket Center (home of Space Camp), Huntsville Depot Museum, Museum of Art, Botanical Garden, Dogwood Manor Bed & Breakfast.

Directions: From east end of I-565 in Huntsville, continue east on U.S. 72 for 2 miles, take left on Moores Mill Rd. for 1 mile, cross second railroad track, left on Chase Rd. for ½ mile to museum on left.

     TRAIN M

Radio frequency: 452.325, 457.325

Site Address: 694 Chase Rd., Huntsville, AL
Mailing Address: PO Box 4163, Huntsville, AL 35815-4163
Telephone: (256) 851-6276 (voice Wed. and Sat., 8 to 2, otherwise recording)
E-mail: fredrrman@aol.com
Website: www.suncompsvc.com/narm/

5

WHITE PASS & YUKON ROUTE
Train ride
36" gauge

DEDMAN'S PHOTO

Description: Built in 1898, the White Pass Railroad is a spectacular mountain railroad. The WP&YR offers round-trip excursions from Skagway to the White Pass Summit, Lake Bennett, and through rail/bus connections to Whitehorse, Yukon.

Schedule: May through September: daily. Summit Excursion–depart Skagway 8:30 a.m. and 1 p.m., 3-hour round trip, and Lake Bennett Adventure 8 a.m. (8-hour round trip). Through service northbound–depart Skagway 8 a.m. (train); arr. Fraser, B.C., 10 a.m. (change to bus); arr. Whitehorse, Yukon, 1 p.m. Through service southbound–depart Whitehorse, Yukon, 1:30 p.m. (bus); arr. Fraser, B.C., 2:30 p.m. (change to train); arr. Skagway, Alaska, 4:30 p.m. Steam train–June through August: every other Saturday, departs at 8 a.m.

Admission/Fare: Summit Excursion–adults, $82; children, $41. Through service–adults, $95; children, $47.50. Bennett steam train–adults, $156; children, $78. Bennett diesel train–adults, $128; children, $64. Reservations recommended.

Locomotives/Rolling Stock: 1947 Baldwin no. 73 2-8-2; 8 101 Alco diesels; 11 GE diesels; 63 passenger cars; 1 open observation car; 1898 rotary snowplow no. 1.

Nearby Attractions: Klondike Gold Rush National Historical Park.

Radio frequency: 160.325

Site Address: Second and Spring Streets, Skagway, AK
Mailing Address: PO Box 435, Skagway, AK 99840
Telephone: (907) 983-2217 and (800) 343-7373
Fax: (907) 983-2734
E-mail: info@whitepass.net
Website: www.whitepassrailroad.com

ARIZONA RAILWAY MUSEUM
Museum,
Standard gauge

Schedule: Labor Day to Memorial Day: Saturday and Sunday, 12 to 4 p.m. Tours can be arranged.

Admission/Fare: Donations.

Locomotives/Rolling Stock: Magma no. 10 Baldwin DRS-6-1500; Southern Pacific 2562 (ARM no. 1) 30-ton Plymouth; SP 7130 and 7131 derrick and toolcar; "Imperial Manor" sleeper, Santa Fe 2870; coach "Janemarie" Rock Island private car; SP 5984 horse car; Southern Railway office car "Desert Valley"; 14 other cars of various models.

Special Events: Cotton Festival and Ostrich Festival.

Nearby Attractions: San Marcos Hotel, America West Arena, Bank One Ballpark, Scottsdale Railroad Park, Casa Grande ruins.

Directions: U.S. 60 south on Arizona Ave., U.S. 10 east on Chandler Blvd. approximately 8 miles.

    M arm

Site Address: 399 N. Delaware Ave., Chandler, AZ
Mailing Address: PO Box 842, Chandler, AZ 85244
Telephone: (480) 821-1108

Arizona, Clarkdale

VERDE CANYON RAILROAD
Train ride, museum
Standard gauge

TOM JOHNSON

Description: Arizona's longest running nature show. The four-hour scenic ride includes bald and golden eagles, views of Sinagua Indian ruins, waterfowl, wildlife, a 680-foot tunnel, and the upper Verde River.

Schedule: Year-round, schedule varies. Most trains depart at 1 p.m. and return at 5 p.m. During fall and spring there are morning and afternoon trains on Thursday and Sunday. May through September a starlight ride departs at 5:30 p.m., returning at 9:30 p.m.

Admission/Fare: Adults, $39.95; seniors (65+), children (12 and under), $24.95. All first-class, $59.95.

Locomotives/Rolling Stock: EMD FP7 units no. 1510 and 1512, built 1953.

Special Events: Eagle Watch in the canyon, December to March; Sweetheart Trains, February 14-17; Spring in Bloom, March and April; Easter Bunny train, Easter weekend; Throw Mama on the Train, Mother's Day; Throw Papa on the Train, Father's Day; Fire Crack Express, Fourth of July; Fall Colors, September and October; Haunted Halloween Express, October 31; Santa Claus Express, December 26-30.

Directions: From I-17 take Highway 260 north to Cottonwood. Turn left onto Historic Highway 89A and proceed through Cottonwood to Clarkdale depot.

*Coupon available, see coupon section.

Site Address: 300 N. Broadway, Clarkdale, AZ
Mailing Address: 300 N. Broadway, Clarkdale, AZ 86324-2602
Telephone: (928) 639-0010 and (800) 293-7245 (reservations)
Fax: (928) 639-1653
E-mail: info@verdecanyonrr.com
Website: www.verdecanyonrr.com

8

Description: The Arizona Train Depot is a model railroad retail store.

Schedule: Year-round. Mondays, Tuesdays, Thursdays, Fridays, and Saturdays, 9 a.m. to 6 p.m.; Wednesdays, 9 a.m. to 9 p.m.; closed Sundays.

Admission/Fare: None.

Locomotives/Rolling Stock: N, HO, O, and G models only.

Special Events: Summer sale each August.

Directions: Highway 202 to McKellips exit, east about 2 miles to Home, southwest corner of McKellips and Home.

Site Address: 755 E. McKellips Rd. (southwest corner), Mesa, AZ
Mailing Address: 755 E. McKellips Rd., Mesa, AZ 85203
Telephone: (480) 833-9486 and (877) 777-1444
Fax: (480) 834-4644

Arizona, Scottsdale

MCCORMICK-STILLMAN RAILROAD PARK
Train ride, museum,
15" gauge

Description: A 30-acre theme park offering train rides, carousel rides, railroad museum, retail shops, picnic area, two playgrounds, snack stop, Hartley's General Store, and model railroad displays.

Schedule: Year-round. Seven days a week, 10 a.m. to sunset. Call for summer hours.

Admission/Fare: Train or carousel ride–$1 per person for anyone 3 or older. Museum–$1 for anyone 13 and older.

Locomotives/Rolling Stock: 5-inch scale locomotives. Steam–2-8-2, 4-6-0, 2-6-2. Diesel–GP7, SW1; 20 various cars.

Special Events: Railfair, October 14-15. Holiday Lights, December 15-30 (no December 24, 25, 31). Exclusively Little, March 4. Free summer concerts, May 14 through July 16.

Nearby Attractions: Shopping, resorts, restaurants, casino.

Directions: Southeast corner of Scottsdale Rd. and Indian Bend Rd.

Site Address: 7301 E. Indian Bend Rd., Scottsdale, AZ
Mailing Address: 7301 E. Indian Bend Rd., Scottsdale, AZ 85250
Telephone: (480) 312-2312
Fax: (480) 312-7001
Website: www.ci.scottsdale.az.us/mccormickpark/

Arizona, Scottsdale

SCOTTSDALE LIVE STEAMERS
Train ride, display
7½" gauge

MGM

Description: These are 7½" gauge trains–steam, diesel, and electric–on a ½ mile double-loop track within McCormick-Stillman Railroad Park.

Schedule: Every Sunday, noon to 5 p.m.

Admission/Fare: Donation only.

Locomotives/Rolling Stock: Nos. 3, 289, and 556, 2-6-0 Moguls; no. 585, 4-4-2 Atlantic; no. 1297, CN Ten-Wheeler; no. 31, M&I Pacific; various diesels and an electric speeder; an assortment of cars

Special Events: Spring Meet, third weekend in March; Fall Meet, second weekend in October; Holiday Lights, December 13 through January 4.

Nearby Attractions: McCormick-Stillman Railroad Park; several restaurants and hotels.

Directions: Southeast corner of Scottsdale Rd. and Indian Bend Rd. in Scottsdale.

      M

Site Address: 7339 E. Indian Bend Rd., Scottsdale, AZ
Mailing Address: 7339 E. Indian Bend Rd., Scottsdale, AZ 85250
Telephone: (480) 312-2312
E-mail: cabchatter@aol.com
Website: www.scottsdalelivesteamers.org

Description: Beginning at the south end of the Fourth Avenue Business District, the trolleys pass a remarkable variety of shops and restaurants. Turning onto University Boulevard, the cars pass beautifully restored homes, boutiques, and cafes, terminating near the Main Gate of the University of Arizona Campus.

Schedule: Fridays, 6 to 10 p.m.; Saturdays, noon to midnight; Sundays, noon to 6 p.m.

Admission/Fare: One way: adults, $1; children (6-12), $.50. All-day fare: adults, $2.50; children, $1.25. Special Sunday family fare (all riders, one way), $.25 per person. Group charters available.

Locomotives/Rolling Stock: Car 869 (Kyoto, Japan); car 1511 (Brussels, Belgium); others under restoration.

Directions: Take I-10 to Speedway exit, then east to Fourth Ave. and south to Eighth St. The carbarn is west of the corner of Fourth Ave. and Eighth St.

*Coupon available, see coupon section.

Site Address: West of the corner of Fourth Ave. and Eighth St., Tucson, AZ
Mailing Address: PO Box 1373, Tucson, AZ 85702
Telephone: (520) 792-1802
E-mail: OPT-Tucson@att.net
Website: www.oldpueblotrolley.org

Arizona, Williams

GRAND CANYON RAILWAY
Train ride
Standard gauge

AL RICHMOND

Description: Relive the excitement of the Old West aboard a historic train to America's national treasure, the Grand Canyon. After a 2¼-hour journey, passengers have 3¼ hours to explore the canyon before the train returns to Williams. Many passengers spend the night inside Grand Canyon National Park.

Schedule: Year-round. Daily except December 24-25. Williams departure–10 a.m., arrives Grand Canyon National Park 12:15 p.m., departs Grand Canyon 3:30 p.m., returning to Williams at 5:45 p.m.

Admission/Fare: Adults, $58; children age 16 and under, $25. Additional park entrance fee and tax. Upgrades available.

Locomotives/Rolling Stock: Steam: no. 18, 1910 Alco SC-4 2-8-0; no. 29, 1906 Alco SC-3 2-8-0; no. 4960, 1923 Baldwin O1A 2-8-2 Mikado type; diesel: no. 2134 GP7 Electro-Motive Division of GM Corporation, more. Many historic coach and other passenger cars.

Special Events: Memorial Day, steam engine returns to service.

Nearby Attractions: Fray Marcos Hotel and Max & Thelma's Restaurant. Historic downtown Williams and Route 66. Golf. Amtrak now stops in Williams for an all-rail trip to the Grand Canyon.

Directions: I-40 exit 163 (Williams), Grand Canyon Blvd. ½ mile south to Williams depot.

Site Address: 235 N. Grand Canyon Blvd., Williams, AZ
Mailing Address: 1201 W. Route 66, Ste. 200, Flagstaff, AZ 86601
Telephone: (800) THE TRAIN (843-8724)
Fax: (520) 773-1610
E-mail: info@thetrain.com
Website: www.thetrain.com

YUMA VALLEY RAILWAY
Train ride
Standard gauge

Description: A 34-mile, three- to four-hour round trip alongside the Colorado River. Enjoy the native wildlife and agriculture as you journey through the desert in 1922, 1923, or 1950 Pullman coaches pulled by either a 1952 Davenport-Beshler or 1957 GE diesel-electric.

Schedule: October: Saturday, 10 a.m.; November through March: Saturday and Sunday, 1 p.m.; April and May: Sunday, 1 p.m.; June through September: by appointment only.

Admission/Fare: Adults, $13; seniors (55+), $12; children (4-16), $7.

Locomotives/Rolling Stock: 1952 Davenport-Beshler (former U.S. Army); 1957 GE center-cab (former USMC); 1922 Pullman chair car (former Apache Railway); 1923 Pullman club car (former U.S. Army ambulance car); 1950 Pullman Chair Car (former Rhode Island Railroad). Also, in retirement, a 1941 Whitcomb diesel chain-drive 30-ton mining engine (former Apache Railway).

Special Events: Yuma Crossing Day, last weekend of February.

Nearby Attractions: See websites of Yuma Chamber of Commerce and local paper for up-to-date information.

Directions: I-8 to Fourth Ave. exit. Next to Yuma Crossing Park.

            M

Site Address: 100 N. Second Ave., Yuma, AZ
Mailing Address: PO Box 10305, Yuma, AZ 85366-8305
Telephone: (520) 782-1583

EUREKA SPRINGS & NORTH ARKANSAS RAILWAY
Train ride
Standard gauge

GEORGE A. FORERO, JR.

Description: Five-mile round trip excursion trains; also, diesel-pulled dining cars.

Schedule: Excursions, 10 a.m. to 4 p.m. Dining trains, 12 and 5 p.m. daily. Closed Sundays, except Memorial Day, July 4th, and Labor Day weekends.

Admission/Fare: Excursion–adults, $8; children ages 4-10, $4. Lunch–$14.95. Dinner–$23.95. All plus tax.

Locomotives/Rolling Stock: No. 1, 1906 Baldwin 2-6-0, former W.T. Carter; no. 201, 1906 Alco 2-6-0, former Moscow, Camden & San Augustine; no. 226, 1927 Baldwin 2-8-2, former Dierks For. & Coal; six commuter cars, former Rock Island; no. 4742, 1942 EMD SW1.

Nearby Attractions: Tourist town with many opportunities.

Directions: Eureka Springs is 45 miles northeast of Fayetteville, 9 miles south of the Missouri state line. Take Highway 23 north to the city limits.

Site Address: 127 Spring, Eureka Springs, AR
Mailing Address: PO Box 310, Eureka Springs, AR 72632
Telephone: (501) 253-9623
Fax: (501) 253-6406
E-mail: depot@esnarailway.com
Website: www.railroadtrain.com

Arkansas, Fort Smith

**FORT SMITH TROLLEY
MUSEUM**
Trolley ride, museum
Standard gauge

Description: Ride a restored Fort Smith Light & Traction Birney Safety Car over ½ mile of track in the downtown area.

Schedule: May through October: Mondays through Saturdays, 10 a.m. to 5 p.m.; Sundays, 1 to 5 p.m. November through April: Saturdays, 10 a.m. to 5 p.m.; Sundays, 1 to 5 p.m. Tours by appointment.

Admission/Fare: Trolley ride–adults, $1; children, $.50. Museum is free.

Locomotives/Rolling Stock: Fort Smith Light & Traction nos. 205, 224, 10; locomotives Frisco no. 4003 (steam); USAF no. 1246; August Railroad no. 6; ARR no. 7; diner MKT no. 100162; troop sleeper (power car) MKT no. 100186; three cabooses, more.

Nearby Attractions: Fort Smith Historic Site, Fort Smith Museum of History, Civic Center, Fort Smith National Cemetery.

Directions: From west Highway 64 to Garrison Ave., Garrison to S. Fourth St., south four blocks. From east I-54 to Rogers exit, west on Rogers to S. Fourth St., south three blocks to museum.

Site Address: 100 S. Fourth St., Fort Smith, AR
Mailing Address: 100 S. Fourth St., Fort Smith, AR 72901
Telephone: (479) 783-0205 and (479) 783-1237
Fax: (479) 782-9289
E-mail: info@fstm.org
Website: www.fstm.org

Description: Self-guided or interpretive tours upon request. Beautifully restored Victorian depot built in 1885/1886. Operated by the Frisco Railroad 1901 to 1968. Nine exhibits depicting 13 lifesize figures, dressed in historical costumes each with their own audio unit telling their story. Two videos are shown about history of the railroad in Mammoth Spring and life in Mammoth Spring in the 1900s.

Schedule: Year-round. Tuesdays through Sundays, 8 a.m. to 5 p.m. Closed Mondays except Monday holidays.

Admission/Fare: Adults, $2.50; children (6-12), $1.50; age 5 and under are free; special rates for groups of 15 or more with 2 weeks notice; season passes.

Locomotives/Rolling Stock: Wooden Frisco caboose SL-SF no. 1176.

Special Events: Mammoth Spring Park offers events and programs March through October and by request. Call for information.

Nearby Attractions: Mammoth Spring State Park, Mammoth Spring Federal Fish Hatchery, camping, canoeing, trout fishing on Spring River, museums, antique stores.

Directions: Located in Mammoth Spring State Park on Highway 63. Twenty-seven miles south of West Plains, Missouri, and 16 miles north of Hardy, Arkansas.

    Radio frequency: 160.35000

Site Address: U.S. Highway 63, Mammoth Spring, AR
Mailing Address: PO Box 36, Mammoth Spring, AR 72554
Telephone: (870) 625-7364
Fax: (870) 625-3255
E-mail: mammothsprg@arkansas.com
Website: www.arkansasstateparks.com

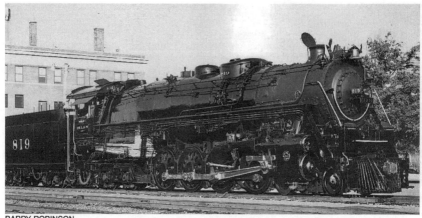
BARRY ROBINSON

Description: Located in the 1.5-acre former Cotton Belt erecting and machine shop. It contains the last two SSW steam locomotives and other railroad equipment and artifacts.

Schedule: Year-round. Mondays through Saturdays, 9 a.m. to 3 p.m. Closed during periods of extremely cold weather. Call before your visit during hottest summer weather.

Admission/Fare: Free; donations appreciated.

Locomotives/Rolling Stock: SSW 4-8-4 no. 819; SSW 2-6-0 no. 336; GP 30; SSW relief crane and outfit train; cabooses; passenger cars; snowplow.

Special Events: Annual Model Train Show and Sale, April. Mainline steam excursions with SSW 819.

Nearby Attractions: Jefferson County Museum in Old Union Station; Band Museum; Arkansas Entertainment Hall of Fame.

Directions: Highway 65, Port Rd. exit.

          M

Site Address: 1700 Port Rd., Pine Bluff, AR
Mailing Address: PO Box 2044, Pine Bluff, AR 71613
Telephone: (870) 535-8819

READER RAILROAD
Train ride
Standard gauge

CHARLES HOOT DESIGN

Description: Reader Railroad, the oldest all-steam standard gauge carrier to operate in the United States, offers a 7-mile, one-hour round trip. Open-platform wooden coaches are drawn by veteran logging engines, operations reminiscent of the railroad's earliest days.

Schedule: Write or call for information.

Admission/Fare: Adults, $6; children 4-11, $3.60; children under 4 ride free with parent. Group rates available. Fares may be slightly higher for special events.

Locomotives/Rolling Stock: No. 7, 1907 Baldwin 2-6-2, former Victoria, Fisher & Western; open-platform wooden coaches; open-air car; caboose.

Directions: Off State Route 24 between Camden and Prescott on Highway 368.

Site Address: Highway 368, off State Route 24 between Camden and Prescott
Mailing Address: PO Box 507, Hot Springs, AR 71902
Telephone: (501) 624-6881
Website: www.movietrains.com and www.ReaderRailroad.com

ARKANSAS & MISSOURI RAILROAD
Train ride
Standard gauge

Description: Enjoy a 134-mile excursion through the Boston Mountains with 2½-hour layover in historic Van Buren, or a 70-mile scenic journey from Van Buren to Winslow.

Schedule: Regular excursions run April through mid-November, with specials throughout the year. The eight-hour excursion departs Springdale at 8 a.m.; the three-hour excursion departs Van Buren at 10:30 a.m.

Admission/Fare: Springdale to Van Buren–April to September: Wednesdays, $33; Saturdays, $38. October: Wednesdays and Fridays, $43; Saturdays, $48. Van Buren to Winslow–April to September: Wednesdays, $20; Saturdays, $22. October: Wednesdays and Fridays, $25; Saturdays, $28.

Locomotives/Rolling Stock: Six T-6s, nos. 12, 14, 15, 17, 18; two RS-1s, nos. 20, 22; one RF-32, no. 42; 12 C-420s; one C-630, no. 4500; all Alco.

Special Events: Mardi Gras of the Ozarks, Saturday before Fat Tuesday; Spring Fest; Feather Fest; Bikes; Blues & Barbecue; annual Air Show; Rodeo of the Ozarks; War Eagle Arts & Craft Show; Trolley Museum Open House; West Fest; annual Christmas Train; Haunting History of the Ozarks; Tales of the Crypt.

Directions: On our website at arkansasmissouri-rr.com

*Coupon available, see coupon section.

Site Address: 306 E. Emma St., Springdale, AR
Mailing Address: 306 E. Emma St., Springdale, AR 72764
Telephone: (479) 751-8600 and (800) 687-8600
Fax: (479) 751-2225
E-mail: Brendab@arkansasmissour-rr.com
Website: www.arkansasmissouri-rr.com

California, Alpine

DESCANSO, ALPINE & PACIFIC RAILWAY

Train ride
24" gauge

MIRAN FLORES

Description: Passengers ride an industrial 2-foot-gauge railway to yesteryear among 100-year-old Engelman oaks in San Diego County's foothills. The train leaves Shade Depot and makes a ½-mile round trip, climbing the 6½-percent grade to High Pass/Lookout and crossing a spectacular 112-foot-long wooden trestle, giving passengers magnificent views of the surrounding area. At Shade Depot and Freight Shed is a display of railroad artifacts, including those of the DA&P. Mail service with mailer's postmark permit canceling is available.

Schedule: June through August: Sundays, 1 to 3 p.m., every half hour. September through May: intermittent Sunday operation. Rides and tours may be scheduled at other times with advance notice; please call to arrange.

Admission/Fare: Free.

Locomotives/Rolling Stock: No. 2, 1935 2½-ton Brookville, SN 2003, powered by original McCormick-Deering 22½-horsepower P-12 gasoline engine, former Carthage (Missouri) Crushed Limestone Company.

Directions: Thirty miles east of San Diego. I-8 exit Tavern Rd., travel south on Tavern 1.9 miles, turn right on South Grade Rd. and travel .6 mile, turn left onto Alpine Heights Rd.; the DA&P is the fifth driveway on the right.

Site Address: 1266 Alpine Heights Rd., Alpine, CA
Mailing Address: 1266 Alpine Heights Rd., Alpine, CA 91901
Telephone: (619) 445-4781
E-mail: dapry@juno.com

GOLDEN GATE LIVE STEAMERS, INC.
Layout
2½", 3¼", 4¾", 7½" gauges

JIM LOWE

Description: We are a club of some 200+ members. Our purpose is to build and operate live steam engines. We offer a ½-mile ride behind 7½" gauge steam engines.

Schedule: Sundays 12-3 p.m., weather permitting.

Admission/Fare: Donations appreciated.

Locomotives/Rolling Stock: Pacific; Atlantic SW-15; various rolling stock.

Special Events: Spring Meet, May 3 and 4; open house for public, June 1; Fall Meet, October 11 and 12.

Nearby Attractions: Redwood Valley Railway 15" gauge; Tilden Park merry-go-round; Little Farm Petting Zoo.

Directions: Fish Ranch Rd. exit of Highway 24, then follow the signs.

 M

Site Address: 2501 Grizzly Peak Blvd., Berkeley, CA
Mailing Address: 130 Pereira Ave., Tracy, CA 95376
Telephone: (209) 835-0263
Website: www.ggls.org

California, Berkeley

REDWOOD VALLEY RAILWAY CORP.
Train ride
15" gauge

Description: A 1¼-mile ride in the East Bay Hills through Redwood groves. Authentic scale narrow gauge steam equipment and trackwork.

Schedule: Year-round. Weekends and holidays, 11 a.m. to 6 p.m., weather permitting. Summer weekdays, mid-June through Labor Day, 12 to 5 p.m.

Admission/Fare: Single-ride ticket, $1.75; five-ride family ticket, $7; under age 2 ride free.

Locomotives/Rolling Stock: No. 4, 1875 2-4-2 "Laurel"; no. 5, 1890 4-4-0 "Fern"; no. 11, 4-6-0 "Sequoia"; no. 2, 0-4-0 gas/hydraulic switcher "Juniper" (current project, no. 7, 1930 2-6-2 "Oak"). Passenger gondolas with wood bodies, truss rods, archbar trucks; D&RGW-style caboose, 4-wheel work "Jimmies," and special purpose work cars.

Nearby Attractions: Tilden Regional Park with antique merry-go-round (with food service), 18-hole golf course, Botanical Gardens, pony rides, Little Farm, Environmental Education Center, hiking trails, picnic areas.

Directions: Tilden Regional Park in Berkeley Hills. Grizzly Peak Blvd. at Lomas Cantadas. Off Highway 24 at Fish Ranch Rd.

Site Address: Grizzly Peak Blvd. at Lomas Cantadas, Berkeley, CA
Mailing Address: 2950 Magnolia St., Berkeley, CA 94705
Telephone: (510) 548-6100
Fax: (510) 841-3609
Website: www.redwoodvalleyrailway.com

California, Bishop

**LAWS RAILROAD MUSEUM
AND HISTORICAL SITE**
Museum
Narrow gauge

BOB HAYDEN

Description: Original 1883 depot and agent's house, including over 20 other historic buildings with exhibits, and 11 acres of mining, farming, and railroad equipment. Located on the original location of the Carson-Colorado and later the Southern Pacific site.

Schedule: Year-round. Daily, 10 a.m. to 4 p.m. except Thanksgiving, Christmas, New Year's Day, and Easter.

Admission/Fare: Suggested $3 donation per person.

Locomotives/Rolling Stock: 1909 Baldwin 4-6-0, former Southern Pacific; Brill motor car, 1927; 12 boxcars; one A frame gondola; one stock car; one combination caboose; postal caboose.

Nearby Attractions: Fishing, skiing, hunting, camping.

Directions: From Bishop follow Highway 6 north 5 miles, then turn right on Silver Canyon Rd.

        M

Site Address: Silver Canyon Rd., Bishop, CA
Mailing Address: Box 363, Bishop, CA 93515
Telephone: (760) 873-5950
Website: www.thesierraweb.com/bishop/laws

California, Buena Park

KNOTT'S THEME PARK
Train ride
Narrow gauge

Description: The Ghost Town & Calico Railway (GT&C) is America's only narrow gauge passenger train operating on a daily, year-round basis. America's first theme park, Knott's is the place to go for family fun! Experience world-class thrills on Ghost Rider, Supreme Scream, and the all-new Xcelerator, a '50s-themed launch coaster that sends riders 0-80 in 2.3 seconds, 20 stories straight up and back down. For a different type of thrill, mosey on over to action-packed Old West Ghost Town or the 6-acre Camp Snoopy children's area, home of Charles Schultz's lovable Peanuts gang. There are six themed areas in all.

Schedule: Open daily except Christmas. Please call (714) 220-5200 or click on www.knotts.com for operating hours.

Admission/Fare: Adults, $44; seniors (60+) and kids 3-11, $32.

Locomotives/Rolling Stock: No. 41 "Red Cliff" Rio Grande Southern; no. 40 "Green River" Denver & Rio Grande and Denver & Rio Grande Western; railway coaches; special cars; Galloping Goose gasoline-driven railway car former Rio Grande Southern; more.

Nearby Attractions: Knott's is 10 minutes from Disneyland Park. The Radisson Resort Knott's Berry Farm is adjacent.

Directions: Please call (714) 220-5200 or click on www.knotts.com for directions.

Site Address: 8039 Beach Blvd., Buena Park, CA
Mailing Address: 8039 Beach Blvd., Buena Park, CA 90620
Telephone: (714) 220-5200
Fax: (714) 220-5124
Website: www.knotts.com

Description: Huge working model railroad passing by your table as you dine. This is a restaurant, deli, and train museum.

Schedule: Mondays through Saturdays, 11 a.m. to 8 p.m. Closed Sundays.

Admission/Fare: No charge for railroad, if dining. $8.50 per table, if not dining.

Nearby Attractions: Only 10 minutes from Roaring Camp Railroad. Just 5 minutes from the Santa Cruz Boardwalk. One mile off Highway 1.

Directions: Exit California Highway 1 on 41st Ave., west one mile, turn left into parking lot at Capitola Station.

Site Address: 1820-F 41st Ave., Capitola, CA
Mailing Address: 1820-F 41st Ave., Capitola, CA 95010
Telephone: (831) 475-0150
Fax: (831) 475-0188
Website: www.thetrainplace.com

**ORANGE COUNTY MODEL
ENGINEERS, INC.**
*Train ride
7.5" gauge*

Description: The Orange County Model Engineers have 18,000 feet of track and offer guided tours of the roundhouse and facilities. Our train rides are about 12 minutes long.

Schedule: Year-round, third Saturday and Sunday of each month, 10 a.m. to 3:30 p.m.

Admission/Fare: Free.

Locomotives/Rolling Stock: SP GS-1 4-8-4; Pennsy K-4 Pacific; 4-6-2 Streamlined Hiawatha Engine; 0-4-2T 3.75″ scale "Joshua"; and many more live steam and diesel locomotives.

Special Events: Annual fall meet, third weekend in September; up to 20 trains operating.

Nearby Attractions: Disneyland, Knott's Theme Park. Easy access to all of Southern California and its myriad of attractions.

Directions: Highway 405 (San Diego) south from Los Angeles. Exit Brookhurst St. south (about 3 miles) to Adams Ave. Left on Adams (east) to Placentia Ave. (about ½ mile) right (south) on Placentia ½ mile to Fairview Park. Station is on the east side of Placentia.

       M

Site Address: 2501 Placentia Ave., Costa Mesa, CA (Fairview Park)
Mailing Address: PO Box 3216, Costa Mesa, CA 92628
Telephone: (949) 54-TRAIN (548-7246)
Fax: (714) 838-8646
E-mail: verno-hb@ix.netcom.com

California, Dunsmuir

RAILROAD PARK RESORT
Dinner train, display
Standard gauge

C. MURPHY

Description: A 28-room caboose motel and restaurant, dinner house in refurbished train cars. RV park and campground on premises.

Schedule: Year-round.

Admission/Fare: Room–$70 to $75 per night. Dinner average $15 per person.

Locomotives/Rolling Stock: Willamette Shay; snowplow, flanger; cabooses; speeders.

Nearby Attractions: Golfing, skiing, camping, hiking, lakes, fishing, boating, and state park.

Directions: I-5, Railroad Park exit. Forty miles north of Redding, just south of city of Dunsmuir.

Site Address: 100 Railroad Park Rd., Dunsmuir, CA
Mailing Address: 100 Railroad Park Rd., Dunsmuir, CA 96025
Telephone: (530) 235-4440
Fax: (530) 235-4470
E-mail: rrp@rrpark.com
Website: www.rrpark.com

**HUMBOLDT BAY & EUREKA
MODEL RAILROAD CLUB**
Layout

Description: This is an 855-square-foot HO gauge layout with 2,000 feet of track. The track goes through and over mountains, valleys, trestles, towns, and railyards. The club was established in 1972 and has been operating at its present site since 1974. The layout portrays Northern California's varied scenery.

Schedule: The club is open Saturday nights from 7:30 to 9 p.m., or at other times by appointment.

Admission/Fare: Free; donations gladly accepted.

Locomotives/Rolling Stock: HO gauge steam and diesel engines, with many varieties of rolling stock provided by members.

Special Events: Spring open house, at the time of the Eureka Rhododendron Festival (April); fall open house around Veterans Day (November); in addition, the members bring out their modular sections for the Redwood Acres Fair, held in June.

Nearby Attractions: Fort Humboldt State park with logging exhibits, Redwood National Park, and various California Redwood parks.

Directions: Off Highway 101 at Seventh and A Streets in Eureka. It's on the second floor, up a flight of stairs.

P   M

Site Address: Seventh and A Streets, Eureka, CA
Mailing Address: 10 W Seventh St. Ste. C, Eureka, CA 95501
Telephone: (707) 825-7689
E-mail: dougtrain@humboldt1.com

NORTHERN COUNTIES LOGGING MUSEUM

Train ride, museum
Standard gauge

MICHAEL KELLOGG

Description: Fort Humbolt State Historic Park includes a logging museum. The exhibit emphasizes historic steam logging equipment used in redwood logging. Several artifacts have been restored to operating condition and are demonstrated on occasion by the Northern Counties Logging Interpretive Association. Two small steam locomotives provide short rides once a month during the summer (cab rides for members).

Schedule: The museum is open daily, 9 a.m. to 5 p.m. Steam trains and equipment operate April 26-27 (Donkey Days), May 17, June 21, July 19, August 16, and September 20, 11 a.m. to 4 p.m.

Admission/Fare: Museum and displays–free. Train rides–adults, $1; children, $.50.

Locomotives/Rolling Stock: Bear Harbor Lumber Co., Marshutz & Cantrell, 1892, 12-ton 0-4-0, no. 1 "Gypsy"; Elk River Mill and Lumber Co., Marshutz & Cantrell, 1884, 9-ton 0-4-0, no. 1 "Falk"; more.

Special Events: School Days, April 23-24; Dolbeer Steam Donkey Days, April 26-27.

Nearby Attractions: Historic military fort adjacent; national and state redwood parks in the area.

Directions: Off Highway 101 at the southern end of Eureka, opposite Bayshore Mall.

Site Address: 3431 Fort Ave., Eureka, CA
Mailing Address: PO Box 6399, Eureka, CA 95502
Telephone: (707) 445-6567
Website: www.visithumboldt.com/loggingmuseum

ROARING CAMP RAILROADS
Train ride
Narrow gauge

Description: Roaring Camp–a 75-minute round trip from Roaring Camp Depot to Bear Mountain redwood forest. The excursion behind the Dixieanna Shay locomotive travels through a magnificent redwood forest. Santa Cruz–One-hour-long journey from the redwood forest to the beach in Santa Cruz. The line runs through a historic part of the city.

Schedule: Roaring Camp–open year-round. Santa Cruz–June through Labor Day, daily; September and October, weekends only.

Admission/Fare: Roaring Camp–adults, $17; children, $12. Santa Cruz–adults, $19; children, $15. Parking, $5.

Locomotives/Rolling Stock: Roaring Camp–1912 Lima 2-truck Shay, 2-truck Heisler, 3-truck Shay, former West Side Lumber. Santa Cruz–Nos. 2600 and 2641, CF7 1500-horsepower diesels, former Santa Fe; no. 20, 50-ton center-cab Whitcomb; passenger cars.

Special Events: Civil War Re-enactment, May 24-26; Hats Off to Dad, June 15; Jumpin' Frog Jamboree, July 4; Day Out with Thomas, September 12-14 and 19-21. Harvest Fair, October 11-12; Holiday Lights, December 5-6, 12-13, 19-21. Call, write, or check website for many more events.

Directions: Off State Route 17/880 to Santa Cruz, Mt. Hermon exit, 3.5 miles to left on Graham Hill Rd., ¼ mile to Roaring Camp.

†See ad on page A-7.

Site Address: Graham Hill Rd. and Roaring Camp Rd., Felton, CA
Mailing Address: PO Box G-1, Felton, CA 95018
Telephone: (831) 335-4484
Fax: (831) 335-3509
E-mail: RCamp448@aol.com
Website: www.roaringcamp.com

California, Fillmore

FILLMORE & WESTERN RAILWAY
Train ride, dinner train
Standard gauge

Description: Day and evening diner car service, 2½- to 3½-hour rides; Murder Mystery dinners on Saturday evenings; barbecue; school field trips; Pumpkinliner; Christmas Tree excursion trains; dance car (with dinner) wine train.

Schedule: Year-round, weekends. Group excursions by prior arrangement.

Admission/Fare: Day excursions: adults, $18; seniors (62+), $16; children, $8; infant-3 years, $5.

Locomotives/Rolling Stock: 1906 Baldwin steam locomotive no. 51; 1891 0-4-0 Porter no. 1 Sespe; 1949 F7 engines nos. 100 and 101; more.

Special Events: Railroad Days Festival, March (Fillmore town festival); Fourth of July (festival, arts and crafts, chili cook-off, etc.); Pumpkinliner, October; Christmas Tree Trains, December.

Nearby Attractions: Six Flags; Magic Mountain; Ventura County Beaches; Santa Barbara.

Directions: I-5 to Highway 126 (Ventura County, California) and Central Ave. in Fillmore. Two blocks north to Main St. Or, I-101 from Ventura, Highway 126 east to Central Ave. Two blocks north to Main St. Free parking.

Site Address: 351 Santa Clara Ave., Fillmore, CA
Mailing Address: PO Box 960, Fillmore, CA 93016
Telephone: (805) 524-2546 and (800) 773-8724
Fax: (805) 524-1838
E-mail: fwry@earthlink.net
Website: www.fwry.com

California, Fish Camp

**YOSEMITE MOUNTAIN-
SUGAR PINE RAILROAD**
Train ride, dinner train, museum
36" gauge

JOSEPH BISPO

Description: The YMSP operates a one-hour narrated steam-powered excursion over a restored section of the Madera Sugar Pine Lumber Co. The 4-mile trip runs through the scenic Sierra Nevada at an elevation of 5000 feet, winds down a 4 percent grade into Lewis Creek Canyon, passes Horseshoe Curve, Cold Spring Crossing, and stops at Lewis Creek Loop. Ex-Westside Lumber Co. Shays provide the motive power for the train. Converted logging cars using sectioned logs are used for passenger cars.

Schedule: Railcars–April through October, daily. Steam train–May through September, daily. April and October, weekends.

Admission/Fare: Railcars–adults, $9.50; children 3-12, $4.75. Steam train–adults, $13; children 3-12, $6.50.

Locomotives/Rolling Stock: 1928 Lima 3-truck Shay, no. 10; 1913 Lima 3-truck Shay, no. 15; Vulcan 1935 10-ton switcher; four model A powered railcars; logging cars; covered and open converted flatcars, more.

Special Events: Moonlight Special with steak barbecue and music every Saturday and Wednesday night in summer; reservations advised. Gold panning, group tours, theme events, and private charters.

Nearby Attractions: Operating in the Sierra National Forest, 4 miles south of Yosemite National Park on Highway 41.

Site Address: 56001 Yosemite Highway 41, Fish Camp, CA
Mailing Address: 56001 Yosemite Highway 41, Fish Camp, CA 93623
Telephone: (559) 683-7273
Website: www.ymsprr.com

33

California, Folsom
(Folsom City Zoo)

FOLSOM VALLEY RAILWAY
Train ride
12" narrow gauge

TERRY GOLD

Description: A ¾-mile ride through a 50-acre city park features vintage wooden freight cars drawn by a ⅛-scale oil fire locomotive representative of late-19th-century steam motive power.

Schedule: February through October: Tuesdays through Fridays, 11 a.m. to 2 p.m.; weekends and holidays, 11 a.m. to 4 p.m. November through January: weekends and school holidays, 11 a.m. to 4 p.m. All are weather permitting.

Admission/Fare: $1.50 per person.

Locomotives/Rolling Stock: 1950 Ottaway Locomotive old-time wooder; truss rod-style freight cars; cattle car; hopper car; five open gondola cars; bobber caboose.

Special Events: Train will operate all day until 10 p.m., week of July 4.

Nearby Attractions: Folsom City Zoo.

Directions: Folsom is approximately 25 miles east of Sacramento off U.S. 50.

Site Address: 50 Natoma St., Folsom, CA
Mailing Address: 121 Dunstable Way, Folsom, CA 95630
Telephone: (916) 983-1873
E-mail: goldtown@juno.com

California, Fort Bragg-Willits

CALIFORNIA WESTERN RAILROAD
THE SKUNK TRAIN
Train ride, dinner train
Standard gauge

GARY RICHARDS

Description: Come ride this historic train through the forest in the heart of Redwood country. We have 3½-hour half-day trips, 8½-hour full-day trips, and 5-hour sunset BBQs.

Schedule: Daily service, March through November; regular service, December through February.

Locomotives/Rolling Stock: No. 45 1924 2-8-2 Baldwin; nos. 64, 65, 66 1955 EMD GP9; coach nos. 655, 656, 657, 658, 659, 696, 697, 698, 699; 1925 M-100; and 1935 M-300.

Nearby Attractions: Fort Bragg is located on the rugged Mendocino Coast. Willits is located at the gateway to the redwoods.

Directions: 3½ hours west of Sacramento; 3 hours north of San Francisco.

Site Address: Fort Bragg and Willits, CA
Mailing Address: PO Box 907, Fort Bragg, CA 95437
Telephone: (707) 964-6371 and (800) 77-SKUNK
Fax: (707) 964-6754
E-mail: skunk@skunktrain.com
Website: www.skunktrain.com

35

NILES DEPOT MUSEUM
Museum, display, layout

Description: Housed in the 1901 Southern Pacific Depot is a museum, along with an N scale and HO scale layout.

Schedule: First and third Sundays of each month, 10 a.m. to 4 p.m.

Admission/Fare: Donation.

Locomotives/Rolling Stock: WP caboose no. 467

Nearby Attractions: The Niles District, home to many antique shops, is two blocks away.

Directions: Between Nursery Ave. and the Sullivan underpass.

Site Address: 36997 Mission Blvd., Fremont, CA
Mailing Address: PO Box 2716, Fremont, CA 94536
Telephone: (510) 797-4449
E-mail: nilesdepot@railfan.net
Website: nilesdepot.railfan.net

SOUTH COAST RAILROAD MUSEUM
Museum
Standard gauge

Description: The centerpiece is the historic Goleta Depot, a Victorian-styled Southern Pacific country station, which is listed on the National Register of Historic Places. The museum features refurnished rooms and station grounds, and a variety of informative displays, including a 300-square-foot HO scale model railroad exhibit. Other attractions include miniature train and handcar rides, Gandy Dancer Theater, picnic grounds, and a museum store and gift shop.

Schedule: Museum–Wednesdays through Sundays, 1 to 4 p.m. Miniature train–1:15 to 3:45 p.m. Handcar–third Saturday of each month, 1:15 to 3:45 p.m.

Admission/Fare: Museum–donations appreciated. Handcar–free. Miniature train–$1.

Locomotives/Rolling Stock: 1960s Southern Pacific bay window caboose no. 4023.

Special Events: Depot Day, fourth Sunday in September, 11 a.m. to 4 p.m.

Directions: Goleta is seven miles west of Santa Barbara, U.S. 101 north exit Los Carneros Rd.

Site Address: 300 N. Los Carneros Rd., Goleta, CA
Mailing Address: 300 N. Los Carneros Rd., Goleta, CA 93117-1502
Telephone: (805) 964-3540
Fax: (805) 964-3549
E-mail: museum@goletadepot.org
Website: www.goletadepot.org

California, Jamestown

Description: Operated by the California State Railroad Museum; one of Hollywood's most popular filming locations. The Historic Sierra Railroad Shops and Roundhouse at Railtown 1897 have been in continuous operation as a steam locomotive maintenance facility for over a century. Our 6-mile, 40-minute round-trip route passes through Gold Country.

Schedule: Open daily 9:30 a.m. to 4:30 p.m., except Thanksgiving, Christmas, and New Year's Day. Steam trains operate weekends April to October (selected dates only in November and December), departing hourly 11 a.m. to 3 p.m. Guided roundhouse tours available daily.

Admission/Fare: Roundhouse tours–adults, $2; children (6-12), $1. Train rides–adults, $6; children (6-12), $3; 5 and under are free.

Locomotives/Rolling Stock: Sierra Railroad 2-8-0 no. 28; 4-6-0 no. 3; combine no. 5; coach no. 6; former Feather River Shay no. 2; former Southern Pacific commuter coaches; more.

Special Events: Spring Wildflower Trains, April and May; Day Out with Thomas, June; Wine & Cheese Special, August; Movie Railroad Days, September.

Directions: Located three blocks east of downtown Jamestown on Highways 49/107, just west of the Highway 120 junction.

Site Address: Fifth Ave. and Reservoir Rd., Jamestown, CA
Mailing Address: PO Box 1250, Jamestown, CA 95327
Telephone: (209) 984-3953
Fax: (209) 984-4936
E-mail: railtown@mlode.com
Website: www.railtown1897.org

Description: The museum is a restored original La Mesa railroad station, built by San Diego, Cuyamaca & Eastern Railway in 1894. It was a winner of the AIA "Orchid" award in 1981 for historic preservation.

Schedule: Open to the public by appointment. Call (619) 595-3031 for information.

Admission/Fare: Free.

Locomotives/Rolling Stock: Mojave Northern Railroad 0-6-0T no. 3 (Davenport, 1923); PFE ice-type refrigerator car no. 11207 (PFE, 1957); Southern Pacific caboose no. 1058 (SP Co., 1941).

Special Events: Back to the '50s, Thursday evenings, June through September; Oktoberfest, first weekend in October; Christmas in the Village, weekend evenings during Christmas season.

Nearby Attractions: Wild Animal Park, San Diego Railroad Museum's Campo Living History Center, Sea World, Balboa Park.

Directions: Ten miles east of San Diego in downtown La Mesa. Accessible via I-8 or State Highway 94 (Spring St. off ramps); La Mesa Blvd. at the railroad tracks.

    M arm

Site Address: 4695 Nebo Dr., La Mesa, CA 91941
Mailing Address: San Diego Railroad Museum, 1050 Kettner Blvd. #5, San Diego, CA 92101-3339
Telephone: (619) 595-3031
Fax: (619) 595-3034
E-mail: sdrmoffice@aol.com. **Website:** www.sdrm.org

LOMITA RAILROAD MUSEUM
Museum, display
Standard gauge

Description: A replica of the Boston & Maine station at Wakefield, Massachusetts. On display are lanterns of the steam era, chinaware, and silverware of the period, scale model live steam engines, spikes, tie date nails, insulators, prints, photographs, postcards, clocks, and a wooden water tower 35 feet high and 14 feet in diameter next to the engine.

Schedule: Year-round. Wednesday through Sunday, 10 a.m. to 5 p.m. Closed Thanksgiving and Christmas.

Admission/Fare: Adults, $2; children under age 12, $1.

Locomotives/Rolling Stock: 1902 Baldwin 2-6-0 (Mogul) no. 1765 with a whale-back tender, former Southern Pacific; 1910 yellow caboose, UP OWR&N; 1913 UP boxcar; 1923 oil tank car, Union Oil Co.; Santa Fe red caboose no. 999531.

Special Events: Golden Spike Day, call or write for details.

Nearby Attractions: South Coast Botanical Gardens, Torrance Cabrillo Museum, San Pedro, Banning House and Drum Barracks, Wilmington.

Directions: 110 (Harbor Freeway) south to Pacific Coast Highway off ramp. Right (west) to Narbonne Ave. Right to second signal. Right (east) one block. Parking on 250th St.

*Coupon available, see coupon section.

     M

Site Address: 250th St. and Woodward Ave., Lomita, CA
Mailing Address: 2137 W. 250th St., Lomita, CA 90717
Telephone: (310) 326-6255

ELDORADO EXPRESS RAILROAD
Train ride
18" gauge

Description: A one-mile round trip in El Dorado Regional Park, with some narration.

Schedule: Fridays, Saturdays, and Sundays, 10:30 a.m. to 4 p.m., weather permitting.

Admission/Fare: Adults and children, $2 each.

Locomotives/Rolling Stock: 1946 locomotive 4-6-2 Pacific; tender; three open cars, each holding 18 persons. Locomotive was once steam, now runs on 4-cylinder gas engine.

Nearby Attractions: Knott's Theme Park, Queen Mary ship.

Directions: El Dorado Regional Park, Long Beach, at 605 Freeway and Spring St.

*Coupon available, see coupon section.

Site Address: 605 Freeway and Spring St., Long Beach, CA
Mailing Address: 4943 Lincoln Ave., Cypress, CA 90630
Telephone: (562) 496-4228

California, Los Angeles

TRAVEL TOWN MUSEUM
Train ride, museum, display, layout
Standard and narrow gauge

Description: An outdoor transportation museum celebrating the history of railroading in the western United States, concentrating on California and specifically on Los Angeles history.

Schedule: Year-round. Weekdays, 10 a.m. to 4 p.m.; weekends, 10 a.m. to 5 p.m.

Admission/Fare: Free.

Locomotives/Rolling Stock: Locomotives, freight cars, cabooses, interurbans and motorcars.

Nearby Attractions: Griffith Park, Los Angeles Zoo, Autry Museum of Western Heritage, Griffith Observatory, Greek Theatre.

Directions: Ventura Freeway exit 134 (Forest Lawn Dr.), located at Griffith Park and Zoo Drives.

Site Address: Griffith Park, 5200 Zoo Dr., Los Angeles, CA
Mailing Address: 3900 W. Chevy Chase Dr., Los Angeles, CA 90039
Telephone: (323) 662-5874
E-mail: TravelTown@rap.lacity.org
Website: www.lacity.org/rap/grifmet/tt/index.htm

California, McCloud

SHASTA SUNSET DINNER TRAIN
Train ride, dinner train
Standard gauge

BOB MORRIS

Description: Four-course gourmet meal served aboard 1916 Illinois Central dining cars. We also offer steam and diesel-powered excursion trains.

Schedule: Call, write, or visit our website for schedule. Special runs on Mother's Day, Father's Day, Thanksgiving, and New Year's Eve.

Admission: Steam excursion train–adults, $15; children under 12, $10. Diesel excursion train–adults, $12; children, $8. Dinner train–$79.95 plus tax and gratuity. Wine-Tasting and Mystery Trains, $89.95 plus tax and gratuity.

Locomotives/Rolling Stock: No. 25 steam engine; no. 18 steam engine; nos. 36, 37, 38 diesel; 1916 IC refurbished cars, open-air and double-decker open-air cars.

Nearby Attractions: Burney Falls, Lake Siskiyou, and Shasta Lake.

Directions: I-5 to Mt. Shasta, California, then 10 miles east on Highway 89 south. In McCloud trains load on Main St. across from the post office and bank.

†See ad on page A-12.

Site Address: Main St., McCloud, CA
Mailing Address: PO Box 1199, McCloud, CA 96057
Telephone: (530) 964-2142 and (800) 733-2141
Fax: (530) 964-2250
E-mail: shastatrains@hotmail.com
Website: www.mctrain.com

NATIONAL CITY DEPOT
Museum, display
Standard gauge

Description: One- and 3-mile rides on the Coronado Belt Line. The museum depicts the Santa Fe and San Diego Electric Railway Company. We have a three-rail (Lionel) layout.

Schedule: Saturday and Sunday, 12 to 4 p.m. Rides on Santa Monica railbus on first full weekend of each month.

Admission/Fare: Adults, $5/10; Children, $3/7. Museum: Adults, $3; Children, $1.

Locomotives/Rolling Stock: Santa Maria Railbus; various LRV/speeders.

Nearby Attractions: National City and Otay (NC&O) no. 1 Car Plaza across the street; Sea World; world-famous San Diego Zoo; Tijuana, Mexico.

Directions: Five miles south of San Diego. Take I-5 south to Bay Marina Dr. exit in National City and turn right. Go west two blocks and the museum is on the right.

Site Address: 922 W. 23rd St., National City, CA
Mailing Address: PO Box 89068, San Diego, CA 92138
Telephone: (619) 474-4400
Fax: (619) 474-4400
E-mail: ncd@trainweb.com
Website: www.trainweb.com/sandiegorail/sdera

California, Nevada City

AL DITTMANN

Description: Contains artifacts and exhibits relating to the historic Nevada
County Narrow Gauge Railroad, including a vintage locomotive and
antique railroad cars being restored by the Transportation Museum
Division. The museum displays and trackwork are in progress. The
grand opening to the public is scheduled for May 18, 2003. Until that
date the museum is open by appointment only.

Schedule: May through October, 10 a.m. to 4 p.m., closed Wednesdays and
Thursdays. (Before May 2003, Saturday and Sunday, 10 a.m. to 4 p.m.,
by appointment only; please call.)

Admission/Fare: Free admission; dontations welcomed.

Locomotives/Rolling Stock: Nevada County Narrow Gauge engine no. 5,
2-6-0, 26-ton Mogul, built 1875 Baldwin Locomotive Works; NCNGRR
tank car no. 187; NCNGRR caboose no. 1, and a lot more; see website.

Special Events: Grand opening to the public, May 18, 2003.

Nearby Attractions: Nevada County Historical Society–Firehouse Museum,
North Star Mining Museum, Searls Historical Library, Grass Valley
Video History Museum, Nevada County Traction Co., three state parks.

Directions: Take Highway 20/49 to Gold Flat exit. Take Gold Flat Rd. to
New Mohawk, go left to Kidder Ct., and right on Kidder Ct.

Site Address: 5 Kidder Ct., Nevada City, CA
Mailing Address: 5 Kidder Ct., Nevada City, CA 95959
Telephone: (530) 470-0902
Fax: (530) 470-0903
E-mail: ncngrr@oro.net
Website: www.ncngrrmuseum.org

California, Nevada City

NEVADA COUNTY
TRACTION COMPANY
Train ride
24" gauge

Description: Take a 3-mile round-trip, 1½-hour train ride. View rolling stock dated from 1888 to early 1900s. Visit a 1850s Chinese cemetery.

Schedule: April, May, November, and December, Friday through Sunday, 12 noon and 2 p.m. June through September, Monday through Friday, 12 noon and 2 p.m.; Saturday, 10 a.m., 2 and 4 p.m.; Sunday, 10 a.m. and 2 p.m. October only, 1 p.m., 12 noon, 2 p.m. and 4 p.m.

Admission/Fare: Adults, $8; children (2-12), $5. In October: adults, $9; children, $6.

Locomotives/Rolling Stock: Argent no. 5 former Stone Machine Co.; Daisy Tenn. 2-6-2, 26-ton Lima Operational West Side Lumber Co.; railbus, 1939 0-4-0 Henschel 14-ton electric speeder; 1959 0-4-0 Plymouth 12-ton 1985 street trolley.

Special Events: Check our website for dates.

Nearby Attractions: Empire Mine State Park, Malahoff Digging State Park, Historical Nevada City (Independent Trail is wheelchair accessible), Sacramento Railroad Museum. Next to Nevada City Museum.

Directions: On Highway 49 and 20, 55 miles northeast of Sacramento. Take Sacramento St. exit, right on Railroad Ave., ⅛ mile on right. Located at Northern Queen Inn upper parking lot.

*Coupon available, see coupon section.

Site Address: 402 Railroad Ave., Nevada City, CA
Mailing Address: 402 Railroad Ave., Nevada City, CA 95959
Telephone: (530) 265-0896 or (530) 265-5824, ext. 262
Fax: (530) 265-0869
E-mail: depotpeople@nccn.net
Website: www.northernqueeninn.com

**HERITAGE JUNCTION
HISTORIC PARK**
Museum, display

Description: We offer a collection of historic structures, including an 1886 Southern Pacific train station.

Schedule: Saturdays and Sundays, 1 to 4 p.m.

Admission/Fare: Free. Donations appreciated.

Locomotives/Rolling Stock: Locomotive 1639 Mogul.

Special Events: Christmas Open House, always second Sunday in December. Cowboy Poetry and Music Festival, March 27-30, 2003.

Nearby Attractions: Magic Mountain, Hart Park.

Directions: Next to Hart Park.

Site Address: 24107 San Fernando Rd., Newhall, CA
Mailing Address: PO Box 221925, Newhall, CA 91322
Telephone: (661) 254-1275
Website: www.scvhs.org

California, Oakdale

Description: The historic Sierra Railroad offers trips out of Oakdale and Sonora. Trips include dinners, lunches, murder mysteries, wild west shows, party trains, Christmas trains, rail and raft trips, and more.

Schedule: Every week, all year.

Admission/Fare: Varies from $20 to $100 per person.

Locomotives/Rolling Stock: GP9 Sierra no. 46, Baldwin S-12 Sierra no. 42; GP20s, nos. 48 and 50; dining and lounge cars.

Special Events: Iron Horse Roundup, celebration of the Old West with emphasis on railroading, annual event on Labor Day weekend.

Nearby Attractions: Yosemite National Park, Railtown 1897, Hershey's Chocolate plant, river trips, fishing, gold country.

Directions: From San Francisco, take 580 and 120 east to Oakdale (100 miles). From Sacramento, take 99 south to Manteca, and 120 east to Oakdale (70 miles). From Los Angeles, take 99 to Turlock and J14 north to Oakdale (300 miles).

*Coupon available, see coupon section.

Site Address: 220 S. Sierra Ave., Oakdale, CA
Mailing Address: 220 S. Sierra Ave., Oakdale, CA 95361
Telephone: (209) 848-2100 or (800) 866-1690
Fax: (209) 848-8595
E-mail: sierrarail@aol.com
Website: www.sierrarailroad.com

IRVINE PARK RAILROAD
Train ride
24" gauge

JOHN FORD

Description: Irvine Park Railroad is located on 500 acres in Irvine Regional Park, the oldest county park in the state of California. The train departs from an old-fashioned depot, where railroad folk songs fill the air. The locomotive will make a scenic one-mile journey around the park during which riders can view two lakes complete with waterfalls and fountains, a grove of oak trees, and the Orange County Zoo. The ride is narrated by the engineer and lasts approximately 12 minutes.

Schedule: Winter–daily, 10 a.m. to 4 p.m. Summer–daily, 10 a.m. to 4:30 p.m. Closed Thanksgiving and Christmas.

Admission/Fare: $3; children under age 1 are free. School group rates are available.

Locomotives/Rolling Stock: A 1/3 scale replica of the 1863 "C.P. Huntington"; four coaches.

Special Events: Christmas train two weeks prior to Christmas. Call for times.

Nearby Attractions: Bicycle and paddleboat rentals, Orange County Zoo, food concessions, pony rides.

Directions: From State Highway 55 take the Chapman Ave. exit and drive east to Jamboree Rd. Turn left into the park entrance.

Site Address: 1 Irvine Park Rd., Orange, CA
Mailing Address: 1 Irvine Park Rd., Orange, CA 92862
Telephone: (714) 997-3968
Fax: (714) 997-0459
Website: www.irvineparkrr.com

ORLAND, NEWVILLE & PACIFIC RAILROAD
Train ride
15" gauge

Description: The ON&P is an all-volunteer railroad operating in the Glenn County Fairgrounds. A one-mile ride takes visitors past the original Orland Southern Pacific depot, the picnic site, and the demonstration orchard, then through a tunnel and along Heritage Trail. The train is normally pulled by a magnificent 5/12-scale live-steam model of the North Pacific Coast's 1875 Baldwin narrow gauge locomotive "Sonoma." The picnic grounds at Deadowl Station are open whenever the train is running. See the former Orland Southern Pacific depot, 1918 Southern Pacific 2-8-0 no. 2852, caboose, schoolhouse, blacksmith shop, print shop, 1920s gas station, miscellaneous steam machinery, and old farm equipment.

Schedule: Saturday and Sunday, 12 noon to 5 p.m. Spring: April 12-13 through May 14-18. Fall: August 30-31, September 1 through October 18-19.

Admission/Fare: $1.

Locomotives/Rolling Stock: No. 12 replica of 1876 Baldwin 4-4-0; no. 2 4-4-0 amusement park type; Davenport switch engine; four open gondolas; covered car.

Special Events: Glenn County Fair, May 15-19; Harvest Festival, October 19-20; Spook Train, October 31; Father's Day, June 16; July 4.

Directions: Glenn County Fairgrounds.

Site Address: 221 E. Yolo St., Orland, CA
Mailing Address: PO Box 667, Orland, CA 95963
Telephone: (530) 865-1168 and (530) 865-9747
Fax: (530) 865-1197

ORANGE EMPIRE RAILWAY MUSEUM
Train ride, museum, display
Standard and narrow gauge

JIM WALKER, JR.

Description: Weekend trains run on our 1.5-mile right-of-way, streetcar rides on a 0.7-mile loop within the museum's property.

Schedule: Museum grounds are open daily 9 a.m. to 5 p.m. Weekends and holidays, trains and streetcars are operated 11 a.m. to 5 p.m.

Admission/Fare: Free admission to museum grounds. All day ride pass–adults, $8; children 5-11, $6; under age 5 are free. Special events may have additional fees.

Locomotives/Rolling Stock: VC Railway 2 Prairie; GF 2 Mogul; UP 2564 Mikado; SP 1474 S4; SP 3100 U25B; UP 942 E8A; and many more.

Special Events: Railfest on the last weekend in April; Railroadiana Swap Meet in March and September; Pumpkin Train in October; and Santa Train in December.

Nearby Attractions: Perris Valley Skydiving Center, Perris Auto Speedway, Lake Perris Recreation Area, March Field Air Museum, Temecula Wineries.

Directions: I-215, exit west onto Fourth St./Route 74, left on "A" St. to museum.

           M arm

Site Address: 2201 S. "A" St., Perris, CA
Mailing Address: PO Box 548, Perris, CA 92570-0548
Telephone: (909) 657-2605
Fax: (909) 943-2676
E-mail: oerm@pe.net
Website: www.oerm.org

GEORGE HALL

Description: Three layouts in O, HO, and N scale. The 10,000-square-foot museum also offers some prototype artifacts and a library.

Schedule: April through December–Saturdays and Sundays, also Memorial Day, Fourth of July, and Labor Day: noon to 5 p.m. Nonoperating, April through December–Wednesdays, noon to 4 p.m., and Fridays, 7:30 to 10 p.m.

Admission/Fare: Adults, $3; children under 14 and seniors, $2; family, $7. Wednesdays and Friday evenings are free.

Locomotives/Rolling Stock: We will have UP baggage car 904253.

Special Events: Holiday Shows: weekend after Thanksgiving; weekends on either side of Christmas.

Directions: Exit I-580 in Richmond at Canal Blvd. from either direction. Turn at signal to Garrard Blvd. (a right from the East Bay, or a left when coming from the San Rafael Bridge). Turn left at the stop sign onto Garrard Blvd. Proceed straight past two stop signs, and the natatorium, and into Ferry Point Tunnel. Dornan Drive is on the other side of the tunnel. We are located about ½ mile past the tunnel on the left across from Miller-Knox Regional Shoreline Park.

*Coupon available, see coupon section.

     M

Site Address: 900-A Dornan Dr., Point Richmond, CA
Mailing Address: PO Box 1243, El Cerrito, CA 94530
Telephone: (510) 234-4884
E-mail: info@gsmrm.org
Website: www.gsmrm.org

RAILWAY & LOCOMOTIVE HISTORICAL SOCIETY, SOUTHERN CALIFORNIA CHAPTER

Museum
Standard and narrow gauge

Description: Former ATSF Arcadia Depot (1895) houses exhibits and a gift shop. There is an outside display of locomotives and rolling stock, including motor cars; ice refrigerator car; caboose; berth and galley section of business car; horse car showing stable section.

Schedule: The second Sunday of every month and the day before, 9 a.m. to 4 p.m. When Easter or Mother's Day falls on the second Sunday, the museum will open on the preceding weekend, same hours. Daily during the Los Angeles County Fair in September. Other times by request.

Admission/Fare: No charge, except during the County Fair, which requires a general fair admission.

Locomotives/Rolling Stock: Union Pacific/Alco 4-8-8-4 Big Boy, no. 4014 (1941); Atchison Topeka & Santa Fe/Baldwin 4-5-4 Hudson, no. 3450 (1927); Union Pacific DD40X diesel-electric, no. 6915.

Special Events: Meetings are held at the Cowan's Room at St. Edmund's Church, 1175 San Gabriel Blvd., San Marino, on the first Tuesday of every month (September-June) at 7:30 p.m.

Nearby Attractions: Fairplex RV Park, NHRA Pomona Drag Strip, NHRA Museum.

Directions: Enter the Fairplex at Gate 1, or Main Gate, off Fairplex Dr.

     M

Site Address: Los Angeles County Fairplex, Pomona, CA
Mailing Address: PO Box 2250, Pomona, CA 91769
Telephone: (909) 623-0190
Website: www.trainweb.org/rlhs

PORTOLA RAILROAD MUSEUM
Museum
Standard gauge

NORMAN HOLMES

Description: A one-mile ride around a balloon turning track through pine forest. On display are more than 90 freight cars representing nearly every car type of the Western Pacific Railroad; several passenger cars; other rolling stock; railroad artifacts in the diesel shop building.

Schedule: Museum–March through mid-December, 10 a.m. to 5 p.m. Train–Memorial Day through Sunday after Labor Day: weekends, 11 a.m. to 4 p.m. Grounds open in winter, weather permitting.

Admission/Fare: Call or write for information.

Locomotives/Rolling Stock: Two steam, 1 electric, and 32 diesels of all types, including 13 former Western Pacific, 6 former Southern Pacific, and 3 former Union Pacific. Manufacturers represented: Alco, Baldwin, Electro-Motive, Fairbanks-Morse, General Electric, Ingersol-Rand, and Plymouth. Steam locomotives are former UP 737, an 1887 4-4-0 and former SP 1215, a 1913 0-6-0.

Special Events: Feather River Railroad Days, July 26-27. Railfan Photographers Day, September 20.

Directions: From State Route 70, travel one mile south on County Road A-15 (Gulling) across river and through town. Follow signs to museum.

†See ad on page A-22.

Site Address: 700 Western Pacific Way, Portola, CA
Mailing Address: PO Box 608, Portola, CA 96122-0608
Telephone: (530) 832-4131 and (530) 832-4532 (run-a-locomotive program reservations)
Fax: (530) 832-1854
Website: www.oz.net/~samh/frrs or www.wplives.com

RIVERSIDE LIVE STEAMERS
Train ride, layout
7½" gauge

Description: We run 1/8-size trains, all steam, on a 6,800-foot track in Hunter Park.

Schedule: Second and fourth Sundays, 10 a.m. to 3 p.m.

Admission/Fare: Donation only.

Special Events: Spring Meet, April 26-27. Fall Meet, October 25-26.

Directions: Corner of Columbia and Iowa, approximately one mile northeast of the junction of California 60/91 and I-215.

   M

Site Address: 1496 Columbia Ave., Riverside, CA
Mailing Address: PO Box 5512, Riverside, CA 92517
Telephone: (909) 779-9024

California, Sacramento　　**CALIFORNIA STATE RAILROAD MUSEUM**
Museum
Standard and 36" gauge

Description: One of the finest interpretive railroad museums in North America, CSRM's 11-acre facilities in Old Sacramento include the 100,000-square-foot museum of railroad history, a reconstructed 1870s Central Pacific passenger station, and an extensive library and archive.

Schedule: Year-round, daily, 10 a.m to 5 p.m. Closed Thanksgiving, Christmas, New Year's Day.

Admission/Fare: Adults, $3; youth and children ages 16 and under, free.

Locomotives/Rolling Stock: More than 30 meticulously restored locomotives and cars on display dating from the 1860s to present. Favorites are Pullman-style sleeper, streamlined dining car, 1870s Victorian coaches, and a railway post office.

Special Events: Day Out with Thomas, April and December; Sacramento Jazz Jubilee, Memorial Day weekend; Gold Rush Days, Labor Day weekend; Train Time for Santa, Thanksgiving weekend and December; also regular changing exhibits primarily spring, summer, and fall.

Nearby Attractions: Old Sacramento (California's largest concentration of restored 19th-century commercial structures), state capitol, Sutter's Fort, Crocker Art Museum, dining, shopping, and lodging.

Directions: In Old Sacramento, adjacent to I-5 exit "J" St.

arm　　TRAIN　　　　　Radio frequencies: 160.335 and 160.440

Site Address: Corner of Second and "I" Streets, Old Sacramento, CA
Mailing Address: 111 "I" St., Sacramento, CA 95814
Telephone: (916) 445-6645
Fax: (916) 327-5655
E-mail: foundation@californiastaterailroadmuseum.org (general)
Website: www.californiastaterailroadmuseum.org

California, Sacramento   **CALIFORNIA STATE RAILROAD MUSEUM**
SACRAMENTO SOUTHERN RAILROAD
Train ride
Standard gauge

Description: Sacramento Southern is the excursion railroad of the California State Railroad Museum. Built as a subsidiary of the Southern Pacific at the turn of the century, the museum trains have been in regular service since 1984. A 6-mile, 40-minute round trip takes passengers along the Sacramento River on vintage 1920s coaches and open-air excursion cars.

Schedule: Steam–April through September: weekends, 11 a.m. to 5 p.m., departing hourly; selected special event weekends, October through December. Diesel-powered school trains–April through June and October through December: Tuesdays and Fridays by reservation.

Admission/Fare: Adults, $6; youth 6-12, $3; children under age 6, free.

Locomotives/Rolling Stock: No. 10 1942 Porter 0-6-0T, former Granite Rock Company; no. 4466, 1920 Lima 0-6-0, former Union Pacific; more.

Special Events: Day Out with Thomas, April and December; Sacramento Jazz Jubilee, Memorial Day weekend; Gold Rush Days, Labor Day weekend; Train Time for Santa, Thanksgiving weekend and December.

Nearby Attractions: Old Sacramento (California's largest concentration of restored 19th-century commercial structures), state capitol, Sutter's Fort, Crocker Art Museum, dining, shopping, and lodging.

Directions: Northern terminus is the reconstructed Central Pacific Railroad Freight Depot at Front and "K" Streets in Old Sacramento.

Radio frequencies: 160.335 and 160.440

Site Address: Front and "K" Streets, Sacramento, CA
Mailing Address: 111 "I" St., Sacramento, CA 95814
Telephone: (916) 445-6645
Fax: (916) 327-5655
E-mail: foundation@californiastaterailroadmuseum.org
Website: www.californiastaterailroadmuseum.org

California, San Diego   **SAN DIEGO MODEL RAILROAD MUSEUM**
Museum

Description: The San Diego Model Railroad Museum is the largest permanent operating model railroad train exhibition in North America, with over 24,000 square feet of exhibit space. The museum features four sections of layout in N scale, HO scale, and O scale and Lionel three-rail toy trains.

Schedule: Tuesdays through Fridays, 11 a.m. to 4 p.m.; weekends, 11 a.m. to 5 p.m.; closed Mondays.

Admission/Fare: Adults, $4; seniors (60+), $3; children under 15 are free.

Locomotive/Rolling Stock: The rolling stock changes each day with different operators.

Special Events: Family Days every month (usually on the third Sunday) with crafts, videos, and special model train operation.

Nearby Attractions: San Diego Zoo, Balboa Park museums, Amtrak station.

Directions: Highway 163 south to the Park Blvd. exit. Take a left at the exit ramp and go north on Park Blvd. Turn left on Space Theater Way. Parking is behind the museum building.

*Coupon available, see coupon section.

Site Address: Balboa Park, 1649 El Prado, San Diego, CA
Mailing Address: 1649 El Prado, San Diego, CA 92101
Telephone: (619) 696-0199
Fax: (619) 696-0239
E-mail: sdmodrailm@abac.com
Website: www.sdmodelrailroadm.com

California, San Diego

SAN DIEGO RAILROAD MUSEUM
Train ride, dinner train, museum, display
Standard gauge

Description: Over 80 pieces of railroading equipment are located at the Campo Depot. Tours, steam and diesel train rides, dinners, brunches, wine tours, and specialty events are available.

Schedule: Campo Depot, year-round: weekends and select holidays, 10 a.m. to 4 p.m. Miller Creek, 1½ hour rides: weekends, 11 a.m. and 2:30 p.m. Ticket to Tecate, six-hour adventure: selected Saturdays. Dinner trains and wine tours, selected Saturdays; brunch trains, selected Sundays.

Admission/Fare: Miller Creek rides–adults, $12; children, $3. Ticket to Tecate–adults, $40; children, $20. Dinner, $75; brunch, $35; wine tour, $90.

Locomotive/Rolling Stock: Steam and diesel locomotives, passenger cars, boxcars, tank cars, cabooses, speeders, track equipment, and more.

Special Events: Spring Festival, Santa Trains, Three Kings Train, Boxcar BBQ.

Nearby Attractions: Lodging, campgrounds, restaurants, parks, and museums.

Directions: I-8 east 50 miles, exit at Buckman Springs Rd., south 10 miles. Road ends at Highway 94, turn right. Turn left at Forrest Gate Rd., turn left at second driveway, to the Depot parking lot.

Site Address: Highway 94 and Forrest Gate Rd., Campo, CA (weekends)
Mailing Address: 1050 Kettner Blvd., San Diego, CA 92101 (weekdays)
Telephone: (619) 595-3030 (days) and (619) 478-9937 (weekends)
Fax: (619) 595-3034
E-mail: sdrmoffice@aol.com
Website: www.sdrm.org

California, San Francisco　　　**GOLDEN GATE RAILROAD MUSEUM**
Museum, display
Standard gauge

Description: We are a hands-on museum, dedicated to the preservation of vintage steam and diesel locomotives and equipment from the San Francisco Bay Area. We offer a rent-a-locomotive program for steam and diesel.

Schedule: Year-round, weekends, 10 a.m. to 4 p.m. Call to confirm.

Admission/Fare: Adults, $5; children, $2.

Locomotive/Rolling Stock: SP Baldwin P8 4-6-2 no. 2472; SF Belt Railway Alcos nos. 25 and 49; FM H12-44 diesel switcher; assorted diesel locomotives; large assortment of passenger cars and rolling stock.

Special Events: SP Railroad Retirees Reunion, last weekend in June; rent-a-locomotive program (learn to run steam and diesel locomotives), by appointment; Spring and Fall Steam Festivals, May and October; special events as announced.

Nearby Attractions: PacBell Park baseball, city of San Francisco.

Directions: Highway 101 to Cesar Chavez St. (Army St.); east to Evans Ave. to Hunters Point Shipyard, Building 809. See website.

*Coupon available, see coupon section.

          Radio frequency: 160.635

Site Address: Bldg. 809, Hunter's Point Naval Shipyard, San Francisco, CA
Mailing Address: PO Box 881686, San Francisco, CA 94188-1686
Telephone: (415) 822-8728
Fax: (415) 822-8739
E-mail: info@ggrm.org
Website: www.ggrm.org

California, San Jose

KEN MIDDLEBROOK

Description: The non-profit CTRC is developing a railroad museum that will include several relocated railroad structures. Visitors can watch the extensive restoration of steam locomotive no. 2479. A nearby bay window caboose displays the organization's activities and current museum development. The CTRC, in partnership with the History Museums of San Jose, also operates the Trolley Barn in Kelley Park.

Schedule: Year-round: Saturdays 9 a.m. to 4 p.m. and by appointment.

Admission/Fare: Donations appreciated.

Locomotives/Rolling Stock: 1923 Baldwin 4-6-2; Southern Pacific no. 2479; 1941 65-ton diesel; Kaiser cement no. 0002; two passenger cars; two cabooses, MP 13522 and SP 1589.

Nearby Attractions: Kelley Park, Children's Discovery Museum, Tech Museum.

Directions: Santa Clara County Fairgrounds, Tully Rd., 2 miles west of U.S. Highway 101.

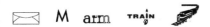

Site Address: 344 Tully Rd., San Jose, CA
Mailing Address: PO Box 403, Campbell, CA 95009
Telephone: (408) 293-2276
Website: www.ctrc.org

California, San Jose

Museum, layout, trolley car ride
Standard gauge

Description: The trolley car operates for rides on ½ mile of track.

Schedule: Year-round, Saturdays and Sundays. Closed holidays.

Admission/Fare: Adults, $6; seniors, $5; youth, $4; under age 5 are free.

Locomotives/Rolling Stock: Trolley car no. 124 ex-San Jose; no. 143 Birney; 168 ex-Porto; horse car no. 7 ex-San Francisco.

Nearby Attractions: Many attractions within a radius of 40 miles.

Directions: Located in Kelley Park, which is a short distance from Highways 280, 680, and 101. Take the no. 73 bus from downtown San Jose.

Site Address: 1650 Senter Rd., San Jose, CA
Mailing Address: 1650 Senter Rd., San Jose, CA 95112
Telephone: (408) 293-2276
Fax: (408) 287-2291

TRAIN TOWN
Train ride
15" gauge

Description: Train Town is a 10-acre railroad park filled with thousands of trees, animals, lakes, bridges, tunnels, waterfalls, and historic replica structures. Fifteen-inch-gauge live-steam locomotives and diesel replicas pull long passenger trains through the park. Railroad shops and a complete miniature town, built to the same 1/4 scale as the railroad. Full-sized rail equipment includes Santa Fe caboose no. 999648; Union Pacific caboose no. 25155; and Southern Pacific's first steel caboose, no. 11.

Schedule: June 1 through Labor Day, daily. Year-round, Fridays through Sundays. Closed Christmas and Thanksgiving. Call or write for hours.

Admission/Fare: Adults, $3.75; seniors and children 15 months to 15, $3.25.

Locomotives/Rolling Stock: Replica of no. 5212, 1937 Alco J-1a 4-6-4, former New York Central; no. 1, 1960 Winton Engineering 2-6-0; SW 1200, 1992 custom locomotive; no. 401, 1975 gas-electric motor car.

Directions: Sonoma is in wine country, less than an hour north of San Francisco. Train Town is on Broadway (Highway 12), one mile south of the Sonoma Town Square.

Site Address: 20264 Broadway, Highway 12, Sonoma, CA
Mailing Address: PO Box 656, Sonoma, CA 95476
Telephone: (707) 996-2559
Fax: (707) 966-6344
Website: www.traintown.com

California, Suisun City

Museum
Standard gauge

BART NADEAU

Description: A 9.5-mile interurban round trip over re-electrified Sacramento Northern Railway interurban in rural Solano County.

Schedule: Year-round, weekends, 10:30 a.m. to 5 p.m. June through Labor Day, Wednesdays through Sundays, 10:30 a.m. to 5 p.m.

Admission/Fare: Adults, $7; seniors (65 and over), $6; children age 14 and under, $4.

Locomotives/Rolling Stock: Wood interurbans: Peninsular Railway no. 52; Petaluma & Santa Rosa no. 63; Sacramento Northern no. 1005. Steel interurbans: Napa Valley no. 63; key units 182 and 187. Crandic III steel locomotives: CCT no. 7; SN nos. 652, 654; many streetcars; more.

Special Events: Special Montezuma Hills Trains in April, Pumpkin Patch Trains in October, Santa Trains in December.

Nearby Attractions: Marine World, Africa USA.

Directions: On Highway 12. I-80, 12 miles from the Suisun/Rio Vista exit; or I-5, 23 miles from the Rio Vista/Fairfield exit.

Site Address: 5848 State Highway 12, Suisun City, CA
Mailing Address: 5848 State Highway 12, Suisun City, CA 94585
Telephone: (707) 374-2978
Fax: (707) 374-6742
Website: www.wrm.org

64

NILES CANYON RAILWAY
Dinner train
Standard gauge

ALAN FRANK

Description: A one-hour and 10-minute ride through scenic Niles Canyon, which is the final leg of the original transcontinental railroad.

Schedule: First and third Sundays year-round, additional Sundays in the summer. Check our website.

Admission/Fare: Adults, $8; seniors, $7; children 3-12, $4; under 3 free.

Locomotives/Rolling Stock: Eleven diesels, eight steam locomotives, seven cabooses, passenger coaches, dome car, diner, all-day lunch car, boxcars, flatcars, reefers, tank cars, and MOW equipment.

Special Events: April Wine-Tasting and Wild Flower Trains; June and September, big and small kids run model trains; December, Train of Lights.

Nearby Attractions: Southeast corner of the San Francisco Bay Area.

Directions: One mile west of I-680 on route 84. Check our website for map.

Site Address: 6 Kildare Rd., Sunol, CA
Mailing Address: PO Box 2247, Niles Station, Fremont, CA 94536
Telephone: (925) 862-9063
Fax: (408) 249-3120
E-mail: alnethie@aol.com
Website: www.ncry.org

California, Woodland

YOLO SHORTLINE
RAILROAD COMPANY
Train ride
Standard gauge

RICHARD JONES

Description: A 28-mile, two-hour round trip between Woodland and West Sacramento over former Sacramento Northern Interurban track. Crosses 8,000-foot Fremont Trestle and offers views of the Sacramento River and scenic Yolo County farmlands and wetlands. The railroad also offers specials to Clarksburg.

Schedule: Spring Specials, March 18 and 25 and April 22 and 29. Regular season, May through October, weekends and major holidays. We also offer birthday parties, weddings, and private charters.

Admission/Fare: Adults, $13; seniors, $11; children (4-14), $8; family $35; family pizza fare, $55; diesel cab ride, add $10; steam cab ride, add $25.

Locomotives/Rolling Stock: No. 1233, former Southern Pacific 0-6-0 switcher; nos. 131, 132, 133 GP-9 EMD diesels, former Southern Pacific.

Special Events: Great Train Robberies, Lunch Cruises, Pizza Trains; steam engine runs third weekend every month.

Nearby Attractions: Hayes Truck and Tractor Museum, Southern Pacific Depot (under restoration), Woodland Opera House.

Directions: I-5 or Highway 113, Main St. exit, one mile west to E. Main and Thomas Streets. Twenty minutes north of Sacramento.

Radio Frequency: 160.260

Site Address: 341 Industrial Way, Woodland, CA
Mailing Address: 341 Industrial Way, Woodland, CA 95776
Telephone: (530) 666-9698
Fax: (530) 666-2919
E-mail: jasdavis@pacbell.net
Website: www.ysrr.com

California, Yermo

RICHARD JONES

Description: An 8- to 10-minute amusement ride in Calico Ghost Town.

Schedule: 364 days a year, 9 a.m. to 5 p.m.

Admission/Fare: Adults, $2.50. Special rate for schoolchildren, $1.

Special Events: Civil War, Presidents' weekend in February; Spring Festival, Mother's Day weekend; Calico Days, October 10-12; Halloween weekend; Harvest Festival, November.

Nearby Attractions: Calico Ghost Town; regional parks in San Bernardino County; original silver mine town, operated in the 1890s.

Directions: Take I-15 to Ghost Town Road exit just 10 minutes north of Barstow, California. Main St. to sign for C.O. Railroad.

Site Address: 36600 Ghost Town Rd., Calico, CA
Mailing Address: PO Box 638, Yermo, CA 92398
Telephone: (760) 254-2117
Fax: (760) 254-2005

California, Yreka

YREKA WESTERN RAILROAD
Train ride, museum, layout
Standard gauge

Description: Tourist excursion through Shasta Valley to railroad/cattle town of Montague. One-hour layover in Montague, 3½-hour tour.

Schedule: Memorial Day weekend through mid-June, weekends only. Mid-June through Labor Day weekend, Wednesday through Sunday. Labor Day weekend through the last Sunday in October, weekends only. Train leaves at 11 a.m. and returns at 2:30 p.m.

Admission/Fare: Adults, $12.50; seniors (60+), $10.75; children (3 through 12), $6.

Locomotives/Rolling Stock: GM EMD SW-8 no. 21; Baldwin steam locomotive 2-8-2 Mikado no. 19.

Special Events: Wild Goose Chase 2-mile and 10K race, Hot Air Balloon Fair, dinner trains.

Directions: I-5 Yreka central off-ramp, east of freeway.

Site Address: 300 E. Miner St., Yreka, CA
Mailing Address: PO Box 660, Yreka, CA 96097
Telephone: (800) 973-5277 and (530) 842-4146
Fax: (530) 842-4148

Colorado, Canon City

ROYAL GORGE ROUTE RAILROAD
Train ride
Standard gauge

RON RUHOFF

Description: Experience the grandeur of traveling by train through the spectacular Royal Gorge on the Royal Gorge route. The train operates alongside the Arkansas River from Canon City, traveling over the famous "Hanging Bridge" where the canyon rim towers 1,000 feet above. This is a 24-mile, two-hour round trip ride.

Schedule: Mid-May through mid-October: three departures daily at 9 a.m., 12 noon, and 3 p.m. Mid-October through mid-May: every Saturday and Sunday (except Christmas) at 12 noon.

Admission/Fare: Round trip: adults, $29.65; children (2-13), $18.15; under 3, no charge if carried on lap.

Locomotives/Rolling Stock: FC&NW EMD F7A nos. 402, 403; VIA Rail CC&F passenger car nos. 3225, 5497, 5541, 5562, 5580, 5586, club car 650.

Nearby Attractions: Royal Gorge Bridge, rafting, horseback riding, fishing, camping.

Directions: Located at the Santa Fe Depot, 401 Water St. (one block south on Third St. off Highway 50). Canon City is 45 miles southwest of Colorado Springs.

Site Address: 401 Water St., Canon City, Co 81212
Mailing Address: PO Box 859, Georgetown, CO 80444
Telephone: (303) 569-2403 and (888) RAILS-4-U
Fax: (303) 569-2894
E-mail: info@royalgorgeroute.com
Website: www.royalgorgeroute.com

Colorado, Cimarron

NPS PHOTO BY LISA LYNCH

Description: At Cimarron, 20 miles east of Montrose, a historic narrow gauge railroad exhibit with engine no. 278, its coal tender, a boxcar, and a caboose sit on a stone and steel trestle one mile into the Cimarron River Canyon. At the Cimarron Visitor Center, a cattle car, sheep car, outfit car, hoist car, livestock corral, and interpretive panels illustrate early mountain railroad operations of the Denver & Rio Grande.

Schedule: Year-round.

Admission/Fare: Free.

Locomotives/Rolling Stock: Locomotive no. 278, C-16 280, 1882/Baldwin Locomotive Works, Philadelphia, Pennsylvania; tender and D&RGW 0577 caboose.

Nearby Attractions: Black Canyon of the Gunnison National Park, Curecanti National Recreation area.

Directions: Cimarron is 20 miles east of Montrose on U.S. Highway 50. The exhibit can be seen from the highway. Follow Curecanti National Recreation Area signs.

Site Address: U.S. Highway 59, Cimarron, CO
Mailing Address: Curecanti NRA, 102 Elk Creek, Gunnison, CO 81230
Telephone: (970) 249-1914 ext. 23 and (970) 641-2337 ext. 205
Fax: (970) 641-3127
E-mail: cure_vis_mail@nps.gov
Website: www.nps.gov/cure

Colorado, Colorado Springs

PIKE'S PEAK HISTORICAL STREET RAILWAY FOUNDATION, INC.
Ride, museum, display
Standard gauge

Description: This interpretive center displays street railway history with a strong emphasis on Colorado Springs street railway history. We also offer a lecture on history and the return of streetcars to Colorado Springs. There are several trips over a 500-foot test track. The operation and history of the car are explained during the ride. You can visit a working car house (former Rock Island Engine House) built in 1888, see cars under restoration, and take a guided tour of the cars on hand and the shop area.

Schedule: Year-round, Saturdays, 10 a.m. to 4 p.m. Closed Thanksgiving, Christmas, and New Year's week. Other times please write or call. Group tours, please call ahead for special showing.

Admission/Fare: Adults, $2; children 12 and under, $1.

Locomotives/Rolling Stock: Nine Southeastern Pennsylvania Transportation Authority PCCs (Philadelphia) 1947; Los Angeles Railways PCC 1943; Colorado Springs double truck, 1901 Laclede Car Co.; Ft. Collins Municipal Railway, single truck, 1919 Birney, American Car Co.; Colorado Springs double truck, 1901 J. G. Brill Car Co.

Directions: I-25, exit Fillmore St. east, south on Tremont St., west on Polk St. When forced to turn south, you will automatically be on Steel Dr. The site is located at the end of Steel Dr.

       arm M

Site Address: 2333 Steel Dr., Colorado Springs, CO
Mailing Address: PO Box 544, Colorado Springs, CO 80901
Telephone: (719) 475-9508 and (719) 471-2619
Fax: (719) 475-2814
Website: colospringstrolleys.home.att.net.

PATRICIA STAUFFER

Description: Tours of private Pullman railcar of railroad magnate David Moffat. The car was named for his only child, Marcia.

Schedule: Memorial Day through Labor Day, Mondays through Fridays, 9 a.m. to 5 p.m.

Admission/Fare: Donations accepted.

Locomotives/Rolling Stock: Private Pullman car of David Moffat–Moffat Railroad.

Nearby Attractions: Adjacent to City Park and the wave pool.

Directions: Directly across from Moffat County Visitor's Center.

Site Address: 360 E. Victory Way, Craig, CO
Mailing Address: 360 E. Victory Way, Craig, CO 81625
Telephone: (800) 864-4405
Fax: (970) 824-0231
E-mail: craigcoc@craig-chamber.com
Website: www.craig-chamber.com

CRIPPLE CREEK AND VICTOR NARROW GAUGE RAILROAD
Train ride
Narrow gauge

Description: A 4-mile, 45-minute round trip over a portion of the old Midland Terminal Railroad. The train runs south out of Cripple Creek past the old MT wye, over a reconstructed trestle and past many historic mines to the deserted mining town of Anaconda.

Schedule: Mid-May through mid-October: daily, 9:30 a.m. to 5:30 p.m., departing every 45 minutes.

Admission/Fare: Adults, $9; seniors, $8; children 3-12, $5; under age 3 are free.

Locomotives/Rolling Stock: No. 1 1902 Orenstein & Koppel 0-4-4-0; no. 2 1936 Henschel 0-4-0; no. 3 1927 Porter 0-4-0T; no. 13 1946 Bagnall 0-4-0T.

Nearby Attractions: Cripple Creek District Museum, Mueller State Park.

Directions: From Colorado Springs west on Highway 24 to Highway 67 south to Cripple Creek. Trains leave from former Midland Terminal Railroad Bull Hill Depot.

Site Address: 520 E. Carr, Cripple Creek, CO
Mailing Address: PO Box 459, Cripple Creek, CO 80813
Telephone: (719) 689-2640
Fax: (719) 689-3256
Website: ccvngrailroad.webjump.com

Description: Self-guided museum tours.

Schedule: Year-round, Mondays through Saturdays, 9 a.m. to 5 p.m.

Admission/Fare: Adults, $6; youth 12-18, $4; children 6-11, $3.

Locomotives/Rolling Stock: UP Big Boy locomotive 4005 (4-8-8-4); Pikes Peak diner 804; UP rotary snowplow 099-900099; CBQ business car C&S no. 300; CNW locomotive no. 444; Forney locomotive; German locomotive no. 7.

Nearby Attractions: Near downtown Denver, the Denver Coliseum, and the National Western Stock Show grounds. Short distance from many attractions.

Directions: From I-25 exit on I-70 east, then exit on Brighton Blvd. and go southwest two blocks. Turn right into the museum driveway when you see the sign.

Site Address: 4303 Brighton Blvd., Denver, CO
Mailing Address: 4303 Brighton Blvd., Denver, CO 80216
Telephone: (303) 297-1113
Fax: (303) 297-3113
E-mail: forney@frii.net
Website: www.forneymuseum.com

Colorado, Denver

PLATTE VALLEY TROLLEY
Train ride
Standard gauge

JOHN HAMMOND

Description: The Denver Sightseeing route, about 4 miles round trip, lasts 30 minutes. The Route 84 Excursion includes Denver Sightseeing plus an additional 5 miles, with three blocks of street running and several trestles.

Schedule: Memorial Day through Labor Day, 11:15 a.m. to 4:15 p.m., with the Route 84 Excursion departing at 12:15 p.m. weekdays and 3:15 weekends.

Admission/Fare: Sightseeing Route–adults, $2; children and seniors, $1. Route 84 Excursion–adults, $4; seniors, $3; children, $2.

Locomotives/Rolling Stock: Comaco reproduction Brill open trolley, diesel-powered, no. 1977.

Nearby Attractions: Children's Museum, Colorado's Ocean Journey Aquarium, Six Flags Amusement Park.

Directions: I-25 exit 211, 23rd St. Turn east to Water St. and follow the signs. Park at the Children's Museum.

*Coupon available, see coupon section.

Site Address: 2121 Children's Museum Dr., Denver, CO
Mailing Address: PO Box 481244, Denver, CO 80240-1244
Telephone: (303) 458-6255
Fax: (303) 369-5691
E-mail: mail@denvertrolley.org
Website: www.denvertrolley.org

Colorado, Denver

THE SKI TRAIN
Train ride
Standard gauge

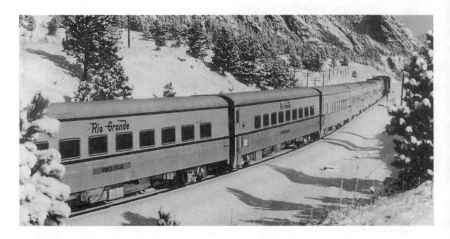

Description: A 130-mile round trip on the historic Moffat Line between Denver and Winter Park Resort.

Schedule: Weekends, December through April. Saturdays only, June through August.

Admission/Fare: $45.

Locomotives/Rolling Stock: Varies.

Directions: Train departs from Denver Union Station.

Site Address: Denver Union Station, Denver, CO
Mailing Address: 555 17th St., Ste. 2400, Denver, CO 80202
Telephone: (303) 296-4754
Fax: (303) 298-8881
Website: www.skitrain.com

GALLOPING GOOSE HISTORICAL SOCIETY OF DOLORES, INC.
Train ride, museum, display, layout
36" gauge

Description: The ride is 320 feet; by request, up and back, 640 feet.

Schedule: May 15 through October 15, Monday through Saturday, 9 a.m. to 5 p.m.

Admission/Fare: Free. Donations accepted.

Locomotives/Rolling Stock: RGS motor no. 5 (Galloping Goose).

Special Events: Memorial Day, Raft Days, Escalante Days, Railfest.

Nearby Attractions: Mesa Verde, Anasazi Heritage Center, McPhee Reservoir.

Directions: Southwest Colorado, 45 miles west of Durango Highway 145 north.

Site Address: 421 Railroad Ave., Dolores, CO
Mailing Address: PO Box 297, Dolores, CO 81323
Telephone: (970) 882-7082
Fax: (970) 882-2224
E-mail: gghs5@fone.net
Website: doloresgallopinggoose5.org

Colorado, Durango

DURANGO & SILVERTON
NARROW GAUGE RAILROAD
Train ride, museum
Narrow gauge

ROBERT ROYEM

Description: Steam-powered narrow gauge railroad through the scenic San Juan mountains of Colorado. The 90-mile round trip begins in Durango and takes about 9 hours, with a 2¼-hour layover in Silverton for lunch.

Schedule: Summer (Silverton) schedule starts second weekend in May; daily, 8:15 a.m. Cascade Canyon Winter Trains run November 27 to second weekend in May; 12 noon. Closed Christmas. Call for information.

Admission/Fare: Silverton round trip–adults, $60; children ages 5-11, $30; parlor car (over 21), $99. Winter Cascade Canyon–adults, $45; children, $22; parlor car (over 21), $75. All tickets include admission to the D&SNGRR Museum (fares subject to change).

Locomotives/Rolling Stock: Locomotives nos. 473, 476, 478, 480, 481, 482, 486, 493, 498, 42; B-2 Cinco Animas, B-3 Nomad, more.

Special Events: Narrow Gauge Days, May; Iron Horse Bicycle Classic, May; Annual Railfest, August; Photo Special, September; Holiday Trains, New Year's Eve Moonlight Train, December.

Directions: At the intersection of U.S. Highways 550 and 160 in southwest Colorado. Depot is at the far south end of Main Ave.

†See ad on page A-10.

Site Address: 479 Main Ave., Durango, CO
Mailing Address: 479 Main Ave., Durango, CO 81301
Telephone: (970) 247-2733 and (888) TRAIN-07
Fax: (970) 259-9349
E-mail: info@durangotrain.com
Website: www.durangotrain.com

FORT COLLINS
MUNICIPAL RAILWAY
Train ride
Standard gauge

Description: Trolley ride; 3-mile round-trip ride in peaceful residential setting on original right-of-way.

Schedule: Weekends and holidays, May through September, noon to 5 p.m.

Admission/Fare: Adults, $1; seniors, $.75; children under 12, $.50.

Locomotives/Rolling Stock: 1919 Birney single-track streetcar, Ft. Collins car no. 21.

Special Events: Mother's Day, Father's Day, Fourth of July.

Nearby Attractions: Rocky Mountain National Park, Colorado State University, Poudre Canyon.

Directions: From I-25 take exit 269 (Colorado 14, Mulberry St.) west to Jackson St. Right on Jackson St. to Oak St. Left on Oak St. to Depot at Roosevelt St. in City Park.

     M arm

Site Address: Roosevelt St., Fort Collins, CO
Mailing Address: PO Box 635, Fort Collins, CO 80522
Telephone: (970) 224-5372
Website: www.fortnet.org/trolley

GEORGETOWN LOOP RAILROAD
Train ride
Narrow gauge

RON RUHOFF

Description: A 6.5-mile, 70-minute round trip over the right-of-way of the former Colorado & Southern. The train travels through scenic, mountainous terrain and over the reconstructed Devil's Gate Viaduct, a spectacular 96-foot-high curved trestle. The Georgetown Loop Railroad is a project of the Colorado Historical Society.

Schedule: Memorial Day weekend through first weekend in October: daily. Silver Plume (exit 226)–9:20 and 10:40 a.m., 12, 1:20, 2:40, and 4 p.m. Devil's Gate (exit 228)–10 and 11:20 a.m., 12:40, 2:00, and 3:20 p.m.

Admission/Fare: Adults, $15.95; children (3-15), $10.45. Mine tour–adults, $6; children, $4. Charters and group rates available. Tickets must be purchased at the Old Georgetown Station, 1106 Rose St., Georgetown.

Locomotives/Rolling Stock: Lima 3-truck Shay, nos. 8, 12, 14; more.

Nearby Attractions: Old Georgetown Station, Historic Georgetown, and Silver Plume

Directions: I-70 exit 228 for Devil's Gate or exit 226 for Silver Plume. Tickets must be purchased at Old Georgetown Station, 1106 Rose, Georgetown.

Radio frequency: 161.115

Site Address: 1106 Rose St., Georgetown, CO
Mailing Address: PO Box 217, Georgetown, CO 80444
Telephone: (303) 569-2403 and (800) 691-4FUN
Fax: (303) 569-2873
E-mail: info@georgetownloop.com
Website: www.georgetownloop.com

COLORADO RAILROAD MUSEUM
Museum
Standard and 36" gauge

BOB JENSEN

Description: An extensive collection of Colorado railroad memorabilia and over 70 historic cars and locomotives, both standard and narrow gauge. It is the home of the Denver HO Model Railroad Club and the Denver Garden Railway Society. "Galloping Goose" motorcars operate on selected weekends.

Schedule: Museum–June through August, daily, 9 a.m. to 6 p.m.; September through May, 9 a.m. to 5 p.m. Train–call, fax, or write for schedule. HO model railroad–first Thursday of every month, 7:30 to 9:30 p.m. Richardson Railroad Research Library–Tuesdays through Saturdays, 11 a.m. to 4 p.m.; Thursdays to 9 p.m.

Admission/Fare: Adults, $6; seniors, $5; children under age 16, $3; families (parents and children under age 16), $14.50.

Locomotives/Rolling Stock: Three RGS "Galloping Geese" motorcars; D&RGW Baldwin 1890 2-8-0 no. 683; Rio Grande Zephyr EMD F9s 5771 and 5762; Chicago Burlington & Quincy 4-8-4 no. 5629; Santa Fe Super Chief 1937 observation car Navajo; more.

Nearby Attractions: Coors Brewery, Buffalo Bill Museum, Blackhawk and Central City casinos.

Directions: Twelve miles west of downtown Denver. I-70 westbound exit 265 or eastbound exit 266 to W. 44th Ave.

Site Address: 17155 W. 44th Ave., Golden, CO
Mailing Address: PO Box 10, Golden, CO 80402
Telephone: (303) 279-4591 and (800) 365-6263
Fax: (303) 279-4229
E-mail: mail@crrm.org
Website: www.crrm.org

LEADVILLE, COLORADO & SOUTHERN RAILROAD
Train ride
Standard gauge

BARBARA MALLETTE, THE LEADVILLE PICTURE COMPANY

Description: The 22.5-mile, 2.5-hour train trip follows the headwaters of the Arkansas River to an elevation of 11,120 feet, over an old narrow gauge roadbed converted to standard gauge in the 1940s. The train leaves from the restored 1894 railroad depot (formerly Colorado & Southern, built originally for the Denver, South Park & Pacific) in Leadville, the highest incorporated city in the United States. We offer enclosed, open, and sun cars along with snacks, souvenirs, and restrooms in the boxcars.

Schedule: Memorial Day weekend through September.

Admission/Fare: Adults, $24; children 4-12, $12.50; age 3 and under are free. Group rates available for 20 or more.

Locomotives/Rolling Stock: 1955 EMD GP9 no. 1714, former Burlington Northern; EMD GP-9 no. 1918.

Nearby Attractions: National Mining Museum, Matchless Mine, Leadville's historic mining district, Tabor Opera House, San Isabel National Forest.

Directions: Located 25 miles south of I-70 on Highway 91, Copper Mountain exit. Travel south to Leadville, turn east on E. Seventh St. to depot.

Site Address: 327 E. Seventh St., Leadville, CO
Mailing Address: Box 916, Leadville, CO 80461
Telephone: (719) 486-3936
Fax: (719) 486-0671
E-mail: info@leadville.train
Website: www.leadville-train.com

MANITOU & PIKE'S PEAK RAILWAY
Train ride
Standard gauge (cog)

Description: The M&PP, the highest cog railway in the world, was established in 1889 and has been operating continuously since 1891; it celebrated its centennial of passenger operations in June 1991. A 3¼-hour round trip takes passengers to the summit of Pike's Peak (elevation 14,110 feet) from Manitou Springs (elevation 6,575 feet) and includes a 40-minute stop at the summit.

Schedule: Daily; May through mid-June, September and October, 9:20 a.m. and 1:20 p.m. Mid-June through August, every 80 minutes, 8:00 a.m. to 5:20 p.m.

Admission/Fare: Adults, $26; children 3-11, $14. July through August 15: adults, $27; children, $14.50. Children under 3 free if held on lap. One-way tickets sold on space-available basis.

Locomotives/Rolling Stock: Twin-unit diesel hydraulic railcars and single-unit diesel electric railcars.

Special Events: Occasional steam-up of former M&PP steam locomotive no. 4, built by Baldwin in 1896, and runs of streamliner no. 12, built in 1946.

Directions: Six miles west of Colorado Springs.

Radio frequency: 161.55 and 160.23

Site Address: 515 Ruxton Ave., Manitou Springs, CO
Mailing Address: PO Box 351, Manitou Springs, CO 80829
Telephone: (719) 685-5401
Fax: (719) 685-9033
E-mail: info@cograilway.com
Website: www.cograilway.com

Colorado, Morrison   **TINY TOWN RAILROAD**
Train ride
15" gauge

Description: Tiny Town Railroad, a 1/4 scale live-steam railroad, takes passengers from its full-sized station on a one-mile loop around Tiny Town. Started in 1915, Tiny Town is the oldest miniature town in the United States. It features more than 100 handcrafted, 1/6-sized structures laid out in the configuration of town, rural, and mountainous areas.

Schedule: Memorial Day through Labor Day: daily. May, September, and October: weekends. 10 a.m. to 5 p.m. Train runs continuously.

Admission/Fare: Display–adults, $3; children 3-12, $2; children under age three are free. Train–$1.

Locomotives/Rolling Stock: 1970 standard-gauge 4-6-2 "Occasional Rose" propane-fired; 1970 narrow-gauge 2-6-0 "Cinderbell" coal-fired; 1954 F-unit "Molly," gas-powered; 1952 A- and B-unit "Betsy" gas-powered. Open amusement-park-style cars, propane tank car and caboose.

Nearby Attractions: Red Rocks Park and Dinosaur Ridge.

Directions: Approximately 30 minutes southwest of Denver, off Highway 285.

Site Address: 6249 S. Turkey Creek Rd., Morrison, CO
Mailing Address: 6249 S. Turkey Creek Rd., Morrison, CO 80465
Telephone: (303) 697-6829

Colorado, Pueblo

PUEBLO LOCOMOTIVE & RAIL HISTORICAL SOCIETY INC., PUEBLO RAILWAY MUSEUM
Museum
Standard and narrow gauge

RICHARD M. HOLMES

Description: Static displays, museum car, and gift shop. Take a motor car or hi-rail ride on the old Pueblo Union Depot passenger tracks on selected weekends. Restoration work is ongoing on former ATSF steam locomotive no. 2912. There is fantastic trainwatching on the BNSF and UP main, adjacent to the museum.

Schedule: Tuesdays, tours by appointment. Thursdays and Fridays, 12:30 to 4 p.m. Saturdays, 9:30 a.m. to 4 p.m.

Admission/Fare: Guided tour–adults, $2; children are free.

Locomotives/Rolling Stock: ATSF Baldwin 4-8-4 Northern no. 2912; Colorado Fuel and Iron, GE 25-ton diesel no. 11; Colorado & Southern caboose no. 10538; Colorado & Wyoming locomotive simulator training car no. 100; Denver & Rio Grande Western caboose no. 01432; Southern Pacific bay window caboose no. 4773; more.

Special Events: Open House, weekend following Memorial Day. Pueblo Railfest, September 28-29.

Nearby Attractions: Lake Pueblo State Park, Pueblo Weisbrod Aircraft Museum, Union Ave. Historic District.

Directions: I-25, exit First St. West to Union Ave., south to "B" St., right turn on "B." Museum is located behind and to the west of the depot. Parking available behind the depot.

Site Address: 200 W. "B" St., Pueblo, CO
Mailing Address: PO Box 322, Pueblo, CO 81002
Telephone: (719) 250-0381
Fax: (719) 564-3460
E-mail: BVaneystation1@aol.com
Website: www.pueblorail.com

Colorado, Ridgway

RIDGWAY RAILROAD MUSEUM
Museum
Narrow gauge

JIM PETTENGILL

Description: An educational museum highlighting Ouray County's three railroads: Rio Grande Southern, Denver & Rio Grande, and Silverton Railroad. See photos, a diorama, galloping goose no. 1, and rolling stock.

Schedule: From October 15 to May 15, Monday through Saturday, noon to 4:30 p.m. From May 15 to October 15, daily, noon to 4:30 p.m. Other times by appointment.

Admission/Fare: Donations accepted.

Locomotives/Rolling Stock: RGS Motor no. 1 (galloping goose no. 1); D&RG boxcar no. 3130; D&RG stock car no. 5574; "posse car" prop used in *Butch Cassidy and the Sundance Kid.*

Special Events: Picnic in the Trainyard, outdoor F scale demonstration and picnic fund raiser, early June; Ouray County Railroad Days, demonstrations, symposium, guided field trips, late September.

Nearby Attractions: Spectacular mountain scenery, hiking, jeeping, winter sports, Ridgway State Park, Ouray County Historical Society Museum, outstanding fall colors.

Directions: At the southwest corner of U.S. highways 550 and 62 in Ridgway.

    M

Site Address: 151 Racecourse Rd., Ridgway, CO
Mailing Address: PO Box 588, Ridgway, CO 81432
Telephone: (970) 626-5181 (Chamber of Commerce)
Website: www.ridgwayrailroadmuseum.org

Colorado, Silverton

OLD HUNDRED GOLD MINE TOUR
Train ride
24" gauge

W.R. JONES

Description: This is a ⅔-mile mine train ride and one-hour underground guided mine tour with mining demonstrations. Free gold and silver panning are included. There are mining artifact and rail equipment displays.

Schedule: Daily, May 10 through mid-October. Tours depart hourly, 10 a.m. through 4 p.m.

Admission/Fare: Adults, $14.95, seniors (60+) $13.95, children 5-12, $7.95.

Locomotives/Rolling Stock: Ex-Campbird, Goodman diesel-mechanical; ex-Sunnyside, Greensburg 4-ton battery electric; ex-N.J. Zinc/ Greensburg 6-ton battery electric, various mine cars and rail-mounted mining equipment.

Special Events: Hardrockers Holidays mining contests, second weekend in August.

Nearby Attractions: Durango & Silverton Narrow Gauge Railroad, Mayflower Gold Mill National Historic landmark.

Directions: Five miles east of Silverton on Hwy. 110 and County Road 4-A.

*Coupon available, see coupon section.

Site Address: 721 C.R. 4-A Silverton, CO
Mailing Address: PO Box 430, Silverton, CO 81433-0430
Telephone: (970) 387-5444 and (800) 872-3009
Fax: (970) 387-5579
E-mail: old100@minetour.com
Website: www.minetour.com

Connecticut, Danbury

DANBURY RAILWAY MUSEUM
Train ride, museum, display, layout
Standard gauge

RON FREITAG

Description: Over 50 pieces of equipment representing 11 different northeastern railroads. Vintage train rides in the yard to the only operating turntable in Connecticut. N scale layout of Danbury yard, gift shop, library (by appointment) and displays in our 1903 station.

Schedule: Train rides–Saturdays, April through early November; Sundays also in July and August. Open January through March, Wednesday through Saturday, 10 a.m. to 4 p.m.; Sunday, 12 noon to 4 p.m. April through December, 10 a.m. to 5 p.m.; Sunday, 12 noon to 5 p.m.

Admission/Fare: Adults, $5; seniors, students, NRHS, $4; children 5-12, $3.

Locomotives/Rolling Stock: NH 0673 Alco RS-1; NH 32 Budd RDC-1; DRMX 7589 (NH 1402) Alco RS-11; B&M 1455 Alco 2-6-0; NYC 4096 EMD E9; NYC 1390 Alco FPA; NYC 2013 EMD FL9; NH 2006 EMD FL9; LIRR 617 (NH 0428) Alco FA; CDOT 605 RS3m; more.

Special Events: Every weekend in March, Budd car 50th Anniversary; Easter Bunny Trains, April 12-13, 18-19; Haunted Railyard, October 24-26; Holiday Express to New York City, December 6; Santa Trains, December 13-14, 20-21.

Nearby Attractions: Railroad Museum of New England, Valley Railroad, Military Museum, Danbury Fair Mall, many restaurants.

Directions: I-84 exit 5, right on Main St., left on White St.

Site Address: 120 White St., Danbury, CT
Mailing Address: PO Box 90, Danbury, CT 06813-0090
Telephone: (203) 778-8337
Fax: (203) 778-1836
Website: www.danbury.org/drm

88

Connecticut, East Haven

SHORE LINE TROLLEY MUSEUM
Museum
Standard gauge

G. BOUCHER

Description: The Shore Line Trolley Museum operates the sole remaining segment of the historic 103-year-old Branford Electric Railway. The 3-mile round trip passes woods, salt marshes, and meadows along the scenic Connecticut shore.

Schedule: Memorial Day through Labor Day: daily. May, September, and October: weekends and holidays. April and November: Sundays. Hours 10:30 a.m. to 4:30 p.m. Cars depart every 30 minutes.

Admission/Fare: Unlimited rides and guided tours–adults, $6; seniors, $5; children 2-15, $3; under age 2 are free.

Locomotives/Rolling Stock: Connecticut Co. suburban no. 775; Montreal no. 2001; Johnstown no. 357; Brooklyn (New York) convertible no. 4573; Third Avenue no. 629.

Special Events: Santa Days, Thanksgiving to Christmas on weekends.

Nearby Attractions: Yale University, Foxwoods Casino.

Directions: I-95 exits 51 north or 52 south and follow signs.

*Coupon available, see coupon section.

        M arm

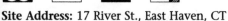

Site Address: 17 River St., East Haven, CT
Mailing Address: 17 River St., East Haven, CT 06512-2519
Telephone: (203) 467-6927 and (203) 467-7635 group sales
Fax: (203) 467-7635
E-mail: BERASLTM@aol.com
Website: www.bera.org

Connecticut, East Windsor

CONNECTICUT TROLLEY MUSEUM
Trolley ride, museum, display
Standard gauge

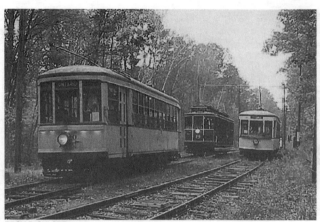

TROY D. SULSER

Description: A 1.5-mile trolley ride through the countryside.

Schedule: April through Memorial Day: Saturday, 10 a.m. to 4 p.m.; Sunday, 12 noon to 4 p.m. Memorial Day through Labor Day: Wednesday through Friday, 10 a.m. to 4 p.m.; Saturday, 10 a.m. to 4 p.m.; Sunday, 12 noon to 4 p.m. Labor Day through December: Saturday, 10 a.m. to 4 p.m.; Sunday, 12 noon to 4 p.m. Closed Thanksgiving, Christmas Eve, and Christmas Day.

Admission/Fare: Adults, $6; seniors (62+), $5; youth ages 3-12, $3; under age 2 are free. Group rates are available.

Trolleys: No. 1326, former Connecticut Co.; nos. 4, 2056, and 2600, former Montreal Tramways; no. 1850, former Rio de Janeiro; no. 451, former ITPCC car.

Special Events: Halloween program: Little Pumpkin Patch. Trolley rides, games, each child receives a pumpkin. Last three weekends in October, Saturdays 10 a.m. to 4 p.m., Sundays 12 noon to 4 p.m. Winterfest: 1.5-mile trolley ride through tunnel of lights. Day after Thanksgiving through December, Fridays through Sundays, 6 to 9 p.m.

Directions: Between Hartford, Connecticut, and Springfield, Massachusetts. I-91, exit 45, ¾ mile east on Route 140.

*Coupon available, see coupon section.

Site Address: 58 North Rd. (Route 140), East Windsor, CT
Mailing Address: PO Box 360, East Windsor, CT 06088-0360
Telephone: (860) 627-6540
Fax: (860) 627-6510
Website: www.ceraonline.org

Connecticut, Essex

ESSEX STEAM TRAIN AND RIVERBOAT RIDE
Train ride, display
Standard gauge

Description: A 1.5-hour excursion through the scenic Connecticut River valley with views of the river and wetlands. The passenger trains consist of restored 1920s-era coaches. You can connect with a riverboat ride for a 2½-hour train-boat combination excursion.

Schedule: Mid-June through Labor Day, daily. May through mid-June, September, and October: Wednesday through Sunday.

Admission/Fare: Train and boat–adults, $18.50; children 3-11, $9.50. Train only–adults, $10.50; children 3-11, $5.50; under age 3 free. Parlor car–extra fare. Open car and caboose (when available)–extra fare. Senior discounts. Group rates available. All tickets sold at Essex station only. Essex Clipper dinner train–$52.95 per person, gratuity and beverages extra.

Locomotives/Rolling Stock: No. 40, Alco 2-8-2, no. 97, Alco 2-8-0; more.

Special Events: A Day Out with Thomas, Easter Eggspress, Eagle Festival Special, Your Hand on the Throttle, Polar Express Santa Special.

Directions: From New York and Boston, I-95 to exit 69 and north on State Route 9 to exit 3. From Hartford, I-91 south to exit 22S and south on State Route 9 to exit 3. Follow signs to Essex Steam Train.

*Coupon available, see coupon section.

Site Address: Near junction of State Routes 9 (exit 3) and 154 in Essex, CT
Mailing Address: PO Box 452, Essex, CT 06426
Telephone: (860) 767-0103
Fax: (860) 767-0104
Website: www.essexsteamtrain.com

CONNECTICUT ANTIQUE MACHINERY ASSOCIATION, INC.
Museum
36" gauge

JOHN STAUFFER

Description: Exhibits show the development of the country's agricultural and industrial technology from the mid-1800s to the present. Exhibits include a collection of large stationary steam engines, large internal combustion engines; an oil field pumphouse; mining museum; agricultural displays of tractors and farm implements; reconstructed Cream Hill Agricultural School buildings (forerunner to the University of Connecticut). A stretch of 3-foot gauge track is in operation during the popular Fall Festival.

Schedule: Memorial Day through Labor Day, weekends and by appointment.

Admission/Fare: Adults, $4; children (5-12), $2; under age 5 are free.

Locomotives/Rolling Stock: No. 4 Argent Lumber Co. Porter 2-8-0; no. 5 Hawaii Railway Co. Baldwin 2-4-2; no. 16 Hutton Brick Co. DL Plymouth; no. 18 Wickwire Spencer Vulcan limited clearance 0-4-0-T; no. 6 Waynesburg & Washington 1894 coach; nos. 1132 and 1331 Denver & Rio Grande 1902 high-side gondolas; no. 111 Tionesta Valley Railway 1917 caboose.

Special Events: Spring Gas Up, first Sunday in May. Fall Festival, last full weekend in September.

Directions: One mile north of village on Route 7 adjacent to Housatonic Railroad.

          M

Site Address: Route 7, Kent, CT
Mailing Address: PO Box 1467, New Milford, CT 06776
Telephone: (860) 927-0050
Website: www.ctamachinery.com

Connecticut, Thomaston

NAUGATUCK RAILROAD/
RAILROAD MUSEUM OF NEW ENGLAND
Train ride
Standard gauge

HOWARD PINCUS

Description: A 17.5-mile round trip over a former New Haven Railroad line, from the 1881 Thomaston Station along the scenic Naugatuck River and past 100-year-old New England brass mills, on to the face of the Thomaston Dam. The original Naugatuck Railroad opened this route in 1849. The Naugatuck Railroad is operated by the not-for-profit Railroad Museum of New England.

Schedule: Starting May 26, weekends, 1 and 3 p.m. Earlier in May, operation for groups of 45 or more. During the fall: 11 a.m., 1 and 3 p.m.

Admission/Fare: Adults, $9.95; seniors, $8.95; children 3-12, $6.95. Group rates and charters available.

Locomotives/Rolling Stock: New Haven RS-3 no. 529; New Haven U25B no. 2525; Naugatuck GP-9 no. 1732; Canadian National open-window heavyweight coaches from 1920s.

Special Events: Occasional excursions over entire 19.6-mile route between Waterbury and Torrington. Also, engineer-for-an-hour program.

Nearby Attractions: Amusement parks, vineyards, state parks.

Directions: I-84, exit 20 to north on Route 8, exit 38 Thomaston.

Site Address: E. Main St., Thomaston, CT
Mailing Address: PO Box 400, Thomaston, CT 06787-0400
Telephone: (860) 283-RAIL
Fax: (203) 269-3364
E-mail: rrexc@snet.net
Website: www.rmne.org

Connecticut, Willimantic

ROBERT A. LA MAY

Description: Tour a railroad village and railroad equipment; the tour lasts approximately one hour. An 1850 replica pump car is available for rides, and there are ongoing restoration projects.

Schedule: May through November, 10 a.m. to 4 p.m.; open holidays during the same hours.

Admission/Fare: Adults and seniors, $3; children 12 and under are free.

Locomotives/Rolling Stock: CERR no. 0800 44-ton; CERR 25-ton; CV RS-11 no. 3608; CV S-4 no. 8081; B&M RDC no. 6152; MEC railbus no. 10; Pfizer SW8 no. 2; New Haven baggage no. 3841; New Haven coach no. 4414; New Haven coaches nos. 8673 and 8695; CV boxcar no. 43022; CV flatcar no. 4287; CV cabooses nos. 4029 and 4052; New Haven caboose C618; and Trackmobile carmover.

Nearby Attractions: Windham Textile and History Museum, Jillson House Museum.

Directions: Located off Route 32 (Bridge St.) in downtown Willimantic.

Site Address: 55 Bridge St. (Rt. 32), Willimantic, CT
Mailing Address: PO Box 665, Willimantic, CT 06226
Telephone: (860) 456-9999
E-mail: webmaster@cteastrrmuseum.org
Website: www.cteastrrmuseum.org

Delaware, Wilmington

WILMINGTON & WESTERN RAILROAD
Train ride, dinner train
Standard gauge

SETH JACKSON

Description: A ten-mile, 1¼-hour round trip over a portion of former Baltimore & Ohio Landenberg Branch from Greenbank Station to Mt. Cuba. Occasional trips to Yorklyn and Hockessin are also offered.

Schedule: April through December: Saturdays and/or Sundays, one- and two-hour excursions along the Red Clay Valley. Call or write for timetable.

Admission/Fare: Varies, please call or write for information. Caboose rentals, group rates, and private charters are available.

Locomotives/Rolling Stock: Two SW-1 EMD switchers; 1909 Alco steam 4-4-0; 1907 Baldwin 0-6-0; 1910 Canadian Locomotive Co. 2-6-0; 1929 PRR railcar.

Special Events: Easter Bunny Special, Santa Claus Express, Dinner and/or Murder Mystery Trains, Civil War Weekend.

Nearby Attractions: Longwood Gardens, Hagley Museum, Kalmar Nyckel, Winterthur Museum.

Directions: I-95, exit 5, follow Route 141 north to Route 2 west, then follow Route 41 north. Greenbank Station is on Route 41 just north of Route 2, 4 miles southwest of Wilmington.

*Coupon available, see coupon section.

          M

  Radio frequency: 160.755

Site Address: 2201 Newport-Gap Pike, Route 41, Wilmington, DE
Mailing Address: PO Box 5787, Wilmington, DE 19808
Telephone: (302) 998-1930
Fax: (302) 998-7408
E-mail: schedule@wwrr.com
Website: www.wwrr.com

Florida, Fort Myers

FORT MYERS HISTORICAL MUSEUM

Museum

Description: Relive the rich history of southwest Florida. Walk with the prehistoric animals of the area, live with the Calusa Indians. Ever wondered how Thomas Edison traveled here? Experience it yourself as you tour the "Esperanza," our private Pullman railcar.

Schedule: Tuesdays through Saturdays, 9 a.m. to 4 p.m.

Admission/Fare: Adults, $6; seniors, $5.50; children under 12, $3.

Locomotives/Rolling Stock: Pullman Standard Car & Manufacturing Co. 1929/30 "Esperanza" no. 6242.

Special Events: Open year-round for tours (closed Sundays and Mondays).

Nearby Attractions: Thomas A. Edison winter home, Henry Ford winter home, Burroughs home, baseball spring training camps for Boston Red Sox and Minnesota Twins, Sanibel Island beaches.

Directions: Take I-75, to exit 138 (Martin Luther King Jr. Blvd.), drive 5 miles west to downtown Fort Myers to Jackson St. Turn left and go one block to Peck St.

*Coupon available, see coupon section.

Site Address: 2300 Peck St., Fort Myers, FL
Mailing Address: 2300 Peck St., Fort Myers, FL 33901
Telephone: (239) 332-5955
Fax: (239) 332-6637
E-mail: msantiago@cityftmyers.com

Florida, Fort Myers

MURDER MYSTERY DINNER TRAIN ON THE SEMINOLE GULF RAILWAY
Train ride, dinner train
Standard gauge

Description: A freight railroad serving southwest Florida that offers excursion trains (20-mile, 2-hour round trip) and dinner trains (30-mile, 3½-hour round trip).

Schedule: Excursion trains–year-round, Wednesdays and weekends. Murder mystery dinner train–five nights a week: Wednesday through Saturday, 6:30 p.m.; Sunday, 5:30 p.m.

Admission/Fare: Excursion train–adults, $7 and up; children 3-12, $4 and up. Dinner train theater, $47.98 and up.

Locomotives/Rolling Stock: GP9s; Alco C-425; EMD F7 and F9; local freight railroad (115 miles).

Special Events: Christmas rail/boat trips in December.

Nearby Attractions: Edison and Ford winter homes, Edison lab and museum, Red Sox and Minnesota Twins spring training, former ACL City Station (Fort Myers Historical Museum), beaches and water attractions.

Directions: Excursion and dinner trains depart from Colonial Station near the Colonial Blvd. (State Route 884) and Metro Parkway intersection in Fort Myers, 3 miles west of I-75 exit 22.

*Coupon available, see coupon section.

Site Address: Station on Colonial Blvd. at Metro Pkwy., Fort Myers, FL
Mailing Address: 4410 Centerpointe Dr., Ste. 207, Fort Myers, FL 33916
Telephone: (239) 275-8487 and (800) SEM-GULF
Fax: (239) 275-0581
E-mail: RSVP@semgulf.com
Website: www.semgulf.com

Florida, Fort Myers

RAILROAD MUSEUM OF SOUTH FLORIDA'S TRAIN VILLAGE
Train ride
7½" gauge

MICHAEL MULLIGAN

Description: Miniature train ride–a 1½-mile round trip through tropical county park, tunnel, bridges, villages, gardens, around lakes.

Schedule: Weekdays, 10 a.m. to 2 p.m.; Saturdays, 10 a.m. to 4 p.m.; Sundays, 12 noon to 4 p.m. Closed Christmas Day and Thanksgiving Day. August through September, weekends only.

Admission/Fare: $2.50; children 5 and under, $.50.

Locomotives/Rolling Stock: Museum piece Atlantic Coast Line 0-4-0 no. 143 and tender, built in 1904, cosmetically restored.

Special Events: Haunted Express, last two weeks of October, 6:30 to 9 p.m. nightly. Holiday Express, month of December, 6:30 to 9 p.m. nightly.

Nearby Attractions: Fort Myers Beach, Sanibel Island, Edison Winter Home, Fort Myers Historical Museum.

Directions: Take I-75 to the Daniels Rd. exit. Also, Southwest Florida Regional Airport, west 4 miles to Lakes Park Regional Park.

      M

Site Address: 7330 Gladiolus Dr., Fort Myers, FL
Mailing Address: PO Box 7372, Fort Myers, FL 33911-7372
Telephone: (239) 267-1905

Florida, Miami

GOLD COAST RAILROAD MUSEUM
Train ride, museum, display, layout
24" gauge

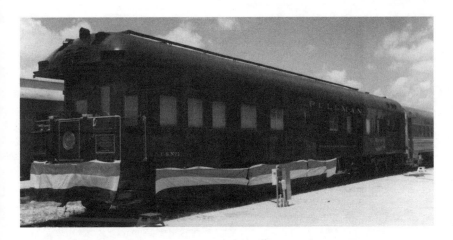

Description: Two-foot equipment operates Saturday and Sunday; standard gauge operates on the second weekend of each month. On a 58-acre site, you can see model trains and a covered trainshed with 20 pieces of equipment, including a variety of locomotives, passenger cars, and freight cars. Additional equipment is in the yard.

Admission/Fare: Adults, $5; children, $3; under 3 free. Train ride–2-foot gauge, $2; standard gauge, $5.

Locomotives/Rolling Stock: For a detailed listing of our equipment, please see our website.

Nearby Attractions: Miami Metro Zoo (on the same property), Coral Castle, Monkey Jungle, Florida Everglades Park.

Directions: Florida Turnpike south to exit 16; follow the signs. Or U.S. 1 south to SW 152nd St., turn right at the intersection, and follow the signs.

*Coupon available, see coupon section.

       M

Site Address: 12450 SW 152nd St., Miami, FL
Mailing Address: 12450 SW 152nd St., Miami, FL 33177
Telephone: (305) 253-6300
Fax: (305) 233-4641
E-mail: Through website
Website: http://goldcoast-railroad.org

Florida, Milton

**WEST FLORIDA
RAILROAD MUSEUM**
Museum, layout

Description: The West Florida Railroad Museum is a former L&N depot/freighthouse with a static display of two cabooses, boxcar, a flatcar, and three heavyweight passenger cars. It houses a model railroad club HO layout (with a theme of the '50s and '60s) and offers miniature train rides.

Schedule: Open Fridays and Saturdays from 11 a.m. to 3 p.m. or by appointment for group visits.

Admission/Fare: Free.

Locomotives/Rolling Stock: L&N diner "Globe Coffee House"; L&N passenger car no. 1652 (museum office car); L&N passenger car no. 2715; L&N caboose no. 1148; St. Louis, San Francisco (Frisco) caboose no. 1102; L&N boxcar no. 18050; L&N flatcar no. 21107.

Special Events: Depot Days, second weekend (Saturday and Sunday) of November, arts & crafts, music, food, amusements.

Nearby Attractions: National Museum of Naval Aviation (Pensacola), Gulf Breeze, Florida Zoo, Gulf Islands National Seashore.

Directions: I-10 to exit 8 (old), Bagdad. Then go north 3 miles on county route 191 to the railroad crossing and depot.

Site Address: 206 S. Henry St., Milton, FL
Mailing Address: PO Box 770, Milton, FL 32572
Telephone: (850) 623-3645

**ORLANDO & MOUNT
DORA RAILWAY**
Train ride
Standard gauge

Description: Operates over a 37-mile segment between Orlando and Mount Dora. Take a day trip on the Mount Dora Limited between Orlando and Mount Dora, or a one-hour ride on 1928 "Dora Doodlebug" motor car.

Schedule: Year-round.

Admission/Fare: Doodlebug–adults, $12; seniors, $11; children (under 12), $8. Mount Dora Limited–adults, $40; seniors, $35; children (under 12), $20.

Locomotives/Rolling Stock: 1928 Brill Interurban converted to Edwards gas-mechanical M-201; no. 4 Baldwin 2-6-2, Reader Railroad; two coaches, combine, and open-air gondola car; Illinois Central "Calumet Club," no. 3378.

Special Events: Art Festival, Craft Fair, Pumpkin Train, Santa Express.

Directions: Located 30 minutes north of Orlando. Take Highway 441 north, go left on Donelly St. We're on the corner of Alexander St. and Third Ave.

Site Address: 150 W. Third Ave., Mount Dora, FL
Mailing Address: 150 W. Third Ave., Mount Dora, FL 32756
Telephone: (352) 735-4667
Fax: (352) 735-6255
Website: www.mtdoratrain.com

Florida, Palm Beach

THE FLAGLER MUSEUM
Museum

© FLAGLER MUSEUM

Description: Whitehall, a 55-room Gilded Age estate and National Historic Landmark, was the winter home of Henry M. Flagler, developer of the Florida East Coast Railway that linked the east coast of Florida. Experience life during America's Gilded Age through the eyes of one of its most important citizens, Henry Flagler. Flagler, with partners John D. Rockefeller and Samuel Andrews, founded Standard Oil. Displays and exhibits focus on the contributions Flagler made to the state of Florida by building the Florida East Coast Railway and developing tourism and agriculture as the state's major industries.

Schedule: Year-round. Tuesdays through Saturdays, 10 a.m. to 5 p.m. Sundays, noon to 5 p.m. Closed Thanksgiving, Christmas Day, and New Year's Day.

Admission/Fare: Adults, $8; children 6-12, $3. Free on Founder's Day.

Locomotives/Rolling Stock: FEC Car no. 91, Henry Flagler's private railcar, built in 1886.

Special Events: Whitehall Lecture Series, February and March. Founder's Day, June 5. Flagler Museum Music Series, December through April. Holiday tours, December.

Nearby Attractions: Museums, zoo, Atlantic Ocean.

Directions: I-95 to exit 52 (Okeechobee Blvd.). Travel 3 miles across Intracoastal Waterway, left on Cocoanut Row. Museum is ¾ mile on left.

        M

Site Address: Cocoanut Row and Whitehall Way, Palm Beach, FL
Mailing Address: PO Box 969, Palm Beach, FL 33480
Telephone: (561) 655-2833
Fax: (561) 655-2826
E-mail: flagler@emi.net
Website: www.flagler.org

Florida, Winter Garden

CENTRAL FLORIDA RAILROAD MUSEUM
Museum, display, layout

Description: A large museum emphasizing the history of Florida railroads (Operated by Central Florida Chapter, NRHS). It is located in the former Tavares & Gulf Railroad station.

Schedule: Sundays, 2 to 5 p.m. Closed major holidays.

Admission/Fare: Free, donations appreciated.

Locomotives/Rolling Stock: Clinchfield caboose.

Special Events: Railroad Show in October and April in Apoka, Florida.

Nearby Attractions: Winter Garden Heritage Museum, Orlando attractions, West Orange Trail (built on ex-Orange Belt, ex-Plant System, ex-ACL line), several city parks and restaurants, Citrus Tower.

Directions: Turnpike to Winter Garden exit, east on State Route 50 to Dillard St., left on Dillard, left on Story Rd., right on Boyd St. to museum.

Site Address: 101 S. Boyd St., Winter Garden, FL
Mailing Address: 101 S. Boyd St., Winter Garden, FL 34787
Telephone: (407) 656-8749
E-mail: irvl@peoplepc.com

Florida, Winter Haven

Description: This tropical showplace includes Cypress Junction, where ten high-speed model trains tour tiny replicas of U.S. landmarks–Miami, New Orleans, Mt. Rushmore–on 1,100 feet of track.

Schedule: Year-round, daily, 10:30 a.m. to 5 p.m. Extended hours during special seasons.

Admission/Fare: Entrance price to theme park–adults, $34.95 plus tax; children (6-17), $19.95 plus tax; kids free.

Locomotives/Rolling Stock: Santa Fe no. 3571; B&O or Chessie System BTO no. 3597; Seaboard System no. 6378; Lehigh Valley no. 211; Atlantic Coast Line C-O no. 47124.

Nearby Attractions: Bok Tower, Fantasy of Flight, and all Orlando attractions.

Directions: I-4 to U.S. 27 south to 540 west. Located in central Florida.

Site Address: 2641 S. Lake Summit, Winter Haven, FL
Mailing Address: PO Box 1, Cypress Gardens, FL 33884
Telephone: (863) 324-2111 and (800) 282-2123
Fax: (863) 324-7946
E-mail: publicrelations@cypressgardens.com
Website: www.cypressgardens.com

BLUE RIDGE SCENIC RAILWAY
Train ride, display, layout

DICK HILLMAN

Description: A 3½-hour round trip (includes layover) along the Toccoa River to McCaysville, Georgia, on the old L&N Hook and Eye Division. The gift shop is located in a 100-year-old depot in downtown Blue Ridge.

Schedule: February through mid-December: Friday, Saturday, Sunday, and Monday departures, daily in October.

Admission/Fare: Adults, $25 and up; seniors, $20 and up; children, $12.50 and up, year-round. Send for further schedule information for changes.

Locomotives/Rolling Stock: Various diesel locomotives available to us through our parent company, Georgia Northeastern Railroad. GP7 no. 2097; GP9 no. 6576; GP10 no. 7529; GP10 no. 7562; GP18 no. 8704; GP18 no. 8705; GP20 no. 316; GP20 no. 4125; SW1 no. 77, 1947; NW1 no. 81, 1948.

Nearby Attractions: Amicalola Falls State Park; Helen, Georgia (alpine village), surrounded by national forests, hiking and biking trails; Ocoee Whitewater Center.

Directions: Ninety miles north of Atlanta and 85 miles southeast of Chattanooga, Tennessee.

Site Address: 241 Depot St., Blue Ridge, GA
Mailing Address: 241 Depot St., Blue Ridge, GA, 30513
Telephone: (706) 632-9833, and (800) 934-1898
Fax: (706) 258-2756
Website: www.brscenic.com

SOUTHEASTERN RAILWAY MUSEUM
Train ride, display
Standard gauge

Description: Visitors meet rail history "hands on" through the display of over 90 pieces of retired railway rolling stock, including a World War II troop kitchen, railway post office, the 1911 Pullman "Superb" used by President Warren Harding, a modern office car, vintage steam locomotives, restored wooden cabooses. Short on-site train ride aboard vintage cabooses.

Schedule: April through November: Thursday, Friday, Saturday, 10 a.m. to 5 p.m. December through March: Saturdays, 10 a.m. to 5 p.m. Train rides complimentary with admission.

Admission/Fare: Adults, $6; seniors and children 2-12, $4; under age 2 are free.

Locomotives/Rolling Stock: 1950 and 1941 HRT GE 44-ton nos. 2 and 5; 1943 Georgia Power Porter 0-6-0T no. 97; 1954 CRR caboose no. 1064; SOU caboose XC7871; SCL caboose no. 01077.

Directions: I-85 northwest of Atlanta to west on exit 104 (Pleasant Hill Rd.) for 3.5 miles to U.S. 23 (Buford Highway). North ¼ mile to Peachtree Rd., turn west to museum entrance.

Site Address: 3595 Peachtree Rd., Duluth, GA
Mailing Address: PO Box 1267, Duluth, GA 30096
Telephone: (770) 476-2013
Fax: (770) 926-6095
E-mail: admin@srmduluth.org
Website: www.srmduluth.org

Georgia, Kennesaw

SOUTHERN MUSEUM OF CIVIL WAR AND LOCOMOTIVE HISTORY
Museum
Standard gauge

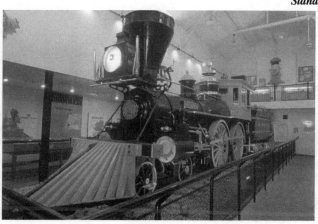

Description: The Andrews Raid and the Great Locomotive Chase, one of the unusual episodes of the Civil War, has been much publicized over the years. In 1972 the famous locomotive "The General" was enshrined in a museum just 100 yards from the spot where she was stolen on April 12, 1862. Now the extensively renovated museum will collect, preserve, and interpret artifacts relating to the role of steam locomotives in Southern history. Renovations are scheduled to be completed at the end of 2002.

Schedule: Please call or see website for information.

Admission/Fare: Please call or see website for information.

Locomotives/Rolling Stock: Rodgers 4-4-0 no. 3, "The General"; two 0-4-0 Glover Machine Works locomotives.

Nearby Attractions: Kennesaw Mountain National Battlefield Park, Marietta History Museum, Gone with the Wind Museum, Pickett's Mill Battlefield State Park.

Directions: I-75 north (from Atlanta) exit 273 (Wade Green Rd.), west 2.3 miles. Museum is on right.

*Coupon available, see coupon section.

†See ad on page A-2.

Site Address: 2829 Cherokee St., Kennesaw, GA
Mailing Address: 2829 Cherokee St., Kennesaw, GA 30144
Telephone: (770) 427-2117
Fax: (678) 354-7580
E-mail: hharris@kennesaw.ga.us
Website: www.kennesaw.ga.us and www.southernmuseum.org

Georgia, Savannah

**ROUNDHOUSE RAILROAD
MUSEUM**
Museum, display, layout

PAINTING BY T.J. SCYPINSKI

Description: Savannah's Roundhouse Railroad Museum is the oldest and most complete antebellum railroad manufacturing and repair facility still standing in the U.S. and is a National Historic Landmark. Construction of the site began in 1845 and 13 of the original structures are still standing, including the massive roundhouse and operating turntable and the 125-foot smokestack. There are permanent exhibits in five of the structures on site.

Schedule: Year-round, daily. Self-guided tours, 9 a.m. to 4 p.m.

Admission/Fare: Adults, $4; seniors and children, $3.50.

Locomotives/rolling stock: Wrightsville & Tennille no. 223, 1907; Central of Georgia "Old Maude," 1886; Georgia Power "goat," 1913, our only operating steam locomotive; Holly Hill Lumber Co. no. 15, 1914. Savannah & Atlanta Railway GP35 diesel-electric no. 2715; Central Railroad & Banking Co. inspection car no. 2; Melbourne Tramways type W5 car no. 756; Birney Car no. 630; many freight cars.

Nearby Attractions: Savannah History Museum and Savannah's Historic District of Homes and Museums.

Directions: I-16 east to Martin Luther King Jr. Blvd. exit. Left on Martin Luther King Jr. Blvd., and then left on Harris St.

*Coupon available, see coupon section.

Site Address: 601 W. Harris St., Savannah, GA
Mailing Address: 601 W. Harris St., Savannah, GA 31401
Telephone: (912) 651-6823
Fax: (912) 651-3194
E-mail: rjusten@chsgeorgia.org
Website: www.chsgeorgia.org

HAWAIIAN RAILWAY SOCIETY
Train ride, museum, display
36" gauge

MARK D. BRUESHABER

Description: A 6½-mile, 90-minute ride along OR&L track from Ewa to Kahe Point, where passengers can witness the surf crashing against the rocks. The train passes former Barbers Point Naval Air Station, Ko'Olina Golf Course, and more. Fully narrated trip provides railroading history of the area.

Schedule: Sunday, 12:30 and 2:30 p.m. (weather permitting). Call for information.

Admission/Fare: Adults, $8; seniors and children ages 2-12, $5; under age 2 are free.

Locomotives/Rolling Stock: Two Whitcomb diesel-electrics, nos. 302 and 423; converted U.S. Army flatcars; parlor car no. 64.

Special Events: Halloween rides. Call or write for information.

Nearby Attractions: Ihilani Resort; Ko'Olina Golf Course; Paradise Cove Luau.

Directions: Freeway H-1, exit 5A, continue on 76 (Fort Weaver Rd.) south to Renton Rd., take a right on Renton Rd., and left on Fleming Rd.

†See ad on page A-4.

       arm TRAIN M

Site Address: 91-1001 Renton Rd., Ewa Town, HI
Mailing Address: PO Box 60369, Ewa Station, Ewa, HI 96706
Telephone: (808) 681-5461
Fax: (808) 681-4860
E-mail: HawaiianRailway@aol.com
Website: members.aol.com/hawaiianrailway//index.html

Hawaii, Lahaina (Maui)

LAHAINA, KAANAPALI & PACIFIC RAILROAD
Train ride, dinner train
36" gauge

Description: The "Sugar Cane Train" chugs its way through the colorful history and breath-taking scenes of Maui by bringing back memories, sounds, and experiences of turn-of-the-century sugar plantation life. The sugar trains of the past were used to transport sugar cane from the fields to the mills and were a popular means of transportation for sugar workers in the early 1900s. Passengers are taken on an entertaining and historical tour by one of our singing conductors. The train stations are designed to resemble turn-of-the-century boarding platforms and are a delightful glimpse at Hawaii's historical and cultural past.

Schedule: Daily, 10:15 a.m. to 4:30 p.m.

Admission/Fare: Call or write for information.

Locomotives/Rolling Stock: No. 1, "Anaka," 1943 Porter 2-4-0 and no. 3, "Myrtle," 1943 Porter 2-4-0, both former Carbon Limestone Co.; no. 45, "Oahu," 1959 Plymouth diesel, former Oahu Railway; nine 19th-century King Kalakaua replica nostalgic coaches; two non-operational displays of Oahu 5 and Oahu 86 from Oahu Railway; more.

Nearby Attractions: Historic town of Lahaina, Maui, and resort area of Kaanapali.

Directions: Lahaina Station located near Pioneer Mill, turn off Highway 30 at Hinau St., turn right at Limahana St.

Site Address: 975 Limahana Pl., Ste. 203, Lahaina, Maui, HI
Mailing Address: 975 Limahana Pl., Ste. 203, Lahaina, Maui, HI 96761
Telephone: (800) 499-2307, (888) LKP-MAUI, and (808) 661-0089 (recording)
Fax: (808) 661-8389
E-mail: info@sugarcanetrain.com
Website: www.sugarcanetrain.com

CANYON COUNTY HISTORICAL MUSEUM
Museum, layout

Description: Built in 1903, this train depot is now the home of the Canyon County Museum. Used as a depot until 1926, and then as offices for the Union Pacific Railroad, the building now houses displays of both Canyon County and Union Pacific memorabilia.

Schedule: Year-round, Tuesday through Saturday, 1 to 5 p.m.

Admission/Fare: Free. Suggested donation: Adults, $1, children $.50.

Locomotives/Rolling Stock: Union Pacific Caboose no. 25076, can be toured; steam crane circa 1917.

Special Events: Snake River Stampede, Good Old Dayz Celebration, starts second weekend in July, includes rodeo, entertainment, lots of family activities, parade.

Nearby Attractions: War Hawk Air Museum, WWII memorabilia; Celebration Park, petroglyphs and interpretive center; Oregon trail sites, several throughout Treasure Valley area; Old Fort Boise, replica of old fort.

Directions: I-84 take Garrity exit, turn left on Garrity Rd. to 16th Ave., then turn left at Lakeview Park. Go over overpass and turn right on first street. Turn right on 12th Ave., and go one block to Front St. to Depot museum.

      M

Site Address: 1200 Front St., Nampa, ID
Mailing Address: 1200 Front St., Nampa, ID 83651
Telephone: (208) 467-7611
E-mail: canyondepomuseum@netzero.net

Idaho, Wallace

**NORTHERN PACIFIC DEPOT
RAILROAD MUSEUM**
Museum

Description: The museum offers pictorial exhibits and railroad artifacts.

Schedule: April, 9 a.m. to 5 p.m., Monday through Saturday; May, 9 a.m. to 5 p.m., daily; June through August, 9 a.m. to 7 p.m., daily; September, 9 a.m. to 5 p.m., daily; October, 9 a.m. to 3 p.m. Closed October 15 for season.

Admission/Fare: Adults, $2; seniors, $1.50; children 6-16, $1; under 6 are free; family, $6. For tour information, please call.

Special Events: Depot Day Festival and Car Show, Saturday before Mother's Day.

Nearby Attractions: Mine Tour, Mining Museum, Oasis Bordello Museum.

Directions: I-90, exit 62, Wallace, Idaho.

*Coupon available, see coupon section.

Site Address: 219 Sixth St., Wallace, ID
Mailing Address: PO Box 469, Wallace, ID 83873
Telephone: (208) 752-0111
Fax: (208) 753-9361

HISTORIC PULLMAN FOUNDATION
Museum

Description: The Historic Pullman Foundation operates the Pullman Visitor Center, which gives an overview of George Pullman, the Pullman Company, and Mr. Pullman's town, built in the 1880s, which still exits.

Schedule: Year-round. Monday through Friday, 12 noon to 2 p.m.; Saturday, 11 a.m. to 2 p.m.; Sunday, 12 noon to 3 p.m.

Admission/Fare: Adults, $3; students, $2 suggested donation. Group tours available; call (773) 785-3828.

Special Events: Annual Pullman House Tour, second weekend in October, 11 a.m. to 5 p.m. First Sunday guided walking tours, 12:30 and 1:30 p.m., May through October.

Nearby Attractions: Museum of Science and Industry, Downtown Chicago, riverboat casinos, Sandridge Nature Center, South Suburban Geneology Society, Ridge Historic District, International Harborside Golf Course, River Oaks Mill, Calumet Park Beach, East Side Historical Society, Wolf Lake.

Directions: I-94 to 111th St. (exit 66A), travel west four blocks. Metra Electric stops at 111th St./Pullman, 115th St./Kensington, and downtown Chicago.

Site Address: 11141 S. Cottage Grove Ave., Chicago, IL
Mailing Address: 1000 E. 111th St., 10th Floor, Chicago, IL 60628-4614
Telephone: (773) 785-3828 and (773) 785-8181
Fax: (773) 785-8182
E-mail: foundation@pullmanil.org and tours@pullmanil.org
Website: www.pullmanil.org

MUSEUM OF SCIENCE AND INDUSTRY
Museum, display, layout
Standard gauge

Description: The Museum of Science and Industry is one of the nation's preeminent centers for informal science and technology education. The Great Train Story, the museum's new model railroad exhibit, is a 3,500-square-foot layout that depicts the railroad's winding journey between Chicago and Seattle.

Schedule: Hours of operation for the museum are: Monday through Saturday, 9:30 a.m. to 4 p.m.; Sundays, 11 a.m. to 4 p.m.

Admission/Fare: Adults, $9; seniors, $7.50; children 3-11, $5. Chicago residents receive a discount.

Locomotives/Rolling Stock: Engine 999 was the first vehicle to go over 100 mph. The *Pioneer Zephyr* was the first streamlined diesel-electric train.

Nearby Attractions: Soldier Field, Navy Pier, Shedd Aquarium, Field Museum, Adler Planetarium, Art Institute, Wrigley Field, Comiskey Park.

Directions: By car–take Lake Shore Dr. south to 57th St. By train–Metra trains stop at the 55th/56th/57th Street station, two blocks from the Museum's north exit. Turn left as you exit the station. Chicago South Shore & South Bend trains stop at the 59th Street station.

         M

Site Address: 57th St. and Lake Shore Dr., Chicago, IL
Mailing Address: 57th St. and Lake Shore Dr., Chicago, IL 60637
Telephone: (773) 684-1414
Fax: (773) 684-2907
Website: www.msichicago.org

AMERICAN ORIENT EXPRESS
Train ride
Standard gauge

Description: Luxury rail vacations across the U.S., Canada, and Mexico by vintage streamliner train. Eight- to eleven-day programs.

Schedule: Operating season, January through November.

Admission/Fare: Prices based on tour and accommodations. Fares start at $2,890 per person. Vintage Pullman based on double occupancy.

Nearby Attractions: Tours include Antebellum South; Transcontinental Journey; Pacific Coast Explorer; Great Trans-Canada Rail Journey; Autumn in New England and Quebec; Southwest and Mexico's Copper Canyon; Great Northwest and Rockies; National Parks of the West.

Site Address: Varies.
Mailing Address: 5100 Main St., Suite 300, Downers Grove, IL 60515
Telephone: (800) 320-4206 and (630) 663-4550
Fax: (630) 663-1595
Website: www.americanorientexpress.com

ELIZABETH DEPOT MUSEUM
Museum

Description: Depot museum displaying artifacts of the Chicago Great Western Railroad. This depot serviced the nearby Winston Tunnel, the longest railroad tunnel in Illinois. The museum features a model of the tunnel.

Schedule: May through October, weekends, 1 to 4 p.m.

Admission/Fare: Free.

Special Events: Great Western Day, first Saturday in May, featuring additional displays and activities relating to the railroad.

Nearby Attractions: Apple River Fort, also in downtown Elizabeth; Mississippi Palisades State Park, Apple River Canyon State Park.

Directions: Three miles east of the Great River Road on U.S. Highway 20; turn right on Myrtle St. at the Veterans' Monument in downtown Elizabeth.

      M

Site Address: Myrtle St., Elizabeth, IL
Mailing Address: PO Box 353, Elizabeth, IL 61028-0353
Telephone: (815) 858-2098
E-mail: elizabethdepot@yahoo.com

Illinois, Freeport

SILVER CREEK & STEPHENSON RAILROAD
Train ride, display
Standard gauge

STEVE SNYDER

Description: The turn-of-the-century Silver Creek Depot is a tribute to an important part of our country's transportation history. On display are lanterns, locks and keys, whistles, sounders, tickets, couplers, and more, representing railroads from across the country. The 4-mile train trip travels through Illinois farmland and stands of virgin timber known as "Indian Gardens," crossing Yellow Creek on a 30-foot-high cement and stone pier bridge.

Schedule: May 25-26; June 14-15; July 4, 25-27; September 1-2, 27-28; October 11-12, 25-26; 11 a.m. to 4 p.m. on the hour.

Admission/Fare: Adults, $5; children (under 12), $3.

Locomotives/Rolling Stock: 1912, 36-ton Heisler; 1941 bay-window caboose, former Chicago, Milwaukee, St. Paul & Pacific; 1889 wooden caboose with cupola, former Hannibal & St. Joseph, reported to be the oldest running caboose in Illinois; 1948 caboose, former Illinois Central Gulf; covered flatcar; 14-ton Brookville switch engine; 12-ton Plymouth switch engine; and work cars.

Directions: Intersection of Walnut and Lamm Roads, ½ mile south of Stephenson County Fairgrounds.

        M

Site Address: 2954 W. Walnut Rd., Freeport, IL
Mailing Address: PO Box 255, Freeport, IL 61032
Telephone: (815) 232-2306
E-mail: peggy1@mwci.net

Illinois, Kankakee

KANKAKEE MODEL RAILROAD CLUB
AND MUSEUM
Museum, display, layout

GLENN JOHNSON

Description: Display area features railroad memorabilia and a full-size Pullman coach. We have running layouts of model trains in G, O, HO, and N scales, and we're developing a new layout in the·building across the parking lot.

Schedule: Saturdays, 11 a.m. to 4 p.m. Sundays, 12 noon to 4 p.m.

Admission/Fare: Free, though donations are accepted.

Locomotives/Rolling Stock: 1947 Pullman stainless-steel coach. Its original owner was Illinois Central Railroad; it spent many years leased to Santa Fe and ended up with Amtrak.

Special Events: We host an annual March swap meet.

Nearby Attractions: Kankakee River State Park; several restaurants; many golf courses in Kankakee County.

Directions: One block south of Highway 17 in downtown Kankakee, in historic, registered, Kankakee railroad depot.

Site Address: 197 S. East Ave., Kankakee, IL
Mailing Address: 197 S. East Ave., Kankakee, IL 60901
Telephone: (815) 929-9320
Fax: (815) 932-4136

MONTICELLO RAILWAY MUSEUM
Train ride, museum
Standard gauge

DAVID MARSHALL

Description: A 7-mile round trip on former Illinois Central and Illinois Terminal trackage. Passengers board at either the Illinois Central depot at the museum or the 1899 Wabash depot downtown Monticello. Visitors view displays located both inside and outside railcars.

Schedule: May through October: weekends and holidays. Museum site departures: Saturdays, 11 a.m., 12:30, 2, and 3:30 p.m.; Sundays, 12:30, 2, and 3:30 p.m. Wabash depot departures: Saturdays, 11:30 a.m., 1 and 2:30 p.m.; Sundays, 1 and 2:30 p.m. Charters, private cars, on request.

Locomotives/Rolling Stock: 1907 Southern Railway Baldwin 2-8-0 no. 401; 1916 Mississippi Eastern Baldwin 4-6-0 no. 303; 1953 Wabash EMD F-7A no. 1189; 1959 CN MLW FPA-4 no. 6789; 1955 LIRR Alco RS-3 no. 301; more.

Special Events: Throttle Times; Caboose Days, August. Railroad Days, September. Ghost Train, October. Lunch with Santa, December.

Nearby Attractions: Allerton Park, nearby Amish and Lincoln sites.

Directions: I-72 exit 166, Market St. Turn onto Iron Horse Pl. at traffic light, go past Best Western to museum.

P 🚌 ✳ ☕ 🎋 ✉ M arm TRAIN 🚆

Site Address: 993 Iron Horse Pl., Monticello, IL
Mailing Address: PO Box 401, Monticello, IL 61856-0401
Telephone: (217) 762-9011 (weekends) and (800) 952-3396 (weekdays)
E-mail: mrm@prairienet.org
Website: www.prairienet.org/mrm

Illinois, Peoria (Dunlap)

WHEELS O' TIME MUSEUM
Museum

TOM MITCHELL

Description: Steam locomotive, combine car, caboose, and switcher, plus three buildings displaying antique autos, fire trucks, tractors, clocks, musical devices, toys, clothing, and much more.

Schedule: May through October: Wednesdays through Sundays, 12 to 5 p.m. Summer holidays.

Admission/Fare: Adults, $4.50; children, $2.00. Under 3 free.

Locomotives/Rolling Stock: Rock Island Pacific no. 886; Milwaukee Road combine car; TP&W caboose.

Nearby Attractions: Wildlife Prairie Park, Lakeview Museum.

Directions: On Route 40, north of Peoria, 2 miles north of the Route 6 intersection.

Site Address: 11923 N. Knoxville, Peoria, IL
Mailing Address: PO Box 9636, Peoria, IL 61612-9636
Telephone: (309) 243-9020
E-mail: wotmuseum@aol.com
Website: wheelsotime.org

120

Description: Rochelle provides an area for train watching for everyone. Two busy mainline railroads (UP and BNSF) cross on the diamonds, averaging 80 to 90 trains in a 24-hour period. Gift shop and heated restrooms are available for all your needs.

Schedule: Park open 365 days a year. Gift shop open every day except Monday and Tuesday, year-round.

Admission/Fare: Free.

Locomotives/Rolling Stock: Whitcomb locomotive on display for the children's enjoyment.

Nearby Attractions: Magic Waters is only a half-hour drive away in Rockford.

Directions: From north and south, take I-39 to Illinois 38 exit west. From east and west, take I-88 to Illinois 251 north.

Site Address: 124 N. Ninth St., Rochelle, IL
Mailing Address: 124 N. Ninth St., Rochelle, IL 61068
Telephone: (815) 562-8107
E-mail: atsf525@aol.com
Website: www.rochellerailroadpark.tripod.com

Description: Forty-five minute trolley ride with historic narrative.

Schedule: June through August, Tuesdays and Thursdays, 11 a.m. to 3 p.m.; weekends, noon to 3 p.m.

Admission/Fare: Adults, $3.50; youth 5-17, $3; 4 and under free; resident discount of 50 cents per rider.

Locomotives/Rolling Stock: Trolley car no. 36

Nearby Attractions: Forest City Queen riverboat rides, Riverview Ice House.

Directions: I-90 to E. State St. exit. East on State St. to Madison St. Turn north onto Madison St. The trolley station is on the west side of the street.

Site Address: 324 N. Madison St., Rockford, IL
Mailing Address: 324 N. Madison St., Rockford, IL 61107
Telephone: (815) 987-8894; TTY (815) 963-DEAF
Fax: (815) 987-1597

DEPOT RAILROAD MUSEUM
Museum, layout

RICHARD M. SCHROEDER

Description: Displays show the history of the former Chicago & Eastern Illinois and other area railroads. The Baggage Room contains an HO model railroad. The Depot Museum preserves the railroads' history in east central Illinois and western Indiana in a former C&EI Railroad Depot.

Schedule: Memorial Day weekend through last Sunday in September. Weekends, noon to 4 p.m. and by appointment.

Admission/Fare: Free. Donations are appreciated.

Nearby Attractions: Rossville Historical Society Museum, Mann's Chapel, Vermilion County Museum, 15 antique shops in downtown area.

Directions: In Rossville, one block north on Illinois Route 1 to Benton St., east three blocks to CSX transportation tracks.

     M

Site Address: E. Benton St., Rossville, IL
Mailing Address: PO Box 1013, Danville, IL 61834-1013
Telephone: (217) 748-6615
E-mail: djcnrhs@prairienet.org or rickshro@aol.com
Website: http://www.prairienet.org/djc-nrhs/

Illinois, South Elgin

FOX RIVER TROLLEY MUSEUM
Train ride, museum
Standard gauge

JACK SOWCHIN

Description: Ride the historic 107-year-old remnant of an interurban railroad aboard Chicago-area interurban and "L" equipment. Includes operation on the new ½-mile line into the Blackhawk Forest Preserve. CNS&M 715 on the new line is shown above.

Schedule: Sundays and holidays (Memorial Day, July 4, and Labor Day), May 11 through November 2. Saturdays, June 28 through Labor Day and October 18 and 25. 11 a.m. to 5 p.m.

Admission/Fare: Adults, $3.50; seniors, $2; children (3-11), $2; under age 3, free. Second ride, $.50. All-day pass, $7.

Locomotives/Rolling Stock: Historic Chicago interurban and "L" equipment including CA&E no. 20; North Shore nos. 715 and 756; CTA nos. 40, 43, 4451, and L202; CRT 5001; AE&FRE no. 5 (diesel).

Special Events: Mother's Day; Spring Caboose Day, June 1; Father's Day; Red, White, and Blue Day, July 4; Trolley Fest and Riverfest, August 16-17; Fall Foliage/Caboose Days October 5 and 12; Pumpkin Trolley, October 18-19 and 25-26.

Directions: Illinois 31 south from I-90 or U.S. 20, or north from I-88. Site is three blocks south of State St. traffic light in South Elgin.

*Coupon available, see coupon section.

       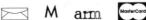

Site Address: 365 S. LaFox St. (Illinois 31), South Elgin, IL
Mailing Address: PO Box 315, South Elgin, IL 60177-0315
Telephone: (847) 697-4676
E-mail: info@foxtrolley.org
Website: www.foxtrolley.org

Illinois, Union (McHenry County)

ILLINOIS RAILWAY MUSEUM
Train ride, museum, display
Standard gauge

Description: More than 400 pieces of equipment and artifacts, operating or on display in car barns and open railyards, including steam, diesel, and electric locomotives; electric interurbans, elevated cars, and streetcars; trolley buses and motor buses, as well as passenger and freight equipment. A 9.5-mile round trip over our 4.8-mile reconstructed Elgin & Belvedere right-of-way is offered, featuring steam or diesel trains and electric interurbans on weekends and streetcars on weekdays.

Schedule: Weekdays, Memorial Day through Labor Day; Saturdays, May through October; Sundays, April through October.

Admission/Fare: Weekends: adults, $8; children 5-11/seniors 62+, $6. Weekdays: adults, $6; children 5-11, $4. Maximum family admission, $35. Higher fares for some special events.

Locomotives/Rolling Stock: No. 2903 Santa Fe 4-8-4; no. 2050 N&W 2-8-8-2; no. 9911A CB&Q EMC E5; no. 6930 UP DDA 40X; Electroliner; many more.

Special Events: Chicago Weekend, June; 4th of July Trolley Pageant; Diesel Days, July; Vintage Transport Day, August; Thomas the Tank Engine, call for details.

Directions: One mile east of Union off U.S. Route 20.

*Coupon available, see coupon section.

†See ad on page A-25.

Site Address: 7000 Olson Rd., Union, IL
Mailing Address: PO Box 427, Union, IL 60180
Telephone: (815) 923-4391 and (815) 923-4000 (recorded message)
Fax: (815) 923-2006
Website: www.irm.org

Illinois, Union (McHenry County)

VALLEY VIEW MODEL
RAILROAD
Layout

Description: This display is modeled after the Chicago & North Western's Northwest line, with accurate track layouts of some of the towns modeled. Three to four trains operate simultaneously over the railroad, which has eight scale miles of track, 20 ever-changing trains, 300 buildings, 64 turnouts, 700 vehicles, 900 people, 84 operating signal lights, 350 pieces of rolling stock, and operating grade crossings with flashers and gates. Extra equipment is on static display in the gift shop.

Schedule: Memorial Day through Labor Day: Wednesdays, Saturdays, and Sundays.

Admission/Fare: Adults, $5; seniors, $4; children, $2.50; age 5 and under are free.

Nearby Attractions: Illinois Railway Museum, Wild West Town, McHenry County Museum.

Directions: From Illinois Railway Museum, travel north ¾ mile on Olson Rd. to Highbridge.

Site Address: 17108 Highbridge Rd., Union, IL
Mailing Address: 17108 Highbridge Rd., Union, IL 60180
Telephone: (815) 923-4135

WATERMAN & WESTERN RAILROAD
Train ride
15" gauge

Description: One-mile ride around a city park.

Schedule: Memorial Day to Labor Day: Sundays 1 to 4 p.m.

Admission/Fare: Summer rides, $1; Pumpkin Train, $4.50; Holiday Lights Train, free, but donation appreciated.

Locomotives/Rolling Stock: 15" gauge F3 built 1990; two 8-passenger gondolas; two 10-passenger steel excursion cars; one caboose; one 8-passenger 1865 coach; one ballast car; one flat car, one Casey Jones railbus; one speeder, one hand pump car.

Special Events: Pumpkin Train, weekends and Fridays in October; Holiday Lights Train, Thursday through Sunday, Thanksgiving to New Year's Eve.

Nearby Attractions: Kids' playground on site.

Directions: Two blocks south of U.S. 30 in downtown Waterman.

*Coupon available, see coupon section.

Site Address: 400 S Birch St. Waterman, IL
Mailing Address: PO Box 217, Waterman, IL 60556
Telephone: (815) 264-7753
Fax: (815) 264-3230
E-mail: wwrr@indianvalley

Indiana, Connersville

WHITEWATER VALLEY RAILROAD
Train ride
Standard gauge

JOHN R. HILLMAN

Description: This line offers a 32-mile, five-hour round trip to Metamora, Indiana, a restored canal town with shops and a working grist mill. A two-hour stopover at Metamora gives passengers a chance to tour the town.

Schedule: May through October: weekends and holidays, 12:01 p.m. May: Wednesday through Friday, 10 a.m.; October: Thursday and Friday, 10 a.m.

Admission/Fare: Adults, $16; children 2-12, $8; under age 2 are free. One-way and group rates available.

Locomotives/Rolling Stock: No. 6, 1907 Baldwin 0-6-0, former East Broad Top; no. 8, 1946 General Electric, former Muncie & Western; no. 11, 1924 Vulcan 0-4-0T; no. 100, 1919 Baldwin 2-6-2; no. 25, 1951 Lima SW7.5; no. 210, 1946 General Electric 70-ton; no. 709, 1950 Lima SW10; no. 2561, 1931 Plymouth 32-ton gas engine; no. 9339, 1948 Alco S1; no. 9376, 1950 Lima SW12, former Baltimore & Ohio; EMD SD-10 no. 532.

Special Events: Metamora Canal Days, first weekend in October; Christmas Trains, November and December. Train-to-Dinner, first and third Fridays of each month May through October.

Nearby Attractions: Whitewater State Park, Brookville Lake, Mary Gray Bird Sanctuary.

Directions: Corner of Fifth and Grand in downtown Connersville (Market St.).

      M

    Radio Frequency: 160.650

Site Address: 455 Market St., Connersville, IN
Mailing Address: PO Box 406, Connersville, IN 47331
Telephone: (765) 825-2054
Fax: (765) 825-4550
Website: www.whitewatervalleyrr.org

NATIONAL NEW YORK CENTRAL
RAILROAD MUSEUM
Museum

TAGMARKS INC.

Description: The museum traces the rich history of the New York Central and its impact on Elkhart and the nation. Extensive hands-on exhibits bring railroading alive.

Schedule: Year-round. Tuesdays through Saturdays, 10 a.m. to 4 p.m.; Sundays 12 noon to 4 p.m. Closed Mondays and major holidays.

Admission/Fare: Adults, $3; seniors (62+) and children 3-12, $2; age 2 and under are free.

Locomotives/Rolling Stock: NYC 3001 L3a Mohawk Alco 1940; NYC 4085 E8 EMD 1953; PRR 4882 GG1; CSS no. 15; six passenger cars; seven freight cars, seven cabooses; six non-revenue.

Nearby Attractions: Northern Indiana Amish Country, Midwest Museum of American Art, Time Was Museum, Woodlawn Nature Center, Ruthmere, RV/MH Museum, Elkhart County Historical Museum.

Directions: Indiana Toll Road (I-80/90) exit 92. Main St. in downtown Elkhart. The museum is in the historic freighthouses next to the Norfolk Southern main line.

  Elkhart

Site Address: 721 S. Main St., Elkhart, IN
Mailing Address: PO Box 1708, Elkhart, IN 46515
Telephone: (574) 294-3001
Fax: (574) 295-9434
E-mail: info@nycrrmuseum.org
Website: www.nycrrmuseum.org

Indiana, Fort Wayne

FORT WAYNE RAILROAD
HISTORICAL SOCIETY
Train ride, museum
Standard gauge

TOM NITZA

Description: Home to steam locomotive 765, currently undergoing a major overhaul by society volunteers. You can tour the facility, talk to the people who maintain and operate this historic rail equipment, sit in the engineer's seat of a 400-ton iron horse and get a conductor's eye view from a 100-year-old caboose. For the ultimate railfan experience, the society offers an Engineer for an Hour program on our diesel locomotive. Several times each year, the society has operating days when you can see railroad equipment in action and ride a vintage caboose.

Schedule: Self-guided tours–March through October, Saturdays, 9 a.m. to 4 p.m. Operating days–in June, August, and December.

Admission/Fare: Museum/self-guided tour, free; train ride, $2 to $4.

Locomotives/Rolling Stock: NKP 2-8-4 Berkshire steam locomotive no. 765; Lake Erie & Fort Wayne 0-6-0 no. 1; NKP wooden caboose no. 141; Wabash wooden caboose no. 2543; N&W wrecker no. 540019; 44-ton Davenport diesel no. 1231; NKP wooden boxcar no. 83047.

Special Events: Annual open house with operating equipment, August; Caboose Ride with Santa, December; Engineer for an Hour program.

Directions: From New Haven take Lincoln Highway/Dawkins Rd. east to Ryan Rd., then left to Edgerton Rd. Turn right, and the society is 1.5 miles on the right.

    M

Site Address: 15808 Edgerton Rd., New Haven, IN
Mailing Address: PO Box 11017, Fort Wayne, IN 46855
Telephone: (219) 493-0765
Website: www.765.org

Indiana, French Lick

FRENCH LICK, WEST BADEN & SOUTHERN RAILWAY
Train ride
Standard gauge

ALAN BARNETT

Description: A 20-mile round trip between the resort town of French Lick and Cuzco, site of Patoka Lake. The train traverses wooded Indiana limestone country and passes through a half-mile tunnel

Schedule: April through October: weekends and Memorial Day, July 4, and Labor Day, 10 a.m., 1 and 4 p.m. June through October: Tuesdays, 1 p.m. November: weekends, 1 p.m.

Admission/Fare: Adults (12 and up), $9; children (3-11), $5.

Locomotives/Rolling Stock: 1947 General Electric 80-ton switcher, 1947 Alco RS-1.

Special Events: Wild West holdups are scheduled for many holiday weekends. Call or write for information.

Nearby Attractions: French Lick Springs Resort.

Directions: Trains depart the old Monon Depot on Highway 56 in French Lick.

Site Address: 1 Monon St., French Lick, IN
Mailing Address: 1 Monon St., French Lick, IN 47432
Telephone: (812) 936-2405 and (800) 74-TRAIN
Fax: (812) 936-2904
E-mail: gabarnett@smithville.net
Website: www.indianarailwaymuseum.org

HESSTON STEAM MUSEUM
Train ride, museum
Various gauges

RON STAHOUIAK

Description: Train rides from full scale to amusement-park size to hobby scale. Each railroad has 2 to 2.5 miles of mainline trackage, all live-steam operation. Operational steam sawmill, steam light plant, more.

Schedule: Memorial Day weekend through Labor Day: Saturdays and Sundays. September through October: Sundays. Noon to 5 p.m.

Admission/Fare: Free admission except Labor Day weekend. Train rides, adults, $3; children, $2.

Locomotives/Rolling Stock: Darjeeling & Himalayan built by Atlas Works; New Mexico Lumber Shay built by Lima Locomotive; Orenstein and Koppel no. 080, German-built in 1938; Koblen Danake Werke no. 040, built in Czechoslovakia 1939; Porter Mogul no. 17 built in 1923.

Special Events: Whistle-Stop Days, Memorial Day weekend; Whistle Fest, July 4; Annual Steam Show, Labor Day weekend.

Nearby Attractions: Lighthouse Mall, Dunes National Lakeshore, Washington Park Beach/Zoo, Blue Chip Casino, charter boat fishing, Door Prairie Auto Museum, motels.

Directions: South of Indiana-Michigan state line. Four miles east of State Road 39 north of LaPorte or south of New Buffalo to 1000 North, turn east, go for about 3 miles.

Site Address: LaPorte County Rd. 1000 North, Hesston, IN
Mailing Address: 2946 Mt. Clair Way, Michigan City, IN 46360
Telephone: (219) 872-5055
Fax: (219) 874-8239
Website: www.hesston.org

CARTHAGE, KNIGHTSTOWN & SHIRLEY RAILROAD
Train ride
Standard gauge

Description: A 10-mile, one-hour round trip from Knightstown to Carthage, Indiana.

Schedule: May through October: weekends, 11 a.m., 1 and 3 p.m.; Fridays, 11 a.m.

Admission/Fare: Adults, $7; children 3-11, $5; under age 3 ride free. Group rates available.

Locomotives/Rolling Stock: No. 215 44-ton GE, miscellaneous coaches and cabooses.

Directions: Thirty miles east of Indianapolis on U.S. 40; three miles out of I-70 on State Route 109.

Site Address: 112 W. Carey St., Knightstown, IN
Mailing Address: 112 W. Carey St., Knightstown, IN 46148
Telephone: (765) 345-5561 and 800-345-2704 (Indiana only)
E-mail: cksrrinc@netzero.net
Website: www.cksrail.com

**JEFFERSON COUNTY HISTORICAL SOCIETY
RAILROAD MUSEUM**
Museum

Madison Railroad Station
Built 1895

© Jefferson County Historical Society 1992

Description: Restored 1895 Pennsylvania Railroad station known for its 2½-story octagon waiting room topped by stained glass windows. View other local railroad memorabilia, civil war and steam boat displays.

Schedule: May 1 through October 31: Mondays through Saturdays, 10 a.m. to 4:30 p.m.; Sundays, 1 to 4 p.m. November through April, weekdays only.

Admission/Fare: $4; youth 16 and under are free.

Locomotives/Rolling Stock: 1920 L&N caboose.

Special Events: Madison in Bloom, last weekend in April and first weekend in May.

Nearby Attractions: Clifty Falls State Park, Lanier Mansion, antique shops, wineries, bed and breakfast, Ohio River.

Directions: Highways 56 and 421, located in downtown historic Madison.

        M

Site Address: 615 W. First St., Madison, IN
Mailing Address: 615 W. First St., Madison, IN 47250
Telephone: (812) 265-2335
E-mail: jchs@seidata.com
Website: www.seidata.com/~jchs

Indiana, Noblesville

**INDIANA TRANSPORTATION
MUSEUM**
Train ride, dinner train, museum, display
Standard gauge

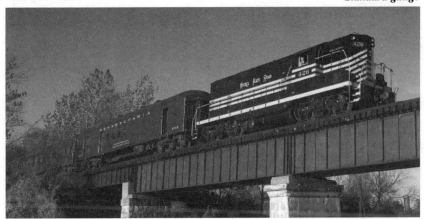

WAYNE WILLIAMS

Description: Many railroad cars are on display. The Henry M. Flagler
private car is open on special occasions. We offer train rides through
rural Hamilton County on weekends.

Schedule: April, May, September, and October: weekends, 10 a.m. to 5 p.m.
Memorial Day through Labor Day: Tuesday through Sunday, 10 a.m. to
5 p.m. Trains run each weekend at 1:30 p.m.

Admission/Fare: Museum–adults, $3; children 3-12, $2. Train fares depend
on event.

Locomotives/Rolling Stock: EMD F7 and F9 diesels; 1918 Baldwin steam
locomotive no. 587, former NKP; 1929 private car, NKP no. 1; 1930
L&N diner; eight stainless-steel coaches from 1937 Santa Fe Scout.

Special Events: Fair Train during Indiana State Fair, August; Atlanta new
Earth Festival, September; Railfan Day, November 21; Polar Bear
Express, December 6-7 and 13-14. Hamiltonian to restaurants in Cicero
and Atlanta, Friday evenings.

Directions: Located 20 miles north of Indianapolis in Forest Park/
Noblesville on State Route 19, just north of the intersection with State
Route 32.

†See ad on page A-11.

Site Address: 325 Cicero Rd., Noblesville, IN
Mailing Address: PO Box 83, Noblesville, IN 46061-0083
Telephone: (317) 773-6000 (recording)
E-mail: nkp587@iquest.net
Website: www.itm.org

Indiana, North Judson

HOOSIER VALLEY
RAILROAD MUSEUM, INC.
Train ride, museum
Standard gauge

M.W. KNEBEL

Description: Established in North Judson since 1988, the organization has been in the process of building the physical plant for a working railroad museum. The collection today consists of 30 pieces of railroad rolling stock. This includes the former 2-8-4 Chesapeake & Ohio steam locomotive no. 2789, which is under roof. We offer short caboose rides May through September. Wheelchair lift equipped.

Schedule: Year-round, Saturdays, 8 a.m. to 5 p.m.

Admission/Fare: No admission fee.

Locomotives/Rolling Stock: C&O 1947 Alco K-4 2-8-4 no. 2789; Erie 1947 Alco S-1 switcher no. 310; EL caboose no. C345; 30 pieces rolling stock.

Nearby Attractions: Tippecanoe River State Park, Bass Lake State Beach, Kersting's Cycle Center & Museum.

Directions: Seventy miles southeast of downtown Chicago, Indiana 10 and 39.

      TRAIN M

Site Address: 507 Mulberry St., North Judson, IN
Mailing Address: PO Box 75, North Judson, IN 46366
Telephone: (574) 223-3834 (treasurer), (574) 946-6499 (secretary), and (574) 896-3950 (museum)
E-mail: hvrm@yahoo.com
Website: http://hvrm.railfan.net

Iowa, Boone

BOONE & SCENIC VALLEY RAILROAD
Train ride, dinner train, museum, display
Standard gauge

FENNER STEVENSON

Description: Fifteen-mile round-trip rides across 156-foot-high bridge and through the Des Moines River Valley. Dinner and dessert trains are 22 miles round trip.

Schedule: Saturdays in May, 1:30 p.m.; Memorial Day through October, daily, 1:30 p.m. Weekends and holidays, 1:30 and 4 p.m. Dinner train, Saturdays, April through mid-December and Fridays, June through October, 5:30 p.m. Dessert train, weekends at 12:30 p.m., June through October.

Admission/Fare: Excursion trains–adults, $12; children 3-12, $5. Dinner trains–$50. Dessert trains–$25.

Locomotives/Rolling Stock: Datong JS8419; Alco S21098; Alco RS1 205; GE 90-ton center-cab 2252; GE 45-ton center-cab 1858; EMD SW2 1003. Charles City Western Electric Car 50; many coaches and cabooses.

Special Events: Pufferbilly Days, weekend after Labor Day; Civil War re-enactment, last weekend in July; Thomas the Tank Engine, late September.

Nearby Attractions: Birthplace of Mamie Doud Eisenhower, Ledges State Park, Don Williams County Park.

Directions: Fifteen miles west of I-30 at Ames, Iowa. Turn north at stop sign and go to 11th St. Turn left, and go six blocks.

Radio frequency: 463.800

Site Address: 225 Tenth St., Boone, IA
Mailing Address: PO Box 603, Boone, IA 50036
Telephone: (515) 432-4249
Fax: (515) 432-4253
E-mail: b&svrr@tdsi.net
Website: www.scenic-valleyrr.com

FRED KELLEY

Description: The hobo story is told in pictures and artifacts throughout the museum. But there is also the story of the railroad's importance, the call of the steam engine, the chance to move on–the story of the town whose people have gotten caught up in the hobo lifestyle.

Schedule: Memorial Day through Labor Day, 10 a.m. to 5 p.m. Other times by appointment.

Admission/Fare: $1 per person.

Special Events: National Hobo Convention, second weekend in August; Draft Horse Show, Labor Day weekend.

Nearby Attractions: Armstrong House, Hancock County Speedway, Agricultural Museum, Grotto of the Redemption.

Directions: Located on Route 18, 31 miles west of Mason City.

Site Address: The old Chief Theater in downtown Britt, IA
Mailing Address: PO 143, Britt, IA 50423
Telephone: (641) 843-9104
E-mail: frank@hobo.com
Website: www.hobo.com

Description: Trainland U.S.A. is an operating toy train museum featuring Lionel trains and accessories. This exhibit represents three eras of time: frontier, steam, and diesel.

Schedule: Memorial Day weekend through Labor Day, 10 a.m. to 6 p.m.

Nearby Attractions: International Wrestling Institute and Museum, Newton Jasper County Historical Museum, Newton, Living History farms, Des Moines.

Directions: Exit 155 off I-80, 2½ miles north on Highway 117.

*Coupon available, see coupon section.

Site Address: 3135 Hwy. 117 N., Colfax, IA
Mailing Address: 3135 Hwy. 117 N., Colfax, IA 50054-7534
Telephone: (515) 674-3813
Fax: (515) 674-3813
E-mail: trainsjudy@aol.com
Website: www.trainlandusa.com

Iowa, Council Bluffs

RAILSWEST RAILROAD MUSEUM
Museum, display, layout

ROBERT HASTINGS

Description: The RailsWest Railroad Museum and HO model railroad are housed in an 1899 former Rock Island depot. The museum contains displays of historic photos, dining car memorabilia, uniforms, and many other interesting items used during the steam era. The 22 x 33-foot model railroad depicts scenery of the Council Bluffs/Omaha area, featuring train lines that served the heartland: Union Pacific; Chicago & Northwestern; Wabash; Chicago Great Western; Wabash, Rock Island; Milwaukee Road; Chicago, Burlington & Quincy.

Schedule: May: weekends, 1 to 5 p.m. Memorial Day through Labor Day: Tuesdays through Saturdays, 10 a.m. to 4 p.m. and Sundays, 1 to 5 p.m. December: weekends, 1 to 5 p.m. Closed major holidays.

Locomotives/Rolling Stock: UP steam locomotive no. 814; CB&Q steam engine no. 915; CB&Q waycar no. 13855; CB&Q Omaha club car; Budd RPO former UP no. 5908; 1967 Rock Island caboose 17130; UP boxcar no. 462536.

Special Events: Depot Days, last weekend in September. Christmas at the Depot, weekends in December

Directions: I-80 exit 3, travel north one mile or I-29 exit Lake Manawa.

*Coupon available, see coupon section.

Site Address: 1512 S. Main St., Council Bluffs, IA
Mailing Address: PO Box 2, Council Bluffs, IA 51502
Telephone: (712) 323-5182

DELMAR DEPOT MUSEUM
Museum
Standard gauge

Description: A restored Victorian-style depot, with displays.

Schedule: Open weekends, 1 to 4 p.m.

Admission/Fare: Free.

Locomotives/Rolling Stock: Caboose CC no. 199506, Illinois Central (Iowa Division).

Special Events: Labor Day events: car show, tractor show, depot opened for viewing.

Nearby Attractions: Masquoketa Caves Park, 15 miles north; drive-in theater, 2 miles west of Delmar.

Directions: Take Highway 561 to Highway 136.

Site Address: 414 Lincoln Ave., Delmar, IA
Mailing Address: Delmar Depot, c/o City Hall, PO Box 175, Delmar, IA 52037
Telephone: (563) 574-4077 and (563) 574-4256 (City Hall)

**SANTA FE DEPOT
HISTORICAL CENTER**
Museum, layout

DAVE SALLEN

Description: The former Santa Fe depot in Fort Madison, a building in the mission revival style, is the nucleus of Fort Madison's historic district. It is a museum of railroad history, firefighting equipment, and fountain pens, reflecting Fort Madison's industrial history. There is a section on the great floods of 1993. Outside is a Santa Fe caboose, open to view.

Schedule: Memorial Day to Labor Day: Wednesday, Thursday, Friday, and Saturday, 12:30 to 4:30 p.m.

Admission/Fare: Adults, $2; children 12 and under, $.50.

Locomotives/Rolling Stock: AT&SF caboose no. 235.

Special Events: Antique car and motorcycle show is third Sunday in May.

Nearby Attractions: Old Fort Madison.

Directions: On U.S. Highway 61 in Fort Madison's Riverview Park.

*Coupon available, see coupon section.

M arm

Site Address: 814 Tenth St., Fort Madison, IA
Mailing Address: PO Box 285, Fort Madison, IA 52627
Telephone: (319) 372-7661 and (319) 372-7363
Fax: (319) 372-1825

Iowa, Mount Pleasant

MIDWEST CENTRAL RAILROAD
Train ride, museum
36" gauge

SCOTT A. WILEY

Description: A one-mile steam train ride encircling the grounds of the Midwest Old Threshers grounds, with two trains and three section cars.

Schedule: August 28 to September 1 in conjunction with the Midwest Old Threshers Reunion; October 11 and 18 (Ghost Train); December 6, 7 (Polar Express).

Admission/Fare: Round trip during Reunion–adult, $2; child, $1. Prices vary for Ghost Train and Polar Express.

Locomotives/Rolling Stock: 1891 Baldwin 2-6-0 Surrey, Sussex & Southhampton Railway no. 6; 1923 Lima three-truck Shay, West Side Lumber no. 9; 1951 Henschel 0-4-0T no. 16; 1935 Vulcan gas mechanical switcher; three vintage speeders; five wooden coaches; wooden caboose; White Pass & Yukon steel caboose no. 903.

Special Events: October 11 and 18, Ghost Train; December 6 and 7, Polar Express.

Nearby Attractions: Midwest Old Thresher Heritage Museum.

Directions: Five blocks south of Highway 34 on Walnut St.

Site Address: McMillan Park, Mount Pleasant, IA
Mailing Address: PO Box 102, Mount Pleasant, IA 52641
Telephone: (319) 385-2912
E-mail: jwcrouch@interl.net
Website: www.mcrr.org

Kansas, Abilene

ABILENE & SMOKY VALLEY RAILROAD
Train ride
Standard gauge

Description: A 1½-hour, 10-mile round trip through the Smoky Hill River Valley from historic Abilene to Enterprise, Kansas. The track crosses the Smoky Hill River on a high steel span bridge.

Schedule: Memorial Day through Labor Day: Tuesdays through Sundays. May, September through October: weekends. Dinner train specials. Call or write for more information.

Admission/Fare: Adults, $8.50; children 3-11, $5.50. Dinner train prices vary. All prices subject to change without notice.

Locomotives/Rolling Stock: 1945 Alco S1; 1945 GE 44-ton; 1945 Whitcomb 45-ton side-rod; more.

Special Events: Abilene–Chisholm Trail Day, Saturday of first full weekend in October. Easter Bunny Train. Santa Claus Train. Call or write for details.

Nearby Attractions: Eisenhower Center, Dickinson County Heritage Center, C.W. Parker Carousel, Greyhound Hall of Fame, Great Plains Theater Festival, Abilene Community Theater.

Directions: I-70 exit 275, south 2 miles on K-15 (Buckeye St.). Park in lot west of Eisenhower Center (shared lot with Greyhound Hall of Fame).

Site Address: 417 S. Buckeye, Abilene, KS
Mailing Address: PO Box 744, Abilene, KS 67410
Telephone: (785) 263-1077, (888) 426-6687, and (888) 426-6689 (reservations)
Fax: (785) 263-1066
Website: www.asvrr.org

Kansas, Baldwin City

MIDLAND RAILWAY
Train ride
Standard gauge

E. N. GRIFFIN

Description: This line was constructed in 1867 as the Leavenworth, Lawrence & Galveston, the first railroad south of the Kansas River. The Midland Railway is a volunteer-operated intrastate common-carrier passenger railroad. Trains operate to the former town site of Norwood for an 11-mile round trip through scenic eastern Kansas farmland and woods.

Schedule: Memorial Day weekend through October, weekends, 11:30 a.m., 1:30 and 3:30 p.m.; and Thursdays, 10:30 a.m.

Fare/Admission: Adults, $9; children ages 4-12, $4; under age 4 ride free. All-day fare (all ages), $18. Discounts for groups of 25 or more.

Locomotive/Rolling Stock: No. 524, 1946 EMD NW2, former Chicago, Burlington & Quincy; no. 142 RS-3M, former Missouri-Kansas-Texas; no. 652 E8, former CRI&P; 8255 RS-3, former NYC-630 and CR&IP E6 no. 630.

Special Events: Maple Leaf Festival, third weekend in October; Halloween Trains, last weekend in October. Railfans Weekend, date to be announced (call for information).

Directions: About 30 miles southwest of Kansas City on U.S. 56 at the 1906 former AT&SF depot, seven blocks west of downtown.

Lawrence   **Radio Frequency:** 160.380

Site Address: 1515 High St., Baldwin City, Kansas
Mailing Address: PO Box 412, Baldwin City, KS 66006
Telephone: (785) 594-6982 and (800) 651-0388
Fax: (816) 873-3387
Website: www.midland-ry.org

**GREAT PLAINS TRANSPORTATION
MUSEUM, INC.**
Museum
Standard

J. HARVEY KOEHN

Description: Museum with outdoor displays of locomotives, cabooses, and cars; indoor displays of artifacts and memorabilia.

Schedule: Year-round, Saturdays, 9 a.m. to 4 p.m.; April through October, Sundays, 1 to 4 p.m.

Admission/Fare: Adults, $3.50; children 3-12, $2.50.

Locomotives/Rolling Stock: ATSF 4-8-4 no. 3768; ATSF SDFP45 no. 93; BN NW2 no. 421; Whitcomb GM-2; Plymouth industrial locomotive; Frisco caboose 876; Central Kansas Railway caboose 1959; CB&Q caboose 13519; ATSF coach, baggage caboose 2312; MoPac caboose 13495; UP caboose no. 24538; ATSF baggage car 190006.

Nearby Attractions: In the heart of historic Old Town.

Directions: Across from Wichita Union Station.

*Coupon available, see coupon section.

      M arm

Site Address: 700 E. Douglas Ave., Wichita, KS
Mailing Address: 700 E. Douglas Ave., Wichita, KS 67202
Telephone: (316) 263-0944

MY OLD KENTUCKY DINNER TRAIN
Dinner train

Description: Thirty-five-mile round trip through the Kentucky countryside. Fine dining and whisper-perfect service aboard vintage 1940s dinner train.

Schedule: Year-round operation. Lunch on Saturdays, 12 noon; dinner, Tuesday through Saturday, 5 p.m. Schedule subject to change.

Admission/Fare: Lunch, $42.95 plus tax, per person; dinner, $59.95 plus tax, per person.

Locomotives/Rolling Stock: Two FP7A units nos. 1940 and 1941; Budd diner 1940 era, nos. 011 (formerly Eisenhower family car), 007, 777 and 021.

Special Events: Bourbon Festival, September. Murder Mysteries, fall and spring.

Nearby Attractions: Bardstown is a major historical site with many attractions; home to "My Old Kentucky Home."

Directions: Forty-five minutes south of Louisville on Highway 31E.

Site Address: 602 N. Third St., Bardstown, KY
Mailing Address: PO Box 279, Bardstown, KY 40004
Telephone: (502) 348-7300
Fax: (502) 348-7780
E-mail: info@rjcorman.com
Website: www.kydinnertrain.com

HARDIN SOUTHERN RAILROAD
Train ride, display
Standard gauge

Description: This line is a working common-carrier railroad offering seasonal Nostalgia Train passenger service for a two-hour, 18-mile journey to the past. Built in 1890, the railroad was once a portion of the Nashville, Chattanooga & St. Louis Railway's Paducah main line through the Jackson Purchase in western Kentucky. The railroad is a designated Kentucky State Landmark. Today's trip features the rural farms and lush forests of the Clarks River Valley.

Schedule: May 25 through October 31: weekends, mid-day and late afternoon.

Admission/Fare: Adults, $10.25; children 3-12, $6.50. Tour, group, and charter rates available.

Locomotives/Rolling Stock: No. 863, 1940 Electro-Motive Corporation SW1, former Milwaukee Road; no. 4 Baldwin 1914 2-6-2 steam locomotive; air-conditioned coaches.

Special Events: Easter, Mother's Day, Halloween, Christmas.

Nearby Attractions: Land Between the Lakes National Recreation Area.

Directions: In western Kentucky, southeast of Paducah via I-24 and State Route 641; 6 miles from the Tennessee Valley Authority's Land Between the Lakes National Recreation Area. Hardin is located at junction of Routes 641/80. Depot is on Route 80 in the center of town.

Site Address: Hardin, KY
Mailing Address: PO Box 20, Hardin, KY 42048
Telephone: (270) 437-4555
Fax: (270) 753-7006
E-mail: office@hsrr.com
Website: www.hsrr.com

KENTUCKY RAILWAY MUSEUM
Train ride, dinner train, museum, display, layout
Standard gauge

ELMER KAPPELL

Description: Twenty-two-mile round trip through Rolling Fork River valley.

Schedule: March through May, weekends; June through September, Tuesday through Sunday; October through December, weekends. Call for trip times.

Admission/Fare: Adults and teens, $12.50; children 3-12, $8; under 3, free; cab rides, $25. Steam weekends, adults and teens, $15; children 3-12, $8; under 3, free; cab rides, $35.

Locomotives/Rolling Stock: L&N 4-6-2 no. 152; Monon BL-2 no. 32; SF CF-7 no. 2546; USA F-M H-12-44 no. 1846; L&N 2554; L&N 2572; SAL 821; MKT 884; TC 8038 (diner); other locomotives and rolling stock on display.

Nearby Attractions: My Old Kentucky Home State Park, Historic Bardstown, Mammoth Cave National Park, Lincoln birthplace (national historic site), Lincoln boyhood home, Maker's Mark Distillery (national landmark), Bernheim Forest.

Directions: Three-and-one-half miles east of I-65 at exit 105 (Boston exit); 12 miles south of Bluegrass Parkway at exit 21 (New Haven exit).

Radio Frequency: 160.545

Site Address: 136 S. Main St., New Haven, KY
Mailing Address: PO Box 240, New Haven, KY 40051
Telephone: (502) 549-5470 and (800) 272-0152
Fax: (502) 549-5472
E-mail: kyrail@bardstown.com
Website: www.kyrail.org

Description: The Paducah Railroad Museum, operated by the Paducah chapter of the N.R.H.S., is a railroad history museum that includes maps, photographs, tools, signals, and dispatching and communications equipment.

Schedule: Saturdays, 10 a.m. to 4 p.m., and by appointment.

Admission/Fare: Free, contributions appreciated.

Nearby Attractions: Museum of American Quilters Society, River Heritage Museum, other history museums, Ohio and Tennessee River vistas, Kentucky and Barkley Lakes, Land Between the Lakes Recreation Area.

Directions: Located at Third and Washington St., on the I-24 downtown loop. Get off I-24 at the U.S. 68 or U.S. 60 exits.

Site Address: Washington St. at Third St., Paducah, KY
Mailing Address: PO Box 1194, Paducah, KY 42002-1194
Telephone: (270) 442-4032
E-mail: wrj@hcis.net
Website: www@paducahrr.org

BIG SOUTH FORK SCENIC RAILWAY
Train ride
Standard gauge

Description: Three- to 4½-hour round trips into the gorge of the Big South Fork National Park. Each trip includes stopovers at restored Blue Heron and Barthell Mining Camps. Also includes admission to McCreary County Museum in Stearns.

Schedule: April: Thursday and Friday, 10 and 11 a.m.; Saturday, 10 and 11 a.m. and 2:30 p.m. May through September: Wednesday through Friday, 10 and 11 a.m.; Saturday, 10 and 11 a.m. and 2:30 p.m.; Sunday, 11 a.m. and 2:30 p.m. Memorial Day and Labor Day, 11 a.m. October, same as May through September, but add Tuesday to weekday schedule. November, first two Saturdays, 10 and 11 a.m. and 2:30 p.m.

Admission/Fare: Adults, $15; seniors, $14; children (3-12), $7.50.

Locomotives/Rolling Stock: Nos. 102 and 105, 1942 Alcos; open cars; caboose.

Special Events: July 3rd Evening Run; Halloween Trains, last three Fridays and Saturdays in October; Cumberland Heritage Day in mid-October (call).

Nearby Attractions: Cumberland Falls State Park, Big South Fork National River and Recreation Area, Daniel Boone National Forest, Lake Cumberland, Mill Springs Battlefield, Kentucky Splash, Historic Rugby.

Directions: One mile west of U.S. 27 on State Route 92.

Site Address: 100 Henderson St., Stearns, KY
Mailing Address: PO Box 368, Stearns, KY 42647
Telephone: (800) 462-5664 and (606) 376-5330
Fax: (606) 376-5332
E-mail: bsfsry@highland.net
Website: www.bsfsry.com

BLUEGRASS RAILROAD MUSEUM
Train ride
Standard gauge

Description: The Bluegrass Railroad Museum offers a 1½-hour, 11½-mile round-trip train ride through horse, cattle, and tobacco farms, over an ex-Southern Railway branch line that was built by the Louisville Southern Railroad in 1889.

Schedule: May 27, 2002, to October 28, 2002, open weekends only. Saturdays, 1:30 and 3:30 p.m.; Sundays, 1:30 p.m.

Admission/Fare: Adults, $8; seniors, $7; children under 12, $6. Special events: Adults, $10; seniors, $9; children, $8.

Locomotives/Rolling Stock: Alco MRS1s nos. 2043 and 2086; Fairbanks Morse H12-44 1849, former U.S. Army; L&N caboose no. 1086; Southern caboose X741.

Special Events: Book Bandits Robbery, June 1, 2; Wild West Train Robbery, June 22, 23; Civil War Train Robbery, August 7, 8; Clown Daze, October 5, 6; Halloween, October 18, 19, 25, 26; Santa Train, December 7, 8, 14, 15. (Special events have special hours; please call for information.)

Directions: Woodford County Park off U.S. 62 (Tyrone Pike).

Radio frequency: **160.275, 161.160, 160.500, 161.190**

Site Address: Versailles, Kentucky
Mailing Address: PO Box 27, Versailles, KY 40383-0027
Telephone: (859) 873-2476 and (800) 755-2476
Website: www.bgrm.org

DEQUINCY RAILROAD MUSEUM
Museum

Description: Nestled among tall pines at the beginning of Louisiana's foothills in north Calcasieu County, the city of DeQuincy was at the intersection of two major railroads in 1895. Its turn-of-the-century beginnings have been preserved, including two major historical landmarks–the All Saints Episcopal Church and the Kansas City Southern Railroad Depot. Both structures are on the National Register of Historic Places, and the depot now houses the railroad museum. There are a vintage caboose, a passenger coach, and a host of railroad artifacts. We now have a play train, available for rental for birthday parties.

Schedule: Mondays through Fridays, 9 a.m. to 4 p.m.; weekends, 12:00 to 4 p.m.

Admission/Fare: Museum–free, donations appreciated. Train rental–$20.

Locomotives/Rolling Stock: No. 124 0-6-0 steam engine, built 1913 by America Locomotive Co. 0-6-0 type, does not run; Pullman railcar no. 4472, built 1947, 85 feet in length; MP caboose no. 3487, built 1929.

Special Events: Louisiana Railroad Days Festival, second weekend in April.

Nearby Attractions: Sam Jones State Park, 20 miles; horse racing, 10 miles; Gulf fishing, 40 miles; two large casinos, 20 miles; hunting, all over.

Directions: On Highway 12, 27 miles north of Lake Charles; 60 miles from Texas state line.

Lake Charles, LA

Site Address: 400 McNeese, DeQuincy, LA
Mailing Address: PO Box 997, DeQuincy, LA 70633
Telephone: (337) 786-2823 and (337) 786-7113

HENRY TAVES

Description: Guided tours of a historic sawmill complex. The commissary offers exhibits and a gift shop. The motor car ride is ¾ mile.

Schedule: Year-round, 9 a.m. to 5 p.m., except Thanksgiving and Christmas.

Admission/Fare: Admission is charged.

Locomotives/Rolling Stock: 4-6-0 Red River & Gulf no. 106; 2-6-0 Meridian Lumber co. no. 202; 4-6-0 Crowell Long Leaf Lumber Co. no. 400

Nearby Attractions: Alexander State Forest (camping), 11 miles; restaurants, 3 miles.

Directions: From I-49 take exit 66 and travel west on State Route 112 to Forest Hill; follow signs 3.3 miles south on State Route 497. The site is halfway between Forest Hill and Glenmora on State Route 497.

*Coupon available, see coupon section.

          M

Site Address: 77 Long Leaf Rd., Long Leaf, LA
Mailing Address: PO Box 101, Long Leaf, LA 71448-0101
Telephone: (318) 748-8404
Fax: (318) 748-8404

Maine, Alna
(Sheepscot Station)

JOHN MCNAMARA

Description: Restoration of the WW&F Railway on original roadbed, using some original equipment. Our trains are pulled by either a 1904 Vulcan steam engine or a 1960 Plymouth diesel on a round trip over 2 miles long. We have a museum, car shop, and gift shop.

Schedule: Saturdays, year-round; Sundays, Memorial Day through Labor Day weekends. Also Memorial Day and Labor Day. All hours are 9 a.m. to 5 p.m.

Admission/Fare: Steam train ride–adults, $4; children, $2. Diesel–adults, $3; children, $1.50. Museum–free.

Locomotives/Rolling Stock: WW&F no. 9 (ex-SR&RL no. 6) Portland Co. 1891; WW&F no. 10 Vulcan 1904; Brookville no. 51; Plymouth no. 52; coach no. 31; flatcar no. 118; boxcar no. 309; caboose no. 320.

Special Events: Tracklaying and work sessions, April 25-27 and October 10-13; annual picnic, August 8-10; Halloween Trains, Oct. 25; Victorian theme Christmas, December 20.

Nearby Attractions: Boothbay Railway Museum, Boothbay; local beaches.

Directions: From south and west: I-95 to Brunswick, north on Rt. 1 to Wiscasset, north on Rt. 218 4.5 miles, left on Cross Rd. From east–south on Rt. 1 to Newcastle, right on Sheepscot Rd., follow signs.

    M arm

Site Address: 97 Cross Rd., Alna, ME
Mailing Address: PO Box 242, Alna, ME 04535
Telephone: (207) 882-4193
Website: www.wwfry.org

COLE LAND TRANSPORTATION MUSEUM
Museum
Standard gauge

Description: Two hundred Maine antique land transportation vehicles, as well as 2,000 photographs of life in early Maine communities, enlarged, displayed, and captioned. Home of the Maine State World War II veterans memorial.

Schedule: May 1 through November 11, daily, 9 a.m. to 5 p.m.

Admission/Fare: Adults, $5; seniors, $3; under 19, free.

Directions: From I-95, take exit 45B. Turn left at the traffic light and follow the signs.

Site Address: 405 Perry Rd., Bangor, ME
Mailing Address: 405 Perry Rd., Bangor, ME 04401
Telephone: (207) 990-3600
Fax: (207) 990-2653
E-mail: mail@colemuseum.com
Website: www.colemuseum.org

Maine, Boothbay   **BOOTHBAY RAILWAY VILLAGE**
Train ride, museum
24" gauge

Description: Two-foot gauge steam train rides around a re-created historic village Exhibits include Maine narrow gauge history; rural village exhibits; restored historic buildings such as railroad stations, town hall, general store; and an exceptional antique auto exhibit.

Schedule: Memorial Day through Columbus Day, 9:30 a.m. to 5 p.m.

Admission/Fare: Adults, $7; children 12 and under, $3.

Locomotives/Rolling Stock: Four Henschel 0-4-0T locomotives, nos. 12313 (1913), 22486 (1934), 24022 (1938, display only), and 24023 (1938); two Baldwin 0-4-0ST locomotives (1895, display); Plymouth 4-ton 0-4-0 Buda gasoline engine; Ford Model T Inspection vehicle; three boxcars, nos. 312, 147, 132; combine no. 33; open and closed coaches; more.

Special Events: Father's Day, June 15; Antique Engine Meet, July 5-6; Annual Fundraising Auction, July 19; Antique Auto Days, July 19-20; Children's Day, August 17; Maine Narrow Gauge Railroad Day, September 21; Fall Foliage Festival (craft fair), October 11-12; Ghost Train, October 24-25; Christmas trains.

Nearby Attractions: The Boothbay and mid-coast regions are rich in museums, shops, and scenery.

Directions: Take U.S. Route 1 to Wiscasset, then Route 27 south to Boothbay, 8 miles on the left.

[♿] [P] 🚌 ✳ ☕ [🎏] M arm TRAIN

Site Address: Route 27, Boothbay, ME
Mailing Address: PO Box 123, Boothbay, ME 04537
Telephone: (207) 633-4727
Fax: (207) 633-4733
E-mail: staff@railwayvillage.org
Website: www.railwayvillage.org

Maine, Kennebunkport

SEASHORE TROLLEY MUSEUM
Train ride
Standard gauge

Description: A 25-minute, 3.5-mile trolley ride. Fifty-four streetcars on display in three car barns and Restoration Shop.

Schedule: May 3 until Memorial Day, weekends; Memorial Day through Columbus Day, daily; the rest of October, weekends.

Admission/Fare: Adults, $7.50; seniors, $5.50; children (6-16), $5.00; 5 and under, free.

Locomotives/Rolling Stock: Restored streetcars, interurbans, subways, buses, PCC cars.

Special Events: Mother's Day, May. Father's Day, June. Trolley Parade, July 4. Trolley Birthday Celebration, August. Pumpkin Patch weekend, September.

Nearby Attractions: Downtown Kennebunkport and several beautiful beaches.

Directions: Maine Turnpike, Kennebunkport exit. Left onto Route 35 to downtown Kennebunkport. Left on Route 1, north for 2.8 miles. Right at traffic light onto Log Cabin Rd. Museum is 1.7 miles on left.

Radio frequency: 160.470

Site Address: 195 Log Cabin Rd., Kennebunkport, ME
Mailing Address: PO Box A, Kennebunkport, ME 04046
Telephone: (207) 967-2800
Fax: (207) 967-0867
E-mail: carshop@gwi.net
Website: www.trolleymuseum.org

Description: Oakfield Station has been restored to its original condition. Exhibits include hundreds of photographs dating back to the beginning of the Bangor & Aroostook Railroad in 1891. You'll see the building of this epic rail line through some of the most rugged terrain in the East. Other memorabilia include vintage signs and advertising pieces, signal lanterns, original railroad maps, telegraph equipment, newspapers chronicling the area's history, restored mail cars, and a rejuvenated C-66 caboose. Railroad history lives at Oakfield Station.

Schedule: Memorial Day weekend through Labor Day: Saturdays, 12 to 4 p.m.; and Sundays, 1 to 4 p.m.

Admission/Fare: Donations appreciated.

Locomotives/Rolling Stock: BAR C-66 caboose.

Nearby Attractions: Restaurants and lodging.

Directions: I-95 exit 60, turn right for 1 mile, turn left at hardware store, cross bridge, turn right to end of street.

    M

Site Address: Station St., Oakfield, ME
Mailing Address: PO Box 62, Oakfield, ME 04763
Telephone: (207) 757-8575
E-mail: oakfield.rr.museum@ainop.com
Website: www.ainop.com/users/oakfield.rr/

SANDY RIVER & RANGELEY LAKES RAILROAD
DIVISION OF PHILLIPS HISTORICAL SOCIETY
Train ride, museum, display
24" gauge

Description: Ride along the original roadbed of the SR&RL Railroad in 1884 Laconia Coach no. 18, powered by a replica of SR&RL no. 4. Take a trip back in time as you visit our eight-stall roundhouse and see the ongoing restoration of original SR&RL equipment.

Schedule: June 1 and 15; July 6, 19, and 20; August 3, 15, 16, 17, 30, and 31; September 7 and 21; October 4, 5, 11, and 12. Trains depart on the hour, 11 a.m. to 3 p.m. Special 8:30 night trains on August 15 and 16.

Admission/Fare: Train–$3; children under age 13 ride free.

Locomotives/Rolling Stock: SR&RL no. 4 (replica); coaches nos. 17 and 18; cabooses nos. 556 and 559 (a replica of no. 556); flangers nos. 503 and 505; boxcars nos. 86, 59, 155, 73, and 121; tool car no. 562; flatcar; handcars; two Brookvilles; a Plymouth; MEC coach no. 170; Concord & Montreal coach no. 77.

Special Events: Phillips Old Home Days, August 15-17.

Nearby Attractions: Stanley Museum, Nordica Homestead, Logging Museum in Rangeley, Small Falls, Mount Blue State Park.

Directions: Eighteen miles north of Farmington on State Route 4. Cross the bridge in downtown Phillips and up the hill (Bridge St.) ½ mile.

*Coupon available, see coupon section.

     M

Site Address: Bridge St., Phillips, ME
Mailing Address: PO Box B, Phillips, ME 04966
Telephone: (207) 778-3621
Fax: (207) 779-1901
E-mail: awberry@prexar.com
Website: www.srrl-rr.org

**MAINE NARROW GAUGE RAILROAD
COMPANY AND MUSEUM**
Train ride, museum, display
24" gauge

EMMONS LANCASTER

Description: A 3-mile round trip along the edge of Casco Bay.

Schedule: Museum, seven days a week. Closed Thanksgiving and Christmas.

Admission/Fare: Museum–free, donations accepted. Rides–adults, $5;
children, $3.

Locomotives/Rolling Stock: No. 8 Bridgton steam locomotive; nos. 3 and 4
Monson steam locomotives; no. 1 Edaville diesel; coaches from
Bridgton/Harrison; Sandy River Railroad; Edaville.

Special Events: Flower Show Steam Trains, March; Boat Show Steam Trains,
March; Memorial Day weekend, July 4th; and Steamfest, September.

Nearby Attractions: Portland's "Old Port" shopping area, walking trail, children's museum, many restaurants.

Directions: Old Portland Co. site Highway 295 to exit 7, Franklin St. Turn
left on Fore St.

       M arm TRAIN

  Radio frequency: 160.245

Site Address: 58 Fore St., Building 6, Portland, ME
Mailing Address: 58 Fore St., Building 6, Portland, ME 04101-4842
Telephone: (207) 828-0814
Fax: (207) 879-6132
E-mail: mngrr@clinic.net
Website: www.mngrr.rails.net

Maryland, Baltimore **THE B&O RAILROAD MUSEUM**
Museum, layout

Description: Over 20 new exhibits and events celebrating 175 years of American railroading, now through July 2003.

Schedule: Daily, 10 a.m. to 5 p.m. Closed major holidays.

Admission/Fare: Adults, $8; seniors (60+), $7; children 2 through 12, $5.

Locomotives/Rolling Stock: Over 250 pieces of rolling stock.

Special Events: Call for dates and times.

Nearby Attractions: Camden Yards, Ravens' Stadium, Babe Ruth Museum, ten blocks from the Inner Harbor.

Directions: Take I-95 to 395 to Martin Luther King Blvd. Follow signs to museum.

*Coupon available, see coupon section.

†See ad on inside back cover.

     M arm

Site Address: 901 W. Pratt St., Baltimore, MD
Mailing Address: 901 W. Pratt St., Baltimore, MD 21223
Telephone: (410) 752-2490
Fax: (410) 752-2499
E-mail: info@borail.org
Website: www.borail.org

BALTIMORE STREETCAR MUSEUM
Train ride
5'4½" gauge

ANDREW S. BLUMBERG

Description: Relive rail transit in the city of Baltimore from 1859 to 1963 through a 15-car collection (13 electric, 2 horse-drawn). Cars operate over 1¼-mile round-trip trackage. The Visitors' Center contains displays and the Trolley Theatre, a streetcar mockup and video presentation.

Schedule: June 1 through October 31, weekends. November 1 through May 31, Sundays. Hours are noon to 5 p.m.

Admission/Fare: Adults, $6; seniors and children 4-11, $3; family, $24.

Locomotives/Rolling Stock: No. 417, circa 1888 single-truck closed car; no. 554, 1896 single-truck summer car, no. 1050, 1898 single-truck closed car and no. 264, 1900 double-truck convertible car, all Brownell Car Co.; no. 1164, 1902 double-truck summer car; no. 3828, 1902 double-truck closed car; no. 4533, 1904 single-truck closed car; and no. 6119, 1930 Peter Witt car, all J.G. Brill Co.; no. 3715, 1913 double-truck crane; no. 7407, 1944 Pullman-Standard PCC car; more.

Special Events: Mother's, Father's, and Grandparent's Days. Museum Birthday Celebration. Tinsel Trolley, December; more. Call, write, or check website for more information.

Nearby Attractions: B&O Railroad Museum.

Directions: One block west on Lafayette Ave. to Falls Rd.

*Coupon available, see coupon section.

Site Address: 1901 Falls Rd., Baltimore, MD
Mailing Address: PO Box 4881, Baltimore, MD 21211
Telephone: (410) 547-0264
Fax: (410) 547-0264
Website: www.baltimoremd.com/streetcar/

Description: 1910 restored Pennsylvania Railroad depot, interlocking tower, caboose, and model trains. Collections illustrate local rail history, 1870 to today, alongside Amtrak/MARC corridor.

Schedule: Saturdays and Sundays, 12 to 4 p.m.

Admission/Fare: Free.

Locomotives/Rolling Stock: N&W caboose no. 518303, built 1922.

Special Events: Spring Fling, last Sunday in April; Fall Fest, last Sunday in September; Train Spotting Day, Sunday of Thanksgiving weekend.

Nearby Attractions: Five sites in City of Bowie Museums and near National Capital Trolley Museum and B&O Railroad Museum. Close to Patuxent State Park. Enjoy dinner at the Railroad Inn.

Directions: U.S. 50 or U.S. 295 to Maryland Route 197 for Bowie. Route 564 to Old Bowie. Route 564 becomes Eleventh St. The museum is at Eleventh and Chestnut on the south side of the rail line.

Site Address: 8614 Chestnut Ave., Bowie MD
Mailing Address: 12207 Tulip Grove Dr., Bowie MD 20715
Telephone: (301) 809-3088
Fax: (301) 809-2308
E-mail: museums@cityofbowie.org
Website: www.cityofbowie.org/comserv/museums.htm

**BRUNSWICK RAILROAD
MUSEUM**
Museum, layout

Description: Brunswick yards handled all B&O passenger and freight on the east-west main line. The 863 feet of track in an interactive HO layout traces the route from Washington, D.C., to Brunswick. Railroad artifacts include numerous historic photographs, tools, signals, equipment, and uniforms; exhibitions of life circa 1900 in a railroad town; women's and labor history. At the same site is the National Park Service C&O Canal Historical Park Visitor Center.

Schedule: Year-round: Saturdays, 10 a.m. to 4 p.m.; Sundays, 1 to 4 p.m. April through September: additional Thursdays and Fridays, 10 a.m. to 2 p.m.

Admission/Fare: Adults, $5; seniors, $4; children age 6 and up, $2.50.

Special Events: Railroad History Days, first full weekend in April. Railroad Days, first full weekend in October. Victorian Christmas, weekend after Thanksgiving.

Nearby Attractions: Harper's Ferry Toy Train Museum, Walkersville Southern Railroad, River and Trail Outfitters, Potomac and Shenandoah expeditions and ski tours.

Directions: From Washington, D.C.–I-270 north to U.S. 340 west to Brunswick. From Baltimore–I-70 west to I-340 west to Brunswick. From Leesburg, Virginia–U.S. 15 north to U.S. 340 west.

Site Address: 40 W. Potomac St., Brunswick, MD
Mailing Address: 40 W. Potomac St., Brunswick, MD 21716
Telephone: (301) 834-7100
Website: www.brrm.org

Maryland, Chesapeake Beach

Description: The CBRM preserves and interprets the history of the Chesapeake Beach Railway, which brought people from Washington, D.C., to the resorts of Chesapeake Beach and North Beach from 1900 until 1935. The museum exhibits photographs and artifacts of the railroad and resort.

Schedule: May 1 through September 30: daily, 1 to 4 p.m. April and October: weekends only. By appointment at all other times.

Admission/Fare: Free.

Locomotives/Rolling Stock: The CBR chair car "Dolores" is undergoing restoration by the museum staff and volunteers. Only one half of "Dolores" survives; it is the only known CBR rolling stock to survive.

Special Events: Right of Way Hike, April 5 (rain date April 12); Antique Car Show, May 18; Bay Breeze Summer Concerts, June 12, July 10, August 14, September 11, 7:30 p.m; summer children's programs, mid-June through mid-August, Thursdays, 10 a.m.; Holiday Open House, December 7.

Nearby Attractions: Chesapeake Beach Water Park, Bayfront Park, Breezy Point Beach and Campground.

Directions: From Washington's Capital Beltway–I-95 to Route 4 south. From Baltimore Beltway–I-695 to Route 301 south to Route 4 south. Left on Route 260, right on Route 261 to museum.

       M

Site Address: 4155 Mears Ave., Chesapeake Beach, MD
Mailing Address: PO Box 1227, Chesapeake Beach, MD 20732
Telephone: (410) 257-3892

Maryland, Colesville **NATIONAL CAPITAL TROLLEY MUSEUM**
Streetcar ride, museum
Standard gauge

JAMES HOGAN

Description: See "Streetcar Communities" and visit "From Streetcars to Light Rail," a computer-based exhibit. Enjoy a 1¾-mile, 20-minute round trip in Northwest Branch park on cars selected from the museum's collections.

Schedule: January 2 through November 30: weekends, 12 to 5 p.m. June 15 to August 15: Thursdays and Fridays, 11 a.m. to 3 p.m. October 1 to November 15 and March 15 to May 15: Thursdays and Fridays, 10 a.m. to 2 p.m. December: weekends, 5 to 9 p.m.

Admission/Fare: Full fare, $3; reduced fare (2-17 years of age and 65+ years), $2; under age 2, free.

Locomotives/Rolling Stock: JTCo no. 352; TTC no. 4603; European trams, Washington streetcars.

Special Events: Snow Sweeper Day, March 22. Cavalcade of Street Cars, April 27. Fall Open House, October 19. Holly Trolleyfest, December.

Nearby Attractions: Brookside Gardens, Sandy Spring Museum, Montgomery County Historical Society, nation's capital.

Directions: On Bonifant Rd. between Layhill Rd. (Route 182) and New Hampshire Ave. (Route 650), north of Wheaton.

*Coupon available, see coupon section.

     M arm

Site Address: 1313 Bonifant Rd., Colesville, MD
Mailing Address: 1313 Bonifant Rd., Colesville, MD 20905
Telephone: (301) 384-6088
Fax: (301) 384-2865
E-mail: nctm@dctrolley.org
Website: www.dctrolley.org

Maryland, Cumberland

**WESTERN MARYLAND SCENIC
RAILROAD**
Train ride
Standard gauge

Description: From May through mid-December, our 1916 restored Baldwin steam engine and our vintage diesel locomotives travel the scenic mountains of western Maryland on a stunning 32-mile round trip between Cumberland's restored Western Maryland Railway Station and the 1891 Old Depot in Frostburg.

Schedule: Steam–May 7 through September 28, Friday through Sunday, 11:30 a.m.; October 1-26, Thursday through Sunday, 11:30 a.m. and October 4, 11, and 18, 4:30 p.m.; November 1 through December 7, weekends, and Friday, November 28, 11:30 a.m. Diesel–May 7 through September 28, Thursday, 11:30 a.m.; October 1-26, Monday through Wednesday, 11:30 a.m.

Admission/Fare: Standard–adult, $19; seniors, $17; children 12 and under, $10; children under 2 or not occupying a seat, free. First class (Sundays only, includes lunch)–adult, 37.50; seniors, $35.50; children, $17.50; children without lunch, $10.

Locomotives/Rolling Stock: 1916 Baldwin 280 no. 734; Atlantic Coastline no. 850, Florida East Coast no. 851; PRR diner no. 1155; more.

Special Events: Many special events throughout the year. Call, write, or check our website for information.

Directions: Take I-68, exit 43C to Harrison St. to the station.

Site Address: Cumberland, MD
Mailing Address: 13 Canal St., Cumberland, MD 21502
Telephone: (301) 759-4400 and (800) 872-4650
Fax: (301) 759-1329
E-mail: wmsrinfo@wmsr.com
Website: www.wmsr.com

**ELLICOTT CITY B&O RAILROAD
STATION MUSEUM**
Museum, layout

Description: Oldest railroad station in America. Forty-foot layout of the first 13 miles of the B&O.

Schedule: Fridays, Saturdays, Mondays, 11 a.m. to 4 p.m.; Sundays, 12 to 5 p.m. Closed Mondays after Labor Day. Call for hours.

Admission/Fare: Adults, $4; seniors and students, $3; children 12 and under, $2.

Locomotives/Rolling Stock: 1927 Class I-5D caboose; speeder car; hand car.

Special Events: Seasonal programs.

Directions: Corner of Maryland Ave. and Main St. in historic Ellicott City.

Site Address: 2711 Maryland Ave., Ellicott City, MD
Mailing Address: 2711 Maryland Ave., Ellicott City, MD 21043
Telephone: (410) 461-1944
Fax: (410) 461-1944
E-mail: ecbostation@aol.com
Website: www.ecbo.org

Maryland, Hagerstown **HAGERSTOWN ROUNDHOUSE MUSEUM**
Museum, layout

CRYSTAL SPRECHER

Description: Memories of the Western Maryland Railway Complex, arti-facts, photos, and displays. Trains for kids to run. Model train layouts, gift shop.

Schedule: Year-round, Friday through Sunday, 1 to 5 p.m.; closed Easter.

Admission/Fare: Adults, $3; children under 13, $.50.

Locomotives/Rolling Stock: Western Maryland Railway diesel locomotive VO-1000, 1944, no. 132; Hagerstown & Frederick trolley no. 168.

Special Events: Railroad Heritage Days, June; excursions, summer and fall; Trains of Christmas, December and January.

Nearby Attractions: Antietam National Battlefield, Hagerstown City Park, Hager House, Museum of Fine Arts, C&O Canal, Fort Frederick.

Directions: I-81 to exit 2, U.S. 11 north to museum; I-70 to exit 32; U.S. 40 west to U.S. 11, south to museum.

Site Address: 300 S. Burhans Blvd. (U.S. 11), Hagerstown, MD
Mailing Address: PO Box 2858, Hagerstown, MD 21741-2858
Telephone: (301) 739-4665
Fax: (301) 739-5598
Website: www.roundhouse.org

CHARLES LEE MOZINGO

Description: Our museum houses a large O gauge model railroad display, with all the sights and sounds of the real thing . . . and tons of memorabilia. We have a collection of rare and unusual items from Lionel and Marx. Much of the collection is pre-World War II.

Schedule: Weekends, 12 noon to 6 p.m.; Mondays and Fridays, 10 a.m. to 8 p.m.; Tuesdays and Thursdays, 10 p.m. to 6 p.m. Closed Wednesdays.

Admission/Fare: Adults, $2.50; children under 12, free with adult.

Nearby Attractions: Antietam Battlefield, Western Maryland Roundhouse Museum, Hagerstown City park, with steam engine on display and eight cabooses.

Directions: Close to I-81 and I-70 interchange; check our website.

Site Address: 360 S. Burhans Blvd., Hagerstown, MD
Mailing Address: 360 S. Burhans Blvd., Hagerstown, MD 21740
Telephone: (301) 745-6681
Fax: (301) 766-4697
E-mail: conniemo@mris.com
Website: www.the-train=room.com

Massachusetts, Beverly

WALKER TRANSPORTATION COLLECTION
BEVERLY HISTORICAL SOCIETY
& MUSEUM
Display

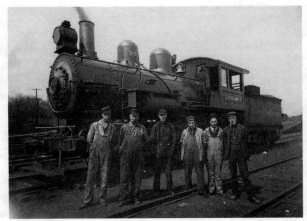

O. C. LEONARD

Description: Repository of photos/negatives, slides, maps, documents, artifacts, some models relating to most modes of transportation in Massachusetts/Eastern New England.

Schedule: Year-round (except for week between Christmas and New Year's), Wednesday evenings, 7 to 10 p.m., or by prior appointment.

Admission/Fare: Free. Donations requested. Annual supporter: $25.

Nearby Attractions: Historic Salem, Massachusetts, and renowned Peabody-Essex Museum. John Hale Farm and historic Balch House are located in Beverly.

Directions: U.S. Route 1A, North; WTC at Beverly Historical Society & Museum in Beverly, housed in historic John Cabot house.

    M

Site Address: 117 Cabot St., Beverly, MA
Mailing Address: 117 Cabot St., Beverly, MA 01915
Telephone: (978) 922-1186 (weekdays and Wednesday nights)
E-mail: info@beverlyhistory.org
Website: www.walkertrans.org

Description: Five-and-a-half-mile train ride through a 1,300-acre cranberry plantation. Children's rides, Wheels & Fun Museum, and much more.

Schedule: June: weekends, 10 a.m. to 5 p.m. July and August: Friday through Monday, 10 a.m. to 5 p.m. September and October: weekends, 10 a.m. to 5 p.m. November and December: weekdays, 4 to 9 p.m.; weekends, 2 to 9 p.m.

Admission/Fare: $17 per person.

Locomotives/Rolling Stock: 1949 GE diesel; 1951 Whitcomb diesel; 1938 Hudswell-Clark steam; no. 11 combine 1900; no. 21 coach 1901; no. 26 coach 1986.

Nearby Attractions: Plymouth Plantation, Super Sports, Plymouth War Museum.

Directions: Take Highway 495 south to Route 58 north. Get off at exit 2, go 3½ miles; Edaville USA is on the left.

*Coupon available, see coupon section.

Site Address: 7 Eda Ave., Carver, MA
Mailing Address: PO Box 825, Carver, MA 02330
Telephone: (508) 866-8190 and (877) Edaville
Fax: (508) 866-7921
E-mail: bjohnson@edaville.org
Website: www.edaville.org

**OLD COLONY AND FALL RIVER
RAILROAD MUSEUM**
Museum

JACK DARMODY

Description: The museum, located in railroad cars that include a renovated
Pennsylvania Railroad coach, features artifacts of the New Haven, Penn
Central, Conrail, Amtrak, and other New England railroads.

Schedule: April 19 through June 20 and September through November 16:
Saturdays, 12 to 4 p.m.; and Sundays, 10 a.m. to 2 p.m. July 1 through
September 2: Thursdays through Sundays, 12 to 5 p.m.

Admission/Fare: Adults, $2.50; seniors, $2; children 5-12, $1; under age 5
are free. Group rates available.

Rolling Stock: Pennsylvania P-70 coach; no. 42 New Haven RDC
"Firestone"; New Haven 40-foot boxcar no. 33401; New York Central
N7B caboose no. 21052.

Special Events: Annual Railroad Show, third weekend in January. Fall River
Celebrates America waterfront festival, mid-August.

Nearby Attractions: Battleship Cove (six warships on display), Marine Museum
at Fall River, Heritage State Park, Fall River Carousel.

Directions: The museum is located in a railroad yard at the corner of Central
and Water Streets, across from the entrance to Battleship Cove.

            M

Site Address: 2 Water St., Fall River, MA
Mailing Address: PO Box 3455, Fall River, MA 02722-3455
Telephone: (508) 674-9340
E-mail: railroadjc@aol.com
Website: www.ocandfrrailroadmuseum.com

CAPE COD CENTRAL RAILROAD
Train ride, dinner train
Standard gauge

Description: Two-hour scenic excursion and luncheon train from Hyannis to the Cape Cod Canal. Three-hour elegant dinner trains. See cranberry bogs, salt marshes, sand dunes, kettle ponds, and Cape Cod Bay.

Schedule: Scenic trains–May through October, daily except Monday. Dinner train–April through December.

Admission/Fare: Adults, $15; seniors (62+), $13; children 3-11, $11. Dinner train–$57 per person.

Locomotives/Rolling Stock: NYC RS-3, rebuilt by Amtrak into RS-3M, Cape Cod Central no. 1201; Bayline Railroad chopnose GP-7s (two); three ex-LIRR coaches (scenic train), built in 1964 by Pullman; two ex-CN, ex-VIA coaches built by Canadian Car and Foundry in 1938, converted into table cars in early 1990s (dinner train); ex-Illinois Central parlor-lounge car built in 1917, used on dinner trains.

Nearby Attractions: Boat lines, beaches, and many other area attractions.

Directions: Take route 6 to exit 7. Go left off the exit and follow for approximately 3 miles to Route 28. Cross Route 28 and continue straight to the end of the road. At Main St. turn right. The depot is on the right at the corner of Main and Center Streets.

Radio Frequency: 160.305

Site Address: 252 Main St., Hyannis, MA
Mailing Address: 252 Main St., Hyannis, MA 02601
Telephone: (508) 771-3800
Fax: (508) 771-1355
Website: www.capetrain.com

Massachusetts, Lenox

BERKSHIRE SCENIC RAILWAY
Train ride, museum, display, layout
Standard gauge

Description: Twenty-mile round trip between Lenox and Stockbridge, Massachusetts, along the Housatonic River. The museum is located in the restored Lenox Station. Restored New York, New Haven & Hartford NE-5 caboose; Fairmont speeder and track gang train; displays about Berkshire railroading history; railroad videos; exhibit of photos and artifacts about Gilded-Age Berkshire "Cottages" in restored coach.

Schedule: May through October, weekends and holidays. Call or write for specific train times.

Admission/Fare: Adults, $12; seniors, $10; children 3-12, $5.

Locomotives/Rolling Stock: GE 50-ton switcher no. 67; Maine Central Alco S-1 no. 954; New York Central EMD SW8 no. 8619.

Special Events: Halloween Special, Santa Special, and more. Contact the museum for specific information.

Nearby Attractions: Tanglewood, summer home of the Boston Symphony Orchestra; the Norman Rockwell Museum; Hancock Shaker Village. Located in the center of the Berkshire Hills, America's premier cultural resort.

Directions: U.S. 7/20 to Housatonic St., travel east 1.5 miles.

  Radio frequency: 161.400

Site Address: Willow Creek Rd., Lenox, MA
Mailing Address: PO Box 2195, Lenox, MA 01240
Telephone: (413) 637-2210
Fax: (518) 392-2225
E-mail: wordworks@taconic.net
Website: www.berkshirescenicrailroad.org

**SHELBURNE FALLS TROLLEY
MUSEUM**
Trolley ride, museum, display, layout

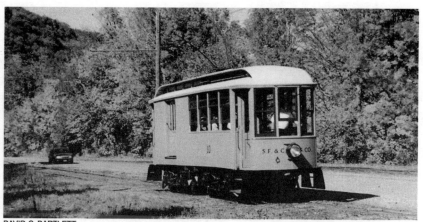

DAVID C. BARTLETT

Description: Museum with 15-minute trolley ride continuously and interpretive talk by motorman/conductor; locomotive, caboose, handcar, trolley, and railroad displays.

Schedule: Memorial Day to November, weekends and holidays, 11 a.m. to 5 p.m.

Admission/Fare: Adults, $2; children under 6, free.

Locomotives/Rolling Stock: 1896 Wason trolley car no. 10; 1934 Baldwin saddle tank steam locomotive; 1910 Central Vermont caboose no. 4015; 1937 Bangor & Aroostook "American Flyer" coach; handcar.

Special Events: Trolleyfest Day, Amherst Railway Society Appreciation Day.

Nearby Attractions: Bridge of Flowers, glacial potholes, Historic Deerfield, artisans' studios, craft shops.

Directions: Route 91 or Route 2 to Greenfield. Go west on Route 2 approximately 8 miles to Shelburne Falls. Follow the signs to the Buckland side of Shelburne Falls. Take Depot St. to the railyard next to the tracks.

*Coupon available, see coupon section.

      M arm

Site Address: 14 Depot St., Buckland, MA
Mailing Address: PO Box 272, Shelburne Falls, MA 01370
Telephone: (413) 625-9443 and (413) 624-0192
E-mail: trolley@sftm.org
Website: www.sftm.org

Massachusetts, Wenham

WENHAM MUSEUM
Museum

Description: Model train room with seven operating layouts and railroad artifacts.

Schedule: Tuesdays through Sundays, 10 a.m. to 4 p.m. Closed Mondays and major holidays.

Admission/Fare: Adults, $5; seniors (65+), $4; children (2-16), $3.

Locomotives/Rolling Stock: Models only.

Special Events: Annual Railroad Hobby Show, first weekend in January.

Nearby Attractions: Wenham Tea House and shops, numerous historical sites and museums in region. Beautiful beaches, scenic drives, quaint towns.

Directions: Route 128 north to exit 20A (Route 1A north). Follow Route 1A north for 2.3 miles. The museum is on the right next to Town Hall.

*Coupon available, see coupon section.

   M

Site Address: 132 Main St., Wenham, MA
Mailing Address: 132 Main St., Wenham, MA 01984
Telephone: (978) 468-2377
Fax: (978) 468-1763
E-mail: info@wenhammuseum.org
Website: www.wenhammuseum.org

JUNCTION VALLEY RAILROAD
Train ride
14⅛" gauge

LILLIAN STENGER

Description: The ride, more than 2 miles long, travels 22 feet down into a valley, around a lake, over 865 feet of bridges and trestles, and through a 100-foot tunnel, playground, and picnic area. We have a 10-stall round-house with turntable, five-track switchyard, railroad shops, and railroad hobby shop.

Schedule: Train rides–mid-May through Labor Day: Mondays through Saturdays, 10 a.m. to 6 p.m.; Sundays, 1 to 6 p.m. September through October 7: weekends, 1 to 5 p.m. Railroad hobby shop open year-round.

Admission/Fare: Adults, $5.25; seniors, $5; children, $4.50. Special events fares are higher. Group rates available.

Locomotives/Rolling Stock: No. 1177 GP45; no. 333 SW1500; no. 4 Plymouth; no. 300 SW1500 booster unit; no. 5000 WS4A; no. 7000 WS4A; no. 6000 WS4B; no. 555 MP15; no. 8000 W54B; 65 railroad cars of all types. All are built ¼ the size of their prototype.

Special Events: Opening Day balloon launch. Valley of Flags, July 4. Railroad Days, June 28-29, July 26-27, August 23-24. Halloween Spook Ride, October, and more.

Directions: I-75, Bridgeport exit, head south for 2 miles. Located 5 miles west of historic Frankenmuth.

*Coupon available, see coupon section.

Site Address: 7065 Dixie Highway, Bridgeport, MI
Mailing Address: 7065 Dixie Highway, Bridgeport, MI 48722
Telephone: (517) 777-3480
Fax: (517) 777-4070
Website: http://gtesupersite.com/jvrailroad

Michigan, Capac

CAPAC COMMUNITY MUSEUM
Museum, display, layout

KEMPF MODEL CITY

Description: 1912 Grand Trunk Depot Museum with railroad and other historical artifacts from around the area. We also have the Kempf Model City and a Grand Trunk Western caboose

Schedule: May through September, Saturdays and Sundays, 1 to 4 p.m.

Admission/Fare: Donations.

Locomotives/Rolling Stock: GTW caboose no. 78899; C&O speeder.

Nearby Attractions: Motels in Imlay City; campground on Beech Grove Road in Emmett; ½ hour away from Pt. Huron, Michigan, and Canada.

Directions: Just ¼ mile east of the Village of Capac off Capac Rd. on the south side of Downey Rd. (M-21).

   M

Site Address: 401 E. Kempf Ct., Capac, MI
Mailing Address: 401 E. Kempf Ct., Capac, MI 48014
Telephone: (810) 395-2859

Michigan, Charlotte

CHARLOTTE SOUTHERN RAILROAD
OLD ROAD DINNER TRAIN
Train ride, dinner train
Standard gauge

Description: This working, common-carrier freight and passenger railroad offers 7-mile, 2½-hour round trips from downtown Charlotte over a former New York Central line. The Old Road Dinner Train features traditional impeccable dining-car service, including an elegant five-course dinner and cash bar, and murder mystery.

Schedule: Year-round. Call for information; charters anytime.

Admission/Fare: Dinner train fares vary; call for current pricing.

Locomotives/Rolling Stock: GE 44-tonner no. 3, 1956, the last one built, former Dansville & Mt. Morris Railroad; dining cars "Butternut Creek" and "Battle Creek," both former Canadian National, nos. 5208 and 2502, built 1937 and 1954; baggage-generator car no. 5674, former Union Pacific, 1958; RPO no. 105, former Canadian National, 1924; coaches nos. 2957 and 2959, former Long Island 1956.

Special Events: Frontier Days, September. Santa Train. Special trips, senior charters, and bus tour group charters with or without meals.

Nearby Attractions: Michigan State Historical Museum in Lansing.

Directions: 451 N. Cochrane St. is at the north end of downtown Charlotte's main street. Charlotte is 15 miles southwest of Lansing, just off I-69 exit 61.

Lansing

Site Address: 451 N. Cochrane St., Charlotte, MI
Mailing Address: PO Box 265, Charlotte, MI 48813
Telephone: (888) 726-8277
Fax: (248) 583-3194
E-mail: ihswabash@msn.com
Website: www.murdermysterytrain.com

Michigan, Clinton

**SOUTHERN MICHIGAN
RAILROAD SOCIETY**
Train ride, museum
Standard gauge

ERNEST JESCHKE

Description: Ride the rails on the historic Clinton Branch of the former New York Central. The 11 miles of track pass twice over the River Raisin, on a wooden trestle bridge north of Tecumseh or the all-steel trestle south of Tecumseh. Some trips board at Clinton, some at Tecumseh.

Schedule: May through September: Sundays, 11 a.m. and 2 p.m. Fall color tours: weekends, 11 a.m., 1:30 and 4 p.m. Call for details.

Admission/Fare: May through September–adults, $8; seniors, $7; children (2-12), $5. Fall color tours–adults, $15; seniors, $10; children (2-12), $8. Special prices for Mother's and Father's Day, Anniversary, Holiday runs.

Locomotives/Rolling Stock: Regular passenger service–1943 GE 44-ton WM diesel no. 75; 1926 Chicago South Shore & South Bend commuter car no. 1; NYC gondola no. 726456; 1952 NYC bay window caboose no. 21692. Other–GM 1960 GMDH-2 prototype; 1938 Plymouth no. 1; more

Special Events: Mother's and Father's Day weekend excursions; Anniversary Special, August 9 and 10; Clinton Fall Festival, last weekend of September, shuttle between Tecumseh and Clinton; fall color tours, weekends in October; Holiday Train, first two weekends in December.

Directions: Clinton–take US 12 to Clinton and turn south two blocks on Division St.; or take M-53 south from Chelsea and I-94. Tecumseh–take M-50 to Tecumseh. Board the train at the corner of Evans and M-50.

Site Address: 320 S. Division St. Clinton, MI (corner of Clark and Division)
Mailing Address: 320 S. Division, PO Box K, Clinton, MI 49236
Telephone: (517) 456-7677
Fax: (517) 456-7677
E-mail: trains@southernmichiganrailroad.org
Website: www.southernmichiganrailroad.org

Michigan, Dearborn

**HENRY FORD MUSEUM AND
GREENFIELD VILLAGE RAILROAD**
Train ride
Standard gauge

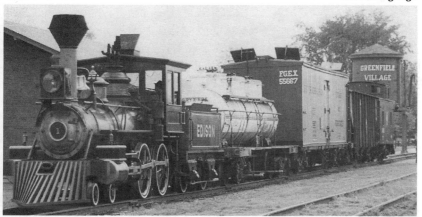

E.J. GULASH

Description: The Greenfield Village Railroad offers a 2½-mile, 35-minute narrated circuit of the world-famous Greenfield Village in open-air passenger cars. While riding you will hear interpretations of the history of the
village, its occupants and the railroad. The Henry Ford Museum, a general museum of American history occupying about 12 acres under one
roof, contains a huge transportation collection, including the widely
acclaimed "Automobile in American Life" exhibit. Greenfield Village is
an 81-acre outdoor museum comprising more than 80 historic structures. A new visitor experience is a recreation of the Detroit, Toledo &
Milwaukee roundhouse; a six stall repair facility from 1884. Visitors can
get an up close look at repairs taking place on the trains of Greenfield
Village. Also at the site are 1941 Lima 2-6-6-6 no. 1601; a 1902
Schenectady 4-4-2; an 1858 Rogers 4-4-0; an 1893 replica of the "DeWitt
Clinton"; 1909 Baldwin 2-8-0, former Bessemer & Lake Erie no. 154.

Schedule: Call or write for information.

Admission/Fare: Call or write for information.

Locomotives/Rolling Stock: No. 1, 1876 Ford Motor Co. 4-4-0 (rebuilt
1920s); no. 3, 1873 Mason-Fairlie 0-6-4T, former Calumet & Hecla Mining;
no. 8, 1914 Baldwin 0-6-0, former Michigan Alkali Co.

Directions: One-half mile south of U.S. 12 (Michigan Ave.) between
Southfield and Oakwood Blvd. (freeway M39).

         M TRAIN

 Dearborn

Site Address: 20900 Oakland Blvd., Dearborn, MI
Mailing Address: PO Box 1970, Dearborn, MI 48121
Telephone: (313) 271-1620
Website: www.hfmgv.org

MICHIGAN AUSABLE VALLEY RAILROAD
                                        Train ride
                                        16" gauge

Description: A 1½-mile, 18-minute scenic ride on a 1/4 scale passenger train that runs through part of the Huron National Forest and overlooks beautiful AuSable Valley. You will pass through a 115-foot wooden tunnel and over two wooden trestles, one over 220 feet long, to view the wooded valley below. The MAV Railroad is also home to Schrader's Railroad Gift Catalog. You will find one-of-a-kind items from past and present catalogs in the quaintly designed Railroad Depot Gift Shop.

Schedule: Weekends and holidays *only,* Memorial Day weekend through Labor Day: 10 a.m. to 5 p.m. First two weekends in October: fall color.

Admission/Fare: $3; children under age 2 are free.

Locomotives/Rolling Stock: 1/4 scale 16-inch Hudson steam locomotive 4-6-4 no. 5661, built by E.C. Eddy of Fairview and formerly run on the Pinconning & Blind River Railroad; two F7 diesel hydraulic locomotives built by Custom Locomotive, Chicago, Illinois; nine 1/4 scale passenger streamline coaches.

Nearby Attractions: Huron National Forest, canoe ride National Scenic AuSable River, campgrounds, nature hikes.

Directions: North on I-75, exit 202 onto M-33, north to Fairview. Turn south at blinker light in Fairview and go 3.5 miles south on Abbe Rd.

*Coupon available, see coupon section.

Site Address: 230 S. Abbe Rd., Fairview, MI
Mailing Address: 230 S. Abbe Rd., Fairview, MI 48621
Telephone: (989) 848-2229
Fax: (989) 848-2240

HUCKLEBERRY RAILROAD
Train ride
Narrow gauge

MARTY KNOX

Description: Steam locomotive and historic wooden coaches depart from 1860s Crossroads Depot for an 8-mile excursion. The route borders Mott Lake and crosses a 26-foot trestle. Huckleberry Railroad is operated in conjunction with Crossroads Village, living history museum of 34 buildings and paddle-wheel riverboat.

Schedule: Mid-May through August, Tuesdays through Sundays. September, weekends. Weekdays, 10 a.m. to 5 p.m.; weekends and holidays, 11 a.m. to 5:30 p.m. Call for dates and hours for October through December.

Admission/Fare: Village, train, and boat–adults (13-59), $13.25; seniors (60+), $12.25; children (3-12), $8.50; age 2 and under free.

Locomotives/Rolling Stock: Baldwin 4-6-0 HRR no. 2; Baldwin 2-8-2 HRR no. 464; Plymouth diesel HRR no. 5; caboose and 14 historic coaches.

Special Events: Weekend events throughout summer, Halloween and Christmas trains. Railfans weekend, August.

Nearby Attractions: Timber Wolf Campground, Stepping Stone Falls, outlet shopping, Genesee Belle paddle-wheel riverboat dinner and lunch cruises.

Directions: Just north of Flint, Michigan. I-475 off either I-75 or I-69 to exit 11, follow signs to railroad and Crossroads Village.

          M arm

Site Address: 6140 Bray Rd., Flint, MI
Mailing Address: 5045 Stanley Rd., Flint, MI 48506
Telephone: (810) 736-7100 and (800) 648-7275
Fax: (810) 736-7220
E-mail: parkswebteam@co.genesee.mi.us
Website: geneseecountyparks.org

Michigan, Flushing

**FLUSHING AREA HISTORICAL
SOCIETY & CULTURAL CENTER**
Museum
Narrow gauge

Description: The collection includes items of the area's historical past, including permanent displays of railroad items. Other displays change periodically.

Schedule: May through first Sunday in December, open Sundays. Closed holiday weekends.

Admission/Fare: Free.

Nearby Attractions: There are several antique shops in the area.

Directions: Take I-75 to exit 122 (Pierson Rd.) and go west approximately five miles. Pierson Rd. becomes Main St. in Flushing.

    M

Site Address: 431 W. Main St., Flushing, MI
Mailing Address: PO Box 87, Flushing, MI 48433
Telephone: (810) 487-0814 (recording)
Website: www.flushinghistorical.org

Michigan, Iron Mountain

IRON MOUNTAIN IRON MINE
Train ride
24" gauge

Description: Designated a Michigan Historical Site, the Iron Mountain Iron Mine offers guided underground tours by mine train. Visitors travel 2,600 feet into the mine to see mining demonstrations and the history of iron mining in Michigan's Upper Peninsula. Mining equipment dating from the 1870s is shown and explained.

Schedule: June 1 through October 15, daily, 9 a.m. to 5 p.m.

Admission/Fare: Adults, $7; children 6-12, $6; children under 6 are free. School and group rates available.

Locomotives/Rolling Stock: Electric locomotive and five cars.

Directions: Nine miles east of Iron Mountain on U.S. 2.

Site Address: Iron Mountain, MI
Mailing Address: PO Box 177, Iron Mountain, MI 49801
Telephone: (906) 563-8077
E-mail: ironmine@uplogon.com
Website: www.ironmountainironmine.com

Michigan, Lake Linden

COPPER COUNTRY RAILROAD
HERITAGE CENTER
Layout
36" gauge

Description: The line is currently under construction. Total length, 1.4 miles, including interpretative program on copper milling.

Schedule: Layout open Tuesdays and Thursdays, 10 a.m. to 4 p.m.

Admission/Fare: Museum, depot, layout, $5.

Locomotives/Rolling Stock: 1915 Porter 0-4-0 tank engine used by Calumet & Hecla; caboose Soo Line no. 261; C&H plow/flanger no. 2; C&H flanger (both constructed by C&H Mining) offsite exhibits; Q&TL RR 2-6-0 and 2-8-0; various other 36″ gauge equipment, Russell snow-plow C&H.

Special Events: Railroad Days, third weekend in August.

Nearby Attractions: Lake Linden Village campground (hook-ups, swimming beach, boat launch), Quincy Mine Hoist, McClain and Port Wilkens State Parks, Keweenaw National Historical Park, 40 miles by boat to Isle Royale National Park.

Directions: Take U.S. 41 or M-26 to Houghton, cross Portage Lift Bridge to M-26 (right), 10 miles on southwest side of Lake Linden.

Site Address: 5500 Highway M-26, Lake Linden, MI
Mailing Address: PO Box 127, Lake Linden, MI 49945
Telephone: (906) 296-4121
Fax: (906) 296-0862
E-mail: richard@raildreams.com

Michigan, Mount Clemens

MICHIGAN TRANSIT MUSEUM
Train ride, museum, display
Standard gauge

TIMOTHY D. BACKHURST

Description: A 45-minute round trip onto the trackage of the Selfridge Air National Guard Base on 1920s interurban rapid transit cars. Optional stop at Selfridge Military Air Museum. At a separate site, the Mount Clements Depot Museum, where Thomas A. Edison learned telegraphy.

Schedule: Train–end of May through end of October, Sundays. Depot Museum–year-round, weekends, 1 to 4 p.m.

Admission/Fare: Train–adults, $6; children 4-12, $3. Air Museum–$3. Depot Museum–free (donations welcome).

Locomotives/Rolling Stock: U.S. Army Alco S1 no. 1807; BLH RST4C no. 4040; South Shore interurban no. 11; Chicago Rapid Transit ("L" cars) nos. 4442, 4450; DSR PCC no. 268; TTC PCC no. 4601; GTW caboose no. 77058; numerous freight and work equipment.

Special Events: Fall color tours on train, October. Polar Express Train–for information, call (586) 286-9336.

Directions: Train ride–from Mount Clemens take Gratiot north 1 mile to Joy Blvd., turn right, go ¼ mile to Joy Park (back of park). Depot–¾ mile west of downtown Mount Clemens on Cass Ave., between Gratiot and Groesbeck Avenues.

*Coupon available, see coupon section.

       M arm TRAIN

Site Address: Depot Museum, 200 Grand Ave., Mount Clemens, MI
Mailing Address: PO Box 12, Mount Clemens, MI 48046
Telephone: (586) 463-1863
Fax: (586) 463-9814
E-mail: tbackhurst@bignet.net
Website: www.mtmrail.com

189

MICHIGAN STATE TRUST FOR RAILWAY PRESERVATION, INC.
Museum
Standard gauge

STEAM RAILROADING INSTITUTE

Description: A museum atmosphere with steam railroad equipment displayed in an interactive educational format. Classroom programs explain railroading's impact on our economy and culture.

Schedule: Saturdays, 10 a.m. to 5 p.m. Occasional events as announced. Weekdays and Sundays by appointment.

Admission/Fare: $3 per person.

Locomotives/Rolling Stock: Pere Marquette 2-8-4 no. 1225; Flagg Coal Co. 0-4-0T no. 75; Pullman Sleeper C&O no. 2624; classroom car, ex-Amtrak baggage no. 1316; two museum display cars, ex-Amtrak passenger nos. 1610 and 1614; tool car, ex-C&O troop sleeper no. 1701; aux. tank car, ex-Rock Island tender no. 5000; Pere Marquette caboose no. A909; wooden boxcar PM no. 88305; two Ann Arbor Railroad boxcars, nos. 1314 and 4633; two GTW "idler" flatcars nos. 54263 and 54262; more.

Special Events: Engineer-for-an-Hour program allows the public to drive a steam locomotive; some restrictions apply. Weekend or day "rail camp": a railroading experience for groups. Reservation required for both programs.

Nearby Attractions: Huckleberry Railroad, Durand Union Station, Curwood Castle.

Directions: Take I-69 to M-52 or M-71. Follow map route north to Owosso.

Radio frequency: 160.575

Site Address: S. Washington St. at Howard
Mailing Address: PO Box 665, Owosso, MI 48867
Telephone: (989) 725-9464
Fax: (989) 723-1225
E-mail: mstrp@shianet.org
Website: www.mstrp.com

Michigan, Port Huron

THOMAS EDISON DEPOT MUSEUM
Museum, display
Standard gauge

T. J. GAFFNEY

Description: Museum dedicated to Thomas Alva Edison's boyhood in Port Huron. Displays are set in the 1858 CD&CGT Jct. RR Depot he worked out of as a news butcher. Displays also include an 1870s-era combine from the Grand Trunk Railroad, with a re-creation of Edison's train-borne laboratory and printing press. While you're in Port Huron, be sure to visit the Huron Lightship and Port Huron Museum.

Schedule: Summer hours: Monday through Sunday, 1 to 4:30 p.m.; Fridays, 1 to 8 p.m. Winter hours: Wednesday through Sunday, 1 to 4:30 p.m.

Admission/Fare: Depot Museum only–adults, $3; seniors and students, $2. Passport to all three Port Huron Museum sites–adults, $5; seniors and students, $3. Tour group discounts available.

Locomotives/Rolling Stock: Former Grand Trunk Western combine no. 7365, nee no. 3244; Chicago & Grand Trunk Railway coach no. 1842.

Special Events: February 11, Thomas Edison's birthday; October 21, celebration of invention of electric light.

Nearby Attractions: Huron Lightship; Port Huron Museum; Main Street Port Huron; Huron Lady Cruises; Tall Ship Highlander Sea; Pine Grove Park.

Directions: Take I-94 or I-69 to Hancock St. exit. Turn right and go five blocks until you reach Gratiot Ave. (M-25). Go right on Gratiot, until it ends in the Thomas Edison Inn parking lot. We are located to your left.

     M

Site Address: 510 Edison Pkwy. (beneath Blue Water Bridges), Port Huron, MI
Mailing Address: c/o Port Huron Museum, 115 Sixth St., Port Huron, MI 48060
Telephone: (810) 982-0891, ext. 15
Fax: (810) 982-0053
E-mail: depot@phmuseum.org   **Website:** www.phmuseum.org

HERB MCCULLAGH

Description: An educational and research facility dedicated to the preservation and enhancement of railroad technology and lore. Operating diesel locomotives, caboose(s), Armstrong interlocking tower, combine coach (under restoration), 1907 Pere Marquette depot, HO model train.

Schedule: Open April through November, second and fourth Sundays; June and July, every Sunday; also by appointment. Hours, 1 to 5 p.m. December through March, closed; also closed holidays.

Admission/Fare: Individual, $2; family rate, $5; children under 5 are free.

Locomotives/Rolling Stock: GP-9 locomotives (operable) GTW 4428 and GTW 4433; GE 25-tonner U.S. Navy dock locomotive built 1942 (under restoration); C&O cabooses 903577, 900342, 900977 (latter two under restoration); combine C&O 911245 (under restoration) converted to MW cook car by C&O.

Nearby Attractions: Frankenmuth; Junction Valley 1/4 scale railroad; Japanese gardens, children's zoo; waterslide and wave pool.

Directions: I-75 to exit 149 (M-46 West–Holland Ave.) Follow through city and across river. Left at first traffic light (Michigan Ave.) and follow across tracks. Turn right at museum sign. Follow to Maple and turn right.

       M

Site Address: 900 Maple St., Saginaw, MI
Mailing Address: 900 Maple St., Saginaw, MI 48602
Telephone: (517) 790-7994
Website: www.rypn.org/svrhs

TOONERVILLE TROLLEY, TRAIN AND BOAT TOURS
Train ride
24" gauge

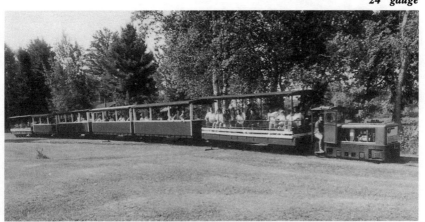

Description: Enjoy a 6½-hour train and boat tour to Tahquamenon Falls or 1¾-hour wilderness train ride, 5½ miles one way. Longest 24″ rail in the country.

Schedule: June 15 through October 6. Please call for schedule.

Admission/Fare: For the 6½-hour trip to falls–adults, $27; children 6-15, $13.50; under 6, free. For the 1¾-hour train ride–adults, $12; children 6-15, $6; under 6, free.

Locomotives/Rolling Stock: Two 1964 Plymouth 5-ton diesels; 1957 Plymouth 5-ton gas; 11 passenger cars.

Nearby Attractions: Oswald's Bear Ranch, Whitefish Point lighthouse, logging museum.

Directions: East of Newberry, Michigan, just off M-28 at Soo Junction. One hour from Mackinac Bridge or Sault Ste. Marie.

Site Address: Soo Junction, MI
Mailing Address: 5883 County Road 441, Newberry, MI 49868
Telephone: (888) 77-TRAIN or (906) 293-3806
E-mail: soojunction@portup.com
Website: www.destinationmichigan.com/toonerville-trolley.html

**THE GRAND TRAVERSE
DINNER TRAIN**
Dinner train

ANTHONY BEAVERSON

Description: Three-hour dining excursions through northern Michigan. We travel 60 miles and serve a five-course gourmet meal.

Schedule: Year-round, with the number of excursions relative to the seasons. Weekday departures, 12:30 and 6:30 p.m. Weekend departures, 12 noon and 6 p.m.

Admission/Fare: During the high season, dinner train–adult, $75; children, $37.50. Train ride–$10 per ticket.

Locomotives/Rolling Stock: EMD 567BC F7 diesel electric no. 1951; EMD 645BC F7 diesel electric no. 1950; GTDR 100; GTDR 300; articulated Pullman dining coaches.

Special Events: Valentine's Day, Bunny Hops, Mother's Day, Father's Day, Thanksgiving, Victorian Christmas, Santa Rides, New Year's; Victorian High Tea.

Directions: Corner of Eighth and Woodmere Ave.

Site Address: 642 Railroad Place, Traverse City, MI
Mailing Address: 642 Railroad Place, Traverse City, MI 49686
Telephone: (231) 933-3768 and (888) 933-3768
Fax: (231) 933-5440
E-mail: gtdt@dinnertrain.com
Website: www.dinnertrain.com

SPIRIT OF TRAVERSE CITY
Train ride
15" gauge

LAUREN VAUGHN

Description: The Spirit of Traverse City, an oil-fired, 1/4 scale replica of a 4-4-2 steam locomotive, pulls passengers in three open-air cars on a ⁹⁄₁₀-mile loop through the Clinch Park Zoo marina and beach. Provides scenic views of West Grand Traverse Bay.

Schedule: May 24 through September 8 and September 13-14, 20-21. Daily, 10 a.m. to 4:30 p.m.

Admission/Fare: Adults, $1; children 5-12, $.50; under 5 are free.

Locomotives/Rolling Stock: "Spirit of Traverse City" no. 400 oil-fired 4-4-2 steam locomotive, three open-air passenger cars.

Special Events: Family Fun Day, June 1: $.25 rides, popcorn, and zoo admission.

Nearby Attractions: Clinch Park Zoo, Grand Traverse Heritage Center, Great Lakes Children's Museum, Dennos Museum, beaches, golf course, campgrounds, and more.

Directions: On U.S. 31 (Grandview Pkwy.) at Cass St. in downtown Traverse City on West Grand Traverse Bay.

*Coupon available, see coupon section.

Site Address: 100 E. Grandview Pkwy., Traverse City, MI
Mailing Address: 625 E. Woodmere Ave., Traverse City, MI 49686
Telephone: (231) 922-4910
Fax: (231) 941-7716
E-mail: tcparks@megsinet.net
Website: www.traverse.net/traversecity/services/train.htm

IRONWORLD DISCOVERY CENTER
Museum

Description: Ironworld Discovery Center, perched on the edge of the Glen open-pit iron mine, showcases the iron range's rich industrial, cultural and ethnic history. Included in the Ironworld experience is a 2.5-mile rail trip along the edge of Glen Mine.

Schedule: June through September.

Admission/Fare: Rates vary.

Locomotives/Rolling Stock: Two 16-ton electric trolleys; 45-ton diesel electric switching locomotive; caboose; boxcar, three observation cars; miscellaneous railroad repair equipment.

Special Events: Call for more specific information.

Nearby Attractions: For more information, please contact the Iron Trail Convention and Visitor's Bureau at (800) 777-8497.

Directions: Highway 169 west in Chisholm, Minnesota.

Site Address: Highway 169 west, Chisholm, MN
Mailing Address: PO Box 392, Chisholm, MN 55719
Telephone: (218) 254-7959 and (800) 372-6437
Fax: (218) 254-7972
E-mail: marketing@ironworld.com
Website: www.ironworld.com

**END-O-LINE RAILROAD PARK
AND MUSEUM**
Museum, display, layout

Description: A working railroad yard including a rebuilt enginehouse on its original foundation, an original four-room depot, a water tower, an 1899 section-foreman's house, and an outhouse. The turntable, built in 1901 by the American Bridge Company and still operable, is the only one left in Minnesota on its original site. A general store and one-room schoolhouse can also be seen. A replica of the coal bunker is used as a picnic shelter and gift shop. The buildings contain various exhibits and displays of railroad artifacts, photographs, memorabilia, and equipment. The freight room in the depot has an HO scale model train layout of the railroad yards in Currie, complete with steam engine sound effects, authentic structures, and local countryside. A bicycle/pedestrian paved pathway connects the railroad park to Lake Shetek State Park (6 miles round trip).

Schedule: Memorial Day through Labor Day: Mondays through Fridays, 10 a.m. to 12 noon and 1 to 5 p.m.; weekends, 1 to 5 p.m. Last tour 4 p.m.

Admission/Fare: Adults, $3; students, $2; household, $10.

Locomotives/Rolling Stock: Georgia Northern steam engine no. 102; Grand Trunk Western caboose; Brookville diesel switcher, more.

Nearby Attractions: Lake Shetek State Park, Laura Ingalls Wilder Museum, Pipestone National Monument, campgrounds.

Directions: Highway 30 to Currie, go ¾ mile north on County Road 38.

Site Address: 440 N. Main St., Currie, MN
Mailing Address: 440 N. Mill St., Currie, MN 56123
Telephone: (507) 763-3708
E-mail: louise@endoline.com
Website: www.endoline.com

Minnesota, Dassel　　　　**THE OLD DEPOT RAILROAD MUSEUM**
Museum

Description: A former Great Northern depot built in 1913 is filled with rail-road memorabilia and pictures. This 33 x 100-foot country depot has two waiting rooms, an agent's office, and a large freight room, as well as a full basement. Authentic recorded sounds of steam locomotives and the clicking of the telegraph key create the realistic feel of an old small-town depot. Items displayed include lanterns, telegraph equipment, semaphores, and other signals; section crew cars, a hand pump car, and a velocipede; tools and oil cans; depot and crossing signs; buttons, badges, service pins, and caps; a large date-nail collection; and many baggage carts. Also included are children's toy trains, an HO scale model railroad, and many railroad advertising items. Interpretation of the items is provided. Static 1/2 scale train on display.

Schedule: Memorial Day through October 1, daily, 10 a.m. to 4:30 p.m.

Admission/Fare: Adults, $2.50; children under age 12, $1; babies free.

Locomotives/Rolling Stock: Caboose; two boxcars.

Special Events: Red Rooster Day, Labor Day.

Directions: Fifty miles west of Minneapolis on U.S. Highway 12. Fourteen miles north of Hutchinson on State Highway 15.

*Coupon available, see coupon section.

Site Address: 651 W. Highway 12, Dassel, MN
Mailing Address: PO Box 99, Dassel, MN 55325
Telephone: (320) 275-3876
Fax: (320) 275-3933

Minnesota, Duluth

**LAKE SUPERIOR &
MISSISSIPPI RAILROAD**
Train ride
Standard gauge

DAVE SCHAUER

Description: A 90-minute train ride on historic right-of-way in antique coaches.

Schedule: Weekends, June 14 to September 1; fall colors, weekends September 27-28 and October 4-5. Call for dates or changes.

Admission/Fare: Adults, $8; seniors (55 and up), $7; children (12 and under), $6.

Locomotives/Rolling Stock: GE center-cab 50-ton; ACF coach 1914; Pullman coach 1912; flatcar 1928.

Nearby Attractions: Duluth Zoo is across the street.

Directions: Go west on Grand Ave. to Fremont St., turn left (behind "Little Store").

*Coupon available, see coupon section.

    M  Radio frequency: 160.380

Site Address: 6930 Fremont St., Duluth, MN
Mailing Address: PO Box 16211, Duluth, MN 55816-0211
Telephone: (218) 624-7549
Fax: (218) 728-6303
Website: www.lsmrr.org

Minnesota, Duluth   **LAKE SUPERIOR RAILROAD MUSEUM**
Train ride, dinner train, museum, display, layout
Standard gauge, narrow gauge, HO

BRUCE OJARD PHOTOGRAPHY

Description: The Lake Superior Railroad Museum has one of the largest and most diverse collections of railroad artifacts, including the Great Northern's famous "William Crooks" locomotive and cars of 1861; Northern Pacific Railway no. 1, The "Minnetonka" built in 1870; the Soo line's first passenger diesel, FP7 no. 2500A; Duluth, Missabe & Iron Range 2-8-8-4 no. 227, displayed with revolving drive wheels and recorded sound; an 1887 steam rotary snowplow; other steam, diesel, and electric engines; a Railway Post Office car; a dining-car china exhibit; freight cars; work equipment; an operating electric single-truck streetcar; and much railroadiana.

Schedule: Museum–year-round. Train/trolley–Memorial Day weekend through Labor Day weekend. Hours: Memorial Day to Mid-October, 9:30 a.m. to 6 p.m. Mid-October to Memorial Day, 10 a.m. to 5 p.m. Monday through Saturday and 1 p.m. to 5 p.m. Sunday.

Admission/Fare: Combination tickets (museum and train), $6 to $20.

Special Events: Steam train weekends.

Nearby Attractions: Downtown Duluth, Canal Park, Duluth waterfront; Bayfront Park.

Directions: I-35 exit downtown Duluth/Michigan St.

Site Address: 506 W. Michigan St., Duluth, MN
Mailing Address: 506 W. Michigan St., Duluth, MN 55802
Telephone: (218) 733-7590
Fax: (218) 733-7596
E-mail: museum@lsrm.
Website: www.lsrm.org

Minnesota, Duluth

NORTH SHORE SCENIC RAILROAD
Train ride, dinner train
Standard gauge

TIM SCHANDEL

Description: Formerly the Duluth Missabe & Iron Range Railway's Lake Front Line, this railroad's 26 miles of track run between the depot in downtown Duluth, along the Lake Superior waterfront, and through the residential areas and scenic woodlands of northeastern Minnesota to the Two Harbors Depot, adjacent to DM&IR's active taconite yard and ship-loading facility. The line offers 1½-, 2½-, and 6-hour round trips with departures from Duluth.

Schedule: To Lester River–Memorial Day to Labor Day, Sunday through Thursday, 12:30 and 3 p.m.; Friday and Saturday, 10 a.m., 12:30 and 3 p.m. Pizza train–Wednesday through Saturday, 6:30 p.m. Two Harbors–Friday and Saturday, 10:30 a.m. Reduced schedule, Labor Day to mid-October.

Admission/Fare: Lester River–adults, $9.50; children, $5. Pizza train–adults, $16.50; children, $11.50. Two Harbors–adults, $18; children, $8.

Locomotives/Rolling Stock: DM&IR SD18 no. 193; GN SD45 no. 400; GN NW5 no. 192; Soo Line FP7 no. 2500; DM&IR and GN coaches; more.

Special Events: Steam excursions, dinner trains, murder mystery train, beer tasting train.

Directions: Duluth Depot, Michigan St., downtown Duluth.

Radio frequency: 160.920

Site Address: 506 W. Michigan St., Duluth, MN
Mailing Address: 506 W. Michigan St., Duluth, MN 55802
Telephone: (218) 722-1273 and (800) 423-1273
Fax: (218) 733-7596
E-mail: museum@lsrm.org
Website: www.lsrm.org

Minnesota, Excelsior

MINNESOTA TRANSPORTATION MUSEUM
LAKE MINNETONKA DIVISION
Museum, streetcar
Standard gauge

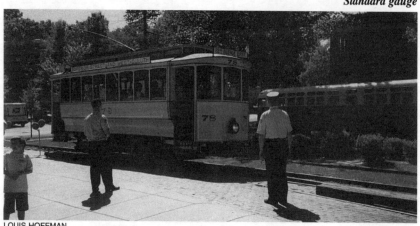

LOUIS HOFFMAN

Description: At the Minnesota Transportation Museum, Lake Minnetonka Division Streetcar Ride, you'll take a 15-minute ride (approximately a half mile) on a historic streetcar and tour our restoration carbarn.

Schedule: Memorial Day weekend through mid-October: Thursdays, 3 to 6 p.m.; Saturdays, 10 a.m. to 4 p.m.; Sundays, 1 to 4 p.m.

Admission/Fare: $1; age 4 and under, free.

Locomotives/Rolling Stock: Duluth Railway no. 78.

Special Events: Farmer's market every Thursday.

Nearby Attractions: Steamboat Minnehaha.

Directions: Highway 7 west, right onto County Road 19; right onto Water St., board streetcar at Lyman Park on right side of street.

Site Address: 328 Lake St., Excelsior, MN
Mailing Address: 328 Lake St., Excelsior, MN 55331
Telephone: (952) 474-2115 and (800) 711-2591
Fax: (952) 474-2192
E-mail: lmdminne78@qwest.net
Website: www.mtmuseum.org

MINNESOTA TRANSPORTATION MUSEUM COMO-HARRIET STREETCAR LINE

Train ride, museum
Standard gauge

LOUIS HOFFMAN

Description: A 2-mile, 15-minute round trip on a restored portion of the former Twin City Rapid Transit Company's historic Como-Harriet route. Streetcars operate over a scenic line through a wooded area between Lakes Harriet and Calhoun. This is the last operating portion of the 523-mile Twin City Lines system, abandoned in 1954. The Linden Hills Station, a re-creation of the 1900 depot located at the site, houses changing historical displays about electric railways in Minnesota.

Schedule: May 16 through September 7: weekends, holidays, 12:30 p.m. to dusk. Mondays through Fridays, 6:30 p.m. to dusk. May 4 through 12 and September 13 through 28: weekends, 12:30 p.m. to dusk. October 4 through 26: weekends, 12:30 to 5 p.m.

Admission/Fare: $1.50; children under age 4 are free. Chartered streetcars–$65 per half hour.

Locomotives/Rolling Stock: No. 265, 1915 Duluth St. Railway (TCRT Snelling Shops, St. Paul); no. 322, 1946 Twin City Lines PCC (St. Louis Car Co.); no. 1300, 1908 Twin City Lines (Snelling Shops).

Special Events: Halloween Ghost Trolley, October 24-26 and 31.

Nearby Attractions: Lake Harriet Park.

Directions: I-35W, 46th St. west to Lake Harriet Parkway, parkway to west shore at Linden Hills Station. Metro transit routes 6 and 28.

St. Paul   **Radio frequency: 161.355**

Site Address: 2330 W. 42nd St., Minneapolis, MN
Mailing Address: 193 E. Pennsylvania Ave., St. Paul, MN 55101-4319
Telephone: (651) 228-0263 and (800) 711-2591
Website: www.mtmuseum.org

Minnesota, Minneapolis   **MINNESOTA TRANSPORTATION MUSEUM**
MINNEHAHA DEPOT
Museum, display

ERIC MORTENSEN, MINNESOTA HISTORICAL SOCIETY

Description: Built in 1875, the Minnehaha Depot replaced an even smaller Milwaukee Road depot on the same site. Milwaukee Road agents quickly nicknamed the depot the "Princess" because of its intricate architectural details. Until Twin City Rapid Transit Company streetcars connected Minnehaha Falls Park to the city, as many as 13 passenger trains per day served the depot. It remained in service, primarily handling freight, for many years. Located at the south end of the Canadian Pacific South Minneapolis branch, operated by the Minnesota Commercial Railway, once a through route to the south, the depot occasionally hosts visiting private cars. Visitors may tour the depot, which appears much as it did when in service as a typical suburban station. Exhibits include telegraphy demonstrations and historic photographs of the depot and its environs.

Schedule: Memorial Day weekend through Labor Day weekend: Sundays and holidays, 12:30 to 4:30 p.m.; other times by advance reservation.

Admission/Fare: Donations appreciated; $25 for group tours outside scheduled hours.

Nearby Attractions: Fort Snelling State Park, Historic Fort Snelling, Mall of America.

Directions: In Minnehaha Falls Park just off State Highway 55 (Hiawatha Ave.). Metro transit routes 7 and 20.

St. Paul

Site Address: 4926 Minnehaha Ave., Minneapolis, MN
Mailing Address: 193 E. Pennsylvania Ave., St. Paul, MN 55101-4319
Telephone: (651) 228-0263 and (800) 711-2591
Website: www.mtmuseum.org

NORTH STAR RAIL, INC.
FRIENDS OF THE 261
Train ride
Standard gauge

VICTOR HAND

Description: North Star Rail, Inc., operates a day-long steam-powered excursion over various Class 1 railroads.

Schedule: Varies with trip. Call or write for information.

Admission/Fare: Varies. Reservations recommended.

Locomotives/Rolling Stock: No. 261 1944 Alco 4-8-4, former Milwaukee Road class S3, leased to North Star Rail by the National Railroad Museum in Green Bay, Wisconsin.

Site Address: Minneapolis, MN
Mailing Address: 4322 Lakepoint Ct., Shoreview, MN 55126
Telephone: (651) 765-9812
Fax: (651) 490-1985 (call first)
Website: www.261.com

Minnesota, St. Paul

**JACKSON STREET
ROUNDHOUSE**
Train ride, museum, display
Standard gauge

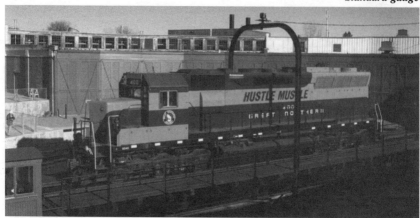

Description: The roundhouse at Jackson St. and Pennsylvania Ave. was built by the Great Northern Railroad in 1907 to service their passenger-service steam locomotives. It was part of the historic Jackson Street shop complex, which was founded just after the Civil War. The turntable has been restored, and the roundhouse is open to visitors all year long. Children can enjoy a miniature train ride.

Schedule: Saturdays, 10 a.m. to 5 p.m.; Sundays, 1 to 5 p.m.

Admission/Fare: $3 per person; $10 per family.

Locomotives/Rolling Stock: "The Gopher," steam engine of Casey Jones, no. 2156; many more diesel and steam locomotives in restoration.

Special Events: Family Day, quarterly.

Nearby Attractions: Minnesota State Capitol.

Directions: On Pennsylvania Ave. between Jackson St. and 35E.

       M

Site Address: 193 E. Pennsylvania Ave., St. Paul, MN
Mailing Address: 193 E. Pennsylvania Ave., St. Paul, MN 55708
Telephone: (651) 228-0263
E-mail: petit@augsburg.edu
Website: www.mtmuseum.org

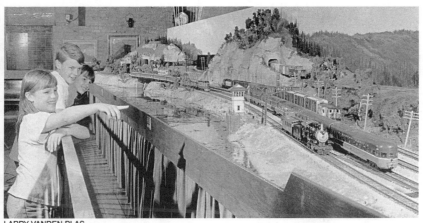

LARRY VANDEN PLAS

Description: Operating 3,000-square-foot O scale model of Minneapolis, St. Paul, and Mississippi River from the 1930s to the 1950s, plus one of the best displays of railroad art, maps, and photographs. Located in former Northern Pacific Como Shops, now Bandana Square.

Schedule: Year-round, Sundays 12 noon to 5 p.m. Closed Mondays. Tuesdays, 11 a.m. to 3 p.m. and 6 to 8 p.m. Wednesdays and Thursdays, 11 a.m. to 3 p.m. Fridays, 11 a.m. to 7 p.m. Saturdays 10 a.m. to 6 p.m.

Admission/Fare: $2; under 5, free.

Locomotives/Rolling Stock: Full-size GTW 0-8-0 in front of building.

Special Events: Night Trains, Circus Train Day, Northern Pacific Day, Great Northern Day, Soo Line Day, etc. Check or request schedule.

Nearby Attractions: Restaurants, gift, hobby, book and art shops located in Bandana Square. Como Park (zoo, picnic, etc.) within a mile. The Mall of America, Gibbs Farm.

Directions: In Bandana Square, on north side of Energy Park Dr., between Lexington and Sneling Avenues, one mile north of I-94.

Site Address: 1021 Bandana Blvd. East, St. Paul, MN
Mailing Address: 1021 Bandana Blvd. East, Suite 222, St. Paul, MN 55108
Telephone: (651) 647-9628
E-mail: tcmrm@tcmrm.org
Website: www.tcmrm.org

Minnesota, Two Harbors

**LAKE COUNTY HISTORY AND
RAILROAD MUSEUM**
Museum

Description: A museum with railroad exhibits. Two locomotives, a three-spot and a Mallet, are on the grounds.

Schedule: May 1 through October 31: Monday through Saturday, 9 a.m. to 5 p.m.; Sunday, 10 a.m. to 3 p.m.

Admission/Fare: $2 per person; $1 ages 9 to 17.

Locomotives/Rolling Stock: Baldwin Locomotive three-spot, built 1882, no. 3; Baldwin Locomotive Mallet (Yellowstone) no. 229.

Nearby Attractions: Two Harbors Lighthouse Museum.

Directions: From Highway 61 turn right onto Waterfront Drive; go seven blocks to the depot.

*Coupon available, see coupon section.

Site Address: 520 South Ave., Two Harbors, MN
Mailing Address: PO Box 128, Two Harbors, MN 55616
Telephone: (218) 834-4898
Fax: (218) 834-7198
E-mail: lakehist@lakenet.com

Description: Museum with Great Northern steam locomotive and depot.

Schedule: Memorial Day through Labor Day: weekdays, 9 a.m. to 5 p.m.; weekends, 1 to 5 p.m.; September through May: weekdays, 9 a.m. to 5 p.m.

Admission/Fare: Free.

Locomotives/Rolling Stock: Great Northern 2523 P-2 class Baldwin.

Nearby Attractions: Schwanke Tractor and Car Museum.

Directions: 610 N.E. Business 71, Willmar, Minnesota. Follow the signs at the north, south, and east edges of the city.

Site Address: 610 N.E. Highway 71, Willmar, MN
Mailing Address: 610 N.E. Highway 71, Willmar, MN 56201
Telephone: (320) 235-1881
E-mail: kandhist@wecnet.com

Mississippi, Vaughan

CASEY JONES MUSEUM
Museum

Description: Casey Jones Railroad Museum State Park is located near the site of Casey Jones's famous train wreck. The museum contains railroad memorabilia and photos, as well as parts of the trains that were in the accident.

Schedule: Year-round, Monday through Friday, 8 a.m. to 4 p.m.; Wednesday and Saturday, 8 a.m. to 12 noon.

Admission/Fare: Adults and seniors, $1; under 12, $.50.

Locomotives/Rolling Stock: 1923 steam engine no. 841.

Nearby Attractions: Holmes County State Park, 17 miles north of museum.

Directions: One mile east of I-55, and 32 miles north of Jackson, Mississippi.

Site Address: 10901 Vaughan Rd., #1, Vaughan, MS
Mailing Address: 10901 Vaughan Rd., #1, Vaughan, MS 39179
Telephone: (662) 673-9864
Fax: (662) 673-9864

**BELTON, GRANDVIEW & KANSAS
CITY RAILROAD COMPANY**
Train ride, museum

GARY HANOLD

Description: Six-mile round trip aboard a NYC coach used in the movie
Biloxi Blues. The train is pulled by a B&O GP9. Static displays include
two steam engines and numerous other rolling stock.

Schedule: May through October, weekends, 2 p.m. Charter trips available.

Admission/Fare: $7 per person; 2 and under, free.

Locomotives/Rolling Stock: B&O GP9 no. 6142; Frisco 1918 Baldwin
2-10-0 no. 1632 (Russian decapod); Okmulgee no. 5 Alco 2-8-0; KCS
observation lounge; ATSF instruction car; Wabash heavyweight and baggage car; NYC no. 4365 1920 coach; MoPac 1972 wide vision caboose;
UP 1928 wood CA-1 caboose.

Special Events: Ice cream train, Fridays, 7 p.m. Pumpkin Patch Express,
October. Children's Halloween trains on Halloween weekend. Specialty
and discount days.

Nearby Attractions: Pres. Truman's farm home, Kansas City, Missouri, West-
port entertainment area, KC Royals baseball, several switching yards.

Directions: From 435 and Highway 71, take U.S. 71 south to Route Y.
Follow Route Y through traffic light to Commercial St., turn right and
go 4 blocks. Yards and depot are on your left.

*Coupon available, see coupon section.

Site Address: 502 Walnut, Belton, MO
Mailing Address: 502 Walnut, Belton, MO 64012
Telephone: (816) 331-0630
E-mail: bgkcrr@aol.com
Website: www.orgsites.com/mo/beltonrailroad

Missouri, Branson

BRANSON SCENIC RAILWAY
Train ride
Standard gauge

Description: This railway operates a 40-mile, 1¾-hour round trip through the Ozark foothills over the former Missouri Pacific White River Route, now operated by the Missouri & North Arkansas Railroad. Most trips take passengers south into Arkansas, across Lake Taneycomo and two high trestles, and through two tunnels. The original 1906 Branson depot houses the railway's ticket office, waiting room, gift shop, and business offices.

Schedule: Excursions–mid-March through mid-December: 9 and 11:30 a.m., 2 and 4:30 p.m. Dinner train–May through December: Saturdays 5 p.m.

Admission/Fare: Call (800) 2TRAIN2 for fares.

Locomotives/Rolling Stock: BSRX 98, 1951 EMD F9PH, rebuilt 1981; BSRX 99, 1972 EMD GP30M, rebuilt 1982; PPCX 800603 "Silver Eagle," 1949 Budd 60-seat coach; BSRX3118 "Silver Lake," 1951 Budd buffet lounge; BSRX 9540, "Silver Island," 1947 Budd dome lounge; BSRX 8503, "Silver Chef," 1956 Budd 48-seat diner; PPCX 800287 "Silver Garden," 1952 Budd lounge observation; other passenger cars.

Special Events: Downtown see Plumb Nellie Days and Fiddler's Contest.

Nearby Attractions: Theme park, historic downtown, restaurants, flea market, crafts festivals, lake, campgrounds, lodging.

Directions: Downtown Branson, ¾ mile east of U.S. 65.

Site Address: 206 E. Main St., Branson, MO
Mailing Address: PO Box 924, Branson, MO 65615
Telephone: (417) 334-6110 and (800) 2TRAIN2
Fax: (417) 336-3909
Website: www.bransontrain.com

Missouri, Branson   **SILVER DOLLAR CITY THEME PARK**
Train ride
Narrow gauge

Description: The Silver Dollar Steam Train takes guests on a fun-filled 20-minute trip back to the 1880s on a tour through the splendid Ozark Mountains.

Schedule: April through December, departures every 30 minutes. Days of operation vary with operation of theme park.

Admission/Fare: Free with paid admission to theme park.

Locomotives/Rolling Stock: 1938 engine no. 13 Orenstein 2-4-0, Koppel, Germany; 1934 engine no. 43 Orenstein 2-4-0, Koppel, Germany; 1940 engine no. 76 2-4-0, Germany.

Special Events: Sing-Along Steam Train (caroling rides) during Old Time Christmas, November and December.

Nearby Attractions: Branson, Missouri.

Directions: Highway 76, approximately 5 miles west of Branson.

Site Address: Silver Dollar City Theme Park, West Highway 76, Branson, MO
Mailing Address: 399 Indian Pt. Rd., Branson, MO 65616
Telephone: (800) 952-6626
Website: www.silverdollarcity.com

Missouri, Glencoe
(Wildwood)

WABASH FRISCO & PACIFIC RAILWAY
"THE UNCOMMON CARRIER"

Train ride
12" gauge

DAVID J. NEUBAUER

Description: A 2-mile, 30-minute round trip over a former Missouri Pacific right-of-way along the scenic Meramec River through wooded areas and over three bridges. Two and, sometimes, three trains are operated consecutively with meets out on the line.

Schedule: May through October, Sundays, 11:15 a.m. to 4:15 p.m.

Admission/Fare: $3; children under age 3 ride free. No reservations.

Locomotives/Rolling Stock: Nine steam locomotives: no. 102, 2-6-2 (coal); no. 171 (coal), oldest on the line, built 1907; no. 180 4-4-0 (coal); no. no. 300 4-4-2 (oil); no. 400 4-6-2 (oil); no. 401 4-6-2 (coal); no. 403 4-6-2 (coal); no. 534, 4-6-4 (oil); no. 535, 4-6-4 (coal); photo above shows the former 434, now the 534. Also five "diesel replicas," powered by gasoline, 37 cars, roundhouse, shop, three turntables, and a wye.

Special Events: Member's Day, fourth Saturday in June.

Nearby Attractions: Museum of Transportation, 10 miles away; UP and BN main lines in Eureka; new Route 66 State Park.

Directions: Twenty-five miles west of St. Louis. I-44 (Eureka), exit 264, north on Route 109 for 3.5 miles to Old State Rd., make two right turns to depot on Washington-Grand Avenue.

*Coupon available, see coupon section.

 Kirkwood

Radio frequency: 151.955

Site Address: Foot of Washington-Grand Ave, Wildwood, MO
Mailing Address: 1569 Ville Angela Ln., Hazelwood, MO 63042-1630
Telephone: (636) 587-3538
E-mail: jmjrr@apci.net
Website: www.wfprr.com

Missouri, Kirkwood

FRIENDS OF LANDMARK KIRKWOOD STATION (F.O.L.K.S.)
Train ride, dinner train, display

RICHARD A. EICHHORST

Description: F.O.L.K.S. supports the Kirkwood Amtrak station by providing passenger amenities. The station, built in 1893, is listed in the national register of historic places. The exhibits are provided by the Museum of Transportation and the American Association of Railroaders, Inc.

Schedule: Daily, 8 a.m. to 8 p.m.

Admission/Fare: Station, free. Fares for excursions vary according to destination and activity.

Special Events: Kirkwood Jct. Festival, May; Kirkwood Station Celebration, first Sunday in November; train watchers gather every Saturday and Sunday afternoon. Sightseeing and dinner excursions on Amtrak trains are offered each month.

Nearby Attractions: Museum of Transportation; Route 66 State Park; Wabash, Frisco & Pacific Railway.

Directions: In downtown Kirkwood at Kirkwood (Lindbergh) Blvd.

Site Address: 110 W. Argonne Road, Kirkwood, MO
Mailing Address: PO Box 221122, Kirkwood, MO 63122
Telephone: (314) 752-3148

GARY CHILCOTE

Description: Patee House Museum was headquarters for the Pony Express in 1860. The former hotel is now a museum of communications and transportation featuring a steam locomotive, mail car, antique cars, trucks, fire trucks, buggies, and wagons. On the grounds is the Jesse James Home, where the outlaw was killed.

Schedule: April through October, daily 10 a.m. to 5 p.m. and 1 to 5 p.m. on Sundays. November through March, open weekends and for special tours.

Admission/Fare: Adults, $4; seniors, $3.50; students ages 6-17, $2.50; under age 6 are free with family.

Locomotives/Rolling Stock: 1892 Baldwin 4-4-0 no. 35, backdated by Burlington in 1933 to resemble Hannibal & St. Joseph locomotive no. 35.

Nearby Attractions: Home of Jesse James, Pony Express Museum, Doll Museum.

Directions: From Highway 36 take the 10th St. exit, follow 10th St. north to right on Mitchell to 12th St.

Site Address: 1202 Penn, St. Joseph, MO
Mailing Address: PO Box 1022, St. Joseph, MO 64502
Telephone: (816) 232-8206
Fax: (816) 232-3717
Website: www.stjoseph.net/ponyexpress/

Missouri, St. Louis

**AMERICAN ASSOCIATION OF
RAILROADERS**
Train ride, dinner train
Standard

RICHARD A. EICHHORST

Description: Sponsors more than 50 rail activities each year. These events include industry tours, one-day sightseeing excursions, dinner excursions, mystery destination adventures, and mainline Amtrak tours. The organization also charters private sleepers, coaches, and observation cars for operation on Amtrak trains and regional railroads. Several train tours in Canada and at least one extended European tour are scheduled each year. The highlight of 2002 was a first-class rail tour across Canada from Halifax on the Atlantic Ocean to Vancouver on the Pacific Ocean.

Schedule: Year-round. At least three activities every month.

Admission/Fare: Varies. Determined by distance, activities, and amenities.

Locomotives/Rolling Stock: The organization prides itself on often being the "first" or "last" rail organization to ride certain lines and/or equipment. Frequently charters trains and/or private cars.

Special Events: An annual slide show the first weekend in March to preview the previous year. The "Nostalgia Program" brings back historic subjects from the last 35 years. Several excursions (free for members) aboard the organization's 1958 GM PD4104 Trailways bus.

Directions: Sent with tickets.

*Coupon available, see coupon section.

Site Address: St. Louis and Kirkwood, MO; Alton, IL
Mailing Address: 4351 Holly Hills Blvd., St. Louis, MO 63116
Telephone: (314) 752-3148

Missouri, St. Louis   **AMERICAN RAILWAY CABOOSE HISTORICAL EDUCATIONAL SOCIETY, INC. (A.R.C.H.E.S.)**

Caboose museum
Standard gauge

RICHARD A. EICHHORST

Description: The Caboose Museum has at least one of their 30 "cabeese" on display at any given time. While a permanent location is being planned, the equipment is stored at ten different locations in Missouri and Illinois. Some of these cabooses are on loan to other rail museums. In addition to the interpretive center that is open to the public, ARCHES is an international association with members in 33 states and Canada. The members have printed a 220-page book, "Cabeese in America," which lists over 5,000 cabooses that have been preserved and are used for other purposes. List price is $24.95, discounted to members.

Schedule: The cabeese in Ferguson, Missouri, are open on: April 5, May 3, June 7, July 5, August 2, September 6, and October 4. Write for information on the annual meeting and special events.

Admission/Fare: Dues start at $15.

Cabooses: A&S, ATSF, B&O, C&O, C&NW, CC, CGW, Essex Terminal, Frisco, IC, Manufacturers, Milwaukee, Missouri Pacific, N&W, RI, Soo, more.

Special Events: Caboose Chili Cook-off, Caboose Chase excursions, Santa on Amtrak, Rail Caboose tours, one Western Caboose tour and one Eastern tour each year. Charters and special trains.

Directions: Varies. Write for specific date information.

*Coupon available, see coupon section.

       M

 St. Louis & Kirkwood, MO / Alton, IL

Site Address: St. Louis, MO
Mailing Address: PO Box 2772, St. Louis, MO 63116
Telephone: (314) 752-3148
E-mail: arches.org

TOURIST TRAINS 2003
GUEST COUPONS
Arranged alphabetically by state

VERDE CANYON RAILROAD
With coupon: 10% off coach tickets--based on availability
Valid April 2003 through March 2004

OLD PUEBLO TROLLEY
With coupon: Buy one admission, get equal price admission free
Valid April 2003 through March 2004
Maximum discount 1 person per coupon

ARKANSAS MISSOURI RAILROAD
Regular price: Adults $38, seniors $34.20, children $34.20
With coupon: Adults $34, seniors $32, children $32
Valid April 2003 through March 2004

LOMITA RAILROAD MUSEUM
With coupon: Buy one admission, get equal price admission free
Valid April 2003 through March 2004
Maximum discount 1 person per coupon

ELDORADO EXPRESS RAILROAD
Regular price: Adults $2, seniors $2, children $2 (ages 1-3, $1)
With coupon: Adults $1, seniors $1, children $1
Valid April 2003 through March 2004

NEVADA COUNTY TRACTION CO. L.L.C.
With coupon: Buy one admission, get equal price admission free
Valid April 2003 through March 2004
Maximum discount 1 person per coupon

SIERRA RAILROAD GOLDEN SUNSET DINNER TRAIN
With coupon: $5 off the price of any trip
Valid April 2003 through March 2004

GOLDEN STATE MODEL RAILROAD MUSEUM
Regular price: Adults $3, seniors $2, children $2, family $7
With coupon: Adults $2, seniors $1, children $1, family $5
Valid April 2003 through March 2004

SAN DIEGO MODEL RAILROAD MUSEUM
Regular price: Adults $4
With coupon: Adults $3
Valid April 2003 through March 2004

GOLDEN GATE RAILROAD MUSEUM
With coupon: Buy one admission, get equal price admission free
Valid April 2003 through March 2004
Maximum discount 1 person per coupon

PLATTE VALLEY TROLLEY
Regular price: Adults $2
With coupon: Adults $1
Valid April 2003 through March 2004

OLD HUNDRED GOLD MINE TOUR
Regular price: Adults $14.95, seniors $13.95, children $7.95
With coupon: Adults $13.95, seniors $12.95, children $6.95
Valid April 2003 through March 2004
Maximum discount 4 persons per coupon

OLD PUEBLO TROLLEY TUCSON, AZ **TOURIST TRAINS 2003** GUEST COUPON	**VERDE CANYON RAILROAD** CLARKDALE, AZ **TOURIST TRAINS 2003** GUEST COUPON
LOMITA RAILROAD MUSEUM LOMITA, CA **TOURIST TRAINS 2003** GUEST COUPON	**ARKANSAS MISSOURI RAILROAD** SPRINGDALE, AR **TOURIST TRAINS 2003** GUEST COUPON
NEVADA COUNTY TRACTION CO. L.L.C. NEVADA CITY, CA **TOURIST TRAINS 2003** GUEST COUPON	**ELDORADO EXPRESS RAILROAD** LONG BEACH, CA **TOURIST TRAINS 2003** GUEST COUPON
GOLDEN STATE MODEL RAILROAD MUSEUM POINT RICHMOND, CA **TOURIST TRAINS 2003** GUEST COUPON	**SIERRA RAILROAD GOLDEN SUNSET DINNER TRAIN** OAKDALE, CA **TOURIST TRAINS 2003** GUEST COUPON
GOLDEN GATE RAILROAD MUSEUM SAN FRANCISCO, CA **TOURIST TRAINS 2003** GUEST COUPON	**SAN DIEGO MODEL RAILROAD MUSEUM** SAN DIEGO, CA **TOURIST TRAINS 2003** GUEST COUPON
OLD HUNDRED GOLD MINE TOUR SILVERTON, CO **TOURIST TRAINS 2003** GUEST COUPON	**PLATTE VALLEY TROLLEY** DENVER, CO **TOURIST TRAINS 2003** GUEST COUPON

TOURIST TRAINS 2003
GUEST COUPONS
Arranged alphabetically by state

SHORE LINE TROLLEY MUSEUM
Regular price: Adults $6, seniors $5, children $3
**With coupon: Adults $5.50,
seniors $4.50, children $2.50**
Valid April 2003 through March 2004
Maximum discount $3 per coupon

CONNECTICUT TROLLEY MUSEUM
Regular price: Adults $6, seniors $5, youth $3
With coupon: Adults $5, seniors $4, youth $2.50
Valid April 2003 through March 2004

ESSEX STEAM TRAIN/VALLEY RAILROAD
Regular price: Adults $18.50, children $9.50
With coupon: Adults $16.50, children $8.50
Valid April 2003 through March 2004

WILMINGTON & WESTERN RAILROAD
**With coupon: Buy one admission, get
equal price admission free**
Valid April 2003 through March 2004
Maximum discount 1 person per coupon

FORT MYERS HISTORICAL MUSEUM
Regular price: Adults $6, seniors $5.50
With coupon: Adults $5, seniors $4.50
Valid April 2003 through March 2004

MURDER MYSTERY DINNER TRAIN ON THE SEMINOLE GULF RAILWAY
Excursion train regular price: Adults $13.95 + tax,
children $8.95 + tax
**With coupon: Family of 4 (2 adults, 2 children)
$29.95 + tax**
Valid April 2003 through March 2004

GOLD COAST RAILROAD MUSEUM
**With coupon: Buy one admission, get
equal price admission free**
Valid April 2003 through March 2004
Maximum discount 2 persons per coupon

SOUTHERN MUSEUM OF CIVIL WAR AND LOCOMOTIVE HISTORY
With coupon: $1 off regular admission
Valid April 2003 through March 2004

ROUNDHOUSE RAILROAD MUSEUM
Regular price: Adults $4, seniors $3.50, children $3.50
With coupon: Adults $3, seniors $2.50, children $2.50
Valid April 2003 through March 2004

NORTHERN PACIFIC DEPOT RAILROAD MUSEUM
Regular price: Adults $2, seniors $1.50, children $1
**With coupon: Adults $1.50, seniors $1,
children $0.50**
Valid April 2003 through March 2004

FOX RIVER TROLLEY MUSEUM
**With coupon: Buy one ticket and get one
ticket of same or lesser value free**
Valid April 2003 through March 2004
Maximum discount 1 person per coupon

ILLINOIS RAILWAY MUSEUM
**With coupon: $1 off each adult,
$0.50 off each child (5-11) admission in your party.**
Not to be used in conjunction with any other coupon,
group rate, senior admission, or other discount rate.
Valid April 2003 through March 2004
Not valid for A Day Out With Thomas

CONNECTICUT TROLLEY MUSEUM
EAST WINDSOR, CT
TOURIST TRAINS 2003
GUEST COUPON

SHORE LINE TROLLEY MUSEUM
EAST HAVEN, CT
TOURIST TRAINS 2003
GUEST COUPON

WILMINGTON & WESTERN RAILROAD
WILMINGTON, DE
TOURIST TRAINS 2003
GUEST COUPON

ESSEX STEAM TRAIN/VALLEY RAILROAD
ESSEX, CT
TOURIST TRAINS 2003
GUEST COUPON

MURDER MYSTERY DINNER TRAIN ON THE SEMINOLE GULF RAILWAY
FORT MYERS, FL
TOURIST TRAINS 2003
GUEST COUPON

FORT MYERS HISTORICAL MUSEUM
FORT MYERS, FL
TOURIST TRAINS 2003
GUEST COUPON

SOUTHERN MUSEUM OF CIVIL WAR AND LOCOMOTIVE HISTORY
KENNESAW, GA
TOURIST TRAINS 2003
GUEST COUPON

GOLD COAST RAILROAD MUSEUM
MIAMI, FL
TOURIST TRAINS 2003
GUEST COUPON

NORTHERN PACIFIC DEPOT RAILROAD MUSEUM
WALLACE, ID
TOURIST TRAINS 2003
GUEST COUPON

ROUNDHOUSE RAILROAD MUSEUM
SAVANNAH, GA
TOURIST TRAINS 2003
GUEST COUPON

ILLINOIS RAILWAY MUSEUM
UNION, IL
TOURIST TRAINS 2003
GUEST COUPON

FOX RIVER TROLLEY MUSEUM
SOUTH ELGIN, IL
TOURIST TRAINS 2003
GUEST COUPON

TOURIST TRAINS 2003
GUEST COUPONS
Arranged alphabetically by state

WATERMAN & WESTERN RAILROAD
With coupon: Buy one admission, get
equal price admission free
Valid April 2003 through March 2004
Maximum discount 4 persons per coupon

TRAINLAND U.S.A.
With coupon: Buy one admission, get
equal price admission free
Valid April 2003 through March 2004
Maximum discount 4 persons per coupon

RAILSWEST RAILROAD MUSEUM
With coupon: Buy one admission, get
equal price admission free
Valid April 2003 through March 2004
Maximum discount 1 person per coupon

SANTA FE DEPOT HISTORICAL CENTER
Regular price: Adults $2, children $0.50
With coupon: Adults $1, children $0.25
Valid April 2003 through March 2004
Maximum discount 10 persons per coupon

GREAT PLAINS TRANSPORTATION MUSEUM
With coupon: Buy one admission, get
equal price admission free
Valid April 2003 through March 2004
Maximum discount 1 person per coupon

SOUTHERN FOREST HERITAGE MUSEUM
Regular price: Adults $6, seniors $6, children $3
With coupon: Adults $5, seniors $5, children $2.50
Valid April 2003 through March 2004

SANDY RIVER AND RANGELEY LAKES RAILROAD
Regular price: Adults $3, seniors $3
With coupon: Adults free, seniors free
Valid April 2003 through March 2004
Maximum discount 1 person per coupon

B&O RAILROAD MUSEUM
Regular price: Adults $8, seniors $7, children $5
With coupon: Adults $7, seniors $6, children $4
Valid April 2003 through March 2004
Maximum discount 1 person per coupon

BALTIMORE STREETCAR MUSEUM
With coupon: Buy one admission, get
equal price admission free
Valid April 2003 through March 2004
Maximum discount 4 persons per coupon

NATIONAL CAPITAL TROLLEY MUSEUM
With coupon: Buy one admission, get
equal price admission free
Valid April 2003 through March 2004
Maximum discount 1 person per coupon

EDAVILLE U.S.A.
Regular price: Adults, seniors, children $17
With coupon: Adults, seniors, children $15
Valid April 2003 through March 2004

SHELBURNE FALLS TROLLEY MUSEUM
Regular price: Adults $2, seniors $2
With coupon: Adults $1, seniors free
Valid April 2003 through March 2004

TRAINLAND U.S.A. COLFAX, IA **TOURIST TRAINS 2003** GUEST COUPON	**WATERMAN & WESTERN RAILROAD** WATERMAN, IL **TOURIST TRAINS 2003** GUEST COUPON
SANTA FE DEPOT HISTORICAL **CENTER** FORT MADISON, IA **TOURIST TRAINS 2003** GUEST COUPON	**RAILSWEST RAILROAD MUSEUM** COUNCIL BLUFFS, IA **TOURIST TRAINS 2003** GUEST COUPON
SOUTHERN FOREST HERITAGE **MUSEUM** LONG LEAF, LA **TOURIST TRAINS 2003** GUEST COUPON	**GREAT PLAINS TRANSPORTATION** **MUSEUM** WICHITA, KS **TOURIST TRAINS 2003** GUEST COUPON
B&O RAILROAD MUSEUM BALTIMORE, MD **TOURIST TRAINS 2003** GUEST COUPON	**SANDY RIVER AND RANGELEY** **LAKES RAILROAD** PHILLIPS, ME **TOURIST TRAINS 2003** GUEST COUPON
NATIONAL CAPITAL TROLLEY **MUSEUM** COLESVILLE, MD **TOURIST TRAINS 2003** GUEST COUPON	**BALTIMORE STREETCAR MUSEUM** BALTIMORE, MD **TOURIST TRAINS 2003** GUEST COUPON
SHELBURNE FALLS TROLLEY **MUSEUM** SHELBURNE FALLS, MA **TOURIST TRAINS 2003** GUEST COUPON	**EDAVILLE U.S.A.** CARVER, MD **TOURIST TRAINS 2003** GUEST COUPON

TOURIST TRAINS 2003
GUEST COUPONS
Arranged alphabetically by state

WENHAM MUSEUM
Regular price: Adults $5, seniors $4, children $3
With coupon: Adults $4, seniors $3, children $2
Valid April 2003 through March 2004

JUNCTION VALLEY RAILROAD
Regular price: Adults $5.25, seniors $5, children $4.50
With coupon: Adults $4.70, seniors $4.50, children $4.05
Valid April 2003 through March 2004
Maximum discount 10% per coupon

MICHIGAN AUSABLE VALLEY RAILROAD
Regular price: Adults $3, seniors $3, children $3
With coupon: Adults $2, seniors $2, children $2
Valid April 2003 through March 2004

MICHIGAN TRANSIT MUSEUM
Regular price: Adults $6, seniors $6, children $3
With coupon: Adults $5.50, seniors $5.50, children $2.50
Valid April 2003 through March 2004

SPIRIT OF TRAVERSE CITY
With coupon: Buy one admission, get equal price admission free
Valid April 2003 through March 2004
Maximum discount 2 persons per coupon

OLD DEPOT RAILROAD MUSEUM
With coupon: 10% off regular admission
Valid April 2003 through March 2004

LAKE SUPERIOR & MISSISSIPPI RAILROAD
Regular price: Adults $8, seniors $7, children $6
With coupon: Adults $7, seniors $6, children $5
Valid April 2003 through March 2004

LAKE COUNTY HISTORY & RAILROAD MUSEUM
Regular price: Adults $2, seniors $2, children $1
With coupon: Adults $1.50, seniors $1.50, children $0.50
Valid April 2003 through March 2004

BELTON, GRANDVIEW & KANSAS CITY RAILROAD COMPANY
With coupon: Buy one admission, get equal price admission free
Valid April 2003 through March 2004

WABASH FRISCO & PACIFIC STEAM RAILWAY
Regular price: Adults $3
With coupon: Adults $2
Valid April 2003 through March 2004
Maximum discount 6 persons per coupon

AMERICAN ASSOCIATION OF RAILROADERS
Freedom Train (#4449) Poster
Full color, 20" x 24", $25 value
With coupon: $15, includes shipping in a protective tube
Valid April 2003 through March 2004

AMERICAN RAILWAY CABOOSE HISTORICAL EDUCATIONAL SOCIETY, INC.
Book: *Captive Cabeese in America*, $24.95 value
With coupon: $19, includes postage
Valid April 2003 through March 2004

JUNCTION VALLEY RAILROAD BRIDGEPORT, MI **TOURIST TRAINS 2003** GUEST COUPON	**WENHAM MUSEUM** WENHAM, MA **TOURIST TRAINS 2003** GUEST COUPON
MICHIGAN TRANSIT MUSEUM MT. CLEMENS, MI **TOURIST TRAINS 2003** GUEST COUPON	**MICHIGAN AUSABLE VALLEY RAILROAD** FAIRVIEW, MI **TOURIST TRAINS 2003** GUEST COUPON
OLD DEPOT RAILROAD MUSEUM DASSEL, MN **TOURIST TRAINS 2003** GUEST COUPON	**SPIRIT OF TRAVERSE CITY** TRAVERSE CITY, MI **TOURIST TRAINS 2003** GUEST COUPON
LAKE COUNTY HISTORY & RAILROAD MUSEUM TWO HARBORS, MN **TOURIST TRAINS 2003** GUEST COUPON	**LAKE SUPERIOR & MISSISSIPPI RAILROAD** DULUTH, MN **TOURIST TRAINS 2003** GUEST COUPON
WABASH FRISCO & PACIFIC STEAM RAILWAY GLENCOE, MO **TOURIST TRAINS 2003** GUEST COUPON	**BELTON, GRANDVIEW & KANSAS CITY RAILROAD COMPANY** BELTON, MO **TOURIST TRAINS 2003** GUEST COUPON
AMERICAN RAILWAY CABOOSE HISTORICAL EDUCATIONAL SOCIETY, INC. ST. LOUIS, MO **TOURIST TRAINS 2003** GUEST COUPON	**AMERICAN ASSOCIATION OF RAILROADERS** ST. LOUIS, MO **TOURIST TRAINS 2003** GUEST COUPON

TOURIST TRAINS 2003
GUEST COUPONS
Arranged alphabetically by state

MUSEUM OF TRANSPORTATION
**With coupon: Buy one admission, get
equal price admission free**
Valid April 2003 through March 2004
Maximum discount 4 persons per coupon

**NEVADA NORTHERN RAILWAY
MUSEUM**
Regular price: Adults $18, children $12
With coupon: Adults $16, children $10
Valid April 2003 through March 2004

VIRGINIA & TRUCKEE RAILROAD
Regular price: Adults and seniors, $6
With coupon: Adults and seniors, $5
Valid April 2003 through March 2004

HARTMANN MODEL RAILROAD LTD.
Regular price: Adults $6, seniors $5, children $4
With coupon: Adults $5, seniors $4, children $3
Valid April 2003 through March 2004

MODEL RAILROAD CLUB INC
**With coupon: Buy one admission, get
equal price admission free**
Valid April 2003 through March 2004
Maximum discount 2 persons per coupon

SANTA FE SOUTHERN RAILWAY
With coupon: 10% off any tour
Valid April 2003 through March 2004

ARCADE & ATTICA RAILROAD
Regular price: Adults $10, children $7
With coupon: Adults $9, children $6
Valid April 2003 through March 2004

MEDINA RAILROAD MUSEUM
Regular price: Adults $6, seniors $5, children $3
With coupon: Adults $5, seniors $4, children $2
Valid April 2003 through March 2004

ADIRONDACK SCENIC RAILROAD
With coupon: 20% off any purchases in the gift shop
Valid April 2003 through March 2004

WILMINGTON RAILROAD MUSEUM
**With coupon: Buy one admission, get
equal price admission free**
Valid April 2003 through March 2004
Maximum discount 2 persons per coupon

BONANZAVILLE USA
Regular price: Adults and seniors $6, children $3
With coupon: Adults and seniors $5, children $2
Valid April 2003 through March 2004
Maximum discount $1 per coupon

**CUYAHOGA VALLEY SCENIC
RAILROAD**
Regular price: Adults $11, seniors $10, children $7
With coupon: Adults $10, seniors $9, children $6
Valid April 2003 through March 2004

NEVADA NORTHERN RAILWAY
MUSEUM
EAST ELY, NV
TOURIST TRAINS 2003
GUEST COUPON

MUSEUM OF TRANSPORTATION
ST. LOUIS, MO
TOURIST TRAINS 2003
GUEST COUPON

HARTMANN MODEL RAILROAD LTD.
INTERVALE, NH
TOURIST TRAINS 2003
GUEST COUPON

VIRGINIA & TRUCKEE RAILROAD
VIRGINIA CITY, NV
TOURIST TRAINS 2003
GUEST COUPON

SANTA FE SOUTHERN RAILWAY
SANTA FE, NM
TOURIST TRAINS 2003
GUEST COUPON

MODEL RAILROAD CLUB INC
UNION, NJ
TOURIST TRAINS 2003
GUEST COUPON

MEDINA RAILROAD MUSEUM
MEDINA, NY
TOURIST TRAINS 2003
GUEST COUPON

ARCADE & ATTICA RAILROAD
ARCADE, NY
TOURIST TRAINS 2003
GUEST COUPON

WILMINGTON RAILROAD MUSEUM
WILMINGTON, NC
TOURIST TRAINS 2003
GUEST COUPON

ADIRONDACK SCENIC RAILROAD
OLD FORGE, NY
TOURIST TRAINS 2003
GUEST COUPON

CUYAHOGA VALLEY SCENIC
RAILROAD
INDEPENDENCE, OH
TOURIST TRAINS 2003
GUEST COUPON

BONANZAVILLE USA
WEST FARGO, ND
TOURIST TRAINS 2003
GUEST COUPON

TOURIST TRAINS 2003
GUEST COUPONS
Arranged alphabetically by state

TRAIN-O-RAMA

Regular price: Adults $5, seniors $4, children $3
With coupon: Adults $4, seniors $3, children $2
Valid April 2003 through March 2004

LUCAS COUNTY / MAUMEE VALLEY HISTORICAL SOCIETY

Regular price: Adults $5, seniors $4, children $2.50
With coupon: Adults $4.50, seniors $3.50, children $2
Valid April 2003 through March 2004

TOLEDO, LAKE ERIE & WESTERN RAILWAY AND MUSEUM

Regular price: Adults $8, seniors $7, children $4.50
With coupon: Adults $7, seniors $6, children $4
Valid April 2003 through March 2004

OREGON ELECTRIC RAILWAY HISTORICAL SOCIETY

Regular price: Adults $8, seniors $7, children $4
With coupon: Adults $7, seniors $6, children $3
Valid April 2003 through March 2004

OLD MAUCH CHUNK MODEL TRAIN DISPLAY

With coupon: Buy one admission, get equal price admission free
Valid April 2003 through March 2004
Maximum discount 1 person per coupon

LAKE SHORE RAILWAY MUSEUM

With coupon: 10% discount on purchase of $5 or more at the museum gift shop.
Valid April 2003 through March 2004

EAST BROAD TOP RAILROAD

Regular price: Adults $9, children $6
With coupon: Adults $8.50, children $5.50
Valid April 2003 through March 2004

ROCKHILL TROLLEY MUSEUM

With coupon: Buy one admission, get equal price admission free
Valid April 2003 through March 2004
Maximum discount 1 person per coupon

OIL CREEK & TITUSVILLE RAILROAD

With coupon: Buy one admission, get equal price admission free
Valid April 2003 through March 2004
Maximum discount 6 persons per coupon

PENNSYLVANIA TROLLEY MUSEUM

With coupon: $1 off regular admission
Valid April 2003 through March 2004
Maximum discount $1 per coupon

TIOGA CENTRAL RAILROAD

Regular price: Adults $10, seniors $9, children $5
With coupon: Adults $9, seniors $8, children $4
Valid April 2003 through March 2004

CHATTANOOGA CHOO CHOO MODEL RAILROAD MUSEUM

With coupon: $2 off regular admission
Valid April 2003 through March 2004
Maximum discount $2 per coupon

LUCAS COUNTY / MAUMEE VALLEY
HISTORICAL SOCIETY
MAUMEE, OH
TOURIST TRAINS 2003
GUEST COUPON

TRAIN-O-RAMA
MARBLEHEAD, OH
TOURIST TRAINS 2003
GUEST COUPON

OREGON ELECTRIC RAILWAY
HISTORICAL SOCIETY
LAKE OSWEGO, OR
TOURIST TRAINS 2003
GUEST COUPON

TOLEDO, LAKE ERIE & WESTERN
RAILWAY AND MUSEUM
WATERVILLE, OH
TOURIST TRAINS 2003
GUEST COUPON

LAKE SHORE RAILWAY MUSEUM
NORTH EAST, PA
TOURIST TRAINS 2003
GUEST COUPON

OLD MAUCH CHUNK MODEL TRAIN
DISPLAY
JIM THORPE, PA
TOURIST TRAINS 2003
GUEST COUPON

ROCKHILL TROLLEY MUSEUM
ROCKHILL FURNACE, PA
TOURIST TRAINS 2003
GUEST COUPON

EAST BROAD TOP RAILROAD
ROCKHILL FURNACE, PA
TOURIST TRAINS 2003
GUEST COUPON

PENNSYLVANIA TROLLEY MUSEUM
WASHINGTON, PA
TOURIST TRAINS 2003
GUEST COUPON

OIL CREEK & TITUSVILLE RAILROAD
TITUSVILLE, PA
TOURIST TRAINS 2003
GUEST COUPON

CHATTANOOGA CHOO CHOO MODEL
RAILROAD MUSEUM
CHATTANOOGA, TN
TOURIST TRAINS 2003
GUEST COUPON

TIOGA CENTRAL RAILROAD
WELLSBORO, PA
TOURIST TRAINS 2003
GUEST COUPON

TOURIST TRAINS 2003
GUEST COUPONS
Arranged alphabetically by state

TENNESSEE VALLEY RAILROAD

**With coupon: $1 off regular adult price,
$0.50 off regular children's price**
Valid April 2003 through March 2004
Maximum discount 2 persons per coupon

RAILROAD AND HERITAGE MUSEUM

**With coupon: Buy one admission, get
equal price admission free**
Valid April 2003 through March 2004
Maximum discount 2 persons per coupon

OGDEN UNION STATION

**With coupon: Buy one admission, get
equal price admission free**
Valid April 2003 through March 2004
Maximum discount 1 person per coupon

MOUNT RAINIER SCENIC RAILROAD

Regular price: Adults $12.50, seniors $11.50, children $8.50
With coupon: Adults $11.50, seniors $10.50, children $7.50
Valid April 2003 through March 2004

NORTHWEST RAILWAY MUSEUM

**With coupon: Buy one admission, get
equal price admission free**
Valid April 2003 through March 2004
Maximum discount 2 persons per coupon

**CHEAT MOUNTAIN SALAMANDER
RAIL RIDE**

Regular price: Adults $18, seniors $16, children $10
With coupon: Adults $17, seniors $15, children $9
Valid April 2003 through March 2004
Maximum discount 1 person per coupon

**DURBIN & GREENBRIER VALLEY
RAILROAD**

Regular price: Adults $10, seniors $9, children $6
With coupon: Adults $9, seniors $8, children $5
Valid April 2003 through March 2004
Maximum discount 1 person per coupon

EAST TROY ELECTRIC RAILROAD

**With coupon: Buy one admission, get
equal price admission free**
Valid April 2003 through March 2004
Maximum discount 1 person per coupon

CAMP FIVE

Regular price: Adults $15
With coupon: Adults $13.50
Valid April 2003 through March 2004

MID-CONTINENT RAILWAY MUSEUM

Regular price: Adults $11, seniors $10, children $6
With coupon: Adults $9, seniors $8, children $5
Valid April 2003 through March 2004

**OSCEOLA & ST. CROIX
VALLEY RAILWAY**

Regular price: Adults $13, seniors $12, children $7
With coupon: Adults $11, seniors $10, children $6
Valid April 2003 through March 2004

**MINING MUSEUM & ROLLO
JAMISON MUSEUM**

Regular price: Adults $7, seniors $6.30, children $3
**With coupon: Adults $6.30, seniors $5.67,
children $2.70**
Valid April 2003 through March 2004

RAILROAD AND HERITAGE MUSEUM
TEMPLE, TX
TOURIST TRAINS 2003
GUEST COUPON

TENNESSEE VALLEY RAILROAD
CHATTANOOGA, TN
TOURIST TRAINS 2003
GUEST COUPON

MOUNT RAINIER SCENIC RAILROAD
ELBE, WA
TOURIST TRAINS 2003
GUEST COUPON

OGDEN UNION STATION
OGDEN, UT
TOURIST TRAINS 2003
GUEST COUPON

**CHEAT MOUNTAIN SALAMANDER
RAIL RIDE**
CHEAT BRIDGE, WV
TOURIST TRAINS 2003
GUEST COUPON

NORTHWEST RAILWAY MUSEUM
SNOQUALMIE, WA
TOURIST TRAINS 2003
GUEST COUPON

EAST TROY ELECTRIC RAILROAD
EAST TROY, WI
TOURIST TRAINS 2003
GUEST COUPON

**DURBIN & GREENBRIER VALLEY
RAILROAD**
DURBIN, WV
TOURIST TRAINS 2003
GUEST COUPON

MID-CONTINENT RAILWAY MUSEUM
NORTH FREEDOM, WI
TOURIST TRAINS 2003
GUEST COUPON

CAMP FIVE
LAONA, WI
TOURIST TRAINS 2003
GUEST COUPON

**MINING MUSEUM & ROLLO
JAMISON MUSEUM**
PLATTEVILLE, WI
TOURIST TRAINS 2003
GUEST COUPON

**OSCEOLA & ST. CROIX VALLEY
RAILWAY**
OSCEOLA, WI
TOURIST TRAINS 2003
GUEST COUPON

TOURIST TRAINS 2003
GUEST COUPONS

RAILROAD MEMORIES MUSEUM
Regular price: Adults $3, children $0.50
With coupon: Adults $2.50, children $0.25
Valid April 2003 through March 2004

CANADIAN MUSEUM OF RAIL TRAVEL
With coupon: 10% off regular admission
Valid April 2003 through March 2004

**BRITISH COLUMBIA FOREST
DISCOVERY CENTRE**
Regular price: Adults $9, students and seniors $8, children $5
**Group rate (10+) coupon: Adults $7,
students and seniors $6, children $4**
Valid April 2003 through March 2004

ALBERNI PACIFIC RAILWAY
Regular price: Adults $22, seniors $16, children $5
With coupon: Adults $18, seniors $12, children $3
Valid April 2003 through March 2004

**WEST COAST RAILWAY
HERITAGE PARK**
**With coupon: Buy one admission, get
equal price admission free**
Valid April 2003 through March 2004
Maximum discount 4 persons per coupon

**VANCOUVER'S DOWNTOWN
HISTORIC RAILWAY**
**With coupon: Buy one admission, get
equal price admission free**
Valid April 2003 through March 2004
Maximum discount 4 persons per coupon

**ABERFOYLE JUNCTION MODEL
RAILWAY, INC.**
Regular price: Adults $6, seniors $3, children $2
With coupon: Adults $4, seniors $2, children $1
Valid April 2003 through March 2004

**TRAINS TOURISTIQUES DE
CHAUDIERE-APPALACHES**
**With coupon: With purchase of one regular
adult ticket, save 50% on second ticket of equal
or lesser value**
Valid April 2003 through March 2004

WESTERN DEVELOPMENT MUSEUM
**With coupon: Buy one admission, get
equal price admission free**
Valid April 2003 through March 2004
Maximum discount 2 persons per coupon

CANADIAN MUSEUM OF RAIL TRAVEL
CRANBROOK, BC
TOURIST TRAINS 2003
GUEST COUPON

RAILROAD MEMORIES MUSEUM
SPOONER, WI
TOURIST TRAINS 2003
GUEST COUPON

ALBERNI PACIFIC RAILWAY
PORT ALBERNI, BC
TOURIST TRAINS 2003
GUEST COUPON

**BRITISH COLUMBIA FOREST
DISCOVERY CENTRE**
DUNCAN, BC
TOURIST TRAINS 2003
GUEST COUPON

**VANCOUVER'S DOWNTOWN
HISTORIC RAILWAY**
VANCOUVER, BC
TOURIST TRAINS 2003
GUEST COUPON

**WEST COAST RAILWAY
HERITAGE PARK**
SQUAMISH, BC
TOURIST TRAINS 2003
GUEST COUPON

**TRAINS TOURISTIQUES DE
CHAUDIERE-APPALACHES**
VALLEE-JONCTION, QC
TOURIST TRAINS 2003
GUEST COUPON

**ABERFOYLE JUNCTION MODEL
RAILWAY, INC.**
GUELPH, ON
TOURIST TRAINS 2003
GUEST COUPON

WESTERN DEVELOPMENT MUSEUM
MOOSE JAW, SK
TOURIST TRAINS 2003
GUEST COUPON

MUSEUM OF TRANSPORTATION
Museum
Standard gauge

Description: The museum is one of the largest and best collections of transportation vehicles in the world, according to the Smithsonian Institution. See over 70 locomotives, including 34 steamers, the most in North America. Also explore autos, aviation, and riverboat items.

Schedule: Year-round, Tuesday through Sunday, 9 a.m. to 5 p.m. Also open on the following holidays: Martin Luther King Jr. Day, President's Day, Memorial Day, Labor Day, Columbus Day, and Veteran's Day. Closed Thanksgiving, Christmas, and New Year's Day.

Admission/Fare: Adults, $4; seniors (65 and up) and children (5-12), $1.50; group rates for 20 people or more.

Locomotives/Rolling Stock: UP Big Boy no. 4006; UP Centennial no. 6944; N&W Y6a no. 2156; Reading "Black Diamond," GM FTA no. 103; Milwaukee Road bi-polar electric no. E-2; 34 steam, 28 diesel/gas, 10 electric, one gas-turbine locomotives, 30 passenger and 55 freight cars.

Special Events: Transportation Celebration, first weekend in August, free admission and special exhibits. See website for details.

Nearby Attractions: St. Louis Arch, Grant's Farm, Union Station.

Directions: I-270 to exit 8. Take Dougherty Ferry Rd. west 1 mile to Barret Station Rd. (second traffic light), turn left. Museum is ½ mile on right.

*Coupon available, see coupon section.

Site Address: 3015 Barrett Station Rd., St Louis, MO
Mailing Address: 3015 Barrett Station Rd., St. Louis, MO 63122
Telephone: (314) 965-7998
Fax: (314) 965-0242
Website: www.museum of transport.org

Missouri, Springfield

**RAILROAD HISTORICAL
MUSEUM, INC.**
Museum
Standard

Description: This stationary historical train is a museum within a museum, as it contains Frisco steam locomotive no. 4524 with tender, BN Express car, double-deck passenger car, and BN caboose, all enclosed within a 40 x 400 x 8-foot chain-link fence, with railroad antiques, artifacts, and memorabilia, both within the fence and within the cars and locomotive.

Schedule: Saturdays, 2 to 4 p.m., mostly from April through November, weather permitting. (The weather must be sunny and dry and at least 60 degrees.) Also open by special group request.

Admission/Fare: Free. Donations accepted.

Locomotives/Rolling Stock: Frisco steam locomotive, no. 4524 with stoker tender and power boosters; BN express car, no. 976100; double-deck passenger car seating 100 on lower deck and 60 on the upper level; more.

Nearby Attractions: Bass Pro Shop; Dickerson Park Zoo; Grant Beach Park; Wild Animal Paradise, 12 miles east; Branson and Silver Dollar City, 40 miles south.

Directions: From I-44 exit 77, go south on Kansas Expressway, turn east on Division St. Go ¾ mile and turn south on Grant Ave., two blocks to 1400 N. Grant, then turn west on Lynn St. to the museum entrance at Grant Beach Park.

Site Address: Grant Beach Park, 1400 N. Grant Ave., Springfield, MO
Mailing Address: 3661 S. Fort, Springfield, MO 65807
Telephone: (417) 882-9106

FOEREST TRENT

Description: Located in a 1910 passenger depot, the Springfield & Ozark Railway is a ¼ inch, O scale railroad that is modeled after an old branch line that became part of the St. Louis & San Francisco Railway in 1885. This 20 x 66-foot layout is a point-to-point, with reversing loops and a yard at each end. Up to four mainline and four yard trains can be operated simultaneously.

Schedule: The trains operate on the first Tuesday of every month, 7:30 p.m. until around 9 p.m., except on holidays; then operation is moved to the following Tuesday.

Admission/Fare: Free. Tax-deductible donations accepted.

Special Events: Extra holiday operations on the following Tuesdays: December 10, 17, and 24.

Nearby Attractions: BN-SF main line, Amtrak station in Kirkwood, The Magic House, Museum of Transport, St. Louis Live Steamers, Six Flags Over St. Louis, the Wabash Frisco & Pacific Railroad, Gateway Arch.

Directions: Three miles west of St. Louis, Missouri, on the north side of I-44. Use exit 280 (Elm Ave.). Travel north ⅛ mile to stoplight at Big Bend Blvd. Turn left and travel about two blocks, cross the railroad tracks, and you are there.

Site Address: 8833 Big Bend Blvd., Webster Groves, MO
Mailing Address: 855 Windemere Ave., Des Peres, MO 63131-4531
Telephone: (314) 966-5227
E-mail: kc0esl@juno.com
Website: www.geocities.com/bbrrclub/

KYLE BREHM

Description: Historic Great Northern Railroad Inn with caboose cottages.

Schedule: Year-round, 7 a.m. to 10 p.m.

Nearby Attractions: Glacier National Park, Middle Fork of the Flathead River.

Directions: On southern tip of Glacier National Park off Highway 2 between East and West Glacier in Essex.

Site Address: 290 Izaak Walton Inn Rd., Essex, MT
Mailing Address: 290 Izaak Walton Inn Rd., Essex, MT 59916
Telephone: (406) 888-5700
Fax: (406) 888-5200
E-mail: stay@izaakwaltoninn.com
Website: www.izaakwaltoninn.com

CHARLIE RUSSELL CHEW-CHOO DINNER TRAIN
Dinner train

CHERIE NEUDICK

Description: A 3½-hour narrated dinner train ride through the heart of Montana.

Schedule: Year-round: June through September, Saturdays. Special trains occasionally.

Fare/Admission: Adults, $85; children 12 and under, $50.

Locomotives/Rolling Stock: Five stainless-steel Budd RDC cars

Special Events: Polar Express children's ride. Date to be announced.

Nearby Attractions: Many within a two-hour drive.

Directions: Go 2.7 miles north of Lewistown on Highway 191, then west approximately 8 miles on Montana Highway 426, near mile marker 19.

Site Address: 408 NE Main St., Lewistown, MT
Mailing Address: Chamber of Commerce, PO Box 818, Lewiston, MT 59457
Telephone: (406) 538-2527
Fax: (406) 538-5437
E-mail: lewchamb@lewistown.net
Website: www.lewistownchamber.com

MONTANA ROCKIES RAIL TOURS
Train ride
Standard gauge

Description: Daylight excursion train travels on original NPRR between Sandpoint, Idaho, and Livingston, Montana. We offer two-day trips on board with available motorcoach trips into Glacier and Yellowstone.

Schedule: June 7 through September 2, Fridays and Saturdays: eastbound from Sandpoint, Idaho. Sundays and Mondays: westbound from Livingston, Montana.

Admission/Fare: Contact sales office at (800) 519-7245 for fares and availability.

Locomotives/Rolling Stock: Largest operators of ripple-sided Budd cars in the U.S. Cars are from Great Northern, NP Railway, CBQ, *Twin Cities Zephyr,* etc.

Nearby Attractions: Off-the-train tours include Yellowstone, Tetons, and Glacier National Parks. There are eight trips eastbound and eight trips westbound.

Site Address: 1055 Baldy Park Ave., Sandpoint, ID
Mailing Address: 1055 Baldy Park Ave., Sandpoint, ID 83864
Telephone: (800) 519-7245 and (208) 265-8618
Fax: (208) 265-8619
E-mail: information@montanarailtours.com
Website: www.montanarailtours.com

HISTORICAL MUSEUM AT FORT MISSOULA
Museum, display, layout
Standard gauge

RAILWAY MUSEUM

Description: County Historical Museum, on 32-acre site, with 13 historic structures depicting the history of western Montana.

Schedule: Memorial Day weekend through Labor Day weekend: Monday through Saturday, 10 a.m. to 5 p.m.; Sunday, 12 noon to 5 p.m. Labor Day weekend to Memorial Day weekend: Tuesday through Sunday, 12 noon to 5 p.m.

Admission/Fare: Adults, $3; seniors, $2; students, $1; children under 6 and members of the Friends of the Historical Museum free; Wednesdays are free.

Locomotives/Rolling Stock: Anaconda Copper Mining Co. Lumber Dept. 1923, Willamette Iron & Steel Works (3-truck Shay type) Const. no. 7; flatcars with log loads; Slide Jammer log loader; ACM "shuttle" car to transport lumberjacks; section motor car.

Special Events: Forestry Day, April 26; Railroad Day, June 14; Frontier Day, August 24; 4th of July Celebration; occasional operation of steam powered sawmill; motor cars on track; model railroad; Willamette cab tours.

Nearby Attractions: A Carousel for Missoula, Rocky Mountain Elk Foundation, Smokejumpers Visitor's Center.

Directions: From I-90 take Reserve St. exit south to South Ave. (traffic signal). Turn right (west) on South Ave. to left at sign for museum.

        M arm

Site Address: Bldg. #322 Fort Missoula, Missoula, MT
Mailing Address: Bldg. #322 Fort Missoula, Missoula, MT 59804
Telephone: (406) 728-3476
Fax: (406) 543-6277
E-mail: ftmslamuseum@montana.com
Website: www.montana.com/ftmslamuseum

Montana, Nevada City

MONTANA HERITAGE COMMISSION
Train ride, museum, display
30" gauge

ANDY LIEDBERG

Description: Operating steam locomotive, rebuilt 30" gauge Mexican 2-8-0, former Ferrocaril Mexicano no. 12, built by Baldwin in 1910. It had been displayed at Edaville for many years. Also, Alder Gulch Short Line, tourist train with open-air cars that operates along Alder Gulch between Nevada City and Virginia City.

Schedule: Memorial Day through Labor Day, weather permitting, beginning at 11 a.m. Last run at 6:15 p.m.

Admission/Fare: C.A. Bovey train–$5. Steam train–$10 round trip.

Locomotives/Rolling Stock: Ferrocaril Mexicano no. 12 steam locomotive, built by Baldwin; C.A. Bovey gas-powered train.

Nearby Attractions: Historic mining towns Virginia and Nevada City.

Directions: State Highway 287 between Ennis and Sheridan, Montana.

Site Address: Nevada City, MT
Mailing Address: PO Box 338, Virginia City, MT 59755
Telephone: (406) 843-5247
Fax: (406) 841-4004
E-mail: juljohnson@state.mt.us

Nebraska, Fairbury

ROCK ISLAND DEPOT
RAILROAD MUSEUM
Museum, display
Standard and 7½" gauge

JEFFERSON COUNTY HISTORICAL SOCIETY

Description: Established in 1996 in the historic Rock Island Depot, which also housed the Western Division Headquarters for the Rock Island Railroad, built in 1914. The collection consists of Rock Island artifacts, from conductors' uniforms and train order hoops to baggage carts and caboose stoves, as well as local history involving the railroad. Includes a model railroad display, separate freight house, and formal gardens.

Schedule: Wednesdays, Thursdays, Saturdays, and Sundays, 10 a.m. to 5 p.m. Closed in January.

Admission/Fare: Suggested donation.

Locomotives/Rolling Stock: Rock Island motor car no. 9047, built 1927. Train ride is 1½" scale, 7½" gauge railroad, operated on Sunday afternoons and during special events.

Special Events: Annual Christmas at the Depot, second weekend in December; Annual Rock Island Rail Days, second weekend in June.

Nearby Attractions: Rock Creek Station State Historical Park, Homestead National Monument, golf, dining, Oregon Trail, camping.

Directions: Seventy-five miles southwest of Lincoln, west on I-80, south on Nebraska Highway 15.

Site Address: 910 Second St., Fairbury, NE
Mailing Address: 910 Second St., Fairbury, NE 68352
Telephone: (402) 729-5131
E-mail: fairburyridepot@alltel.net
Website: www.jeffersoncountyhistory.com

Nebraska, Fremont   **FREMONT & ELKHORN VALLEY RAILROAD**
NRHS NEBRASKA CHAPTER
Train ride, dinner train, museum
Standard gauge

Description: Take a ride through history on a 30-mile round trip from Fremont to Hooper over rails laid in 1869. Ride on cars built in 1924 and 1925. Enjoy the scenic Elkhorn Valley.

Schedule: April 26, 2003 to October 26, 2003. Dinner train, year-round; call for reservations and fares.

Admission/Fare: Adults, $12; children 12 and under, $7; under age 3 ride free.

Locomotives/Rolling Stock: EMD SW1200, Davenport 44-ton no. 1481 under restoration; CB&Q RPO; "Lake Bluff" passenger car; 1927 "Fort Andrew" passenger car; BN wide-vision caboose.

Special Events: Open House, April; fireworks ride in Hooper on the 4th of July; John C. Fremont Days, second weekend in July; Santa Claus runs; others.

Nearby Attractions: Nebraska Railway Museum, May Museum, antique shopping, Motor Plex, Hooper, Nebraska, historical Main St.

Directions: Approximately 35 miles northwest of Omaha. Highway 275, exit 23rd St., travel west through Fremont, turn south on Somers Ave.

Site Address: 1835 N. Somers Ave., Fremont, NE
Mailing Address: PO Box 191, Fremont, NE 68026
Telephone: (402) 727-0615 and (800) 942-7245 (dinner train)
Fax: (402) 727-0615
E-mail: fevr@teknetwork.com
Website: www.geocities.com/heartland/hills/4184/fevr.html

Nebraska, Fremont

FREMONT DINNER TRAIN
Dinner train
Standard gauge

RUDY DANIELS

Description: Thirty-mile round trip up the Elkhorn Valley to the historic town of Hooper, Nebraska.

Schedule: Year-round. November through April, Saturdays, 6:30 p.m. May through October, Saturdays, 7:30 p.m. June through December, Fridays, 7:30 p.m. May through November, Sundays, 1:30 p.m. Occasionally January through April.

Admission/Fare: $39.95-$63.95 (Sunday afternoons; evenings with dinner theater).

Locomotives/Rolling Stock: Power car no. 1315 (ex-Milw. baggage dorm); dining cars no. 101 (ex-IC); no. 102 (ex-CN); no. 104 (ex-CN); no. 765 lounge diner (ex-CN); no. 193 storage car (ex-Milw. parlor); no. 410 power car (ex-Nickel Plate).

Special Events: Valentine's Day; July 4th picnic dinner run, including fireworks display; New Year's Eve.

Nearby Attractions: Fremont Antique District; May Museum; Fremont State Lakes.

Directions: Thirty-five miles northwest of Omaha; 50 miles north of Lincoln; 75 miles south of Sioux City, Iowa.

Site Address: 1835 N. Somers Ave., Fremont, NE
Mailing Address: 650 N. "H," St., Fremont, NE 68025
Telephone: (800) 942-7245
Fax: (402) 727-0915
E-mail: fdt@fremont-online.com
Website: www.dinnertrain.net

**STUHR MUSEUM
OF THE PRAIRIE PIONEER**
Museum, display

Description: Living-history museum with 1890s living Railroad Town including viewable railroad exhibit stock. It features a new walk-through railroad display, including a 1901 steam locomotive, a 1912 caboose, and an 1871 coach.

Schedule: October 16 through April 30: Mondays through Saturdays, 9 a.m. to 5 p.m., Sundays 1 to 5 p.m. May 1 through October 15: 9 a.m. to 5 p.m. daily.

Admission/Fare: Varies by season; call or visit our website for more information.

Special Events: Railroad Days during the summer season; check our website for this year's calendar of events.

Nearby Attractions: Visit www.visitgrandisland.com for our Visitor's Bureau's website.

Directions: Four short minutes north of I-80, exit 312, Grand Island.

Site Address: 3133 W. Highway 34, Grand Island, NE
Mailing Address: 3133 W. Highway 34, Grand Island, NE 68801
Telephone: (308) 385-5316
Fax: (308) 385-5028
E-mail: info@stuhrmuseum.org
Website: www.stuhrmuseum.org

TRAILS & RAILS MUSEUM
Museum

Description: Trails & Rails Museum is a county historical museum with a theme of transportation.

Schedule: June through August, Sundays, 1 to 5 p.m.; Mondays, 10 a.m. to 5 p.m.; Tuesdays through Saturdays, 10 a.m. to 8 p.m. Other times by appointment.

Admission/Fare: Free. Donations accepted.

Locomotives/Rolling Stock: 1903 Baldwin steam locomotive; Union Pacific caboose; flatcar; other railroad items.

Special Events: July, Collections Day; August 17, Living History; December 7-15, Christmas Tree Walk.

Nearby Attractions: Great Platte River Road, Archway Monument, Parks, Fort Kearney.

Directions: Take I-80 to Second Ave., go north to 11 St.

       M

Site Address: 710 W. 11 St., Kearney, NE
Mailing Address: 710 W. 11 St., Kearney, NE 68845
Telephone: (308) 234-3041
E-mail: bchs@kearney.net
Website: www.bchs.kearney.net

OMAHA ZOO RAILROAD
Train ride
30" gauge

AARON ZORKO

Description: Passengers take a guided 1¾-mile, 20- to 30-minute trip through the zoo grounds, seeing hundreds of animals, including many rare and endangered species. Steam is scheduled 11 a.m. to 4 p.m.

Schedule: Seven days a week, Memorial Day through Labor Day. Weekends only April through Memorial Day and Labor Day through October.

Admission/Fare: Adults, $2.50; children under 12, $1.50; under 3 free round trip (subject to change on January 1).

Locomotives/Rolling Stock: Locomotives no. 395-104, 1890 Krauss 0-6-2T; no. 119 1968 Crown 4-4-0 narrow gauge replica of Union Pacific no. 119; passenger cars; 11 open-air coaches; caboose; ballast maintainer; Fairmont MT14 motor car.

Special Events: Member's Day, with free train ride to zoo members; Halloween Terror Train during zoo-sponsored Halloween party, children in costume ride free.

Nearby Attractions: Omaha Royals baseball, Children's Museum, Western Heritage Museum.

Directions: I-80 and Tenth St.

Site Address: 3701 S. Tenth St., Omaha, NE
Mailing Address: 3701 S. Tenth St., Omaha, NE 68107
Telephone: (402) 733-8401
Fax: (402) 733-7868
Website: www.omahazoo.com

NEVADA STATE RAILROAD MUSEUM
Train ride, museum
Standard and narrow gauge

GEORGE A. FORERO, JR.

Description: The Nevada State Railroad Museum houses over 50 pieces of railroad equipment from Nevada's past. Included in the collection are seven steam locomotives and restored coaches and freight cars. The bulk of the equipment is from the Virginia & Truckee Railroad. Museum activities include operation of historic railroad equipment, handcar races, lectures, an annual railroad history symposium, changing exhibits, and a variety of special events. We offer steam train or motorcar rides on weekends, spring through fall, on the museum's one-mile loop track.

Schedule: Open daily, 8:30 a.m. to 4:30 p.m. Closed Thanksgiving, Christmas, and New Year's Day.

Admission/Fare: Adults, $2; children under 18, free. Fares vary.

Locomotives/Rolling Stock: No. 25, 1905 Baldwin 4-6-0; no. 18, "Dayton," 1873 Central Pacific 4-4-0; no. 22, "Inyo," 1875 Baldwin 4-4-0; no. 1, "Glenbrook," 1875 Baldwin narrow-gauge 2-6-0; no. 8, 1888 Cooke 4-4-0; no. 1, "Joe Douglass," 1882 Porter narrow gauge 0-4-2. Coaches nos. 3, 4, 8, 11, 12, 17, and 18, express/mail nos. 14 and 21; caboose-coaches nos. 9, 10, and 15, and 11 freight cars; more.

Nearby Attractions: Nevada State Museum, Nevada State Capitol, Lake Tahoe, Virginia City, Reno.

Directions: Highways 50 and 395, at the south end of town.

        M arm

Site Address: 2180 S. Carson St., Carson City, NV
Mailing Address: 2180 S. Carson St., Carson City, NV 89701
Telephone: (775) 687-6953
Website: www.nsrm-friends.org

Nevada, East Ely

NEVADA NORTHERN RAILWAY MUSEUM
Train ride, dinner train, museum, display
Standard gauge

STEVE FALLON

Description: Explore the East Ely Shops and Yard National Historic District, home to the Nevada Northern locomotive and railcar collection. The Keystone steam excursions are 1¾-hour trips and travel to the historic Robison Copper Canyon Mining District. The Adverse diesel excursion consistently climbs a 1½ percent grade on the old high line to McGill.

Schedule: Excursion trains–Memorial Day to Labor Day, daily except Tuesdays. May and September through December, weekends. Check our website for train times.

Admission/Fare: Keystone and Adverse trips–adults, $18, children (3-12), $12. Lane City and Lavon trips–adults, $12; children, $8. Caboose tickets–regular fare +$10. Walking tours–$3.

Locomotives/Rolling Stock: Three steam locomotives, 8 first-generation diesel locomotives, steam crane, steam-powered rotary snowplow, 50 freight cars, 6 cabooses.

Special Events: Steam Spectacular, February; Wine Trains, June through September; Fourth of July Fireworks Train; more. Check website.

Directions: Ely is located on U.S. 50 in east central Nevada.

*Coupon available, see coupon section.

†See ad on the inside front cover.

Site Address: 1100 Ave. "A," East Ely, NV
Mailing Address: PO Box 150040, East Ely, NV 89315
Telephone: (775) 289-2085 and (866) 407-8326
Fax: (775) 289-6284
E-mail: info@nevadanorthernrailway.com
Website: www.nevadanorthernrailway.com

EUREKA & PALISADE RAILROAD
Train ride
36" gauge

DANIEL MARKOFF

Description: Operates on various railroads for special occasions.

Schedule: Railfest, each August on the Durango & Silverton Narrow Gauge Railroad, Durango, Colorado.

Admission/Fare: Call the Durango & Silverton.

Locomotives/Rolling Stock: American Standard 4-4-0 narrow gauge wood-burning locomotive, built by Baldwin Locomotive Works in 1875 for the Eureka & Palisade Railroad in Nevada.

Special Events: Railfest in August.

Nearby Attractions: Nevada State Railroad Museum.

Directions: Not available for public viewing except during scheduled events.

TRAIN

Site Address: Private
Mailing Address: 820 S. Seventh St., Suite A, Las Vegas, NV 89101
Telephone: (702) 383-3327

Nevada, Virginia City

VIRGINIA & TRUCKEE RAILROAD CO.
Train ride
Standard gauge

Description: A 5-mile round trip from Virginia City to the town of Gold Hill through the heart of the historic Comstock mining region. A knowledgeable conductor gives a running commentary on the area and on the 126-year-old railroad.

Schedule: May 24 through November 2.

Admission/Fare: Adults, $6; children 5-12, $3; children under age 5 ride free.

Locomotives/Rolling Stock: 1916 Baldwin 2-8-0 no. 29, former Longview Portland & Northern; 1907 Baldwin 2-6-2 no. 8, former Hobart Southern; 1888 Northwestern Pacific combine and coach; former Tonopah & Tidewater coach; former Northern Pacific caboose; 1919 0-6-0 no. 30, former Southern Pacific.

Special Events: Party and Night train, once a month during the season.

Nearby Attractions: Historic Virginia City, mines, mansions, shops.

Directions: Twenty-one miles from Reno, 17 miles from Carson City.

*Coupon available, see coupon section.

Site Address: Washington and "F" Streets, Virginia City, NV
Mailing Address: PO Box 467, Virginia City, NV 89440
Telephone: (775) 847-0380

Description: Museum in well-preserved railway station dating from 1874. It contains a station master's office and authentic fixtures and furnishings, as well as a large collection of railroad memorabilia.

Schedule: Summer months: Saturdays, 10 a.m. to 3 p.m.; Sundays, 1 to 3 p.m.; other times by appointment.

Admission/Fare: Free.

Locomotives/Rolling Stock: Wolfeboro (New Hampshire) Railroad caboose.

Special Events: First Sunday in August, annual fair.

Nearby Attractions: Highland Lake with swimming, trout and other cold-water fishing, boating, and sailing. Rails-to-trails recreational trail at site follows old tracks 70 miles from Concord to Hannover, New Hampshire. Mount Sunapee and Mount Kearsarge are nearby.

Directions: I-89, exit 11, or I-93, exit 20, to Route 11. Station is at Potter Pl., ½ mile west of Andover at the intersection of Routes 11 and 4.

        M

Site Address: 105 Depot St., Andover, NH
Mailing Address: PO Box 167, Andover, NH 03216
Telephone: (603) 735-5694

ANN HODSON

Description: Late 19th-century railroad station (built 1869, remodeled 1891), with displays of railroad artifacts.

Schedule: July and August: Saturdays, 1 to 4 p.m.

Admission/Fare: Free.

Special Events: Fall foliage train rides, dates to be announced; Lakes Region Model Train Show, dates to be announced.

Nearby Attractions: Squam Lakes, Ashland Historical Society museums (Whipple House Museum, Glidden Toy Museum).

Directions: From exit 24 on I-93, take Route 3 south ¾ mile to the junction with Route 132; take Route 132 south about ½ mile to the railroad tracks.

    M

Site Address: 69 Depot St., Ashland, NH
Mailing Address: PO Box 175, Ashland, NH 03217
Telephone: (603) 968-3902
E-mail: ashlandrrstation@yahoo.com

New Hampshire, Bretton Woods

THE MOUNT WASHINGTON COG RAILWAY
Train ride
4'8"gauge

Description: Climb aboard the world's first mountain-climbing cog railway to the summit of Mount Washington, the highest peak in the Northeast. Rain or shine, this three-hour round-trip journey on one of seven enclosed and heated coaches is a unique vacation experience for all ages. Visit our new base station with museum, restaurant, and gift shop. This is a National Historic Engineering Landmark, built in 1869.

Schedule: Early May through early November. Call for schedule. Reservations recommended.

Admission/Fare: Adults, $49; seniors, $45; children ages 6-12, $35; under age 6 are free unless occupying a seat.

Locomotives/Rolling Stock: Seven coal-fired steam engines; seven enclosed heated coaches; one speeder.

Directions: Located in the heart of New Hampshire's White Mountains at the base of the Presidential Mountain Range. Take I-93 to exit 35, then Route 3 north and Route 302 east to Cog Railway Base Rd. The site is located 165 miles from Boston and 105 miles from Manchester, New Hampshire.

†See ad on page A-5.

Site Address: Base Rd., Mt. Washington, NH
Mailing Address: Base Rd., Mt. Washington, NH 03589
Telephone: (800) 922-8825 and (603) 278-5404
Fax: (603) 278-5830
E-mail: info@thecog.com
Website: www.thecog.com

GORHAM HISTORICAL SOCIETY
Museum, display, layout
Standard gauge

Description: The old Gorham railroad station now serves as the headquarters of the Gorham Historical Society. This architecturally unique building contains displays on area history. The railroad displays include two locomotives (one steam), a snowplow, and four freight cars; the Quinn-Crocket railroadiana collection; and an HO layout in our 1929 boxcar.

Schedule: May to November, daily, 1 to 5 p.m.

Admission/Fare: Admission is by donation.

Locomotives/Rolling Stock: 1911 Baldwin 0-6-0 steam locomotive; 1949 B&M diesel locomotive; two 1929 boxcars, 1951 Russell snowplow, 1924 boxcar; 1942 caboose.

Nearby Attractions: Mascot Pond and Lead Mine, Glen Ellis Falls; Pinkham Notch Camp; Wildcat Mountain and Gondolas; Glen House Site and Mount Washington Auto Road; Dolly Copp Camping and Recreation Area; Gorham Hill; Shelburne birches.

Directions: Just off the junction of Routes 2 and 16 in downtown Gorham.

         M

Site Address: 25 Railroad St.
Mailing Address: 25 Railroad St., Gorham, NH 03581
Telephone: (603) 466-5570

HARTMANN MODEL RAILROAD, LTD.
Train ride, museum, display, layout

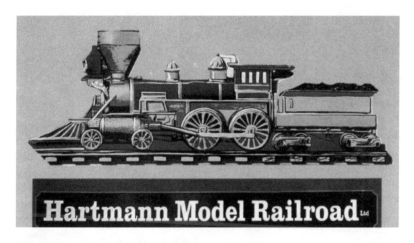

Description: Housed in two buildings, each 8,000 square feet, is a railroad display for all ages. This site features many operating layouts, from G to Z scales, including a replica of Crawford Notch, New Hampshire, in the mid-1950s to early 1960s. Visitors can see several other detailed operating layouts with trains winding through tunnels, over bridges, and past miniature stations and buildings, and Thomas the Tank Engine operates by a light-sensor system. Also on display are about 5,000 model locomotives and coaches, American and European. Come and see our operating outdoor railroad and take a ride with us. Six to eight-minute train ride on 12″ narrow gauge trains, if dry weather.

Schedule: Year-round, daily, 10 a.m. to 5 p.m.

Admission/Fare: Adults, $6; seniors, $5; children ages 5-12, $4; group rates available.

Nearby Attractions: Storyland, 1 mile north; Conway Scenic Railroad, 4 miles south.

Directions: Four miles north of North Conway in the White Mountains.

*Coupon available, see coupon section.

Site Address: Town Hall Rd. and Route 302/16, Intervale, NH
Mailing Address: PO Box 165, Intervale, NH 03845
Telephone: (603) 356-9922
Fax: (603) 356-9958
E-mail: info@hartmannrr.com
Website: www.hartmannrr.com

HOBO RAILROAD
Train ride, dinner train
Standard gauge

Description: The Hobo Railroad features a one-hour and 20-minute train excursion in a natural woodsy setting, along the Pemigewasset River. Our unique specialty offered on most trains is the Hobo Picnic Lunch.

Schedule: Memorial Day through June 30, weekends, 11 a.m. and 1 p.m.; July 1 through Labor Day, daily, 11 a.m. and 1 and 3 p.m.; Labor Day through mid-October, daily, 11 a.m. and 1 p.m.; mid-October through December, select weekends.

Admission/Fare: Adults, $9; children, $7; Hobo Picnic Lunch, $6.95.

Locomotives/Rolling Stock: Alco S-3 no. 1186 (former B&M); Alco S-1 no. 959 (former Maine Central); Alco S-1 no. 958 (former Maine Central). Coaches–former DL&W open-window cars and Boston & Maine Budd RDC coaches (non-powered).

Special Events: Mother's Day, July 4 Family Party Train, Fiddler's Contest, Santa Express Trains, etc. . . .

Nearby Attractions: Clark's Trading Post, Franconia Notch State park, Loon Mountain, Whale's Tale Water Park, Flume Gorge, Lost River Gorge.

Directions: Exit 32 from I-93, Main St., across from McDonald's restaurant.

  Radio frequency: 160.470

Site Address: Main St., Lincoln, NH
Mailing Address: PO Box 9, Lincoln, NH 03251
Telephone: (603) 745-2135
Fax: (603) 745-9850
E-mail: ride@hoborr.com
Website: www.hoborr.com

WHITE MOUNTAIN CENTRAL RAILROAD
Train ride, museum, display

Description: A 30-minute steam train ride in the White Mountains, leaving from a beautiful depot at Clark's Trading Post, traveling over a 1904 covered bridge, and climbing a 2 percent grade through Wolfman's territory. The ticket includes a trained bear show, museum, bumper boats, Merlin's Mansion, and much more.

Schedule: July and August, daily; June and September to mid-October, weekends.

Admission/Fare: Age 6 and up, $10; ages 3-5, $3; under 3, free. Group discounts are available. Price and schedule subject to change without notice.

Locomotives/Rolling Stock: Former International Shoe Co. 2-truck Heisler no. 4; former Beebe River Railroad 2-truck Climax no. 6; former East Branch & Lincoln 2-4-2 Baldwin no. 5; 0-4-0T Porter no. 1; 1898 BM caboose no. 104082; boxcars, flatcars, and log trucks.

Special Events: July 12-13, Wolfman weekend; September 20-21, Railroad Days.

Nearby Attractions: Hobo Railroad, Cog Railway, Conway Scenic Railroad, White Mountain National Forest.

Directions: On Route 3, 1 mile north of North Woodstock; located at Clark's Trading Post.

         arm M

Site Address: Route 3, Lincoln, NH
Mailing Address: PO Box 1, Lincoln, NH 03251
Telephone: (603) 745-8913
Fax: (603) 745-2490
E-mail: info@clarkstradingpost.com
Website: www.clarkstradingpost.com

**New Hampshire, Meredith/
Weirs Beach**

**WINNIPESAUKEE SCENIC
RAILROAD**
*Train ride, dinner train
Standard gauge*

Description: Scenic train rides and lakeside dinner trains along the shores of New Hampshire's largest lake. Ice cream parlor car, party caboose. One- and two-hour rides.

Schedule: Memorial Day through late June, weekends; July 1 to Labor Day, daily; after Labor Day, weekends, fall foliage; select weekends through December.

Admission/Fare: Adults, $9.50; children, $7.50; Hobo Picnic Lunches, $6.95.

Locomotives/Rolling Stock: Alco S-1 no. 1008, former Portland Terminal; EMD GP-7 no. 302, former Rock Island; GE 44-ton no. 2, former U.S. government. Coaches–former DRW open-window cars and Boston & Maine Budd RDC coaches (nonpowered).

Special Events: Mother's Day, fireworks specials, caboose rides, Santa Express Trains, fall foliage specials.

Nearby Attractions: Lake Winnipesaukee, Mount Washington cruises, Funspot, Weirs Beach.

Directions: I-93 exit 23, take Route 104 east to Route 3; Route 3 north for ¼ mile, left onto Mill St.

   Radio frequency: 161.550

Site Address: Main St., Meredith, NH
Mailing Address: PO Box 9, Lincoln, NH 03251
Telephone: (603) 745-2135
Fax: (603) 745-9850
E-mail: ride@hoborr.com
Website: www.hoborr.com

CONWAY SCENIC RAILROAD
Train ride, dinner train, museum,
display, layout
Standard gauge

Description: The Valley Train travels south to Conway and northwest to Bartlett. The Notch Train goes northwest beyond Bartlett through spectacular Crawford Notch to Crawford Depot and Fabyan Station.

Schedule: Valley Train–mid-April through mid-May, also November and December: weekends. Mid-May through mid-October: daily. Notch Train–July 17 through September 6: Tuesday, Wednesday, Thursday, and Saturday. September 9 through October 17: daily.

Admission/Fare: Valley Train–adults, from \$10.50; children 4-12, from \$7.50; under age 4, price varies with destination and seat selection. Notch Train–adults, from \$36; children 4-12, from \$21; under age 4, from \$7, price varies with destination and seat selection.

Locomotives/Rolling Stock: No. 7470, Grand Trunk 0-6-0, former Canadian National; no. 15, 1945 44-ton GE, former Maine Central; no. 573, 1950 GP-7, former maine Central; more.

Special Events: Rites of Spring; Mother's Day; Junior Railroaders' Day; Father's Day; Trains, Planes & Automobiles; Railfans' Days; Pumpkin Patch; Turkey Trotter; Santa Claus Express; Polar Express. Call, write, or check website for dates.

Directions: Route 16/U.S. 302 and Norcross Circle in the heart of North Conway Village. The depot faces Village Park.

          arm TRAIN

Portland **VIA** Montreal **Radio frequency: 161.250** MasterCard VISA

Site Address: Route 16/U.S. 302 and 38 Norcross Circle, North Conway, NH
Mailing Address: PO Box 1947, North Conway, NH 03860-1947
Telephone: (603) 356-5251 and (800) 232-5251
Fax: (603) 356-7606
E-mail: info@conwayscenic.com
Website: www.conwayscenic.com

New Hampshire, North Woodstock

CAFE LAFAYETTE
DINNER TRAIN
Dinner train
Standard gauge

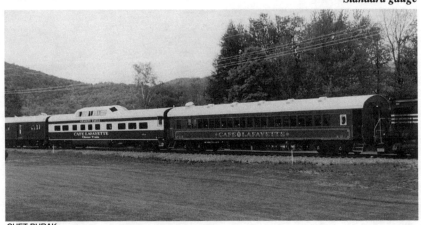

CHET BURAK

Description: Experience a leisurely two-hour evening train ride spent criss-crossing the picturesque Pemigewasset River. As dinner is served, period music keeps time with the rail's rhythmic rumbling. See magnificent mountain vistas and lush New England forests during this 20-mile round trip. After dinner, with the compartment lights down low, watch a dramatic New England sunset outside your window.

Schedule: Mother's Day through last Saturday in October. Call for details.

Admission/Fare: Adults, $55; children, 3-11 $32.95; age 2 and under, $10 minimum.

Locomotives/Rolling Stock: 1923 Pennsylvania Railroad caboose; 1924 Pullman dining car no. 221, former NYC; 1953 Army kitchen car; 1954 CN cafe coach no. 3207; 1952 Pullman dome car, former MoPac/Illinois Central no. 2211; 1946 Pullman sleeper CNR/VIA.

Nearby Attractions: Heart of the White Mountain National Forest, Old Man of the Mountain, Franconia Notch State Park. White Mountain Central Railway, Cog Railroad, Mount Washington, Hobo Railroad, Winnepesaukee Scenic Railroad.

Directions: Take I-93 to exit 32; on Route 112, midway between Lincoln, New Hampshire, and North Woodstock.

Site Address: Route 112, North Woodstock, NH
Mailing Address: RR1 Box 85, Lincoln, NH 03251
Telephone: (603) 745-3500 and (800) 699-3501 (outside NH)
Fax: (603) 745-3535
Website: www.cafelafayette.com or www.nhdinnertrain.com

**KLICKETY KLACK
MODEL RAILROAD**
Layout

Description: Operate a turntable, a quarry train, carnival rides, trolley, Thomas the Tank and Percy; visit a circus, castle, lighthouse, villages and city; see a smoking factory and steam ships in the harbor. All of this is possible at Klickety-Klack, where over two dozen HO, N, and On30 scale trains run over 1,500 feet of track. This miniature collection includes 150 locomotives, 400 freight and passenger cars, 2,000 "people" and much more. This railroad represents over 75,000 hours of work by many dedicated people.

Schedule: July 1 through Labor Day: Mondays through Saturdays, 10 a.m. to 5 p.m. September through June: Thursdays through Saturdays, 10 a.m. to 5 p.m. Closed last week of October and first week of November.

Admission/Fare: Adults, $4; children 3-12, $3.

Nearby Attractions: Mount Washington, New Hampshire lake region.

Directions: At the junction of Routes 28 and 109A.

Site Address: 8 Elm St., Wolfeboro Falls, NH
Mailing Address: PO Box 205, Wolfeboro Falls, NH 03896
Telephone: (603) 569-5384

CAPE MAY SEASHORE LINES
Train ride
Standard gauge

LION PHOTOGRAPHY

Description: Regional/tourist railroad in Cape May County. Operating Budd RDCs in scheduled passenger service. For most recent schedule, fare, locomotives and rolling stock, and special events, please call, write, or check website.

Locomotives/Rolling Stock: Eight Budd RDC1s, former Pennsylvania-Reading Seashore Lines; two RDC9s, former Boston & Maine; Alco/EMD RS2, former Pennsylvania Railroad; EMD GP9, former PRR; three P-RSL P70 coaches, former PRR; two P-RSL P70 coaches, former P-RSL.

Nearby Attractions: Victorian Cape May City, Wildwood Beaches, Boardwalk and Amusement Piers, Cape May Lighthouse, Cap May-Lewes Ferry, Cape May County Park and Zoo, historic Cold Spring Village, Mid-Atlantic Center for the Arts, and Middle Township Performing Arts Center.

Directions: 4-H Fairgrounds Station–off South Dennisville Rd., Middle Township. Cape May Court House–Route 615/Mechanic St. Smith Court House–Elementary School 2 off Pacific Ave. in Cape May Court House (flag stop). Cold Spring–Route 9, Cold Spring. Cape May City–Lafayette St., Cape May City.

P Radio frequency: 161.160

Site Address: Rio Grande, NJ
Mailing Address: PO Box 152, Tuckahoe, NJ 08250-0152
Telephone: (609) 884-2675
Fax: (609) 567-5847
Website: www.cmslrr.com

New Jersey, Farmingdale

**NEW JERSEY MUSEUM OF
TRANSPORTATION, INC.**
Train ride, display
36" gauge

GARY S. CRAWFORD

Description: This is the oldest continuously operated steam preservation railroad in the U.S., established 1952.

Schedule: Weekends, April through October, 12 to 4:30 p.m. Daily, July through August, 12 to 4:30 p.m.

Admission/Fare: $2.50 per person; higher for special events.

Special Events: Easter Express, Palm Sunday and Easter weekends; Railroader's Day, Sunday after Labor Day; haunted Halloween Express (night runs), late October; Christmas Express, four weekends beginning at Thanksgiving.

Nearby Attractions: Historic Allaire Village, Jersey Shore beach attractions.

Directions: Route 524 at Allaire State Park, Allaire, New Jersey. Garden State Parkway exit 98, I-195 exit 31.

      M arm TRAIN

Site Address: Allaire State Park, 4265 Route 524, Wall Township, Monmouth County, NJ
Mailing Address: PO Box 622, Allaire, NJ 07727-0622
Telephone: (732) 938-5524
E-mail: info@njmt.org
Website: www.njmt.org

CARL R. CERAGNO

Description: The museum, housed in the original 1871 Mahwah Depot, features many rare artifacts from ABEX (American Brakeshoe Company), the Erie Railroad, and its successors.

Schedule: Memorial Day through the end of October, Sundays, 2 to 4 p.m.

Admission/Fare: Free.

Locomotives/Rolling Stock: Erie Caboose no. 04940; 1½" scale Erie Pacific-type steam locomotive "The Steven Birch," manufactured in 1918 in Erie Machine Shop, Dunmore, Pennsylvania; 1½" scale Erie boxcar built by Ramapo iron Works, Hillburn, New York.

Nearby Attractions: Mahwah Museum, Suffern Railroad Museum.

Directions: From Route 17 north or south exit onto W. Ramapo Ave. and follow it to E. Ramapo Ave. Old Station Lane is to the left before the railroad underpass.

Site Address: 1871 Old Station Lane, Mahwah, NJ 07430
Mailing Address: 201 Franklin Turnpike, Mahwah, NJ 07430
Telephone: (201) 512-0099

New Jersey, Phillipsburg

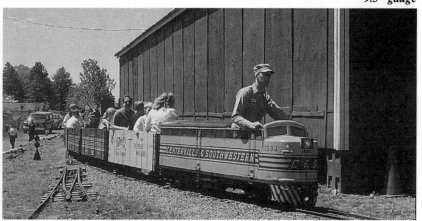

PAUL CARPENITO

Description: Miniature train ride on the Centerville & Southwestern Railroad. Speeder car rides on selected open house days.

Schedule: May 1 through October 1, Sundays, 10 a.m. to 4 p.m. Open houses with train rides in May, July, and September.

Admission/Fare: Donations accepted. Train ride, $1.

Locomotives/Rolling Stock: Ingersoll-Rand GE 45-tonner; L&HR cabooses no. 16 and no. 18; CNJ caboose no. 91197; lowside gondola; L&HR flanger; Centerville & Southwestern, two locomotives and 31 cars.

Special Events: Call for 2003 schedule.

Nearby Attractions: Crayola Factory, Two Rivers Landing Canal and Museum.

Directions: U.S. Route 22, exit at S. Main St., follow over black bridge. Museum entrance is across from Joe's Steak Shop and behind Noto/Wyncoop Funeral Home.

    M

Site Address: Cross St. and Pine Alley, Phillipsburg, NJ
Mailing Address: 292 Chambers St., Phillipsburg, NJ 08805
Telephone: (908) 859-1277 and (610) 826-2580
E-mail: prrh@angelfire.com
Website: www.angelfire.com/nj/prrh

ROBERT SALFI

Description: Large model railroad club featuring fully-scenicked 40 x 40-foot HO scale and 20 x 27-foot N scale operating layouts. 80 x 60-foot expansion of HO layout is under construction. We have a new garden railroad department.

Schedule: Saturdays, 1 to 4 p.m.

Admission/Fare: Adults, $3; children ages 12 and under, $2.

Special Events: Annual Light and Sound Show and Open House, three weekends beginning Thanksgiving weekend. Call or visit our website for details.

Nearby Attractions: Less than one hour from New York City. Many family-oriented activities in our general area, including museums, major and minor league baseball, and other attractions.

Directions: New Jersey Route 22 east, off Jefferson Ave. (behind Home Depot), approximately 3 miles from the Garden State Parkway.

*Coupon available, see coupon section.

Site Address: 295 Jefferson Avenue, Union, NJ
Mailing Address: PO Box 1146, Union, NJ 07083-1146
Telephone: (908) 964-8808 (recorded message)
E-mail: See website for list of e-mail contacts.
Website: www.tmrci.com

New Jersey, Whippany

STEVEN HEPLER

Description: Visit the Whippany Railway Museum, headquartered in the restored 1904 freight house of the Morristown & Erie, with its outstanding collection of railroad artifacts and memorabilia. The railroad yard is complete with the elegant Whippany passenger depot, coal yard, wooden water tank, and historic rail equipment. The museum also features operating model train layouts and a display of ocean liner memorabilia. Train ride is a 10-mile, 45-minute round-trip excursion.

Schedule: April through October, Sundays, 12 noon to 4 p.m.

Admission/Fare: Museum–adults, $1; children under age 12, $.50. Special event train fare–adults, $10; children under age 12, $6.

Locomotives/Rolling Stock: Morris County Central no. 4039, an 0-6-0 built for the U.S. Army by Alco in 1942 and now listed on the national register of historic places; NYS&W no. 150, Whitcomb 20-ton industrial locomotive; railbus no. 10 built in 1918 by the White Motor Company for the Morristown & Erie; and more.

Special Events: Easter Bunny Express, April 12-13, 19; Pumpkin Festival, October 5; Halloween Express, October 25-26; Santa Claus Special, December 6-7, 13-14.

Directions: At the intersection of Route 10 west and Whippany Rd. in Morris County.

     (locomotive no. 4039 only)

Newark & Metropark Sta.   **Radio frequency: 160.230**

Site Address: 1 Railroad Plaza, Rt. 10 West and Whippany Rd., Whippany, NJ
Mailing Address: PO Box 16, Whippany, NJ 07981-0016
Telephone: (973) 887-8177
E-mail: paultup@optonline.net
Website: www.whippanyrailwaymuseum.org

New Mexico, Alamogordo

TOY TRAIN DEPOT

Train ride, museum, display, and layout
16" gauge

HASKELL

Description: Two MTC F-7 16" diesels, Baltimore & Ohio, Union Pacific, transport three-car loads south to Live Tree, Dead Grass, Rosebud, Southhoop, and New Bridge. The round trip is 20 minutes. We also have a large model railroad hobby shop. We have an MTC engineer certification program, which teaches you how to maintain and operate our 16" trains. (We are a 501[c]3 nonprofit foundation.)

Schedule: Year-round, Wednesdays through Sundays, 12 to 4:30 p.m.

Admission/Fare: General admission, museum, $3; train ride, $3. Discounts for large groups with advance reservations.

Locomotives/Rolling Stock: We have five MTC trains. Union Pacific G16; Baltimore & Ohio G16; Western Pacific G16; 1965 steam outline S16; G12 MTC train available for junior engineers to drive.

Special Events: Cottonwood Festival, Alamogordo, New Mexico Labor Day weekend, park/ride.

Nearby Attractions: White Sands National Monument, Dog Canyon Museum, Tularosa Basin Historical Society Museum, Oliver Lee State Park, Lincoln National Forest, guided tours of the Alamogordo Sacramento Mountain Railway roadbed and trestles.

Directions: North end of Alameda Park is located on N. White Sands Blvd. in Alamogordo.

Site Address: 1991 N. White Sands Blvd., Alamogordo, NM
Mailing Address: 1991 N. White Sands Blvd., Alamogordo, NM 88310
Telephone: (505) 437-2855 and (888) 207-3564
E-mail: railfanewmexico@hotmail.com
Website: www.toytraindepot.homestead.com

New Mexico, Chama
Colorado, Antonito

CUMBRES & TOLTEC
SCENIC RAILROAD
Train ride
36" gauge

Description: The Cumbres & Toltec Scenic Railroad is the finest remaining example of the original Denver & Rio Grande narrow gauge railroad, built in the 1880s to reach the mines at Silverton. Unspoiled scenery awaits you as you travel through the spectacular San Juan Mountains. You'll pass over high bridges and through tunnels, alongside ghostly rock formations and restored company towns.

Schedule: Memorial Day weekend through mid-October: daily departures from both Antonito, 10 a.m., and Chama, 10 a.m.

Admission/Fare: Adults, $40-$60; children, $20-$30; senior, handicapped and group discounts.

Locomotives/Rolling Stock: Locomotives–ex-D&RGW K27 463 (BLW 1903, 21788); ex-D&RGW K36 483, 484, 487, 488, and 489 (BLW 1925); and ex-D&RGW K37 497 (BLW 1980), converted to narrow gauge 1930). Rolling stock–passenger cars constructed in the 1970s and 1980s, over 140 pieces of ex-D&RGW equipment from 1880 to 1968.

Special Events: Opening Day, May 26; others to be announced later.

Nearby Attractions: Antonito–Great Sand Dunes National Monument, Taos, Santa Fe, Royal Gorge. Chama–Santa Fe, Durango (D&SNGRR), Mesa Verde.

Radio frequency: 160.305, 161.505

Site Address: U.S. 285, Antonito, CO / 500 Terrace Ave., Chama, NM
Mailing Address: PO Box 789, Chama, NM 87520
Telephone: (505) 756-2151
Fax: (505) 756-2694
E-mail: rrinfo@cumbrestoltec.com
Website: www.cumbrestoltec.com

CLOVIS DEPOT
MODEL TRAIN MUSEUM
Museum, display, layout

PHIL WILLIAMS

Description: The Clovis Depot has been restored to its condition in the 1950-60 era and has displays of historic documents and memorabilia covering its use and the history of the AT&SF in New Mexico along the Belen Cutoff since the turn of the century. Also featured are nine model railroad layouts depicting the history of toy trains, the development of the railroad in both Australia and Great Britain, and the Clovis Yard and adjacent city in 1950-60. Live BNSF train operations can be viewed from the dispatcher's position and platform with some 75-100 trains passing each day. We provide a one-hour guided tour of the museum and model railroad layouts, including running the model trains and other displays.

Schedule: Wednesdays through Sundays, 12 to 5 p.m. Closed September and February, as well as Easter, Thanksgiving, Christmas, and New Year's Day.

Admission/Fare: Call or write for information.

Locomotives/Rolling Stock: Fairmont Railway motor car.

Nearby Attractions: Blackwater Draw Museum, Blackwater Draw Archaeological site, Norman Petty Studios.

Directions: In a restored ATSF passenger depot adjacent to BNSF main line, two blocks west of Main St. on U.S. 60/84.

Site Address: 221 W. First St., Clovis, NM
Mailing Address: 221 W. First St., Clovis, NM 88101
Telephone: (505) 762-0066 and (888) 762-0064
E-mail: philipw@3lefties.com
Website: www.clovisdepot.com

SANTA FE SOUTHERN RAILWAY
Train ride, dinner train
Standard gauge

MARK ROUNDS

Description: The Santa Fe Southern offers 2½-hour, 3½-hour, and 4½-hour excursions with freight movement. Scenic trains year-round; Friday highball and Saturday barbecue dinner trains, April through October.

Schedule: Gift shop/ticket office, 9 a.m. to 5 p.m. Monday through Saturday; 11 a.m. to 5 p.m., Sunday.

Admission/Fare: Adult fares $32 to $55; senior (60+) discount.

Locomotives/Rolling Stock: GP 7 no. 92; GP 7 no. 93; New Jersey no. 1158; Super Chief Club "Acoma"; Santa Fe Pleasure Dome "Plaza Lamy."

Special Events: Valentine's Dinner, February 14; Easter Bunny Train; Fourth of July barbecue and fireworks; Fiesta barbecue; Halloween Ghost Story Train; post-Thanksgiving barbecue; Santa Claus and caroling trains, December 15-24; New Year's Eve dinner, December 31.

Nearby Attractions: Santa Fe downtown, art galleries, museums, fine clothing, restaurants, within walking distance of depot.

Directions: I-25 at St. Francis to Cerrillos, turn right to Guadalupe, turn left, depot on left at Tomasita's Restaurant.

*Coupon available, see coupon section.

Site Address: 410 S. Guadalupe St., Santa Fe, NM
Mailing Address: 410 S. Guadalupe St., Santa Fe, NM 87501
Telephone: (505) 989-8600 and (888) 989-8600
Fax: (505) 983-7620
E-mail: depot@sfsr.com
Website: www.sfsr.com

ARCADE & ATTICA RAILROAD
Train ride, dinner train, museum, layout
Standard gauge

PETER SWANSON

Description: Two-hour excursion ride in coaches built in 1915 and pulled by the only steam locomotive in New York State.

Schedule: Memorial weekend through end of October, hours vary.

Admission/Fare: Adults, $10; children ages 3-11, $7; under 3 free on a lap.

Locomotives/Rolling Stock: 2-8-0 American.

Special Events: Civil War, third weekend in August; children's trains, second Friday in July and August.

Nearby Attractions: Letchworth State Park.

Directions: Three miles east of Route 16 or ½ mile west of Route 98.

*Coupon available, see coupon section.

Site Address: 278 Main St., Arcade, NY (Route 39)
Mailing Address: 278 Main St., Arcade, NY 14009
Telephone: (716) 496-4877 and (585) 492-3100
Fax: (585) 492-0100
E-mail: llk@anarr.com
Website: www.anarr.com

DELAWARE & ULSTER RAILRIDE
Train ride, museum, display
Standard gauge

AARON KELLER

Description: Nineteen miles of rail offering a 1-hour or 1¾-hour trip through the scenic Catskill Mountains. Operates on the route of the historic Ulster & Delaware Railroad.

Schedule: End of May through end of October: weekends; departs 11 a.m., 1, 2:30, and 3:45 p.m. July and August: Wednesdays through Fridays, departs at 11 a.m. and 2 p.m.

Admission/Fare: Short trip–adults, $7; seniors, $6; children, $5; under age 3 ride free. Long trip–adults, $10; seniors, $8; children, $6; under age 3 ride free.

Locomotives/Rolling Stock: D&H no. 5017 RS36 Alco; no. 5106 1953 Alco S-4, former Chesapeake & Ohio; no. 1012 1954 Alco S-4, former Ford Motor Co.; M-405 1928 J.G. Brill Co. diesel-electric rail car, former New York Central; two slat cars with benches, former PRR; two boxcars, former NYC; 44-ton locomotive, former Western Maryland.

Special Events: Train Robberies, Tractor Pulls, Twilight Runs, Fall Foliage, Halloween Train, A Day Out with Thomas, Santa Train.

Directions: Route 28, in Arkville, 45 miles west of New York State Thruway.

Radio frequency: 161.385

Site Address: Route 28, Arkville, NY
Mailing Address: PO Box 310, Stamford, NY 12167
Telephone: (800) 225-4132 and (845) 586-DURR
Fax: (607) 652-2822
Website: www.durr.org

MARTISCO STATION MUSEUM
CENTRAL NEW YORK CHAPTER NRHS
Museum, display, layout

Description: The Martisco Station Museum is a brick Victorian structure erected in 1870 for the New York Central and Hudson River Railroad. Located in a picturesque setting, the restored two-story passenger station houses a collection of railroad mementos of the local area. The adjacent former Pennsylvania Railroad diner houses additional displays. Presently the track passing the station is used five days per week by the Finger Lakes Railway.

Schedule: May through October: Sundays, 1 to 5 p.m.

Admission/Fare: Donations appreciated.

Locomotives/Rolling Stock: Pennsylvania Railroad diner.

Special Events: Christmas at the Station, December.

Directions: New York Route 174, halfway between the villages of Camillus and Marcellus, at the end of Martisco Rd.

      M

Site Address: Martisco Rd., Camillus, NY
Mailing Address: PO Box 229, Marcellus, NY 13108-0229
Telephone: (315) 488-8208
Fax: (315) 487-2849
E-mail: CNYNRHS@aol.com
Website: www.rrhistorical2.com/cnynrhs

CENTRAL SQUARE STATION MUSEUM
CENTRAL NEW YORK CHAPTER NRHS
Museum, display

Description: The Central New York Chapter NRHS is a former joint station of the New York Ontario & Western Railway and the New York Central Railroad, built in 1909. The restored one-story wood passenger station houses a collection of railroad artifacts from the local area.

Schedule: May through October: Sundays, 12 to 5 p.m.

Admission/Fare: Free.

Locomotives/Rolling Stock: 0-4-0 steam locomotive no. 53 American Locomotive Co.; 0-4-0 narrow gauge steam no. 3; Brill car no. M-39; 25-ton GE diesel no. 7; Fairmont Rail motor car; 0-4-0T steam engine from Solvay Process.

Nearby Attractions: St. Lawrence Seaway, Thousand Islands, Adirondack Park.

Directions: Railroad St. in Central Square, off Route 11 south of town, close to Route 81.

       M

Site Address: Railroad St., Central Square, NY
Mailing Address: PO Box 229, Marcellus, NY 13108-0229
Telephone: (315) 488-8208
Fax: (315) 487-2849
E-mail: CNYNRHS@aol.com
Website: www.rrhistorical2.com/cnynrhs

THE CHESTER HISTORICAL SOCIETY
Museum

Description: The Chester Historical Society's charter is for the promotion and preservation of the local history of the town and village of Chester. The town was settled in the early 1700s. The first shipment of fresh milk to New York City by rail was made in 1842 via the Erie Railroad from Chester. The museum is housed in the 1915 Erie Railroad Station on the former Erie main line in Chester. The main line is now an Orange County linear park called the Heritage Trail, running over 10 miles from Monroe to New Hampton for walking, rollerblading, running, and bicycling. This Arts-and-Crafts-influenced passenger station replaced the original 1841 station in 1915. After sitting in disuse for several decades, it opened on June 12, 1999, as Chester's Local History Museum. It houses displays of local history, including items from the various trains and stations that served the Chester community.

Schedule: May through October: Saturdays, 9 a.m. to 1 p.m. Groups by appointment anytime.

Nearby Attractions: Historic Downtown, Heritage Trail, West Point.

Directions: New York State Thruway exit 16. Take Route 17 west 10 miles, exit 126 Chester, straight at light onto Academy Ave. Left on Main St., right at firehouse and continue on Main St. through downtown Chester. The station is on the left.

      M

Site Address: 1915 Erie Railroad Station, 19 Winkler Pl., Chester, NY
Mailing Address: 47 Main St., Chester, NY 10918
Telephone: (845) 469-2591
E-mail: chester.historical@frontiernet.net

ALCO BROOKS RAILROAD DISPLAY
Display
Standard gauge

Description: Located at the Chautauqua County Fairgrounds since 1987, the display features an original Alco-Brooks steam locomotive, a wood-sided boxcar housing displays of Chautauqua County commerce and railroads along with a gift shop, and a restored wooden caboose. Other items of interest at the site are a Nickel Plate work car, an Erie Railroad concrete telephone booth, a New York Central harp switch stand, a Pennsylvania Railroad cast-iron crossing sign, a DAV&P land line marker, and an operating crossing flasher.

Schedule: June 1 through August 31: Saturdays, 1 to 3 p.m., weather permitting. Open daily during special events or by appointment.

Admission/Fare: Donations appreciated.

Locomotives/Rolling Stock: 1916 Alco-Brooks 0-6-0 no. 444, former Boston & Maine; 1907 Delaware & Hudson no. 22020 wood-sided boxcar; 1905 New York Central no. 19224 wooden caboose.

Special Events: Chautauqua County Antique Auto Show and Flea Market, May 16-18. Chautauqua County Fair, July 21-27.

Nearby Attractions: Dunkirk Historical Museum, Dunkirk Lighthouse, Chautauqua Institution.

Directions: I-90, exit 59, to Chautauqua County Fairgrounds.

Site Address: 1089 Central Ave., Chautauqua County Fairgrounds, Dunkirk, NY
Mailing Address: Historical Society of Dunkirk, 513 Washington Ave., Dunkirk, NY 14048
Telephone: (716) 366-3797
E-mail: davrr@netsync.net

New York, Greenport

RAILROAD MUSEUM OF LONG ISLAND, GREENPORT SITE
Museum, display, layout

Description: Located in a historic 1890 LIRR freight station. Displays include photos, artifacts, HO gauge layout of Greenport terminal, operating tower (Bliss), outside "Jaws" snowplow, and 1927 LIRR wooden caboose.

Schedule: Memorial Day weekend through Columbus Day weekend, weekends and holidays. Also, first weekend in December (Santa visit).

Admission/Fare: Adults, $2; children over 5, $1; under 5, free.

Locomotives/Rolling Stock: LIRR/Russell snowplow no. 83, "Jaws"; LIRR/American Car & Foundry Co. caboose (wooden) no. 14.

Special Events: Rail Fest, August, the weekend prior to Labor Day weekend; Santa Visit, first weekend in December.

Nearby Attractions: East End Seaport Museum, Historic Museums of Southold, Vineyards (over 20), charter fishing.

Directions: From New York Route 25 in Greenport, go south two blocks on Fourth St. to the museum, located at the tracks.

Site Address: 440 Fourth St., Greenport, NY
Mailing Address: PO Box 726, Greenport, NY 11944-0726
Telephone: (631) 477-0439
E-mail: secretaryrmli@aol.com
Website: www.rmli.org

ROCHESTER & GENESEE VALLEY RAILROAD MUSEUM

Train ride, museum
Standard gauge

CHRIS HAUF

Description: The museum, housed in a restored 1908 Erie Railroad station, displays railroad artifacts from western New York railroads. On outdoor tracks are a number of railroad cars and diesel locomotives open for display. The museum has tours and track car rides.

Schedule: May through October: Sundays, 11 am. to 5 p.m. Visits at other times by appointment.

Admission/Fare: Adults, $5; seniors, $4; children 5-15, $3.

Locomotives/Rolling Stock: 1946 GE 80-ton diesel, former Eastman Kodak; 1953 Alco RS-3, former Lehigh Valley; 1953 Alco S-4, former Nickel Plate; 1941 GE 45-ton, former Rochester Gas & Electric; Fairbanks-Morse H12-44, former U.S. Army.

Special Events: Diesel Days, mid-August.

Nearby Attractions: Strong Museum, Eastman House, Genesee Country Museum, Frontier Stadium, New York Museum of Transportation.

Directions: All regularly scheduled Sunday tours start at the New York Museum of Transportation. The depot itself is located on Route 251, just west of E. River Rd.

Site Address: 6393 E. River Rd., Henrietta, NY
Mailing Address: PO Box 23326, Rochester, NY 14692-3326
Telephone: (585) 533-1431
E-mail: info@rochnrhs.org
Website: www.rochnrhs.org

HUDSON VALLEY RAILROAD SOCIETY/RAILROAD STATION
Museum, display, layout

LARRY LALIBERTE

Description: This museum is a restoration of a 1914 railroad station by a railroad club. It relates the history of the station and the Roosevelt and Vanderbilt connection and features operating display layouts.

Schedule: Year-round: Mondays, 7 to 10 p.m. Mid-June through mid-September: weekends, 11 a.m. to 5 p.m. Memorial Day and July 4.

Admission/Fare: Free. Donations appreciated.

Nearby Attractions: Franklin Delano Roosevelt home and library, Vanderbilt mansion, Old Rhinebeck Aerodome, bicycle tours, hiking trails, golf course, river tours, Mills Norrie State Park.

Directions: West on W. Market St. from U.S. 9 (historic signs posted on U.S. 9) to bottom of hill. Station in Town Park on right.

Site Address: Riverfront Park, 34 River Road, Hyde Park, NY
Mailing Address: PO Box 135, Hyde Park, NY 12538
Telephone: (845) 229-2338
E-mail: revaul@aol.com
Website: www.hydeparkstation.com

TROLLEY MUSEUM OF NEW YORK
Train ride
Standard gauge

MARILYN JENNINGS

Description: This museum was established in 1955 and moved to its present location in 1983, becoming part of the Kingston Urban Cultural Park. A 2.5-mile, 40-minute round trip takes passengers from the foot of Broadway to Kingston Point, with stops at the museum in both directions. A gas-powered railcar operates on private right-of-way and in-street trackage along Rondout Creek to the Hudson River over part of the former Ulster & Delaware Railroad main line. An exhibit hall features trolley exhibits and a theater.

Schedule: Memorial weekend to Columbus Day, 12 to 5 p.m. Last ride departs at 4:30 p.m. Charters available.

Admission/Fare: Adults, $3; seniors and children, $2.

Locomotives/Rolling Stock: Eleven trolleys; eight rapid transit cars; Whitcomb diesel-electric; Brill model 55 interurban.

Special Events: Shad Festival, May; Mother's Day (moms ride free); Father's Day (dads ride free); Santa Days, December.

Nearby Attractions: Hudson River Maritime Museum, Senate House, Catskill Mountains, Urban Cultural Park.

Directions: In the historic Rondout Waterfront area of Kingston. Call or write for directions or see map on web page.

            M arm Rhinecliffe

 **Radio Frequency: 462.175**

Site Address: 89 E. Strand, Kingston, NY
Mailing Address: PO Box 2291, Kingston, NY 12402
Telephone: (845) 331-3399
E-mail: info@tmny.org
Website: www.tmny.org

New York, Maybrook

MAYBROOK RAILROAD
HISTORICAL SOCIETY
Museum

Description: The museum offers photographs and memorabilia.

Schedule: April through October: weekends, 1 to 4 p.m.

Admission/Fare: Free.

Locomotives/Rolling Stock: Caboose no. C512

Nearby Attractions: Museum Village in Monroe, New York; O&W Railroad Historical Society archives in Middletown; Erie depot and hiking trail in Chester, New York.

Directions: I-84 to exit 5; 2 miles south on Route 208. Located in rear of Maybrook Library.

  M

Site Address: 101 Main St., Maybrook, NY (rear of library)
Mailing Address: PO Box 105, Maybrook, NY 12543
Telephone: (914) 427-2591

MEDINA RAILROAD MUSEUM
Museum

Description: Located in a 1905-06 NYC and HRRR freight depot, the Medina Railroad Museum has a large railroad collection. A 204-foot-long HO scale layout is under construction and operating.

Schedule: Tuesdays through Sundays, 11 a.m. to 5 p.m.

Admission/Fare: Adults, $6; seniors, $5; children under 16, $3.

Locomotives/Rolling Stock: Five 1948 Budd coaches, former NYC Empire State Express coaches from WNY Railway Historical Society; Nickel Plate Road RS11 Alco Diesel 1952 owned by Genesee Valley Transportation.

Special Events: Two-hour, 34-mile rail excursions are on select dates in summer and fall. Call for schedule.

Nearby Attractions: Niagara Falls, Six Flags at Darien Lake, Jell-O Museum.

Directions: Take I-90 to exit 48A, go north on New York Routes 77 and 63 to Medina.

*Coupon available, see coupon section.

        M

Site Address: 530 West Ave., Medina, NY
Mailing Address: 530 West Ave., Medina, NY 14103
Telephone: (716) 798-6106
Fax: (716) 798-1829
E-mail: rrmuseum@tigdata.net
Website: www.railroadmuseum.net

CATSKILL MOUNTAIN RAILROAD
Train ride
Standard gauge

HARRY G. JAMESON III

Description: This railroad, which operates over trackage of the former Ulster & Delaware Railroad, offers a 6-mile, one-hour round trip to Phoenicia along the scenic Esopus Creek, through the heart of the beautiful Catskill Mountains. Tourists, inner-tubers, and visitors interested in fishing or canoeing may ride one way or round trip.

Schedule: Weekends and holidays. May 24 through September 1, 11 a.m. to 5 p.m.; September 6 through October 26, 12 to 4 p.m.

Admission/Fare: Adults, $7; children 4-11, $4; under age 4 are free.

Locomotives/Rolling Stock: No. 1, "The Duck," 1942 Davenport 38-ton diesel-mechanical, former U.S. Air Force; no. 2, "The Goat," H.K. Porter 50-ton diesel-electric, former U.S. Navy; no. 2361, 1952 Alco RS-1, former Wisconsin Central (Soo Line); former 1922 Erie Lackawanna coach.

Special Events: Twilight Limited excursions with music and refreshments at the Empire State Railway Museum; Teddy Bear Train; Leaf Peeper Specials; Halloween Train. Call for schedule.

Nearby Attractions: World's largest kaleidoscope. Tubing the Esopus Creek. Museums, sports activities, restaurants, lodging, campgrounds, state parks, scenic sites.

Directions: New York State Thruway, exit 19 (Kingston). Travel west 22 miles on Route 28 to the railroad depot in Mt. Pleasant.

Site Address: Route 28, Mt. Pleasant, NY
Mailing Address: PO Box 46, Shokan, NY 12481
Telephone: (845) 688-7400
Fax: (845) 657-7257
E-mail: spiegler@netstep.com

**NORTH CREEK RAILWAY
DEPOT MUSEUM**
Museum

TOM RYAN

Description: A restored 1872 train depot that houses a museum with exhibits on regional socioeconomic history, including the history of skiing at Gore Mountain, Theodore Roosevelt's ride to the presidency, mining, logging, and the railroad.

Schedule: May through October, Tuesday through Sunday, 10 a.m. to 4 p.m.

Admission/Fare: Free. Donations accepted. Group tours arranged.

Special Events: Call or check our website for schedule.

Nearby Attractions: Scenic gondola rides, garnet mine tours, Upper Hudson River Railroad Scenic Train Ride.

Directions: Exit 23 Northway to Route 28 to North Creek.

Site Address: 5 Railroad Pl., North Creek, NY
Mailing Address: PO Box 156, North Creek, NY 12853
Telephone: (518) 251-5842
Fax: (518) 251-5812
E-mail: mail@northcreekraildepot.org
Website: www.northcreekraildepot.org

New York, North Creek

UPPER HUDSON RIVER RAILROAD
Train ride, museum
Standard gauge

Description: A two-hour scenic trip along the Hudson River.

Schedule: First weekend in May through late October. Two runs daily in summer.

Admission/Fare: Adults, $12; seniors, $11; children 3-11, $8.

Locomotives/Rolling Stock: Alco RS-36 no. 5019; Alco S-1 no. 5; 1920s CN coaches, CNJ coach, open-air flatcar, LV caboose.

Special Events: Payroll Robberies, July and August Fridays at 1 p.m.; Race the Train, first Saturday in August.

Nearby Attractions: Lake George, with the Great Escape, is a half hour away; Gore Mountain is 5 minutes away; garnet mine tours are 10 minutes away; Adirondack Museum is 40 minutes away.

Directions: Interstate Take I-87 north to exit 23, then take Route 9 through Warrensburg, and Route 28 west 16 miles to North Creek.

Site Address: 3 Railroad Pl., North Creek, NY
Mailing Address: PO Box 343, North Creek, NY 12853
Telephone: (518) 251-5334
Fax: (518) 251-5332
E-mail: info@uhrr.biz
Website: www.uhrr.biz

BULLTHISTLE MODEL RAILROAD SOCIETY, INC., AND MUSEUM

Museum, display, layout

ERIC ROBB

Description: Featured are an operating HO layout of the O&W yards in Norwich circa 1950; O and S gauge antique train layouts; a modern N gauge layout; displays feature historically significant memorabilia.

Schedule: Year-round. Saturdays and Sundays, 1 to 4 p.m., or by appointment.

Admission/Fare: Donation of $2 per person appreciated.

Special Events: Railroad Days, June.

Nearby Attractions: Adirondack Scenic Railroad; Cooperstown & Charlotte Valley Railroad; Chenango County Museum; Northeast Classic Car Museum.

Directions: New York Route 12 to New York Route 23, turn east and go approximately two blocks. Museum is on the left 100 yards past railroad crossing. From east, New York Route 23 to Norwich. Museum is on the right before railroad crossing.

     M

Site Address: 33 Rexford St. (New York Route 23), Norwich, NY
Mailing Address: 33 Rexford St., Norwich, NY 13815
Telephone: (607) 334-7520
E-mail: eled@ascent.net

New York, Old Forge
Utica
Lake Placid
Saranac Lake

ADIRONDACK SCENIC RAILROAD
Train ride, museum
Standard gauge

Description: Rides from one hour to five hours round trip out of Utica, Thendara (one mile south of Old Forge), and Saranac Lake–Lake Placid. Outstanding depots.

Schedule: Varies. Phone (315) 369-6290 (Thendara), (315) 724-0700 (Utica), and (518) 891-3238 (Saranac Lake)

Admission/Fare: Adults, $8 to $28; children $4 to $14.

Locomotives/Rolling Stock: Locomotives: 705 EMD SW1; 8223 Alco RS3; 105 GE 44-ton; 2064 Alco C420; 1508 EMD F7; 4243 Alco C424; 1500 EMD F7; also many passenger cars and work cars (see our website).

Special Events: Rail Fan Days, train robberies, Model Railroad Shows, cocktail runs, Halloween and Santa runs, milk trains, murder mysteries, dinner trains, barbecue trains (see website).

Nearby Attractions: Old Forge Lake Cruises; McCauley Mountain Chairlift Rides; Arts Center/Old Forge; Old Forge Hardware; Enchanted Forest/Water Safari; Great Camp Sagamore; the Adirondack Museum; the W.W. Durant, Raquette Lake Navigation Co.; Adirondack Scenic Railroad, Return Trip. For Lake Placid/Saranac Lake attractions, visit our website.

Directions: Three locations–too complex–send for information.

*Coupon available, see coupon section.

Site Address: Thendara Station, Old Forge, NY; Union Station in Utica, NY; Lake Placid and Saranac Lake train stations
Mailing Address: PO Box 84, Thendara, NY 13472. **Phone:** See above.
Fax: (315) 369-2479
E-mail: train@borg
Website: www.adirondackrr.com

New York, Phoenicia

EMPIRE STATE RAILWAY MUSEUM
Museum, display, layout

Description: This is an all-volunteer membership organization dedicated to bringing alive the history of Catskill Mountain railroads, their people, and the towns they served. The museum is located in a former Ulster & Delaware railroad station, which celebrated its 100th anniversary in 1999.

Schedule: Memorial Day through Columbus Day: weekends and holidays, 11 a.m. to 4 p.m.

Admission/Fare: Suggested donation–adults, $3; seniors and students, $2; children under age 12, $1; families, $5.

Locomotives/Rolling Stock: No. 23, 1910 Alco 2-8-0, former Lake Superior & Ishpeming under restoration; 1920 D&H dining car "Lion Gardner"; 1926 CV autocarrier; 1920 B&M railway post office car.

Special Events: Photo exhibit, lectures, slide shows, Santa Claus Special

Nearby Attractions: Catskill Mountain Railroad, Delaware Ulster rail ride, New York state campgrounds at Woodland Valley and Wilson State Park, hiking, fishing in Catskill Forest Preserve, tube rides on Esopus Creek.

Directions: New York State Thruway to exit 19, then Route 28 west to Phoenicia.

Site Address: Off High St., Phoenicia, NY
Mailing Address: PO Box 455, Phoenicia, NY 12464
Telephone: (845) 688-7501
Website: www.esrm.com

RAILROAD MUSEUM OF LONG ISLAND, RIVERHEAD SITE
Train ride, museum, display
Standard and 16" gauge

Description: Display of three steam locomotives, eight rail cars, two speeders; miniature (16" gauge) 1964-65 World's Fair train ride around the site, museum, gift shop.

Schedule: Year-round, Saturdays, 10 a.m. to 4 p.m. Memorial Day to Columbus weekend, weekends and holidays, 10 a.m. to 4 p.m.

Admission/Fare: Adult, $2; children, $1; under 5, free.

Locomotives/Rolling Stock: Locomotives–LIRR/PRR, G5-S no. 39; LIRR/Alco, RS3 no. 1556; Defiance Coal Co./HK Porter, 0-4-0 no. 1. Railroad cars–LIRR/Alcoa, T62 double-deck passenger car no. 200 (world's first all-aluminum car); LIRR/Morrison International N-22B caboose no. C-68; LIRR/AM Car & Foundry, MB-62 motor RPO no. 4209; LIRR/ACF B-62 baggage no. 7727; LIRR/ACF MPB-54 combine no. 139; LIRR/ACF BM-62 baggage-mail no. 7737; other passenger cars; Reading/Sheffield track car (speeder) ca. 1920; CNJ track car.

Special Events: Railfest, weekend before Labor Day.

Nearby Attractions: Hallockville Museum Farm, aquarium, wineries, Peconic River cruises.

Directions: Long Island Expressway (I-495) exit 72 eastbound, go 4 miles east on New York Route 25 to Griffing Ave., turn north, go three blocks to museum at tracks.

        M

Site Address: 416 Griffing Ave., Riverhead, NY
Mailing Address: PO Box 726, Greenport, NY 11944-0726
Telephone: (631) 727-7920
Fax: (631) 261-6545 and (631) 757-5577 (voice confirmation)
E-mail: secretaryrmli@aol.com
Website: www.rmli.org

**NEW YORK MUSEUM
OF TRANSPORTATION**
Train ride, museum, layout
Standard gauge

CHARLES LOWE

Description: The site includes trolleys, rail and road vehicles, related artifacts and exhibits, an 11 x 21 operating HO model railroad, and a video/photo gallery. A 2-mile track car ride connects with the Rochester & Genesee Valley Railroad Museum, departing every half-hour.

Schedule: Museum–year-round, Sundays, 11 a.m. to 5 p.m. Groups by appointment. Ride–May through October, weather permitting.

Admission/Fare: Adults, $5; seniors, $4; students ages 5-15, $3. Includes entry to NYMT, Rochester & Genesee Valley Railroad Museum, and ride. Lower rates November through April.

Locomotives/Rolling Stock: Rochester & Eastern interurban car no. 157; North Texas Traction interurban car no. 409; P&W cars nos. 161 and 168; Elmira, Corning & Waverly no. 107; Philadelphia snow sweeper no. C-130; Rochester Railway no. 437; Batavia Street Railway no. 33; Alco 0-4-0 no. 47; Genesee & Wyoming caboose no. 8; more.

Special Events: Casey Jones Day, June; Model Steam and Gas Engines, July; Diesel Days, August.

Nearby Attractions: Finger Lakes Region, Niagara Falls, Arcade & Attica Railroad, Genesee Country Museum.

Directions: I-90, exit 46, south 3 miles on I-390, exit 11. Route 251 west 1.5 miles, right on E. River Rd., 1 mile to museum entrance.

        arm M

  Radio Frequency: 160.440

Site Address: 6393 E. River Rd., W. Henrietta, NY
Mailing Address: PO Box 136, W. Henrietta, NY 14586
Telephone: (585) 533-1113
Website: www.nymtmuseum.org

Description: This museum was established under the charter of the Ontario & Western Railway Historical Society in 1984 in a former Erie Railroad caboose. The O&W Railway Festival, first held in August of that year, has since become an annual event. The museum complex consists of an Erie Hack restored O&W caboose, watchman's shanties, the O&W station motif building, and Beaverkill Trout Car Museum. The museum contains displays of O&W memorabilia, other railroadiana, as well as local history displays that show the impact of the O&W on community life, hunting, fishing, farming, tourism, and local industry. The museum is maintained and operated by members of the Roscoe O&W Railway Museum. The Archives center of the history of the Ontario & Western Railway is located in Middletown, New York. For information, e-mail: artrobb@idsi.net.

Schedule: Memorial Day weekend through Columbus Day: weekends, 11 a.m. to 3 p.m.

Admission/Fare: Donations welcomed.

Special Events: O&W Railway Festival, July 12-13, 10 a.m. to 4 p.m.; O&W Penny Social, July 19.

Directions: 7 Railroad Ave.

Site Address: Historic Depot St., 7 Railroad Ave., Roscoe, NY
Mailing Address: PO Box 305, Roscoe, NY 12776-0305
Telephone: (607) 498-5500
E-mail: wilsip@wpe.com
Website: www.nyow.org/museum.html

SALAMANCA RAIL MUSEUM
Museum

Description: Fully restored BR&P depot and freight house. Artifacts and photographs tell the history of railroads in western New York and Pennsylvania. For children, the museum grounds offer the permanent display of a boxcar, a crew camp car, and the chance to explore two cabooses.

Schedule: April through December: Mondays through Saturdays, 10 a.m. to 5 p.m.; and Sundays, 12 to 5 p.m. Closed Mondays in April, October, November, and December.

Admission/Fare: Donations appreciated.

Locomotives/Rolling Stock: B&O caboose; P&WV caboose; Erie crane crew car; Conrail boxcar; Jordan spreader; DL&W electric commuter coach.

Nearby Attractions: Allegany State Park, Seneca Iroquois National Museum, Holiday Valley Summer-Winter Resort, Chautauqua Institution.

Directions: Downtown Salamanca on New York Route 17/U.S. I-86, Route 219.

Site Address: 170 Main St., Salamanca, NY
Mailing Address: 170 Main St., Salamanca, NY 14779
Telephone: (716) 945-3133

JOHN NEHRICH

Description: Five-hundred-foot-long railroad exhibit is a series of some 40-foot connected dioramas depicting historical sites in the upstate New York-Vermont area.

Schedule: Once a month on Saturday afternoon, 12 noon to 4 p.m. Check website or call for upcoming schedule.

Admission/Fare: $5 per person. The exhibit is not for children under 53 inches tall.

Directions: Located opposite Troy High, south of Route 7.

M

Site Address: Davison Hall basement, Burdette Ave.
Mailing Address: RMRRS, RPI Student Union, 110 8th St., Troy, NY 12180
Telephone: (518) 276-2971
Fax: (518) 276-6920
E-mail: mrrs@rpi.edu
Website: railroad.union.rpi.edu/railroad

PIEDMONT CAROLINA MUSEUM
Museum

VIRGIL HURLEY

Description: Our museum is located in a former Piedmont & Northern Railway depot. The outside display consists of railroad cars and a GE 25-ton diesel-electric switcher. The inside displays consist of various articles from the Piedmont & Northern Railway and the Southern Railway, as well as O scale model trains, an HO scale layout, and a gift area.

Schedule: Wednesdays through Saturdays, 10:30 a.m. to 4:30 p.m.; Sundays, 1:30 to 4:40 p.m.

Admission/Fare: Donations are accepted.

Locomotives/Rolling Stock: GE 25-ton diesel-electric switcher, formerly used by Duke Power at their River Bend steam station; Southern Railway caboose no. X662, built in 1951; sleeper-lounge car the "Keystone State," built by Pullman in 1955 for the New York, New Haven & Hartford; more.

Special Events: Third Saturday in May, Belmont's "Garibaldi Days" spring festival across the street in Stowe Park.

Nearby Attractions: Daniel Stowe Botanical Gardens in Belmont; Schiele Museum in Gastonia; Museum of the New South and Discovery Place in Charlotte; Carowinds amusement park in Charlotte on the North Carolina–South Carolina state line.

Directions: Belmont is 10 miles west of Charlotte; the museum is a mile off I-85 in the downtown area.

 M Charlotte

Site Address: 4 N. Main St., Belmont, NC 28012
Mailing Address: Piedmont Carolinas Chapter NRHS, PO Box 11753, Charlotte, NC 28220
Telephone: (704) 825-4403
Website: www.webserve.net/piedmont-nrhs

North Carolina, Blowing Rock

TWEETSIE RAILROAD
Train ride, museum
36" gauge

Description: Wild West theme park with ride on historic coal-fired narrow-gauge railroad. Admission includes amusement rides, live shows, deer park zoo, and many other attractions.

Schedule: May and October, Fridays and weekends. Memorial Day weekend through mid-August, daily.

Admission/Fare: Adults, $24; children ages 3-12, $18.

Locomotives/Rolling Stock: Baldwin 4-6-0 (1917, ex-ET&WNC); Baldwin 2-8-2 (1943, ex-WP&Y).

Special Events: Numerous special events throughout the year, including Thomas the Tank Engine (May 30 through June 8); Ghost Train Halloween Festival, Friday and Saturday nights in October. Details on our website.

Nearby Attractions: Located in a popular resort and vacation area, with many nearby scenic attractions, state and national parks, and the Blue Ridge Parkway.

Directions: Highway 321 between Boone and Blowing Rock.

†See ad on page A-16.

Site Address: Blowing Rock, NC
Mailing Address: PO Box 388, Blowing Rock, NC 28605
Telephone: (828) 264-9061
Fax: (828) 264-2234
E-mail: info@tweetsie.com
Website: www.tweetsie.com

NEW HOPE VALLEY RAILWAY
Train ride, museum, layout
Standard gauge

GRAY LACKEY

Description: Eight-mile round trip over 4 miles of the original Norfolk Southern Railway's Durham Branch with open cars and cabooses. Other equipment and displays at this site.

Schedule: May through December, first Sunday of the month. Departures at 12, 1, 2, 3, and 4 p.m.

Admission/Fare: Adults, $6; children, $4.

Locomotives/Rolling Stock: 80-ton GE and Whtcomb diesels; 45-ton GE diesel; 50-ton Whitcomb diesel; Vulcan 0-4-0T steam engine; cabooses, freight cars.

Special Events: Halloween Train, Santa Claus Train.

Nearby Attractions: Jordan Lake–camping, fishing, boating.

Directions: Eight miles south of Apex on State Route 1011. In Bonsal, turn right on Daisey St., 300 feet on left.

        M arm

Radio frequency: 160.425

Site Address: 5121 Daisey St., Bonsal, NC
Mailing Address: PO Box 40, New Hill, NC 27562
Telephone: (919) 362-5416
E-mail: nhvry@mindspring.com
Website: www.nhvry.org

RON ROMAN

Description: Smoky Mountain Trains Scenic Model Railroad Museum is home of the largest Lionel collection in the Carolinas! The 7,000-piece collection dates back to 1918. Museum highlights include a 24 by 45-foot operating layout containing over a mile of track and a children's activity center.

Schedule: March through December: Monday through Saturday, 8:30 a.m. to 5:30 p.m. Closed sundays.

Admission/Fare: Adults, $8; children under 12, $5; children under 3 free. Discounts may be available.

Special Events: Rail Fest, September 12-14, 2003.

Nearby Attractions: Great Smoky Mountains Railroad, Tweetsie Railroad, Great Smoky Mountains National Park, Blue Ridge Parkway, Cherokee Indian Reservation, Biltmore Estate, Harrah, Casino, whitewater rafting.

Directions: From North Carolina State Highway 74, taken exit 67 into downtown Bryson City. Smoky Mountain Trains is located next to the Great Smoky Mountains Railroad depot.

Site Address: 100 Greenlee St., Bryson City, NC
Mailing Address: PO Box 2390, Bryson City, NC 28713
Telephone: (828) 488-5200
Fax: (828) 488-3162
E-mail: smokymountaintrains@directway.com
Website: www.smokymountaintrains.com

CHARLOTTE TROLLEY, INC.
Trolley ride

Description: A 1.2-mile ride through the historic South End in a vintage streetcar.

Schedule: Year-round. Friday and Saturday, 10 a.m. to 9 p.m.; Sunday, 10 a.m. to 6 p.m.; leaving the barn on the hour and the half hour.

Admission/Fare: Round trip, $2; children, $1; handicap accessible.

Locomotives/Rolling Stock: No. 1 Charlotte Electric Railway by United Electric Car Co. 1914 for Piraeus, Greece; no. 13 Philadelphia Suburban Transp. by St. Louis Car Co. 1949 modified double-end PCC; no. 85 Southern Public Utilities homebuilt 1927; no. 407 South Carolina Power Co. JG Brill 1922 for Virginia Railway & Power Co. (Richmond); four-wheel Birney, was Virginia Railway & Power no. 1520 then Ft. Collins Municipal Railway no. 25-II; Ashville Power & Light no. 117 4-wheel Birney Brill 1927.

Special Events: Monthly pub crawl; annual gala; Volunteer Day, May 20 ; Labor Day barbecue.

Nearby Attractions: Restaurants, shops, galleries, tea house, antiques, and convention center.

Directions: South 1 mile from town on South Blvd. at Atherton Mill.

Site Address: 2104 South Blvd., Charlotte, NC
Mailing Address: 2104 South Blvd., Charlotte, NC 28203
Telephone: (704) 375-0850
Fax: (704) 375-0553
E-mail: clttrolley@aol.com
Website: www.charlottetrolley.org

North Carolina, Dillsboro   **GREAT SMOKY MOUNTAINS RAILROAD**
Train ride, dinner train
Standard gauge

LAVIDGE AND ASSOCIATES

Description: Departures from Dillsboro and Bryson City's historic depot, traveling through scenic mountains of North Carolina. Whitewater rafting packages, gourmet dinner and mystery theater trains.

Schedule: January through December: schedule varies with season. Call or write for schedule and reservations.

Admission/Fare: Adults, $28 and up; children under age 13, $14 and up. Varies seasonally. Steam excursions, add $7 per adult. Ages 21+, $8 upgrade to club car. Some lunch options.

Locomotives/Rolling Stock: No. 1702, 1942 Baldwin 2-8-0, former U.S. Army; nos. 711 and 777, EMD GP7s; nos. 210 and 223, EMD GP35s.

Special Events: Santa Express, featuring the story of "Polar Express," December; Day Out with Thomas event, July/August; spring and fall wine trains.

Nearby Attractions: Smoky Mountains National Park, Cherokee Indian Reservation, Biltmore Estate, whitewater rafting.

Directions: From Asheville, I-40 west to exit 27 to U.S. 74 west. Exit 81 for Dillsboro, or exit 67 for Bryson City. From Atlanta, 85 to 441 North.

†See ad on page A-10.

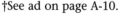

Site Address: 119 Front St., Dillsboro, NC or Depot St., Bryson City, NC
Mailing Address: PO Box 397, Dillsboro, NC 28725
Telephone: (800) 872-4681 and (828) 586-8811
Fax: (828) 586-8806
E-mail: traininfo@gsmr.com
Website: www.gsmr.com

NORTH CAROLINA TRANSPORTATION MUSEUM AT HISTORIC SPENCER SHOPS

Museum
Standard gauge

Description: Thirty-minute narrated train ride around the property. It is steam powered on weekends, April through Labor Day.

Schedule: April through October, museum open Monday through Saturday, 9 a.m. to 5 p.m. and Sundays, 1 to 5 p.m.; November through March, Tuesday through Saturday, 10 a.m. to 4 p.m. and Sundays, 1 to 4 p.m.

Admission/Fare: Train ride–adults, $5; seniors (60+) and children 3-12, $4. Turntable ride–$.50 per person.

Locomotives/Rolling Stock: SR E8 6900; SR FP76133; N&W GP9 620; SRGP302601–all operating. Several more locomotives and cars on display in roundhouse. Operating steam includes Graham County Shay 1925 and BC&G 2-8-0 no. 604.

Special Events: Rail Days, last weekend in April; Steamfest, September 29; A Day Out with Thomas (times vary from year to year).

Nearby Attractions: Dan Nicolas Park, Rowan Museum.

Directions: I-85 exit 79 (Spencer). Follow signs to museum.

Site Address: 411 S. Salisbury Ave., Spencer, NC
Mailing Address: PO Box 165, Spencer, NC 28159
Telephone: (704) 636-2889 and (800) NCTMFUN
Fax: (704) 639-1881
E-mail: nctm<nctrans@vnet.net>
Website: www.nctrans.org

CHARLES KERNAN

Description: Museum housed in the 1900 ACL freight office building. Interact with our extensive artifact collection, model train layouts (HO and Lionel), and children's hands-on learning area. Climb aboard the 1910 Baldwin steam locomotive and red caboose.

Schedule: March 15 through October 14: Monday through Saturday, 10 a.m. to 5 p.m.; Sunday, 1 to 5 p.m. October 15 through March 14: Monday through Saturday, 10 a.m. to 4 p.m.; Closed Thanksgiving, Christmas Eve, Christmas Day, New Year's Day, and Easter Sunday.

Admission/Fare: Adults, $3; seniors (60+)/military, $2.50; children 2-12, $1.50; under 2 and members are free; group rates available.

Locomotives/Rolling Stock: 1910 Baldwin steam locomotive 4-6-0 no. 250; SCL caboose no. 01036 as ACL no. 01983; 1963 RF&P boxcar no. 2379.

Special Events: Model Railroad Show, January; Azalea Festival, April; Riverfest, October.

Nearby Attractions: Battleship U.S.S. *North Carolina,* Fort Fisher State Historical Site, beaches, North Carolina Aquarium

Directions: I-40 east to Route 17 south.

*Coupon available, see coupon section.

 M arm

Site Address: 501 Nutt St., Wilmington, NC
Mailing Address: 501 Nutt St., Wilmington, NC 28401
Telephone: (910) 763-2634
Fax: (910) 763-2634 (call first)
Website: www.wilmington.org/railroad

**WESTERN MINNESOTA STEAM
THRESHERS REUNION**
Train ride

Description: One-and-a-half-mile train ride, operating turntable, scale steam train ride, steam threshing and plowing, steam sawmills, operating steam shovel, and large steam engines.

Schedule: Labor Day weekend, Friday through Monday, 8 a.m. to 8 p.m.

Admission/Fare: Daily ticket, $9; season ticket, $15; 14 years and under, free.

Locomotives/Rolling Stock: Ex Soo Line 0-6-0 switcher no. 353; a Porter 0-4-0; three wooden cabooses; 10 other cars.

Nearby Attractions: Fargo Moorhead, 35 miles; museums, Maplewood State Park, lakes, and campgrounds.

Directions: At Rollag, Minnesota, 10 miles south of Hawley, Minnesota, on Highway 32.

        M

Mailing Address: 2610 First Ave., Fargo, ND 58102
Telephone: (701) 232-4484
Website: www.rollag.com

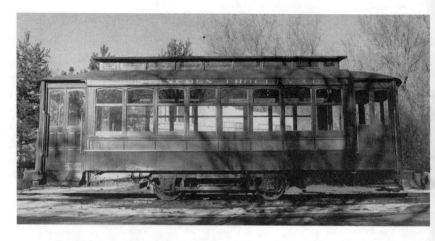

Description: A 9-mile round trip from Mandan to Fort Abraham Lincoln State Park along the Heart River. We have a restored American Car Co. streetcar and an eight-bench open car.

Schedule: Memorial Day through Labor Day: daily departures at 1, 2, 3, 4, 5 p.m.

Admission/Fare: Adults, $5; children 5-10, $3; under 5 are free.

Locomotives/Rolling Stock: American Car Co. streetcar no. 102; eight-bench open car.

Nearby Attractions: Fort Lincoln State Park, Lewis and Clark Riverboats, Mandan Railroad Museum.

Directions: I-94 to Highway 1806 to Third St. SE; east on Third St. SE about five blocks.

Site Address: Third St. SE, Mandan, ND
Mailing Address: 29 Captain Leach Dr., Mandan, ND 58554
Telephone: (701) 663-9018

North Dakota, Mandan

NORTH DAKOTA STATE RAILROAD MUSEUM
Museum, display, layout
Standard gauge

Description: Our museum resides on five acres in northwest Mandan. We have a large collection of railroad artifacts from the region, along with ten pieces of rolling stock, speeder shacks, semaphores, and a 16-ton yard mule from BN.

Schedule: Memorial Day through Labor Day, 1 to 5 p.m. daily.

Admission/Fare: Free.

Locomotives/Rolling Stock: BN 16-ton yard mule; Soo caboose no. 282; BN caboose no. 10411; Soo tank car no. 22511; Soo boxcar no. 135452; BN caboose no. 12591; NP boxcar no. 202124; NP flatcar no. 64027; NP reefer no. 92015; NP boxcar no. 14303; NP boxcar no. 37713.

Nearby Attractions: Trolley, Fort Lincoln State Park, NP Missouri River bridge; Raging Rivers Amusement Park; North Dakota Heritage Center.

Directions: I-94 exit 152, north to Old Red Trail, left to 37th St., left to 30th Ave.

      M

Site Address: 3102 37th St. NW, Mandan, ND
Mailing Address: PO Box 1001, Mandan, ND 58554-1001
Telephone: (701) 663-9322
E-mail: railroad@bix.midco.net
Website: www.geocities.com/ndsrm

North Dakota, Minot

OLD SOO DEPOT TRANSPORTATION
MUSEUM & WESTERN HISTORY
RESEARCH CENTER
Museum

DENNIS LUTZ, M.D.

Description: A museum and research center in a completely restored 1912 Soo Line Depot. The museum focuses on transportation history of the American West, including GN, NP, Soo, Milwaukee Road, and Amtrak.

Schedule: Call or write for information.

Admission/Fare: Donations accepted.

Locomotives/Rolling Stock: Burlington Northern Santa Fe, Canadian Pacific, and Amtrak trains frequently operate beside or across from the building.

Nearby Attractions: Taube Art Museum, Railroad Museum of Minot, Charlie's Main Street Cafe, Dragon Delight.

Directions: North end of Main St. in downtown Minot, along the main line of the Canadian Pacific and Burlington Northern Sante Fe Railroads.

Site Address: 15 N. Main St., Minot, ND
Mailing Address: PO Box 2148, Minot, ND 58702
Telephone: (701) 852-2234

RAILROAD MUSEUM OF MINOT
Museum, layout

Description: Our mission is to preserve, share, and experience this history and future of the region's railroads. We have a 25-foot On30 layout and a 175-foot HO layout.

Schedule: Monday through Wednesday and Friday, 10 a.m. to noon and 1 to 4 p.m.

Admission/Fare: Donations accepted.

Locomotives/Rolling Stock: Burlington caboose no. 12183; Soo Line caboose no. 32; speeder cars; baggage cart; a 50-ton snowplow converted from a locomotive steam tender.

Special Events: Railroad Days, second Friday and Saturday of June; Family Day, last weekend of August.

Nearby Attractions: Soo Line Depot and Carnegie Center.

Directions: Go east on Central Ave., then turn left on First St. NE next to the Soo Line tracks.

Site Address: 19 First St. NE, Minot, ND
Mailing Address: PO Box 74, Minot, ND 58703-0074
Telephone: (701) 852-7091

North Dakota, West Fargo

BONANZAVILLE U.S.A.
Museum
Standard gauge

R.A. YOUNG

Description: The museum includes two vintage train depots; 1883 Northern Pacific no. 684 steam locomotive, the last of the 4-4-0 steam engines; a 1930s Pullman car, a caboose, and a 100-year-old velocipede.

Schedule: Memorial Day through Labor Day: Monday through Saturday, 9 a.m. to 5 p.m.; Sunday, noon to 5 p.m.

Admission/Fare: Adults, $6; children, $3.

Locomotives/Rolling Stock: Northern Pacific steam locomotive no. 684; 1930s Pullman car; caboose; snowplow; velocipede.

Special Events: Wings 'n Wheels, June; Wild West Jamboree, July; Pioneer Days, August.

Nearby Attractions: Red River Zoo, Fargo Air Museum, Heritage Center.

Directions: I-94 in Fargo; located in West Fargo.

*Coupon available, see coupon section.

Site Address: 1351 W. Main Ave., West Fargo, ND
Mailing Address: PO Box 719, West Fargo, ND 58078
Telephone: (701) 282-2822
Fax: (701) 282-7606
E-mail: info@bonanzaville.com
Website: www.bonanzaville.com

Ohio, Bellevue   **MAD RIVER & NKP RAILROAD SOCIETY, INC.**
Museum, display, layout

GEORGE LEADER

Description: Steps and open doors welcome all who come to the hands-on museum.

Schedule: Memorial Day through Labor Day: daily, 1 to 5 p.m.; May, September, and October: weekends only.

Admission/Fare: Adults (age 13 and up), $5; children (4 to 12), $3; under age 4 are free.

Locomotives/Rolling Stock: Alco RSD 12 NKP no. 329; EMD GP30 NKP no. 900; FM H1244 Milw. no. 740; Wabash F7 diesel no. 671; PRR RPO car; NKP dynamometer car; three NKP cabooses; N&W caboose; troop sleeper car; refrigerator cars; four passenger cars, including the first dome car built; and various other cars and equipment.

Special Events: Limited number of bus/rail tours throughout the year. Call for information. Guided tours, if scheduled in advance.

Nearby Attractions: Cedar Point Amusement Park, Sorrowful Mother Shrine, Seneca Caverns, Historic Lyme Village.

Directions: Two blocks south of downtown. Follow our green signs.

Site Address: 353 Southwest St., Bellevue, OH
Mailing Address: 233 York St., Bellevue, OH 44811-1377
Telephone: (419) 483-2222
E-mail: madriver@onebellevue.com
Website: www.onebellevue.com/madriver/

CARROLLTON-ONEIDA-MINERVA RAILROAD
ELDERBERRY LINE
Train ride
Standard gauge

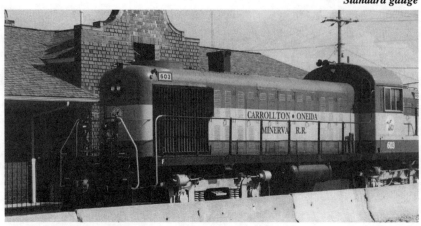

Description: Travel 14 miles between Carrollton and Minerva through areas of light industry, farmland, marshland, and forest, with a one-hour layover in Minerva. The train ride is 28 miles round trip.

Schedule: Mid-June through October: weekends. December: Christmas runs. Call for information and schedules.

Admission/Fare: Adults, $12; children 2-12, $9. Group rates available.

Locomotives/Rolling Stock: 1952 Alco RS-3 locomotive; 1926 ES New Jersey coach; three 1937 coaches, former Canadian.

Special Events: Fall Foliage, October. Christmas trains start Thanksgiving weekend.

Nearby Attractions: Atwood Lodge, sailing, fishing, Pro Football Hall of Fame, McKinley's monument.

Directions: Site is 100 miles south of Cleveland, 25 miles south of Canton, and 60 miles west of Pittsburgh, Pennsylvania.

Site Address: 203 Second St. NW, Carrollton, OH
Mailing Address: 203 Second St. NW, Carrollton, OH 44615
Telephone: (330) 627-2282
Fax: (330) 627-3624
E-mail: elderbrr@raex.com
Website: www.elderberryline.com

DALE W. BROWN

Description: The railroad club is located in a former Cincinnati Union Terminal (CUT) control tower. We have a few museum items.

Schedule: Thursdays, 8 p.m. to 10:30 p.m.; Saturdays, 10 a.m. to 5 p.m.

Admission/Fare: Free. We ask for donations.

Nearby Attractions: Bengals football, Cincinnati Reds baseball, zoo, Newport Aquarium, Kings Island Amusement Park.

Directions: Take I-75 to exits 2A, 1H, or 1F; at Ezzard Charles Drive.

Site Address: 1301 Western Ave., Cincinnati, OH
Mailing Address: PO Box 14157, Cincinnati, OH 45242-7142
Telephone: (513) 561-RAIL (7245)
Website: www.cincinnatirrclub.org

CONNEAUT RAILROAD MUSEUM
Museum
Standard gauge

DALE W. BROWN

Description: Displays of railroad memorabilia and an HO scale model railroad.

Schedule: Memorial Day through Labor Day, daily, 12 to 5 p.m.

Admission/Fare: Donations appreciated.

Locomotives/Rolling Stock: No. 755, 1944 Lima 2-8-4, former Nickel Plate; a 90-ton hopper car and a wooden caboose, both former Bessemer & Lake Erie.

Nearby Attractions: Within a mile of Lake Erie.

Directions: In the old New York Central station at Depot and Mill streets, north of U.S. 20 and I-90. Blue-and-white locomotive signs point the way to the museum.

Site Address: Conneaut, OH
Mailing Address: PO Box 643, Conneaut, OH 44030
Telephone: (440) 599-7878

**THE DENNISON RAILROAD
DEPOT MUSEUM**
*Train ride, museum, layout
N scale*

Description: The museum, restaurant, and gift shop are housed in a restored 1873 Pennsylvania Railroad depot. Train rides from May through December: all-day excursions, murder mysteries, fall foliage trips, and holiday trips.

Schedule: Year-round, Tuesdays through Saturdays, 11 a.m. to 5 p.m. Sundays, 11 a.m. to 3 p.m. Tours by appointment.

Admission/Fare: Range from $7 to $100.

Locomotives/Rolling Stock: See website: www.ohiocentralrr.com for train ride rolling stock. On display: 1940s Thermos Bottle Vulcan engine; caboose; freight cars; C&O engine no. 2700.

Special Events: Railroad festival, third week of May.

Nearby Attractions: Amish Country, Roscoe Village, Zoar and Schoennbrunn (Ohio Historical Society sites).

Directions: Located halfway between Columbus, Ohio, and Pittsburgh, Pennsylvania, 18 miles east of I-77 and 36 miles north of I-70. At the junction of Routes 250, 36, and 800.

Site Address: 400 Center St., Dennison, OH
Mailing Address: PO Box 11, Dennison, OH 44621
Telephone: (740) 922-6776
Fax: (740) 922-0105
E-mail: depot@tusco.net
Website: www.dennisondepot.org

Description: Carvings of the evolution of the steam engine, carved of ivory, ebony, and walnut.

Schedule: Daily, 9 a.m. to 5 p.m. Closed major holidays.

Admission/Fare: Adults, $8.50; students (6-17), $4.

Nearby Attractions: Gateway to Ohio's Amish Country.

Directions: I-77 exit no. 83, east on Route 211 ¼ mile.

          M

Site Address: 331 Karl Ave., Dover, OH
Mailing Address: 331 Karl Ave., Dover, OH 44622
Telephone: (330) 343-7513
Fax: (330) 343-1443
E-mail: info@warthers.com
Website: www.warthers.com

Ohio, Findlay

**NORTHWEST OHIO RAILROAD
PRESERVATION, INC.**
Train ride, display
15" gauge

Description: Live steam 2-6-2 Prairie-type locomotive with open-seat coaches. The ride is approximately one mile.

Schedule: Call or write for information; we are under construction.

Locomotives/Rolling Stock: 1950s Plymouth locomotive; 1890s boxcar; several motorcars (speeders).

Nearby Attractions: Amusement parks, museums, restaurants, campgrounds, state park, scenic sites.

Directions: Northeast corner of I-75 and County Road 99, exit 161.

      M

Site Address: 11600 County Rd. 99, Findlay, OH
Mailing Address: 11600 County Rd. 99, Findlay, OH 45840-9601
Telephone: (419) 423-2995
Fax: (419) 423-4258
E-mail: nworrp@bright.net
Website: www.nworrp.org

Ohio, Hebron   **BUCKEYE CENTRAL SCENIC RAILROAD**
Train ride
Standard gauge

Description: We offer a scenic 1.5-hour round-trip excursion through the rolling hills of central Ohio on the historic Shawnee branch of the old B&O. Travel in vintage passenger coaches or in the open-air gondola. On your journey pass over a steel bridge and two trestles.

Schedule: Memorial Day weekend through mid-October: weekend departures at 1 and 3 p.m.

Admission/Fare: Adults, $7; children (2-12), $5.

Locomotives/Rolling Stock: SW-1 no. 8599; open gondola; four Canadian National coaches.

Special Events: Haunted Halloween Trains, Santa Claus Specials, Wild West/Train Robbery. Call for dates.

Nearby Attractions: Flint Ridge State Park, Buckeye Lake, Dawes Arboretum, Heissy Museum, the Olde Mill, village of Granville.

Directions: I-70, exit Route 13N to Route 40, turn left; or I-70, exit Route 79N to Route 40, turn right. Located on Route 40.

   M

Site Address: 5475 National Road (U.S. Route 40) Hebron, OH
Mailing Address: PO Box 601, Hebron, OH 43025
Telephone: (740) 366-2029
Fax: (614) 891-5847
Website: www.buckeyecentralrailroad.org

Ohio, Independence

Description: The *Scenic Limited* is a 1¾-hour round-trip excursion to the historic village of Peninsula, through the Cuyahoga Valley National Park. Our longer (6½-hour round-trip) excursions go through the park to downtown Akron. Spend the day at Hale Farm and Village or Stan Hywet Hall and Gardens, or visit Quaker Square or Inventure Place.

Schedule: Akron trip–June through August and October, weekends and Wednesdays, 10 a.m. *Scenic Limited*–June through December, weekends; June through August and October, also Wednesdays through Fridays; train departs at 10:15 a.m. and 1 p.m.

Admission/Fare: Akron trip–adults, $20; seniors, $18; children 3-12, $12. *Scenic Limited*–Adults, $11; seniors, $10, children, $7.

Locomotives/Rolling Stock: FPA-4 nos. 14, 15, 800, 6767; 44-ton switcher no. 21; C420 no. 365; RS-18 road/switcher no. 1822; more.

Special Events: Valentine's Day, maple sugaring, Easter Bunny, wine trains, Mother's and Father's Days, 4th of July, fall foliage, Christmas and Santa trains, many more. Call for dates and times.

Directions: Take I-77 to exit 155. Go east on Rockside Rd. 1.2 miles to Canal Rd. Go north on Canal Rd. one block, then turn west on Old Rockside Rd. Boarding site is ⅒ mile on the left.

*Coupon available, see coupon section.

  ♿ Ⓟ 🚌 ✳ ☕ 🎪 🚂 M

Site Address: 1664 W. Main St., Peninsula, OH
Mailing Address: PO Box 158, Peninsula, OH 44264
Telephone: (800) 468-4070
Fax: (330) 657-2080
E-mail: cvsr@cvsr.com
Website: www.cvsr.com

Ohio, Jefferson

AC&J SCENIC LINE RAILWAY
Train ride
Standard gauge

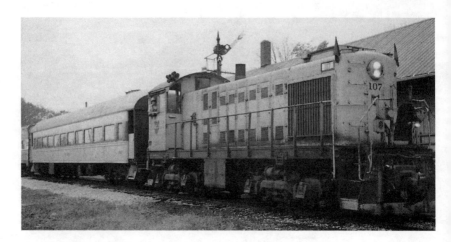

Description: Enjoy a one-hour 12-mile round trip over the last remaining portion of the New York Central's Ashtabula-to-Pittsburgh "High Grade" passenger line. Ride in vintage passenger cars pulled by a first-generation diesel. A family educational adventure.

Schedule: June 14 through October 26, weekends: departures at 12:30, 2, and 3:30 p.m. No reservations needed.

Admission/Fare: Adults, $8; seniors (60+), $7; children (3 to 12), $6; under age 3 are free when not occupying a seat.

Locomotives/Rolling Stock: Alco S2 no. 107; Alco S2 no. 518; Nickel Plate caboose no. 427; Erie Stillman coach no. 1024; Long Island coaches nos. 7133 and 7136; EL AMF baggage car no. 201.

Special Events: Santa Train, December 6 and 7.

Nearby Attractions: Adjacent Jefferson Depot, Victorian Perambulator Museum, Geneva-on-the Lake, Pymatuning Resort area.

Directions: I-90 from east/west exit Ohio 11 south, to Ohio 46 and south to Jefferson, left at second light on E. Jefferson St. to tracks. Or north on Route 11, exit 307 west to Jefferson, right at second light to tracks.

Site Address: E. Jefferson St. at tracks, Jefferson, OH
Mailing Address: PO Box 517, Jefferson, OH 44047-0517
Telephone: (440) 576-6346
Fax: (440) 576-8848
E-mail: acjrscenic@earthlink.net
Website: acjrailroad.com

JEFFERSON DEPOT, INC.
Museum

Description: Jefferson Depot is a restored 1872 Lake Shore & Michigan Southern Railroad station/museum. It features a 1918 PRR caboose, a quaint 1848 church, circuit-rider barn, an 1838 one-room schoolhouse, and a general store; train rides are next door.

Schedule: June through September, Sundays, 1 to 4 p.m. Group tours by appointment. Buses welcome.

Admission/Fare: Adults, $2; children, free.

Special Events: Strawberry Festival and Craft Bazaar, June; fall foliage train/bus trip, October.

Nearby Attractions: Jefferson Depot Historic Village, campgrounds, Pymatuning State Park.

Directions: From I-90, south on I-11 to State Route 46 south to E. Jefferson St. From I-11, north to State Route 307 west to State Route 46 north, to E. Jefferson St.

            M

Site Address: 147 E. Jefferson St., Jefferson, OH
Mailing Address: PO Box 22, Jefferson, OH 44047
Telephone: (440) 293-5532 and (352) 343-8256
E-mail: duttonjg@hotmail.com
Website: http://members.tripod.com/jeffersonhome

Ohio, Marblehead

TRAIN-O-RAMA
Museum, layout

Description: Train-O-Rama is Ohio's largest operating multi-gauge train layout. It is also a gift/hobby store.

Schedule: Year-round; Mondays through Saturdays, 11 a.m. to 5 p.m.; Sundays, 1 to 5 p.m. Extended summer hours: Mondays through Saturdays, 10 a.m. to 6 p.m.; Sundays 1 to 5 p.m.

Fare/Admission: Adults, $5; seniors, $4; children (4-11), $3.

Nearby Attractions: Near East Harbor State Park and Lake Erie Islands; also near Cedar Point.

Directions: State Route 2 to State Route 269 north to Route 163 east. E. Harbor Rd. is Route 163 east.

*Coupon available, see coupon section.

Site Address: 6732 E. Harbor Rd., Route 163 E., Marblehead, OH
Mailing Address: 6732 E. Harbor Rd., Marblehead, OH 43440
Telephone: (419) 734-5856
Fax: (419) 660-0133
E-mail: mail@trainorama.net
Website: www.trainorama.net

MARION UNION STATION ASSOCIATION
Museum, layout

Description: This museum and model railroad club is a train viewer's paradise. Sixty to 70 CSX-NS freight trains pass by daily on average, to the north, south, east, and west.

Schedule: Year-round, Tuesdays through Fridays, 10 a.m. to 2 p.m. May through September, most weekends, 2 to 5 p.m. Model Railroad–Sundays, 2 to 4 p.m.

Admission/Fare: Donations appreciated ($2 per person suggested).

Locomotives/Rolling Stock: Erie/EL caboose no. C-306; 3-ton Plymouth model TLC; AC interlocking tower.

Special Events: Chicken barbecue, first Sunday in October. Model train show, first Saturday in December.

Nearby Attractions: Call Visitor's Bureau at (800) 371-6688.

Directions: Route 309 on west side of Marion (between railroad tracks).

Site Address: 532 W. Center St., Marion, OH
Mailing Address: 532 W. Center St., Marion, OH 43302
Telephone: (740) 383-3768
Fax: (740) 383-3768
E-mail: unionstation@marion.net

**LUCAS COUNTY/MAUMEE VALLEY
HISTORICAL SOCIETY**
Museum

Description: Our costumed docents will be pleased to provide you with a personally guided tour of five historic buildings, including the Clover Leaf Depot (ca. 1888) and caboose.

Schedule: April through December: Wednesdays through Sundays, 1, 2, and 3 p.m.

Fare/Admission: Adults $5; seniors, $4; students, $2.50.

Locomotive/Rolling Stock: Caboose and baggage car.

Nearby Attractions: Fort Meigs State Memorial, Toledo Museum of Art, Toledo Zoo.

Directions: Take Anthony Wayne Trail to Key St. Dead end into River Rd., left on River Rd.

*Coupon available, see coupon section.

    M

Site Address: 1031 River Rd., Maumee, OH
Mailing Address: 1031 River Rd., Maumee, OH 43537
Telephone: (419) 893-9602
Fax: (419) 893-3108
E-mail: mvhs@accesstoledo.com
Website: mvhs@accesstoledo.com

Ohio, Nelsonville

HOCKING VALLEY SCENIC RAILWAY
Train ride, museum
Standard gauge

Description: Hocking Valley Scenic Railway offers a 14-mile round trip at 12 noon and a 22-mile round trip at 2:30 p.m. All regular scheduled trains stop at an 1850s village for 30 minutes.

Schedule: Memorial weekend through first weekend in November: weekends, 12 and 2:30 p.m. Santa Trains: last weekend in November and first three weekends in December; Santa Trains depart at 11 a.m. and 2:30 p.m.

Admission/Fare: 12 p.m.–adults, $8, children 3-12, $5; 2:30 p.m.–adults, $11, children 3-12, $7. Santa trains–adults, $11, children 3-12, $7.50. Fare is subject to change without prior notice.

Locomotives/Rolling Stock: GP7 C&O 5833; BLH switcher 4005; GE 45-ton Industrial 7315; B&O combine "City of Athens"; three RI commuter cars, "City of Logan," "City of Nelsonville," and "Village of Haydenville"; 1941 60-ton center cab Whitcombe.

Special Events: Check website.

Nearby Attractions: Hocking Hills area; Old Man's Cave, campgrounds, Lakes hiking trails Nelsonville; Victorian Square, restored 1800s opera house, famous Dew Hotel, Robbins Crossing 1850s village.

Directions: From Columbus take U.S. 33 east to Nelsonville to the second traffic signal on the right. (U.S. 33 is Canal St. in Nelsonville.)

Site Address: 33 Canal St., Nelsonville, OH
Mailing Address: PO Box 427, Nelsonville, OH 45764
Telephone: (800) 967-7834 and (614) 470-1300
Fax: (740) 753-1152
Website: www.hvsr.com

Ohio, Olmsted Township

TROLLEYVILLE, U.S.A.
Train ride, museum,
Standard gauge

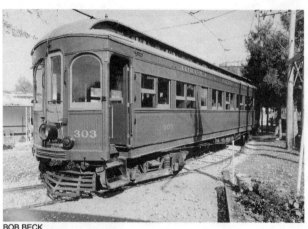

BOB BECK

Description: Streetcars and miscellaneous railroad equipment are on display. The museum is located in the 1875 restored B&O Berea Depot. Ride on over 2.5 miles of track.

Schedule: May through November: weekends. June through September: Wednesdays, Fridays, and weekends.

Admission/Fare: Adults, $5.50; seniors, $4.50; children 3-11, $3.50; 2 and under, free.

Locomotives/Rolling Stock: Thirteen streetcars; 13 interurban; four work cars and locomotives; two boxcars; two cabooses; miscellaneous motorcars.

Special Events: Easter Egg Hunt, 4th of July, Train Shows, Halloween.

Nearby Attractions: Cedar Point, Geauga Lake Amusement Park, Six Flags, Rock and Roll Hall of Fame, Museum of Science and Industry.

Directions: I-480, exit 6A, 2 miles south, west side of road in shopping center.

 **Radio frequency: 43.7**

Site Address: 7100 Columbia Rd., Olmsted Township, OH
Mailing Address: 7100 Columbia Rd., Olmsted Township, OH 44138
Telephone: (440) 235-4725
Fax: (440) 427-1431
E-mail: cliff@trolleyvilleusa.org
Website: www.trolleyvilleusa.org

**ORRVILLE RAILROAD
HERITAGE SOCIETY**
Train ride, museum, display
Standard gauge

ROBERT CUTTING

Description: Mainline trips, all-day rides, 50 to 120 miles in length.

Schedule: Depot open Saturdays, May through October, 10 a.m. to 4 p.m. Trips vary year to year. Send for information.

Admission/Fare: Depot tours, no charge. Mainline trips, fares vary per trip.

Locomotives/Rolling Stock: Ex-New Haven GP-9 PRR; N5C caboose; five Budd passenger coaches; ex-Amtrak baggage car; privately owned caboose and passenger cars; switch block tower.

Special Events: Depot Days, second weekend of June; Open House, Friday and Saturday after Thanksgiving.

Nearby Attractions: Amish Country; Rubbermaid store; Smucker Jam and Jelly store.

Directions: Twelve miles south of I-76; 3 miles north of Route 30, on Route 57.

      M

Site Address: 145 Depot St., Orrville, OH
Mailing Address: PO Box 11, Orrville, OH 44667
Telephone: (330) 683-2426
Fax: (330) 682-2426
Website: www.orrvillerailroad.com

Ohio, Sandusky

**CEDAR POINT &
LAKE ERIE RAILROAD**
Train ride

DAN FEICHT

Description: The Cedar Point and Lake Erie (CP&LE) railroad is a 15-minute train ride that covers a two-mile trip around the Frontiertown section of Cedar Point Amusement Park/resort.

Schedule: To be determined.

Admission/Fare: To be determined.

Locomotives/Rolling Stock: "Myron H."1922 Vulcan 0-4-0 rebuilt as 2-4-0; "Albert" 1910 Davenport 2-6-0; "George R." 1942 H.K. Porter Co. 0-4-0 rebuilt as 2-4-0; "Jennie K." 1909 H.K. Porter Co. 1-4-0 rebuilt as 2-4-0; "Judy K." Vulcan 0-4-0 rebuilt as 2-4-0.

Site Address: 1 Cedar Point Dr., Sandusky, OH
Mailing Address: 1 Cedar Point Dr., Sandusky, OH 44870-5259
Telephone: (419) 627-2350
Fax: (419) 627-2200
E-mail: BEdwards@cedarpoint.com
Website: www.cedarpoint.com

Ohio, Sugar Creek

DOYLE YODER

Description: One-hour narrated rides through Ohio's scenic Amish Country.

Schedule: First Saturday in May through last Saturday in October. Monday through Saturday, closed Sundays. Departure times: 11 a.m., 12:30, 1 and 3:30 p.m.

Admission/Fare: Adults, $9; children (3-12), $6; groups of 15 or more, $7.50 a person; schools (15 or more students), $5 a person.

Locomotives/Rolling Stock: Steam engines Ohio Central no. 1551; Ohio Central no. 1293.

Nearby Attractions: Sugar Creek, known for its Swiss heritage, has restaurants, arts and craft shops, golf course, and a village smithy.

Directions: Take I-77 to exit 83. Go west 6 miles to the traffic light and turn left. Go two blocks to the downtown depot.

†See ad on page A-7.

        TRAIN

Site Address: 111 Factory St., Sugar Creek, OH
Mailing Address: PO Box 427, Sugar Creek, OH 44681
Telephone: (866) 850-4676
Fax: (330) 852-2989
Website: www.amishsteamtrain.com

Ohio, Waterville

TOLEDO, LAKE ERIE & WESTERN RAILWAY AND MUSEUM
Train ride

Description: A 60-minute round-trip train ride between Grand Rapids, Ohio, and Waterville, including a ride across the 909-foot-long Maumee River bridge.

Schedule: May through October, weekends, 1, 2:30, and 4 p.m. June through August, Wednesdays and Thursdays, 10:30 a.m., 12 noon, and 1:30 p.m. All trains depart Grand Rapids.

Admission/Fare: Adults, $8; seniors, $7; children (3-12), $4.50.

Locomotives/Rolling Stock: 1948 Alco S-2.

Special Events: Call or check our website for information on specially scheduled trains.

Directions: The Grand Rapids depot is at Third and Mill Streets next to the Warehouse Antique Mall.

*Coupon available, see coupon section.

Site Address: 49 N. Sixth St., Waterville, OH
Mailing Address: PO Box 168, Waterville, OH, 43566
Telephone: (419) 878-2177
E-mail: info@tlew.org
Website: www.tlew.org

Ohio, Worthington

OHIO RAILWAY MUSEUM
Train ride, museum
Standard gauge

DAVE BUNGE

Description: Museum offers a 3-mile round trip on historic trolley-interurban cars.

Schedule: May through October: Sundays, 1 to 5 p.m.

Admission/Fare: Adults, $4; seniors and children, $3.

Locomotives/Rolling Stock: N&W no. 578 Pacific Steam; OPS no. 21 interurban; passenger cars, street cars, and interurbans.

Special Events: Ghost Trolley, Santa Trolley, State Fair, Twilight Trolley Excursions.

Nearby Attractions: Ohio Historical Museum, Polaris Amphitheatre, Columbus Zoo.

Directions: I-71 to State Route 161 exit, west to Worthington.

    M arm

Site Address: 990 Proprietors Rd., Worthington, OH
Mailing Address: Box 777, Worthington, OH 43085
Telephone: (614) 885-7345
Website: www.ohiorailwaymuseum.org

Oklahoma, Bartlesville (Ramona)

THE TRAIN HOUSE
Display, layout

Description: Trains, trains, and more trains running everywhere! Exhibits include an outdoor G scale garden railroad, a 28 x 48-foot Lionel layout, HO and N scale layouts, and a wagon-train ride through the park.

Schedule: March 15 through September 15: Tuesdays through Saturdays, 10 a.m. to 5 p.m.; Sundays, by appointment. September 15 through March 15: by appointment only.

Admission/Fare: Donations appreciated.

Special Events: Main Line Train Show, first Saturday after 4th of July.

Nearby Attractions: Osage State Park, Woolrock and Woolrock Museum and Buffalo Ranch, Mainline Train Show.

Directions: U.S. 75 to County Road 2700, east 2 miles to stop sign, north 1.5 blocks to entrance.

Site Address: 26811 N. 3990 Rd., Ramona, OK
Mailing Address: 26811 N. 3990 Rd., Ramona, OK 74061
Telephone: (918) 335-2360
E-mail: mariphiloo@aol.com

JOHNNY'S TRAINS
Museum, layout

Description: Our museum of working trains includes a 30 x 40-foot layout with a circus, mountains, and lakes.

Schedule: Year-round, daily, 9 a.m. to 5 p.m.

Admission/Fare: Free; donations appreciated.

Special Events: Cherokee Strips Days, September.

Nearby Attractions: Cherokee Strip Museum; Perry, Oklahoma, is 10 miles away.

Directions: On I-35 to exit 185. Go 10 miles west on Highway 164 and ¼ mile south.

Site Address: Route 1, Box 113, Covington, OK
Mailing Address: Route 1, Box 113, Covington, OK 73730
Telephone: (580) 336-2823

RAILROAD MUSEUM OF OKLAHOMA
Museum, display, layout
Standard gauge

ROBERT CHESTER

Description: This museum, housed in a 1926-27 former Santa Fe freight-house, has one of the largest collections of railroad memorabilia in the midwest. It is focused on preserving historically significant railroad equipment. Recapture the essence of railroad days as you climb aboard a 1925 steam locomotive, wander through cabooses from eight different railroads, and view 12 different types of freight cars.

Schedule: Year-round: Tuesday through Friday, 1 to 4 p.m. Saturdays, 9 a.m. to 1 p.m. Sundays, 2 to 5 p.m. Other times by appointment.

Admission/Fare: A donation of $2 per person is suggested.

Locomotives/Rolling Stock: 1925 Frisco Baldwin 4-8-2 no. 1519; operable 1965 GE 50-ton class BB switcher; renovated BN, NP, RI, MoP, SF, SL&SF, MK&T, and UP cabooses; 1928 automobile boxcar; 1937 three-dome riveted tank car; 1930 boxcar; 1920 gondola with arch-bar trucks.

Special Events: Two model railroad swap meets; Christmas party; Railroad Appreciation Day, April; two caboose excursions each year.

Nearby Attractions: Water park, winery, Science and Discovery Center; Cherokee Strip, Midgley, and Heritage museums.

Directions: Enid is 30 miles west of I-35 in north central Oklahoma on Routes 60, 81, 64, 412. The museum is six blocks northwest of the downtown square.

Site Address: 702 N. Washington, Enid, OK
Mailing Address: 702 N. Washington, Enid, OK 73701
Telephone: (580) 233-3051

Oklahoma, Oklahoma City

KIRKPATRICK AIR SPACE MUSEUM AT OMNIPLEX
Museum, display

Description: The Toy Train Collection features the M.G. Martin Model Train Exhibit, a complete 1,000-square-foot layout that features several toy trains running through a miniature town, including an industrial, agricultural, and amusement area. The layout is maintained and operated by the Toy Train Operating Society, Sooner Division. Our full-size Parlor Car is a 1929 Missouri Pacific Railroad Car built by the Pullman Company and used for executive business. The car has four staterooms, three bathrooms, a dining salon, an observation parlor, a kitchen, and an open observation platform.

Schedule: Museum exhibits open Labor Day through Memorial Day: Tuesday through Friday, 9 a.m. to 5 p.m.; Saturday, 9 a.m. to 6 p.m.; Sunday, 11 a.m. to 6 p.m. Memorial Day through Labor Day: Monday through Saturday, 9 a.m. to 6 p.m.; Sunday, 11 a.m. to 6 p.m.

Admission/Fare: Museum–adults, $7.50; seniors, $6.75; children 6-12, $6; children 3-5, $5.

Nearby Attractions: National Cowboy and Western Heritage Museum, Oklahoma City Zoo, Remington Rack horse racing facility, Softball Hall of Fame, Oklahoma Firefighters Museum.

Directions: Take I-35 to N.E. 50th St. The museum is next door to the Oklahoma City Zoo and directly across from Remington Park.

Site Address: 2100 N.E. 52nd St., Oklahoma City, OK
Mailing Address: 2100 N.E. 52nd St., Oklahoma City, OK 73111
Telephone: (405) 602-6664
Fax: (405) 602-3766
E-mail: ncoggins@omniplex.org; omnipr@omniplex.org
Website: www.omniplex.org

319

Oklahoma, Waynoka

WAYNOKA AIR-RAIL MUSEUM
Museum

WAYNOKA HISTORICAL SOCIETY

Description: The museum, located in a restored Harvey House, has exhibits on the Santa Fe Railroad, Transcontinental air transport, Harvey Houses and Fred Harvey, Railways Ice Co., Waynoka Sand and Gravel Co., German prisoner-of-war paintings, and much more.

Schedule: Tuesday through Friday, 12 noon to 5 p.m. Fridays and Saturdays, 6 to 8 p.m.

Admission/Fare: Adults, $2; children are free.

Locomotives/Rolling Stock: Hudson Bay Railway no. 2511 locomotive built by EMD.

Nearby Attractions: Little Sahara State Park and Curtis Hill for train-watching (50 to 100 trains pass the museum daily).

Directions: From Oklahoma City, west on I-40 to Watonga; take Highway 3 to Seiling, and US 281 north to Waynoka. From Tulsa, west on Highway 412 to U.S. 281, then north 12 miles to Waynoka.

       M

Site Address: 202 S. Cleveland, Waynoka, OK
Mailing Address: PO Box 193, Waynoka, OK 73860
Telephone: (580) 824-1886
E-mail: waynokahs@hotmail.com
Website: www.waynoka.org

YUKON'S BEST RAILROAD MUSEUM
Museum

JOHN SHANNON

Description: The museum contains an extensive display of railroad antiques and artifacts of the Rock Island Line and other railroads.

Schedule: Year-round by chance or appointment. Call or write for information.

Admission/Fare: Free.

Locomotives/Rolling Stock: Rock Island boxcar no. 5542; UP caboose no. 25865.

Directions: On historic Route 66. Main St., across from "Yukon's Best Flour" wheat elevator.

Site Address: Third and Main Streets, Yukon, OK
Mailing Address: 410 Oak Ave., Yukon, OK 73099-2640
Telephone: (405) 354-5079

Oregon, Canby

BERGMAN PHOTOGRAPHY

Schedule: Thursday through Sunday, 1 to 4 p.m. Closed January and February.

Admission/Fare: Free. Donations accepted.

Locomotives/Rolling Stock: Caboose no. HMS7810M.

Special Events: Pancake Breakfast, July 4th. Open House, September. Antique Appraisals, October and April.

Nearby Attractions: Clackamas County Fairgrounds (fair in August), Molalla River State Park, Canby Ferry Crossing, Willamette River, Flower Farmer Miniature Train Rides.

Directions: Highway 99 East and Pine St. Seven miles south of Oregon City.

       M

Site Address: 888 N.E. Fourth Ave., Canby, OR
Mailing Address: PO Box 160, Canby, OR 97013
Telephone: (503) 266-6712
Fax: (503) 266-9775
E-mail: depotmuseum@canby.com
Website: www.canby.com/chamber/depot/depot.htm

Oregon, Canby

PHOENIX & HOLLY RAILROAD
Train ride
15" gauge

FLOWER FARMER

Description: Visitors can ride through acres of flowers at the Flower Farmer and enjoy a 1¾-mile ride with a stopover at "Box Curve" station and pet the farm animals (July through September).

Schedule: May through October: weekends and holidays, 11 a.m. to 6 p.m. Weekdays, groups only. October: open daily, Pumpkin Patch Trips; Haunted Train Rides, last three weeks of October, dusk to 9 p.m.

Admission/Fare: Adults, $3.50; children age 12 and under and seniors (65+), $3. Groups, weekdays by appointment. October Haunted Trains–adults, $3.50; children $3.

Locomotives/Rolling Stock: "Sparky" the diesel locomotive purpose-built; diesel locomotive 5.5" scale; DRG&W side-rod diesel; gondolas; flatcar; caboose.

Special Events: Pumpkin Run to pumpkin patch, month of October. Haunted Train Rides, Christmas lights.

Nearby Attractions: Swan Island, Dahlia Farm, Canby Ferry, state parks, city parks, golf. Swan Island Dahlia Festival, last two weeks in August.

Directions: I-5 to Canby exit, to Holly St., turn left one mile to site.

Site Address: 2512 N. Holly St., Canby, OR
Mailing Address: 2512 N. Holly St., Canby, OR 97013-9118
Telephone: (503) 266-3581
Fax: (503) 263-4027
E-mail: lgarre@canby.com
Website: www.narrowgaugerr.com

**MOUNT HOOD RAILROAD AND
DINNER TRAIN**
Train ride, dinner train
Standard gauge

Description: Built in 1906, this historic railroad takes passengers on four-hour tours from the Columbia Gorge to the foothills of Mt. Hood. The trip aboard the Excursion Train–comprised of 1910-20 Pullman coaches, concession car, and caboose–is narrated one way. The 1940s Dinner & Brunch Train offers excellent four-course dining. Special events occur throughout the year.

Schedule: April through December. Excursion Train–10 a.m. and 3 p.m. Brunch Train–11:50 a.m. Dinner Train–Friday, 6:30 p.m., Saturday, 5:30 p.m. (4:30 p.m. October through December).

Admission/Fare: Excursion Train–adults, $22.95; seniors, $20.95; children, $14.95. Brunch Train–$56. Dinner Train–$69.50. Murder Mystery Dinner Trains–$79.50.

Locomotives/Rolling Stock: Two GP 9s; 1910 and 1920 Pullmans; 1940s dining cars.

Special Events: Festivals, Train Robberies, Circus Train, Christmas Tree Trains, Murder Mystery Trains

Nearby Attractions: Mt. Hood, Columbia River National Scenic Area, biking, hiking, wind surfing, golf, historic hotels.

Directions: Sixty miles east of Portland on I-84, exit 63 right to Cascade St., left to parking lot.

Site Address: 110 Railroad Ave., Hood River, OR
Mailing Address: 110 Railroad Ave., Hood River, OR 97031
Telephone: (800) TRAIN-61 (872-4661) and (541) 386-3556
Fax: (541) 386-2140
E-mail: www.mthoodrr@gorge.net
Website: www.mthoodrr.com

Oregon, Lake Oswego

OREGON ELECTRIC RAILWAY
HISTORICAL SOCIETY
Train ride
Standard

BOB SPARKES

Description: Scenic ride along the river, through a tunnel and over trestles, with some street running in Portland.

Schedule: May through September: Fridays through Sundays and holidays, weather permitting; 10 a.m., 12 noon, 2 and 4 p.m.

Admission/Fare: Round trip–Adults, $8; seniors, $7; children, $4.

Locomotives/Rolling Stock: Blackpool double-deck trolley no. 48; Portland Traction Brill master unit no. 813.

Special Events: Fourth of July fireworks special; Boat Light Parade specials, December (dates variable).

Nearby Attractions: Tillamook Restaurant, Lake Oswego access road, Willamette River along route, tunnel and two high trestles.

Directions: Take I-5 to exit 292, and east to Lake Oswego. The depot is on State St. (east side, south of A St.). Or take I-205 to West Linn and Route 43 north to Lake Oswego.

*Coupon available, see coupon section.

Site Address: 311 N. State St., Lake Oswego, OR
Mailing Address: 3995 Brooklake Rd. NE, Brooks, OR 97303
Telephone: (503) 697-7436
Website: www.trainweb.org

Oregon, Portland

WASHINGTON PARK & ZOO RAILWAY
Train ride
30" gauge

GEORGE BAETJER

Description: Four-mile round trip from the zoo through Washington Park, to the Portland rose gardens and Japanese garden. The Oregon Zoo runs the railway.

Schedule: Seasonal, Memorial Day through September 30.

Admission/Fare: There is an admission fee for the zoo and an additional charge for the train ride. Train ride round trip–adults, $2.75; seniors (65+) and children (3-11), $2.

Locomotives/Rolling Stock: Steam locomotive no. 1; Virginia & Truckee replica; diesel locomotive no. 2, GM Aerotrain replica; diesel locomotive no. 5, "Oregon Express."

Nearby Attractions: Oregon Zoo, Portland Rose Gardens, Japanese Gardens, International Forestry Center, Portland Children's Museum.

Directions: Two miles west of Portland City Center, on U.S. Highway 26. Zoo is on MAX light rail line; get off at Washington Park Station.

       Radio frequency: 151.655

Site Address: Oregon Zoo, 4001 SW Canyon Rd., Portland, OR
Mailing Address: Oregon Zoo, 4001 SW Canyon Rd., Portland, OR 97221
Telephone: (503) 226-1561
Fax: (503) 525-4235
Website: www.oregonzoo.org

326

Oregon, Redmond

CROOKED RIVER DINNER TRAIN
Dinner train
Standard gauge

Description: Three-hour, 38-mile round trip through the scenic Crooked River Valley. A four-course meal is served by characters from the Wild West and a murder mystery or train robbery is performed.

Schedule: Year-round on weekends.

Admission/Fare: Adults, $63 to $75 per person; children 4-12, $39; children 3 and under, $20.

Locomotives/Rolling Stock: 1940s Milwaukee Road railcars.

Special Events: New Year's Eve party train; holiday brunch trains, Easter; holiday mystery trains, December. Railroad Days (with Shay steam engine), September. Mother's Day, Father's Day, Thanksgiving.

Nearby Attractions: Smith Rock State Park, High Desert Museum, Newberry Crater, Lava Cast Forest, Crater Lake.

Directions: Located near intersection of Highway 97 and O'Neil Junction. Follow the signs.

Site Address: 4075 N.E. O'Neil Rd., Redmond, OR
Mailing Address: PO Box 387, Redmond, OR 97756
Telephone: (541) 548-8630
Fax: (541) 548-8702
E-mail: dintrain@coinet.com
Website: www.crookedriverrailroad.com

Oregon, Sumpter Valley

SUMPTER VALLEY RAILROAD
Train ride, museum
36" gauge

Description: A 5-mile one-way or 10-mile round trip.

Schedule: Memorial Day through September: McEwen, 10 a.m., 12:30, and 3 p.m. Sumpter, 11:30 a.m. and 2 p.m. One way only at 4:30 p.m.

Admission/Fare: Adults, round trip, $9, and one way, $6; children 6-16, $6.50/$4.50; families, $20/$15.

Locomotives/Rolling Stock: No. 19 Mikado (oil/steam); no. 3 Heisler (wood/steam); no. 101 diesel switcher; nos. 1101 and 1102 open-air cars; no. 20 coach; no. 5 caboose; nos. 1101 and 1102 Sumpter Valley Ry.; no. 19 American (Sumpter Valley Ry.); no. 3 Heisler (W.H. Eccles Lumber Co.); no. 20 E.M. Eccles; no. 5 Sumpter Valley Ry.; work cars, gondola cars, cabooses, and more.

Special Events: Night trains, round trip with dinner and entertainment: July through September, first Saturdays of each month. Flea market in Sumpter, major holidays in summer.

Nearby Attractions: Oregon Interpretive Center/Museum, Oregon Trail Museum, Phillips Lake with camping.

Directions: Highway 7, 22 miles southwest of Baker City off I-84.

Site Address: Dredge Loop Rd., McEwen, OR
Mailing Address: PO Box 389, Baker City, OR 97814
Telephone: (541) 894-2268 and (541) 523-3453
E-mail: lmcx@eoni.com
Website: www.svry.com

Pennsylvania, Altoona

ALTOONA RAILROADERS
MEMORIAL MUSEUM
Train ride, museum, display, layout
Standard gauge

PETER D. BARTON

Description: America's newest interactive railroad museum reflecting the life and labor of railroad workers.

Schedule: April through October: daily, 9 a.m. to 5 p.m.; November through March: Tuesdays through Sundays, 9 a.m. to 5 p.m. Closed Mondays.

Admission/Fare: Adults, $8.50; seniors, $7.75; children ages 5-18, $5. Combination ticket with Horseshoe Curve National Historic Landmark–adults, $10; seniors, $9; children, $5.50.

Locomotives/Rolling Stock: PRR K4s no. 1361 locomotive; PRR/General Electric GG1 no. 4913; Vulcan Iron Works saddle tank locomotive no. 2826; Baldwin Locomotive Works diesel electric VO-660 no. 6712; Pullman; the "Loretto," private car of Charles Schwab.

Special Events: Railfest, first weekend in October. Holiday program late November and December; call for details. There are programs for youth available.

Nearby Attractions: Horseshoe Curve National Historic Landmark, Allegheny Portage Railroad National Historic Site, East Broad Top Railroad, DelGrosso's Family Park.

Directions: Take I-99 to exit 33.

Site Address: 1300 Ninth Ave., Altoona, PA
Mailing Address: 1300 Ninth Ave., Altoona, PA 16602
Telephone: (814) 946-0834
Fax: (814) 946-9457
E-mail: admin@railroadcity.com
Website: www.railroadcity.com

**PIONEER TUNNEL COAL MINE
AND STEAM TRAIN**
Train ride
Narrow gauge

Description: Scenic ride along the Mahanoy Mountain behind a steam locomotive of the 0-4-0 type built in 1927 by the Vulcan Iron Works of
Wilkes-Barre, Pennsylvania. Guides tell the story of strip mining, boot-
legging and the Centralia Mine Fire. Also available is a tour of a real
anthracite coal mine in open mine cars pulled by a battery-operated
mine motor. Mine guides tell the story of anthracite coal mining.

Schedule: April: weekday mine tours, 11 a.m., 12:30 and 2 p.m. Memorial
Day through Labor Day: daily mine tours and steam train, 10 a.m. to 6
p.m. May, September, October: weekday mine tours, 11 a.m., 12:30 and
2 p.m.; train tours for reserved groups only; weekend mine and train
tours run continuously.

Admission/Fare: Steam train–adults, $5.50; children under age 12, $4.
Mine–adults, $7.50; children under age 12, $5. Group discounts.

Locomotives/Rolling Stock: A spare "lokie" of the 0-4-0 type built by
Vulcan Iron Works; two battery-powered mine motors.

Special Events: Eleventh Annual Pioneer Day, August 16; coal mine tours,
steam train rides, large craft fair, ethnic foods, live music, more.

Nearby Attractions: Pennsylvania Museum of Anthracite Mining.

Directions: I-81, exit 124B (Frackville). Route 61 north to Ashland.

Site Address: 19th and Oak Streets, Ashland, PA
Mailing Address: 19th and Oak Streets, Ashland, PA 17921
Telephone: (570) 875-3850
Fax: (570) 875-3301
Website: www.pioneertunnel.com

Pennsylvania, Bellefonte   **BELLEFONTE HISTORICAL**
                                                      RAILROAD
                                                  Train ride
                                                 Standard gauge

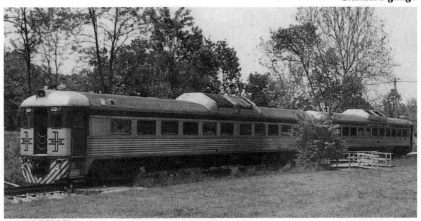

W.M. RUMBERGER

Description: Scheduled and special trips over the 60-mile Nittany & Bald
Eagle Railroad to Lemont, Vail (Tyrone), and Mill Hall. Fall foliage and
Christmas runs offered. The Bellefonte Station, a restored former Pennsylvania Railroad structure built in 1888, houses an operating N gauge
layout of the Bellefonte-Curtin Village route, as well as historical photos
and memorabilia of area railroading. A snowplow and caboose under
restoration are displayed beside the station.

Schedule: May 30 through September 30: weekends and holidays. October
and December: special runs only. Call for information.

Admission/Fare: Adults, $8 and up; children 3-11, $5 and up.

Locomotives/Rolling Stock: No. 9167, 1952 RDC-1; and 1962 No. 1953;
air-conditioned passenger cars. Can be configured for meal service.

Special Events: Spring, Fall, Christmas trains.

Nearby Attractions: Curtin Village, Bald Eagle State Park, Penn State
University, Victorian Bellefonte, Historic Boalsburg, Penns Cave.

Directions: Central Pennsylvania, less than 5 miles from exit 23 and 24,
I-80.

Site Address: The Train Station, Bellefonte, PA
Mailing Address: 320 W. High St., Train Station, Bellefonte, PA 16823
Telephone: (814) 355-0311
Fax: (814) 353-0511
E-mail: countyseat@aol.com

Pennsylvania, Gallitzin   **ALLEGHENY PORTAGE RAILROAD**
NATIONAL HISTORIC SITE
Museum
Standard gauge

NATIONAL PARK SERVICE

Description: This site preserves the remains of the incline railway used to portage canal boats over the Allegheny Mountains. It includes the original railroad trace, inclines, and levels. The park visitor center (film, exhibits, and models) is open year-round. The park also includes the Lemon House Tavern, Engine House Exhibit Shelter, and Staple Bend Tunnel, the first railroad tunnel built in this country.

Schedule: Year-round, daily, 9 a.m. to 5 p.m. Closed Veteran's Day, Thanksgiving, Christmas, New Year's Day, Martin Luther King's Birthday, and President's Day.

Admission/Fare: Adults 17 and older, $3; national park passes honored.

Nearby Attractions: Gallitzin Tunnels, Horseshoe Curve and Altoona Railroad Museum.

Directions: U.S. Route 22, Gallitzin exit, 10 miles west of Altoona.

Site Address: 110 Federal Park Rd., Gallitzin, PA
Mailing Address: 110 Federal Park Rd., Gallitzin, PA 16641
Telephone: (814) 886-6150
Fax: (814) 886-6117
Website: www.nps.gov/alpo/

GETTYSBURG SCENIC RAILWAY
Train ride, museum, display
Standard gauge

Description: Depart from the historic 1884 depot that welcomed thousands of Civil War veterans back to Gettysburg, and enjoy a nostalgic two-hour excursion to Aspers, passing through the renowned Adams County apple orchards. Visit our website for more information and to purchase tickets on line. Special event trains are scheduled throughout the year.

Schedule: June through August: Tuesdays through Sundays, departures every afternoon with an additional evening train on Saturdays. Off-peak season: weekends with afternoon departures.

Admission/Fare: Adults, $20; children 4-15, $10; 3 and under, free; special group rates available.

Locomotives/Rolling Stock: Locomotive PREX 401 EMD F-7A, formerly B&LE 726A; locomotive PREX 402 EMD F-7A, formerly C&NW 406; double-decker open car; combine/snack car; six celestial-roofed heavyweight passenger cars.

Special Events: Civil War Train Raids, July and September; Railfan Package Tour, November; Easter, Apple Harvest, Ghost, and Santa Trains; more.

Nearby Attractions: Renowned Civil War sites and breathtaking scenery. Many fine campgrounds, unique shops, and restaurants.

Directions: Depot is one block off the square in downtown Gettysburg.

Site Address: 106 N. Washington St., Gettysburg, PA
Mailing Address: 106 N. Washington St., Gettysburg, PA 17325
Telephone: (717) 334-6932
Fax: (717) 334-0291
E-mail: scenic@gettysburgrail.com
Website: www.gettysburgrail.com

Pennsylvania, Greenville

GREENVILLE RAILROAD
PARK AND MUSEUM
Museum

Admission/Fare: Free admission.

Locomotive/Rolling Stock: Static equipment. World's largest steam switch locomotive built in 1936 by Baldwin 0-10-2 S/N 61910; antique Erie flatcar; B&LE iron ore car; UP caboose; Wheeling & Lake Erie caboose and B&LE caboose.

Nearby Attractions: Deer and Animal Park, Pymatuning State Park and Dam, Canal Museum, Thiel College, Coneaut Lake Park.

Directions: Fourteen miles east of I-79; 22 miles north of I-80.

Site Address: 314 Main St., Greenville, PA
Mailing Address: 314 Main St., Greenville, PA 16125
Telephone: (724) 588-4004

STOURBRIDGE LINE
RAIL EXCURSIONS
Train ride
Standard gauge

Description: Scenic round-trip rides from Honesdale to Hawley (24 miles) and Honesdale to Lackawaxen-on-the-Delaware (50 miles). The ride parallels the shimmering Lackawaxen River and closely follows the route of the Delaware & Hudson Canal.

Schedule: Easter through early December, on scheduled weekends.

Admission/Fare: Varies by ride.

Locomotive/Rolling Stock: 1949 EMD BL2 no. 54, former Bangor & Aroostook.

Nearby Attractions: Claws 'n Paws Wild Animal Park, Wayne County Historical Society and Museum Shop, Dorflinger Glass Museum, Lake Wallenpaupack, historic downtown Honesdale.

Directions: Northeastern Pennsylvania, 24 miles from Scranton.

Site Address: 303 Commercial St., Honesdale, PA
Mailing Address: 303 Commercial St., Honesdale, PA 18431
Telephone: (570) 253-1960 and (800) 433-9008
Fax: (570) 253-1322
E-mail: waynecoc@sunlink.net
Website: www.waynecountycc.com and www.stourbridgerail.com

**OLD MAUCH CHUNK MODEL
TRAIN DISPLAY**
Layout

Description: This exciting HO scale model train display features 13 separate trains, some pulling as many as 50 railroad cars over nearly 1,100 feet of track. The meticulously designed display also incorporates over 200 scale buildings, 100 bridges, 1,000 streetlights, and moving automobiles into its scenery.

Schedule: Year-round. Call for current hours of operation.

Admission/Fare: Adults, $3; seniors, $2; children, $1; age 4 and under free.

Special Events: Many Jim Thorpe celebrations throughout the year.

Nearby Attractions: Many attractions in the area.

Directions: Located on the second floor of the Hooven Mercantile Company building on Route 209 next to the railroad station at Packer Park in historic Jim Thorpe.

*Coupon available, see coupon section.

Site Address: 41 Susquehanna St. (Route 209), Jim Thorpe, PA
Mailing Address: 68 White Pine Ln., Lehighton, PA 18235-9612
Telephone: (570) 325-4371 and (570) 386-2297
E-mail: jttraindon@yahoo.com
Website: www.geocities.com/omchotd

Pennsylvania, Jim Thorpe

JOHN M. SIMKOVICH

Description: Yesterday's Train Today is a 40-minute ride; the Lake Hauto Special is a 1½-hour ride; our Flaming Foliage Rambles are 2¾ hours.

Schedule: Yesterday's Train Today–mid-May through September, weekends and holidays, 12 noon, 1, 2, and 3 p.m. Lake Hauto Special–July through Labor Day, weekends and holidays, 3 p.m. Flaming Foliage Rambles–October, weekends, 10 a.m. and 2:30 p.m.

Admission/Fare: Yesterday's Train Today–adult, $6; children, $4. Lake Hauto Special–adult, $9; children, $4.50. Flaming Foliage Rambles–Adult, $15; children, $8.

Locomotives/Rolling Stock: CNJ (EMD) F-3 nos. 56 and 57; Conrail (EMD) GP-10 nos. 7545, 7579, and 7580; CP D-10 4-6-0 no. 1098.

Special Events: Easter Bunny Trains, April 18-19; Fall Foliage Festival, October 11-12; Santa Claus Trains, December 6-7, 13-14.

Directions: From I-476, get off at exit 34/74 and go south on Route 209 for 6 miles. From I-80, get off at exit 304 and go north on route 209 for 33 miles.

Radio frequency: 161.2950 and 161.3100

Site Address: 4 Lehigh Ave., Jim Thorpe, PA
Mailing Address: 2434 Butler St., Easton, PA 18042-5303
Telephone: (570) 325-4606
Fax: (610) 250-0968
E-mail: viscount745d@epix.net
Website: www.railtours-inc.com

WANAMAKER, KEMPTON & SOUTHERN, INC.

Train ride
Standard gauge

Description: A 6-mile, 40-minute round trip through scenic Pennsylvania Dutch country over part of the former Reading Company's Schuylkill & Lehigh branch. Restored stations relocated from Joanna and Catasauqua, Pennsylvania; original circa 1874 Wanamaker station; operating HO gauge model layout (Sundays).

Schedule: May through October, weekends. Call or write for detailed schedule.

Admission/Fare: Adults, $6; children 3-11, $3; age 2 and under ride free.

Locomotives/Rolling Stock: No. 2, 1920 Porter 0-4-0T, former Colorado Fuel & Iron; no. 65, 1930 Porter 0-6-0T, former Safe Harbor Water Power; no. 7258 1942 GE diesel electric 45-ton, former Birdsboro Corp.; coaches nos. 1494 and 1474 and combine no. 408, all former Reading Company; coach no. 582, former Lackawanna; assorted freight cars and caboose, former Lehigh & New England; steel and wood cabooses, former Reading.

Special Events: Mother's Day Special, Kids' Fun Weekend, Harvest Moon Special, Halloween Train, Santa Claus Special. Write for schedule.

Nearby Attractions: Hawk Mountain, Crystal Cave.

Directions: Depot is located at Kempton on Routes 143 or 737, a short distance north of I-78. The site is 20 miles west of Allentown.

Site Address: 42 Community Center Rd., Kempton, PA
Mailing Address: PO Box 24, Kempton, PA 19529
Telephone: (610) 756-6469
E-mail: info@kemptontrain.com
Website: www.kemptontrain.com

Pennsylvania, Lancaster

**DUTCH WONDERLAND FAMILY
AMUSEMENT PARK**
Train ride
24" gauge

Description: A 48-acre amusement park geared to families with a variety of rides and attractions. Live shows include the Great American High Diving Show. The Wonderland Special has seating for 56 guests and is a scenic 7-minute ride through the park. We also offer a monorail ride.

Schedule: Spring and fall, weekends; Memorial Day through Labor Day, daily.

Nearby Attractions: Discover Lancaster County History Museum, Old Mill Stream Camping Manor, Wonderland Mini-Golf, Outlets (Tanger and Rockvale).

Directions: Four miles east of Lancaster on Route 30.

Site Address: 2249 Route 30E, Lancaster, PA
Mailing Address: 2249 Route 30E, Lancaster, PA 17602
Telephone: (717) 291-1888 and (866)-FUN at DW (toll-free)
Fax: (717) 291-1595
E-mail: infodw@dutchwonderland.com
Website: www.dutchwonderland.com

Pennsylvania, Marienville

KNOX & KANE RAILROAD
Train ride
Standard gauge

Description: This line offers one round trip each operating day to Kane and the Kinzua Bridge over a former Baltimore & Ohio branch line. Passengers may board at Marienville for a 96-mile, 8-hour trip or at Kane for a 32-mile, 3½-hour trip. The 2,053-foot-long, 301-foot-high Kinzua Bridge, built in 1882 to span the Kinzua Creek Valley, was at the time the highest bridge in the world. It is on the National Register of Historic Places and is a National Historic Civil Engineering Landmark.

Schedule: June and September: Friday through Sunday. July and August: Tuesday through Sunday. Early October: Wednesday through Sunday. Depart Marienville 8:30 a.m.; depart Kane 10:30 a.m.

Admission/Fare: From Marienville–adults, $22; children, $14. From Kane–adults, $16; children, $9. Advance reservations suggested. Box lunches available by advance order, $5.75.

Locomotives/Rolling Stock: No. 38, 1927 Baldwin 2-8-0, former Huntington & Broad Top Mountain; no. 58, Chinese 2-8-2 built in 1989; no. 39, GP-9 built in 1957; Porter Switcher no. 1; steel coaches; open cars; two snack and souvenir cars.

Directions: In northwestern Pennsylvania, about 20 miles north of I-80.

Site Address: S. Forest St., Marienville, PA
Mailing Address: PO Box 422, Marienville, PA 16239
Telephone: (814) 927-6621
Fax: (814) 927-8750
E-mail: info@knoxkanerr.com
Website: www.knoxkanerr.com

MIDDLETOWN & HUMMELSTOWN RAILROAD

Train ride, dinner train, museum
Standard gauge

WENDELL DILLINGER

Description: An 11-mile, 1¼-hour round trip through Swatara Creek Valley with narration and singalongs.

Schedule: Memorial Day through Labor Day, weekends; Thursdays and Fridays in May; Tuesdays, Thursdays, Saturdays, and Sundays in July and August; Sundays only in September; weekends in October.

Admission/Fare: Adults, $10; children 3-11, $5. Add $1 on steam weekends. Special events train pricing varies.

Locomotives/Rolling Stock: Regular train consist: GE 65-ton nos. 1 and 2 with DL&W coaches; freight locomotives NSS Alco T6 no. 1016; WM Alco S6 no. 151; CN 2-6-0 no. 91; three SEPTA PCCs; more.

Special Events: Sweetheart Special; Easter Express; Mother's Special; Colonial Craft Fair; Moonlight Specials; Barbecue Express; Train Robberies; "Civil War Remembered" re-enactment; Fall Foliage Specials and Haunted Trains; Santa Express and New Year's Eve Celebration Train; Hawaiian Luau and '50s Follies Buffet Trains.

Nearby Attractions: Hershey Park, Chocolate World, Pennsylvania Dutch Country, Gettysburg Battlefield.

Directions: Pennsylvania Turnpike, exit 19 to Route 283 to Middletown and Hummelstown exit; go south, turn right on Main St., left on Race St.

Site Address: Race St., Middletown, PA, at railroad track
Mailing Address: 136 Brown St., Middletown, PA 17057
Telephone: (717) 944-4435, ext. 0
Fax: (717) 944-7758
E-mail: riderail@ptdprolog.net
Website: www.800padutch.com/mhrr.html and www.mhrailroad.com

Pennsylvania, New Hope

NEW HOPE & IVYLAND RAILROAD
Train ride, dinner train
Standard gauge

Description: Enjoy a 50-minute, 9-mile round trip to Lahaska, Pennsylvania, and return. Passengers can ride in coach, open-air car, or air-conditioned parlor car.

Schedule: Year-round. Call or visit website for schedule.

Admission/Fare: Adults, $10; seniors, $9; children, $7; under age 2, $1.50.

Locomotives/Rolling Stock: Lancaster & Chester Baldwin Consolidation no. 40; Conrail Penn Central Pennsylvania EMD GP30 no. 2198; CSX family lines GE C30-8 no. 7087.

Special Events: Easter Trains, Father's Day cab ride giveaways; Train Robbery; Halloween trains, Santa Claus trains.

Nearby Attractions: Downtown New Hope, Lambertville, Peddlers Village.

Directions: Take I-95 to New Hope exit 51. Go north 10 miles into downtown New Hope. Turn left on Bridge Street, go one block, and the driveway is on the right.

Site Address: 32 W. Bridge St., New Hope, PA
Mailing Address: 32 W. Bridge St., New Hope, PA 18938
Telephone: (215) 862-2332
Fax: (215) 862-2150
Website: www.newhoperailroad.com

Pennsylvania, North East

LAKE SHORE RAILWAY MUSEUM
Museum, display

RODNEY BLYSTONE

Description: A restored New York Central passenger station built in 1899 by the Lake Shore & Michigan Southern houses an extensive collection of displays. The museum is adjacent to CSX and NS main lines. A passenger/freight station built in 1869 by LS&MS is also on the grounds.

Schedule: Memorial Day through Labor Day: Wednesdays through Sundays, noon to 4 p.m. April 19 through May 25, September, and October: weekends, noon to 4 p.m.

Admission/Fare: Donations appreciated.

Locomotives/Rolling Stock: NYC U25B no. 25001 CSS&SB "Little Joe" electric locomotive; no. 8202 Heisler fireless 0-6-0; heavyweight Pullman sleeping cars; CB&Q heavyweight baggage no. 1530; GN lightweight diner no. 1251; passenger and freight cars, cabooses.

Special Events: Wine Country Harvest Festival, September 27-28. Christmas at the Station, December.

Nearby Attractions: Peek'nPeak Resort, Presque Isle State Park, Lake Erie nature walks, beaches, and marinas.

Directions: At Wall and Robinson Streets. Fifteen miles east of Erie, 2 miles north of I-90, exit 41, three blocks south of U.S. 20.

*Coupon available, see coupon section.

Site Address: 31 Wall St., North East, PA
Mailing Address: PO Box 571, North East, PA 16428-0571
Telephone: (814) 725-1911
Fax: (814) 725-1911
E-mail: lsrhs@velocity.net
Website: www.velocity.net/~lsrhs

Pennsylvania, Philadelphia

**THE FRANKLIN INSTITUTE
SCIENCE MUSEUM**
Museum, display, layout
Standard gauge

Description: The nostalgic Baldwin 60000 steam locomotive has become part of an exciting new attraction. "The Train Factory" transports visitors to an active turn-of-the-century train works where they feel the steam, hear the noise of the machines, and meet some of the people who worked to create America's locomotives. Visitors explore original and modern train technology as they journey through the sections of this exhibit, including The Machine Shop, The Track Shop, Research and Development, Accident Investigation, and the Baldwin 60000 test run. The Franklin Institute is located at 20th St. and the Benjamin Franklin Parkway in downtown Philadelphia, within walking distance of Suburban Station.

Schedule: Year-round, daily, 9:30 a.m. to 5 p.m.

Admission/Fare: Call or check website for information.

Locomotives/Rolling Stock: Baldwin 60000.

Directions: Center city Philadelphia.

30th Street, ¼ mile away

Site Address: 20th St. and the Ben Franklin Parkway, Philadelphia, PA
Mailing Address: 222 N. 20th St., Philadelphia, PA 19103
Telephone: (215) 448-1200
Fax: (215) 448-1235
Website: www.fi.edu

Pennsylvania, Port Clinton

**READING, BLUE MOUNTAIN &
NORTHERN RAILROAD**
Train ride
Standard gauge

Description: Seasonal train rides, usually to view fall foliage and in connection with community festivals.

Schedule: Varies; check website (at the website, click on "Passenger").

Admission/Fare: Check website for information.

Locomotives/Rolling Stock: Steam, when operating: RD6 T-1 no. 2102; GM20 no. 425; modern high-power diesels, usually SD-50s; 1917-era open-window passenger coaches.

Nearby Attractions: Hershey Park, Dorney Park, Allentown.

Directions: Pennsylvania Route 61 to Port Clinton. Two miles north of I-78 near Hamburg, Pennsylvania.

Site Address: 1 Railroad Blvd., Port Clinton, Pa
Mailing Address: 1 Railroad Blvd., Port Clinton, PA 19549
Telephone: (610) 562-2102
Fax: (610) 562-1920
E-mail: passenger@readingnorthern.com
Website: www.rbmnrr.com

Description: The museum is located in two historic buildings at the former southern operating terminus of the East Broad Top Railroad. Exhibits and displays illustrate the history of the East Broad Top Railroad and the men and women who constructed, maintained, and operated the railroad.

Schedule: June through mid-October: Saturdays, 10 a.m. to 5 p.m.; Sundays, 1 to 5 p.m.

Admission/Fare: Free. Donations appreciated.

Locomotives/Rolling Stock: EBT maintenance-of-way handcar; EBT combination passenger-baggage cars nos. 16 and 18 (stored off-site); EBT baggage-express car no. 29 (stored off-site).

Special Events: Summer Open House, June 7-8. EBT Rebirthday Celebration, August 9. Fall Open House and Reunion, October 11-12.

Nearby Attractions: East Broad Top Railroad, Broad Top Area Coal Miners Museum, Raystown Lake.

Directions: Approximately 17 miles southwest of Orbisonia/Rockhill Furnace (EBT and U.S. 522), and 20 miles north of Breezewood (I-70, I-76, and U.S. 30).

     M arm

Site Address: Main St., Robertsdale, PA
Mailing Address: PO Box 68, Robertsdale, PA 16674
Telephone: (814) 625-2388
E-mail: febt@aol.com
Website: www.febt.org

Pennsylvania, Rockhill Furnace **EAST BROAD TOP RAILROAD**

Train ride
36" gauge

Description: The East Broad Top Railroad, chartered in 1856, is the last operating narrow gauge railroad east of the Mississippi. The road hauled coal, freight, mail, express, and passengers for more than 80 years. Today the East Broad Top offers passengers a 10-mile, 50-minute ride through the beautiful Aughwick Valley with its own preserved locomotives; the ride takes passengers from the historic depot at Rockhill Furnace to the picnic grove, where the train is turned. On display are the railroad yard with shops, operating roundhouse, and turntable. Dates, times, and fares are subject to change. Call or write for latest information.

Schedule: June through October: weekends, 11 a.m., 1 and 3 p.m.

Admission/Fare: Adults, $9; children, $6.

Locomotives/Rolling Stock: 1911 Baldwin locomotive 2-8-2 no. 12; 1912 Baldwin locomotive 2-8-2 no. 14; 1914 Baldwin locomotive 2-8-2 no. 15; 1918 Baldwin locomotive 2-8-2 no. 17; all original East Broad Top Railroad.

Special Events: Fall Spectacular, Columbus Day weekend.

Nearby Attractions: Raystown Lake, Rockhill Trolley Museum.

Directions: Pennsylvania Turnpike exit Willow Hill or Fort Littleton.

*Coupon available, see coupon section.

Site Address: Rockhill Furnace, PA
Mailing Address: PO Box 158, Rockhill Furnace, PA 17249
Telephone: (814) 447-3011
Fax: (814) 447-3256

Pennsylvania, Rockhill-Orbisonia   **ROCKHILL TROLLEY MUSEUM**
Trolley ride
Standard

JOEL SALOMON

Description: A 3-mile, 30-minute ride over the former Shade Gap branch of the East Broad Top Railroad aboard a restored trolley. A new 3,000-foot track extension takes riders into Blacklog Narrows.

Schedule: Memorial Day weekend through October, weekends. Weekday tours by arrangement. Trolley rides operate 11 a.m. to 4 p.m.

Admission/Fare: Adults, $4.95; children, $1.95; group rates available; good for unlimited rides on day purchased.

Locomotives/Rolling Stock: York Railway's no. 163, 1924 Brill curveside; no. 1875 1912 open car; no. 311 Johnstown Traction Co. Birney car; Philadelphia and Western no. 205 bullet car; many other trolleys on display; 100-year-old sno-sweeper, snowplow, and more.

Special Events: Ice Cream Night Trolley, July 4th weekend, Labor Day weekend; Fall Spectacular, Columbus Day weekend. Santa's Trolley, first Saturday in December.

Nearby Attractions: East Broad Top Railroad, Raystown Lake, Swigart Antique Car Museum, Altoona Railroaders Museum.

Directions: Twenty miles north of exit 13 of Pennsylvania Turnpike, just off Route 522; opposite the East Broad Top Railroad.

*Coupon available, see coupon section.

Site Address: Meadow St., Rockhill Furnace, PA
Mailing Address: 1003 N. Chester Rd., West Chester, PA 19380
Telephone: (610) 692-4107
E-mail: sgurley@prodigy.net
Website: www.rockhilltrolley.org

KISKI JUNCTION RAILROAD
Train ride
Standard gauge

Description: Take a one-hour scenic ride along the Kiski River on a real working freight shortline railroad. Bring your own picnic lunch, and eat right on the cars with tables as we go. Reservations are required.

Schedule: Memorial Day weekend through Halloween: Tuesdays, 2 p.m. (mixed freight run–discount tickets and half-hour longer ride); Wednesdays, 7 p.m.; weekends, 2 p.m. Group rates and rides available weekdays.

Admission/Fare: Adults, $8; seniors, $7; children 12-17, $6; children 4-11, $4; age 3 and under, free.

Locomotives/Rolling Stock: Alco S1 no. 7135; P&LE cabin car no. 500; KJR transfer cabin no. 200; KJR flatcar no. 44; KJR coach no. 1154.

Nearby Attractions: Crooked Creek State Park.

Directions: Thirty miles northeast of Pittsburgh on the Allegheny and Kiski Rivers. Take Route 66 north out of Leechburg, go two miles to Schenley Rd., turn west, travel 4 miles.

Site Address: 48 Railroad St., Schenley, PA
Mailing Address: PO Box 48, Schenley, PA 15682-0048
Telephone: (724-) 295-5577
E-mail: info@kiskijunction.com
Website: www.kiskijunction.com

Pennsylvania, Scranton

**ELECTRIC CITY TROLLEY
STATION AND MUSEUM**
Museum

AMERICAN VIEWS CLAIRE WAGNER

Description: The museum tells the story of electric traction in the Northeast. A ride one hour in length highlights the north portal of Crown Avenue Tunnel, one of the longest interurban tunnels.

Schedule: Museum–April 1 through November, daily, 9 a.m. to 5 p.m. Ride–April 1 through October, Wednesday through Sunday. We have special events and rides in November and December.

Admission/Fare: To be announced.

Locomotives/Rolling Stock: 1926 Brill trolley car no. 76.

Special Events: Toys for Tots, Thanksgiving weekend; Santa visits, first two weekends in December.

Nearby Attractions: Steamtown National Historic Site, Lackawanna Coal Mine Montage, Red Barons AAA baseball.

Directions: Take I-815 to exit 185; follow signs for Trolley Museum and Steamtown National Historic Site.

†See ad on page A-4.

Site Address: 300 Cliff St., Scranton, PA
Mailing Address: 300 Cliff St., Scranton, PA 18503
Telephone: (570) 963-6590
Fax: (570) 963-6447
E-mail: trolley@lackawannacounty.org
Website: www.ectma.org or www.visitnepa.org

Pennsylvania, Scranton

**STEAMTOWN NATIONAL
HISTORIC SITE**
Train ride, museum, display, layout
Standard gauge

NATIONAL PARK SERVICE

Description: The Historic Site showcases live coal-fired steam locomotives, restored cabooses, freight cars and railroad coaches from the 1920s. You can experience the history of steam railroading in a variety of media, including museum exhibits, film, and guided tours. We offer a 26-mile rail excursion into the foothills of the Pocono Mountains.

Schedule: The park is open year-round, 9 a.m. to 5 p.m. Closed Thanksgiving Day, Christmas, and New Year's Day. Train excursions operate from July 4 through late October.

Admission/Fare: Museum–adults, $6; seniors, $5; children, $3. Excursion–adults, $10; seniors, $8; children, $5 and $4.

Locomotives/Rolling Stock: No. 26 Baldwin 0-6-0 switcher, built 1929; Boston & Maine no. 3713 4-6-2 Pacific, built 1934; Brooks-Scanlon Corp. no. 1 2-6-2 Prairie, built 1914; Bullard Co. no. 2 0-4-0T saddletank, built 1937; Canadian National no. 47 4-6-4T Baltic tank, built 1914; many more.

Special Events: National Park Week, April; Rail Expo, Labor Day; Carbondale Christmas Train and The Polar Express, December.

Directions: Take I-81 to exit 185. Follow the Central Scranton Expwy. into the Center City area. At first stoplight (Jefferson Ave.) turn left. The street bears right and turns into Lackawanna Ave. Go past seven traffic lights; one block further, and the entrance is on the left at Cliff St.

Site Address: Lackawanna Ave. and Cliff St., Scranton, PA
Mailing Address: 150 S. Washington Ave., Scranton, PA 18503
Telephone: (888) 693-9391
E-mail: stea_visitor_information@nps.gov
Website: www.nps.gov/stea

Description: Roadside America, an idea born in June 1903, is a childhood dream realized. More than 60 years in the making by Laurence Gieringer, it is housed in a new, modern, comfortable, air-conditioned building and covers more than 8,000 square feet of space. The display includes 2,570 feet of track for trains and trolleys and 250 railroad cars. O gauge trains and trolleys run among the villages.

Schedule: July 1 through Labor Day: weekdays, 9 a.m. to 6:30 p.m.; weekends, 9 a.m. to 7 p.m. September 6 through June 30: weekdays, 10 a.m. to 5 p.m.; weekends, 10 a.m. to 6 p.m.

Admission/Fare: Adults, $4.50; senior citizens, $4; children 6-11 years old, $2; children 5 and under free.

Directions: Take I-78 to exit 23. We're at 109 Roadside Dr.

Site Address: 109 Roadside Dr., Shartlesville, PA
Mailing Address: P.O. Box 2, Shartlesville, PA 19554
Telephone: (610) 488-6241
Website: www.roadsideamericainc.com

Pennsylvania, Strasburg

CHOO CHOO BARN
TRAINTOWN U.S.A.
Layout

FRED M. DOLE

Description: A 1,700-square-foot display of Lancaster County in miniature, built by hand, mostly by one family. Twenty operating O, HO, and N trains and over 150 animated engines and vehicles.

Schedule: March 23 through January 5: daily, 10 a.m. to 5 p.m. Last tour starts at 4:30 p.m. Closed major holidays.

Admission/Fare: Adults, $5; children 5-12, $3; under age 5 are free.

Special Events: Canned Food Fridays, free admission with non-perishable food item for local food bank, December 6, 13, and 20.

Directions: Located along Route 741 east of Strasburg.

Site Address: Route 741 East, Strasburg, PA
Mailing Address: PO Box 130, Strasburg, PA 17579
Telephone: (717) 687-7911 and (800) 450-2920
Fax: (717) 687-6529 and (800) 886-3819
E-mail: info@choochoobarn.com
Website: www.choochoobarn.com

Description: Five operating layouts, toy trains from the mid-1800s to the present day. Continuous toy train videos.

Schedule: May 1 through October 31, daily; April, November and December, weekends, 10 a.m. to 5 p.m.

Admission/Fare: Adults (13-64), $3; seniors (65+), $2.75; children 6-12, $1.50; under 5, free; family rate, $9.

Nearby Attractions: Choo Choo Barn, Railroad Museum of Pennsylvania, Strasburg Railroad, Hershey Park, Longwood Gardens.

Directions: From U.S. 30: south on Pennsylvania 896, east on Pennsylvania 741, north on Paradise Ln. We are one block from the railroad tracks.

Site Address: 300 Paradise Ln., Strasburg, PA
Mailing Address: PO Box 248, Strasburg, PA 17579-0248
Telephone: (717) 687-8976
Fax: (717) 687-0742
E-mail: toytrain@traincollectors.org
Website: www.traincollectors.org

**RAILROAD MUSEUM
OF PENNSYLVANIA**
Museum

Description: The museum displays a world-class collection of over 100 steam, electric, and diesel-electric locomotives and passenger and freight cars, as well as railroad-related art and artifacts. The 100,000-square-foot Rolling Stock Hall and outdoor restoration Yard exhibit equipment date from 1825 to 1992. Other features of the museum are the Stewart Junction interactive education center, Steinman Station replica passenger depot, and Whistle Stop Shop museum store.

Schedule: Mondays through Saturdays, 9 a.m. to 5 p.m.; Sundays, 12 to 5 p.m. Closed Mondays, November through March, and some holidays.

Admission/Fare: Adults 18-59, $7; seniors (60+), $6; youth 6-17, $5; under age 6 are free. Group rates available with advance reservation.

Locomotives/Rolling Stock: See above.

Special Events: A variety of railroad-themed and holiday events, Members Day, children's days, workshops, educational lectures, museum rambles, and other activities.

Nearby Attractions: Strasburg Railroad, National Toy Train Museum, Choo Choo Barn, Pennsylvania Dutch attractions, Lancaster County area museums and heritage sits.

Directions: Ten miles east of Lancaster on Pennsylvania Route 741.

Site Address: Route 741, Strasburg, PA
Mailing Address: PO Box 15, Strasburg, PA 17579
Telephone: (717) 687-8628
Fax: (717) 687-0876
E-mail: info@rrmuseumpa.org
Website: www.rrmuseumpa.org

STRASBURG RAIL ROAD
Train ride, dinner train, display
Standard gauge

Description: A 45-minute trip into the past. The train travels through beautiful Lancaster County farmland as it journeys from Strasburg to Amtrak's Leaman Place interchange at Paradise. The East Strasburg Station mall features four gift shops, one restaurant, fudge shop, old time portrait studio, and the exquisite "Paradise" business car. Just across the street is the Railroad Museum of Pennsylvania.

Schedule: February 15 through December 29, weekends. March 2 through December 13, daily. December 26 through 31, daily. Times and equipment vary.

Admission/Fare: Adults, $9.50 and up; children 3-11, $4.75 and up. Group rates available.

Locomotives/Rolling Stock: No. 90, 2-10-0 ex-GW; no. 475 4-8-0 ex-N&W; no. 89 2-6-0 ex-GT; no. 31 0-6-0 ex-CN; no. 972 4-6-0 ex-CPR; no. 4 0-4-0 ex-RDG; GE 44-ton ex-PRR 9331; Plymouths nos. 1 and 2; very early 20th-century wooden passenger cars; over a dozen early freight cars; reserved dining car, parlor car, and lounge car seating and service available; open-sided observation cars.

Special Events: A Day Out with Thomas events, Easter Bunny Trains, Pumpkin Trains, Santa Trains. Call for dates.

Directions: On Route 741 one mile east of Strasburg.

Site Address: Route 741, 301 Gap Rd., Strasburg, PA
Mailing Address: PO Box 96, Strasburg, PA 17579
Telephone: (717) 687-7522
Fax: (717) 687-6194
E-mail: srrtrain@strasburgrailroad.com
Website: www.strasburgrailroad.com

OIL CREEK & TITUSVILLE RAILROAD
Train ride

BETTY M SQUIRE

Description: Twenty-seven-mile, 2½-hour train ride through "The Valley That Changed the World."

Schedule: June and September: weekends only, 1 p.m. departure. July and August: Wednesdays, Thursdays, and weekends, 1 p.m. departure. October: Wednesdays, Thursdays, Fridays, 11 a.m. departure. October weekends: 11 a.m. and 3 p.m. departure. All trains depart from 409 S. Perry St., Titusville.

Admission/Fare: Adults, $12; seniors (60+), $11; children (3-12), $8.

Locomotives/Rolling Stock: 1947 Alco S-2 no 75; caboose no. 10 built by Elgin, Joliet & Eastern Railroad approximately 1923; railway post office car.

Special Events: Speeder runs, the third Saturday in August; Santa Express, December 6-7.

Nearby Attractions: Drake Well Museum, Oil Creek State Park, Tyred Wheels Auto Museum.

Directions: Route 8 north or south to Titusville, watch for signs.

*Coupon available, see coupon section.

         M

Site Address: 409 S. Perry St., Titusville, PA
Mailing Address: 7 Elm St., Oil City, PA 16301
Telephone: (814) 676-1733
Fax: (814) 677-2192
E-mail: ocandt@usachoice.net
Website: www.octrr.clarion.edu

Pennsylvania, Washington

PENNSYLVANIA TROLLEY MUSEUM
Train ride, museum, display
5'2½" gauge, standard gauge

SCOTT R. BECKER

Description: A scenic 4-mile round-trip trolley ride, recently extended in length! Also guided tour of carbarn and restoration shop, a film about the trolley era, and an exhibit describing Pittsburgh Railways Co. interurban trolley lines.

Schedule: April through December, weekends; Memorial Day through Labor Day, daily, 11 a.m. to 5 p.m.

Admission/Fare: Adults, $6; seniors (65+), $5; children 2-15, $3.50. Admission includes trolley rides and tours.

Locomotives/Rolling stock: Streetcars from Pittsburgh, Philadelphia, Johnstown, Boston, and New Orleans. Armco Steel/Baldwin Westinghouse 1930 diesel switcher; PA Transformer/HK Porter 1942 diesel switcher.

Special Events: Easter Bunny Trolley, April 12 and 19; Trolley Fair, late June; Pumpkin Patch Trolley, October 11-12, 19-20. Santa Trolley, November 28-30, December 6-7, 13-14. Trolleys & Toy Trains, December 20-21, 26-30.

Directions: Thirty miles southwest of Pittsburgh. Take I-79 south to exit 41 Racetrack Rd. or I-79 north to exit 40 Meadowlands. Follow the museum signs 3 miles.

*Coupon available, see coupon section.

Site Address: 1 Museum Rd., Washington, PA
Mailing Address: 1 Museum Rd., Washington, PA 15301-6133
Telephone: (724) 228-9256 and (877) 228-7655 (toll-free)
Fax: (724) 228-9675
E-mail: store@pa-trolley.org
Website: www.pa-trolley.org

TIOGA CENTRAL RAILROAD
Train ride, dinner train
Standard gauge

RICH STOVING

Description: A 1½-hour excursion through beautiful north central Pennsylvania countryside; 24 miles round trip.

Schedule: May 11 through October 20, weekends; departures at 11 a.m., 1 and 3 p.m.

Admission/Fare: Adults, $10; seniors (60+), $9; children 6-12, $5. Children under 6 free with paying adult.

Locomotives/Rolling Stock: Alco S2 no. 14; Alco R1 no. 62; Alco RS3 no. 506.

Special Events: Wellsboro Rail Days, October 25-26, special trains, longer runs, for rail fans.

Nearby Attractions: Grand Canyon of Pennsylvania, Ives Run Recreation Area, many fine restaurants and Main Street shopping in beautiful Wellsboro.

Directions: Three miles north of Wellsboro on State Route 287. Wellsboro is on U.S. Route 6 east-west, and Pennsylvania Route 287 north-south; 35 miles south of Corning, New York.

*Coupon available, see coupon section.

†See ad on page A-13.

        M

Radio frequency: 160.725

Site Address: Muck Rd., Wellsboro Junction, PA
Mailing Address: PO Box 269, Wellsboro, PA 16901
Telephone: (570) 724-0990
E-mail: info@tiogacentral.com
Website: www.tiogacentral.com

WEST CHESTER RAILROAD

Train ride, dinner train
Standard gauge

Description: A 16-mile round trip from West Chester to Glen Mills. This line is the unused portion of SEPTA's R-3 Elwyn line, which is very scenic as it follows Chester Creek in western Delaware County through eastern Chester County.

Schedule: April, May, September through December: weekends. Charters available year-round. Call for information on specials.

Admission/Fare: Adults, $8; children 2-12, $5.

Locomotives/Rolling Stock: No. 99 EMD GP-9 ex-B&O no. 6499; no. 1803 is DRS-18U Alco former CP 1803; Reading Blue Liners coaches nos. 9114, 9124, 9117, 9107; baggage car former Pennsy B-60 7551; more.

Special Events: Monthly dinner trains; Easter Bunny Express; West Chester Restaurant Festival, third weekend in September; Pratt & Co. Fall Festival, fourth weekend in September; Fall Foliage, October; Holiday Express, November; Santa Express, November and December.

Nearby Attractions: Valley Forge National Park, West Chester Restaurants, Chadds Ford, Brandywine Museum, Winterthur Longwood Gardens.

Directions: Highway 202, exit Gay St./West Chester. Follow Gay to Matlack turning left, one block to Market, left at railroad station, one block on right.

Radio frequency: 160.6050

Site Address: 230 E. Market St., West Chester, PA
Mailing Address: PO Box 385, Yorklyn, DE 19736
Telephone: (610) 430-2233
Fax: (302) 995-5286

Description: Historic Jersey Central train station that was renovated in 1896.

Schedule: Fridays and Saturdays, 9 p.m. to 2 a.m.

Admission/Fare: Night clubs, $7.

Locomotives/Rolling Stock: Various boxcars and passenger cars; antique Amtrak.

Special Events: Farmer's market every Thursday during the summer; several events on the square nearby.

Nearby Attractions: First Union Arena, F. M. Kirby Center for the Performing Arts, Lackawanna Coal Mine Tours.

Directions: Call for directions.

Site Address: 33 Wilkes-Barre Blvd., Wilkes-Barre, PA
Mailing Address: PO Box 2, Wilkes-Barre, PA 18703
Telephone: (570) 825-0000
Fax: (570) 970-9797

Pennsylvania, Williamsport   **THOMAS T. TABER MUSEUM OF THE LYCOMING COUNTY HISTORICAL SOCIETY**
Museum, layout

TERRY WILD STUDIO

Description: History museum with model train exhibit.

Schedule: Open year-round. May 1 through October 31: Tuesdays through Fridays, 9:30 a.m. to 4 p.m.; Saturdays, 11 a.m. to 4 p.m.; Sundays, 1 to 4 p.m. November 1 through April 30: Tuesdays through Fridays, 9:30 a.m. to 4 p.m.; Saturdays, 11 a.m. to 4 p.m. Closed major holidays.

Admission/Fare: Adult, $5; seniors, AARP/AAA, $4; children, $2.50.

Special Events: Toy Train Expo, December 9-10, 12 to 4 p.m. Area collectors have displays and layouts throughout the museum.

Nearby Attractions: Clyde Peeling's Reptile Land, Little League Museum.

Site Address: 858 W. Fourth St., Williamsport, PA
Mailing Address: 858 W. Fourth St., Williamsport, PA 17701-5824
Telephone: (570) 326-3326
Fax: (570) 326-3689
E-mail: lchsmuse@csrlink.net
Website: www.lycoming.org/lchsmuseum

Pennsylvania, Youngwood

**WESTMORELAND SCENIC
RAILROAD**
Train ride
Standard gauge

Description: Train rides on original Pennsylvania lines that were sold to Westmoreland County and operated by Southwest Pennsylvania Railroad.

Schedule: Mid-May through end of October, plus specials at Christmas and Easter.

Admission/Fare: Adults, $10; children, $5 (3-13); 2 and under are free.

Locomotives/Rolling Stock: Diesel: GP-7-U Westmoreland Scenic Railroad; two Union Pacific coaches, 1952.

Special Events: Train Robberies, Civil War, Halloween.

Nearby Attractions: Idawild Park, Pittsburgh Sports Arena, Falling Water.

Directions: Pennsylvania Turnpike, exit 8. Go north on Route 119, then four traffic lights to Depot St. Turn right, go 1½ blocks.

M

Site Address: 1 Depot St., Youngwood, PA
Mailing Address: PO Box 182, New Stanton, PA 15672
Telephone: (724) 925-6543
Website: www.whrr.org

South Carolina, Greenwood

**RAILROAD HISTORICAL
CENTER**
Museum, display
Standard gauge

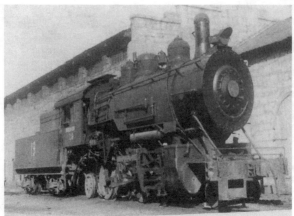

JIMMY WADE

Description: Walk-through of steam engine and other railroad cars. The rolling stock and gardens are open to the public March through December, weather permitting. This is a partnership of the Railroad Historical Center and The Museum (located four blocks to the north at 106 Main St.). There are no restroom facilities.

Schedule: March through December, third Friday and Saturday of each month, weather permitting. Friday 10 a.m. to 4 p.m.; Saturday 2 to 4 p.m.

Admission/Fare: Adults, $2; children and seniors, $1; under 6 free. Free admission to museum members.

Locomotives/Rolling Stock: Baldwin steam locomotive no. 19, ca. 1906; Southern Car Company car no. 2102, 1914; Pullman Standard coach no. 831, 1937; dining car no. 746, ca. 1920; Pullman Standard sleeper no. 5, ca. 1942 "American Liberty"; Southern Car Company parlor/observation car ca. 1914, "Carolina."

Special Events: South Carolina Festival of Flowers (extended hours), mid-June.

Directions: On Main St. next to South Main Street Baptist Church. Park in the church lot and enter through the gate facing Main St. on the north side of the house.

Site Address: 908 S. Main St., Greenwood, SC
Mailing Address: PO Box 3131, Greenwood, SC 29648
Telephone: (864) 229-7093
Website: themuseum@greenwood.net

SOUTH CAROLINA RAILROAD MUSEUM
Train ride, museum, display, layout
Standard gauge

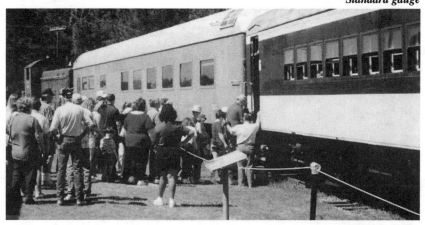

Description: A 7-mile round trip to Greenbrier and return over a portion of the former Rockton & Rion Railway. The route was built in the late 1800s as a quarry line to haul world-famous Winnsboro blue granite from the quarry to the Southern Railway at Rockton.

Schedule: June through October, first and third Saturdays. Museum gallery and yard tours, Sundays 1 to 4 p.m. (No train rides on Sundays.)

Admission/Fare: Adults, $7; children 11 and under, $5; first-class, $11; Caboose rides, when available, $8.

Locomotives/Rolling Stock: No. 2015 and 2028, 1950 SW-8; no. 33, 1946 GE 44-ton, former PRR; no. 76, 1951 Porter 50-ton, former U.S. Navy; no. 82, 1945 GE 45-ton, former U.S. Navy; and no. 44, 1927 Baldwin 4-6-0, former Hampton & Branchville (static display).

Special Events: Easter Bunny Train, Caboose Day, Santa Train. Call, write, or visit our website for exact dates.

Nearby Attractions: Downtown Winnsboro, South Carolina State Museum, Riverbanks Zoo.

Directions: Take State Route 34 from I-26 or I-77 and follow the signs to Winnsboro. Then follow brown signs. The museum is located between State Route 34 and U.S. Highway 321, 3 miles south of Winnsboro.

        M arm TRAIN

Radio frequency: 151.865

Site Address: 110 Industrial Park Rd., Winnsboro, SC
Mailing Address: PO Box 643, Winnsboro, SC 29180
Telephone: (803) 635-9893
E-mail: contactscrm@mindspring.com
Internet: www.scrm.org

South Dakota, Hill City

BLACK HILLS CENTRAL RAILROAD
Train ride
Standard gauge

RICH W. MILLS

Description: Passengers can take a two-hour round-trip journey between Hill City and Keystone. Experience a ride from the past as you travel through the Black Hills, seeing the old mine sights and Harney Peak.

Schedule: Mid-May through early October, daily. Departures added during summer season. Call, write, or e-mail for information.

Admission/Fare: Adults, $18; children 4-12, $10; age 3 and under are free. Group rates available for parties of 20 and up.

Locomotives/Rolling Stock: 1926 Baldwin 2-6-2 no. 104 saddle tank; 1919 Baldwin 2-6-2 no. 7; 1928 Baldwin 2-6-6-2 no. 110; 1880s-1910 passenger cars.

Special Events: Railroad Days, late September.

Nearby Attractions: Mt. Rushmore, Crazy Horse Memorial, Custer State Park, the Badlands.

Directions: Highway 16/385, 24 miles south of Rapid City. Tickets may be purchased at the Hill City Depot, 222 Railroad Ave., which is the truck bypass, or at the Keystone Depot, on the north end of Main St.

Site Address: 222 Railroad Ave., Hill City, SD
Mailing Address: PO Box 1880, Hill City, SD 57745
Telephone: (605) 574-2222
Fax: (605) 574-4915
E-mail: office@1880train.com
Website: www.1880train.com

PRAIRIE VILLAGE
Train ride, dinner train, museum, display
Standard and 24" gauge

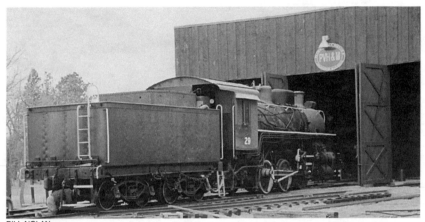

BILL NOLAN

Description: Prairie Village is an assembly of turn-of-the-century buildings. There are steam traction engines, gas tractors, and displays of farm equipment. A 2-mile loop of track is used for train rides. Buildings include the Wentworth Depot, Junius Depot, and roundhouse/turntable.

Schedule: Museum–May through September: daily, 9 a.m. to 6 p.m. Train–June through August and during Railroad Days and Jamboree: Sundays, 2, 3, and 4 p.m.

Admission/Fare: Museum–$5. Train–$3.

Locomotives/Rolling Stock: No. 29 Lima 0-6-0, former D&NE; no. 11 Alco 0-4-0T, ex-Deadwood Central; Orrenstein & Koppel 0-4-0T "Wilhelmine"; Baldwin 60T diesel; GE 80T diesel; rolling stock with snowplow, cabooses and passenger cars.

Special Events: Railroad Days, June. Car Show, August. Fall Jamboree, August.

Nearby Attractions: Camping available on grounds, Lake Herman State Park, Smith-Zimmermann State Museum, Madison.

Directions: Prairie Village is 2 miles west of Madison on Highway 34. From Sioux Falls, take I-29 north to the Madison/Colman exit, then travel west on Highway 34 to Madison.

Site Address: W. Highway 34, Madison, SD
Mailing Address: PO Box 256, Madison, SD 57042-0256
Telephone: (800) 693-3644 and (605) 256-3644
Fax: (605) 256-4588
E-mail: prairiev@rapidnet.com
Website: www.prairievillage.org

Tennessee, Chattanooga

CHATTANOOGA CHOO CHOO
Museum, layout

Description: Opened in 1909 as the Southern Railway's Terminal Station, this depot welcomed thousands of travelers during the golden age of railroads. Today, the restored station is the heart of the Chattanooga Choo Choo Holiday Inn, a 24-acre complex with a full range of entertainment. Forty-eight passenger cars are part of the 360-room hotel; two passenger cars serve as a formal restaurant and meeting/banquet room. A special feature at the complex is the Model Railroad Museum, one of the world's largest HO gauge displays. The model railroad is 174 feet long and 33 feet at its widest point. It has over 3,000 feet of track with up to eight trains running constantly on separate loops. To make the layout come alive there are thousands of lights and dozens of animated features.

Schedule: Daily, 10 a.m. to 8 p.m. May vary seasonally.

Admission/Fare: Adults, $2; children, $1; under age 3 are free.

Nearby Attractions: Tennessee Aquarium, IMAX Theater, Southern Belle Riverboat, Creative Discovery Museum, Coolidge Park, Rock City, Ruby Falls.

Directions: I-24 exit 178, take S. Broad St. split and follow signs to Choo Choo.

*Coupon available, see coupon section.

Site Address: 1400 Market St., Chattanooga, TN
Mailing Address: 1400 Market St., Chattanooga, TN 37402
Telephone: (423) 266-5000
Fax: (423) 265-4635
E-mail: frontdesk@choochoo.com
Website: www.choochoo.com

TENNESSEE VALLEY RAILROAD
Train ride, dinner train, museum, display
Standard gauge

STEVE FREER

Description: Daily, 45-minute round trip through pre-Civil War Missionary Ridge Tunnel. Dixie Land Excursions run on select weekends and most include a dining car luncheon. Special events throughout the year.

Schedule: April through November: Saturdays, 10 a.m. to 5 p.m.; Sundays, 11 a.m. to 5 p.m. Spring and fall weekdays, 10 a.m. to 1 p.m. Summer weekdays, 10 a.m. to 5 p.m.

Admission/Fare: Adults, $11.50; children 3-12, $5.75. Group rates/charters.

Locomotives/Rolling Stock: S160 2-8-0 no. 610; SR KSI 2-8-0 no. 630; SR MSI 2-8-2 no. 4501; K&T 2-8-2 no. 10; CN J7b no. 5288; Alco RSDI nos. 8669 and 8677; EMD GP7 no. 1824 and 1829; Budd RDC nos. 20 and 22.

Special Events: Spring Steam Up, March. Autumn Leaf Specials, October. Polar Express and Christmas Specials, November and December.

Nearby Attractions: Hamilton Place Mall retail center, Chattanooga Regional Airport, Tennessee Aquarium, Rock City, Ruby Falls, Incline Railway, Chattanooga Choo Choo complex, NMRA headquarters, and Kalmbach Memorial Library.

Directions: I-75 exit 4 onto Highway 153 to Jersey Pike (fourth exit), follow brown directional signs ⅛ mile to TVRM.

*Coupon available, see coupon section.

M arm TRAIN MasterCard VISA   Radio frequency: 160.425

Site Address: 4119 Cromwell Rd., Chattanooga, TN
Mailing Address: 4119 Cromwell Rd., Chattanooga, TN 37421-2119
Telephone: (423) 894-8028
Fax: (423) 894-8029
E-mail: info@tvrail.com
Website: www.tvrail.com

COOKEVILLE DEPOT MUSEUM
Train ride, museum, display, layout

Description: A railroad museum housed in an old Tennessee Central Railway depot. Built in 1909, the building is listed on the National Register of Historic Places.

Schedule: Tuesday through Saturday, 10 a.m. to 4 p.m. Closed Fourth of July, Thanksgiving, and Christmas.

Admission/Fare: Free to self-guided museum and cabooses.

Locomotives/Rolling Stock: L&A no. 509 Baldwin Locomotive Works 4-6-0; TC no. 9828 caboose; L&N no. 135 (built by Louisville Shops) caboose. All are static at present.

Special Events: Tennessee Central Rendezvous/Springfest, first Saturday in May; Christmas Open House, second Saturday in December.

Nearby Attractions: Another museum related to community history, three lakes, five state parks, many restaurants, two malls, Tennessee Tech University.

Directions: From I-40 take exit 286 Willow Ave. towards the north. Stay on Willow until you see Broad St. Turn right on Broad and continue until you see the depot on the right.

Site Address: 116 W. Broad St., Cookeville, TN
Mailing Address: PO Box 998, Cookeville, TN 38503
Telephone: (931) 528-8570
Fax: (931) 526-1167
E-mail: depot@cookeville-tn.org

**CASEY JONES MUSEUM
AND TRAIN STORE**
Museum

Description: Visit the home and railroad museum of Casey Jones. Casey was living in this home at the time of his death in 1900. There are three layouts on display in the 1800s baggage car and a replica of no. 382, Casey's engine, along with souvenirs and a hobby shop.

Schedule: Year-round, 9 a.m. to 5 p.m., seven days a week.

Admission/Fare: Adults, $4; seniors, $3.50; children 6-12, $3; children under 6 free. Lifetime passes available.

Locomotives/Rolling Stock: Rogers 4-6-0 locomotive; 1800s M&O baggage car; IC caboose you can sleep in; 1890s sleeper car.

Nearby Attractions: State Park, Shiloh National Military Park, Home of Buford Pusser, Adamsville.

Directions: Take I-40 exit 80A onto 45. We're 45 seconds off Highway 45. Look for the caboose in the sky.

       M

Site Address: 30 Casey Jones Ln., Jackson, TN
Mailing Address: 56 Casey Jones Ln., Jackson, TN 38305
Telephone: (731) 668-1222
Fax: (731) 664-7782
E-mail: ntaylor@caseyjonesvillage.com
Website: www.caseyjones.com

Tennessee, Jackson

NASHVILLE, CHATTANOOGA & ST. LOUIS DEPOT AND RAILROAD MUSEUM
Museum, display, layout

MOORE STUDIOS

Description: The restored NC&StL Depot features a museum that reflects Jackson's history as West Tennessee's railroad hub. A working scale model depicts local railroad heritage. An Amtrak dining car, which seats up to 48 diners, can be rented for catered parties.

Schedule: Year-round, Mondays through Saturdays, 10 a.m. to 3 p.m.

Admission/Fare: Free.

Locomotives/Rolling Stock: Former FEC (Bunn 1947) dining car, "Ft. Matanzas"; Southern caboose X421; C&O caboose 3255.

Nearby Attractions: Brooks Shaw's Old Country Store, Historic Casey Jones Home and Railroad Museum, Pinson Mounds State Archaeological Area, Cypress Grove Nature Park, Chickasaw Rustic State Park, Pringles Park, Home of West Tennessee Diamond Jaxx baseball.

Directions: Turn off Highway 45 bypass onto Martin Luther King Dr. at the Jackson Main Post Office and go one block to S. Royal St. Turn right, proceed one block, depot is on the left.

Site Address: 582 S. Royal St., Jackson, TN
Mailing Address: 582 S. Royal St., Jackson, TN 38301
Telephone: (731) 425-8223
Fax: (731) 425-8682
E-mail: thedepot@cityofjackson.net

RICHARDS DESIGN GROUP

Description: An hour-and-20-minute round-trip excursion aboard our vintage train, which includes our newly restored 1925 steam engine "Lindy." The *Three Rivers Rambler* travels through east Tennessee farmland to the Three Rivers trestle, where the French Broad & Holsten Rivers meet to form the Tennessee River.

Schedule: Saturdays and Sundays, 2 and 5 p.m.

Admission/Fare: Coach–adult, $16.95; seniors 55+, $14.95; children, $9.95; children under under 5, free. Pullman–all ages, $19.95

Locomotives/Rolling Stock: 1925 Baldwin 2-8-0 no. 203, "Lindy"; 1925 Pullman office car "Resplendent"; two 1932 coaches, "Trustworthy" and "Intrepid"; 1940 open-air car (a converted flatcar) "Forthright"; caboose "Desire."

Special Events: Ice Cream Social, July 21.

Nearby Attractions: Gateway Regional Visitor Center, boat and paddleboat rentals, Star of Knoxville Riverboat, Women's Basketball Hall of Fame, three riverfront restaurants, and two historic homes.

Directions: Take I-40 to Knoxville, exit at James White Parkway (388A) to Neyland Dr. (158). Go ½ mile to stoplight at the Tennessee Grill. Park in Tennessee Grill lot C-18, cross Neyland, and walk to train.

Site Address: Neyland Dr. between Tennessee Grill and Calhoun's Restaurant
Mailing Address: 401 Henley St., Suite 5, Knoxville, TN 37902
Telephone: (865) 524-9411
Fax: (865) 546-3717
E-mail: kac@gulfandohio.com
Website: www.threeriversrambler.com

**TENNESSEE CENTRAL
RAILWAY MUSEUM**
Train ride, museum, display, layout
Standard gauge

STEVE JOHNSON

Description: Excursion train, hobby shop, railroad artifacts, modular HO and N scale model railroads.

Schedule: Saturdays, 9 a.m. to 3 p.m. Fifteen to 20 excursion trains scheduled during the year.

Admission/Fare: Museum–free. Excursion train–varies.

Locomotives/Rolling Stock: EMD E8A TCRX 5764; EMD SW8 TC 52; ex-P&LE F7B no. 719; former ATSF coaches; TCRX 4711, 4717, 4719, 4733, 4739; Budd buffet-diner TCRX 3113, 3119; Budd slumbercoach TCRX 2095; Pullman business car TC 102.

Special Events: Excursion trains for Valentine's Day, Easter, July 4th, Fall foliage, Christmas/Santa, more.

Nearby Attractions: Tennessee Titans NFL football, downtown Nashville, Grand Ole Opry House, Opryland Hotel, Nashville Toy Museum, Music Row, Nashville Arena, Opry Mills Shopping Mall.

Directions: Take I-24/40 to eastbound exit 212, Fesslers Ln. Go left onto Fesslers Ln., 0.5 mile to left on Lebanon Rd., proceed 0.8 mile to right on Fairfield Ave., and follow sign to museum site.

Radio frequency: 154.570

Site Address: 220 Willow St., Nashville, TN
Mailing Address: 220 Willow St., Nashville, TN 37210-2159
Telephone: (615) 244-9001
Fax: (615) 244-2120
E-mail: hultman@nashville.com
Website: http://tcry.org

Tennessee, Oak Ridge

SOUTHERN APPALACHIA RAILWAY MUSEUM
Train ride, dinner train, museum, display
Standard gauge

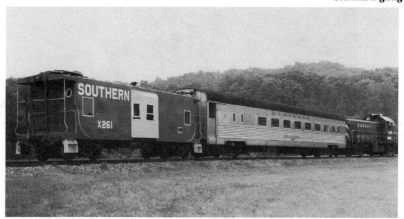

CHRIS WILLIAMS

Description: A 14-mile, 90-minute train ride aboard air-conditioned coaches and dining car, plus caboose. The train travels a former Southern Railway branch line through the former Manhattan Project K-25 facility. There are a limited number of evening dinner trains. Additional short-line railroad charters are conducted across the United States.

Schedule: First and third Saturdays, April through September, plus additional weekends and Sundays in October, November, and December. Departures at 10 a.m., 12, 2 and 4 p.m. Reservations recommended.

Admission/Fare: Adults, $12; children age 12 and under, $8.

Locomotives/Rolling Stock: U.S. Atomic Energy Commission 1951 Alco RS-1 5310; Tennessee Valley Authority, formerly U.S. Army 1943 Alco S-2 7100 and 7125; Central of Georgia 1947; coaches nos. 663, 664, and 665.

Special Events: Sixtieth Anniversary of K-25 Manhattan Project facility, Fabulous Forties Festival, May 17; Halloween Trains, October 25-26.

Nearby Attractions: Museum of Appalachia, Great Smoky Mountains National Park, Big South Fork National River and Recreation Area, Oak Ridge Manhattan Project tours.

Directions: Six miles north of I-40 exit 356 between Knoxville and Nashville at the East Tennessee Technology Park on Highway 58.

           M

Radio frequency: 160.425

Site Address: Highway 58 S., Oak Ridge, TN
Mailing Address: PO Box 5870, Knoxville, TN 37928
Telephone: (865) 241-2140
Fax: (865) 692-9505
E-mail: bjenninl@utk.edu
Website: www.southernappalachia.railway.museum

DOLLYWOOD ENTERTAINMENT PARK
Train ride
36" gauge

RICHARDS & SOUTHERN

Description: The *Dollywood Express,* located in the Village area of Dolly-wood, takes visitors on a 5-mile journey through this scenic park. As passengers ride on the authentic, coal-fired steam train, they can catch a glimpse of the different areas of Dollywood: Dreamland Forest, Rivertown Junction, The Village, Craftsman's Valley, Country Fair, Showstreet, Jukebox Junction, and Adventures in Imagination. The *Dollywood Express* also takes visitors through replicas of a typical turn-of-the-century mountain village and logging community.

Schedule: Thirty-minute rides every hour during park operating hours.

Admission/Fare: Adults, $34; seniors, $30; children 4-11, $25.

Locomotives/Rolling Stock: "Klondike Katie," a 1943 Baldwin 2-8-2, former U.S. Army no. 192; "Cinderella," a 1939 Baldwin 2-8-2, former U.S. Army no. 70; open-air passenger cars.

Special Events: Festival of Nations, early April; Harvest Celebration, October; Smoky Mountain Christmas Festival, mid-November, December. School field trips. Special group rates.

Nearby Attractions: Numerous restaurants, lodging, shopping, and attractions in Pigeon Forge area.

Directions: Call for directions.

Site Address: 1020 Dollywood Ln., Pigeon Forge, TN
Mailing Address: 1020 Dollywood Ln., Pigeon Forge, TN 37863-4101
Telephone: (865) 428-9488 and (800) DOLLYWOOD
Website: www.dollywood.com

**LITTLE RIVER RAILROAD
AND LUMBER COMPANY**
Museum

Description: Restored Shay locomotive, depot, steam sawmill, and collection of railroad and lumber company artifacts and photographs, and interpretive displays tell the story of the community.

Schedule: April, May, and September, weekends; June, July, August, and October, daily; November through March, by appointment only. Open 10 a.m. to 4 p.m.

Admission/Fare: Free. Donations appreciated.

Locomotives/Rolling Stock: Little River Shay no. 2147.

Nearby Attractions: Great Smoky Mountains National Park.

Directions: Take U.S. Highway 321 to Townsend.

Site Address: 7747 E. Lamar Alexander Pkwy., U.S. 321, Townsend, TN
Mailing Address: PO Box 211, Townsend, TN 37882
Telephone: (865) 448-2211
Fax: (865) 448-2312
E-mail: sandy242@aol.com or thurstonphoto@aol.com
Website: www.littleriverrailroad.org

TEXAS PANHANDLE RAILROAD HISTORICAL SOCIETY
Display
Standard gauge

JEFF FORD

Description: The TPRHS has cosmetically restored and maintains former Santa Fe Railway steam locomotive no. 5000. The 2-10-4, better known by its nickname "Madam Queen," was donated to the City of Amarillo in 1957 and placed on display in front of the city's Santa Fe Depot. The TPRHS was formed in 1992 in part to preserve and interpret the locomotive as an important reminder of the Texas Panhandle's railroad heritage.

Schedule: By appointment only.

Admission/Fare: Free. Donations appreciated.

Locomotives/Rolling Stock: 1930 Baldwin, Atchison, Topeka & Santa Fe Railway 2-10-4 no. 5000. The only locomotive of its class.

Nearby Attractions: Palo Duro Canyon State Park, Panhandle-Plains Historical Museum, Sixth Street/Historic Route 66 Antique District, railfan hotspot where BNSF's transcontinental main line crosses BNSF Fort Worth-to-Denver main line.

Directions: I-40, downtown exit north to Third Ave., turn east. Located south of E. Third Ave. on Grant St., downtown Amarillo.

     M

Site Address: E. Third Ave. and Grant St., Amarillo, TX
Mailing Address: PO Box 50422, Amarillo, TX 79159-0422
E-mail: info@tprhs.org
Website: www.tprhs.org

Texas, Arlington

SIX FLAGS OVER TEXAS RAILROAD
Train ride
Narrow gauge

Description: This is a major theme park with trains running along the perimeter of the park.

Schedule: Summer months, daily; spring and fall, weekends. Call for schedule.

Admission/Fare: $37.99 per person. Discounts for guests under 48 inches and seniors.

Locomotives/Rolling Stock: 1901 Dickson 0-4-0T converted 2-4-2 with tender, no. 1280; 1897 H.K. Porter 0-4-4-T converted 2-4-2 with tender, no. 1754.

Special Events: Texas Heritage Crafts Festival, September; Fright Fest, October; Holiday in the Park, December.

Nearby Attractions: Texas Rangers baseball, Six Flags Hurricane Harbor Water Park, Lone Star Park Racetrack, Texas Motor Speedway, Dallas, Fort Worth.

Directions: Located midway between Dallas and Fort Worth in Arlington at the intersection of I-30 and Texas Highway 360.

Site Address: 2201 Rd. to Six Flags, Arlington, TX
Mailing Address: PO Box 90191, Arlington, TX 76004-0191
Telephone: (817) 530-6000
Website: www.sixflags.com

AGE OF STEAM RAILROAD MUSEUM
Museum
Standard gauge

Description: A fine collection of steam and early diesel era railway equipment, including a complete heavyweight passenger train featuring restored MKT dining car and "Glengyle," the oldest all-steel, all-room Pullman.

Schedule: Wednesdays through Sundays, 10 a.m. to 5 p.m.

Admission/Fare: Adults, $5; children age 12 and under, $2.50; 2 years and under, free.

Locomotives/Rolling Stock: Big Boy no. 4018, 1942 Alco 4-8-8-4 and "Centennial" no. 6913, EMD DDA40X, both former Union Pacific; no. 1625, 1918 Alco 2-10-0, former Eagle-Picher Mining Co.; more.

Special Events: State Fair of Texas, September 26 through October 19. A Day Out with Thomas, fall.

Nearby Attractions: The museum is located in Fair Park, a year-round collection of arts and cultural institutions housed in a restored art deco building originally constructed for the 1936 Texas centennial.

Directions: Two miles east of downtown; I-30 westbound, exit 47A right onto Exposition Ave., left on Parry Ave.

Site Address: 1105 Washington St., Fair Park, Dallas, TX
Mailing Address: PO Box 153259, Dallas, TX 75315-3259
Telephone: (214) 428-0101
Fax: (214) 426-1937
E-mail: info@dallasrailwaymuseum.com
Website: www.dallasrailwaymuseum.com

Texas, Dallas

MCKINNEY AVENUE
TRANSIT AUTHORITY
Train ride
Standard gauge

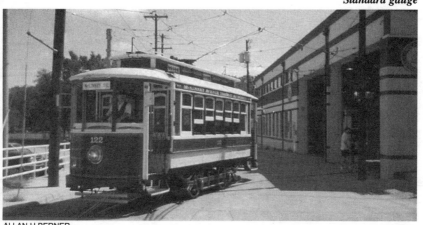

ALLAN H BERNER

Description: Ride vintage streetcars 4.6 miles from Historic Uptown to the Arts District.

Schedule: Monday through Friday, 7 a.m. to 10 p.m.; Saturdays, 10 a.m. to 10 p.m.; Sundays, 12 noon to 10 p.m.

Admission/Fare: Free.

Locomotives/Rolling Stock: No. 186 1913 Stone & Webster standard "turtleback"; no. 636 1920 Dallas Birney, St. Louis Car Co.; no. 122 1906 Brill car; no. 369 1926 Melborne W-2.

Nearby Attractions: Dallas Museum of Art, the Arts District, Gallery Walk District, Antique District, shopping, over 80 unique restaurants.

Directions: One mile north of Downtown in Uptown, along historic McKinney Ave.

Site Address: 3153 Oak Grove Ave., Dallas, TX
Mailing Address: 3153 Oak Grove Ave., Dallas, TX 75204
Telephone: (214) 855-0006
Fax: (214) 855-5250
E-Mail: trolleygirl@juno.com or trolleyguy@juno.com
Website: www.mata.org

381

GULF COAST RAILROAD MUSEUM
Museum
Standard gauge

Description: Features a collection of locomotives, freight and passenger cars with a Texas emphasis. The museum is operated by Gulf Coast Chapter, National Railway Historical Society, Inc.

Schedule: March through November, Saturdays, 11 a.m. to 5 p.m.; and Sundays, 1 to 4 p.m.

Admission/Fare: Adults $3; children 12 and under, $1.50.

Locomotives/Rolling Stock: ATSF "Verde Valley," Pullman; ATSF 3401 Budd RPO; ATSF 1890 Pullman end-door express car; ATSF 2350 Alco S2; MKT 6 cupola caboose; MKT "New Braunfels" coach; KCS "Good Cheer" observation-lounge; GM&O Alton parlor, SP 4696 caboose; HB&T 14 Alco S2; TM 510 Baldwin DS44-750; SP&S 50 baggage; CSOX 2198 tank car; MHAX 1237 helium car.

Special Events: Open House and Railroad Photography Contest in recognition of National Model Railroad month, first two weekends in November. Free admission.

Nearby Attractions: NASA/Space Center in Houston; Center for Transportation & Commerce at Galveston; Six Flags Houston.

Directions: Exit Loop 610 north at McCarty Drive. Go west on McCarty Dr. to Mesa Dr., then left about 1.5 miles to the museum.

    M arm

Site Address: 7390 Mesa Dr., Houston, TX
Mailing Address: PO Box 457, Houston, TX 77001-0457
Telephone: (713) 631-6612
E-mail: tom@kingswayrc.com
Website: www.kingswayrc.com/gcst

Description: Theme park attraction with ten featured roller coasters. The train ride is a complete 2-mile trip around AstroWorld; it takes about 20 minutes and shows all the attractions and history.

Schedule: Open 11 a.m. to closing. Hours vary.

Admission/Fare: General use 48" and taller, $37.99 plus tax; children, $22.99 plus tax; senior citizens, $26.99 plus tax; 2 and under, free.

Locomotives/Rolling Stock: Two diesel locomotives; converted ore car.

Special Events: Fright Fest, Un Dia Padre, Gospel Celebration, Flag Day, concerts, Joy Fest, 4th of July Celebration.

Nearby Attractions: Astrodome, Reliant Stadium.

Directions: On I-610 exit Fannin; southwest of downtown, across from Astrodome complex.

Site Address: 9001 Kirby Dr., Houston, TX
Mailing Address: Attn: Public Relations, 9001 Kirby Dr., Houston, TX 77054
Telephone: (713) 799-8404 and (713) 794-3291 (group sales)
Fax: (713) 799-8945
Website: www.sixflags.com

MARSHALL DEPOT INC.
Museum, display, layout

BILL ROBINSON

Description: Historic Texas & Pacific railway museum and gift shop, with artifacts and photos dating from the 1870s. Our gift shop features Thomas the Tank Engine toys and other memorabilia.

Schedule: Tuesdays through Saturdays, 10 a.m. to 4 p.m. Other times by special request for groups of 12 or more.

Admission/Fare: Adults, $2; students, $1; preschool children, free.

Locomotives/Rolling Stock: UP caboose no. 25687.

Special Events: Stagecoach Days, third weekend in May. Fire Ant Festival, second weekend in October. Wonderland of Lights, Thanksgiving to December 31.

Nearby Attractions: Marshall Pottery, Starr Family Historic Park, Caddo Lake and State Park, Harrison County Court House, Ginocchio Hotel, Harrison County Historical Museum, Michelson Art Museum, T. C. Lindsey store in nearby Jonesville.

Directions: From I-20 exit 617 north on U.S. 59, go 3.8 miles to U.S. 80, west 1 mile (three traffic lights) to North Washington St. Then go north three blocks. Entry is through the pedestrian tunnel.

       M

Site Address: 800 N. Washington Ave., Marshall, TX
Mailing Address: 800 N. Washington Ave., Ste. 1, Marshall, TX 75670
Telephone: (903) 938-9495 and (800) 513-9495 (toll-free)
Fax: (903) 938-8248
Website: www.marshalldepot.org

NEW BRAUNFELS
RAILROAD MUSEUM
Museum

Description: A railroad museum housed in a restored Missouri Pacific depot next to the Union Pacific main line. Displays include a steam locomotive, MP caboose, and numerous railroad artifacts. The museum is run by the Bluebonnet Chapter, NRHS.

Schedule: Thursdays through Mondays, 12 to 4 p.m. (closed Tuesdays and Wednesdays).

Admission/Fare: Admission by donations.

Locomotives/Rolling Stock: 0-6-0 Porter steam switcher; Missouri Pacific caboose no. 13385.

Special Events: Annual Model Railroad Jamboree, April 19; Folkfest, first weekend in May.

Nearby Attractions: Schlitterbahn Water Park, Guadalupe River Recreation, Historic New Braunfels German heritage sites. In San Antonio, the Alamo, Riverwalk, Seaworld and Fiesta Texas Theme Parks.

Directions: Downtown New Braunfels on San Antonio St. at the Union Pacific railroad tracks.

     M

Site Address: 302 W. San Antonio St., New Braunfels, TX
Mailing Address: PO Box 310475, New Braunfels, TX 78131
Telephone: (830) 627-2447
E-mail: lstewart@stic.net
Website: www.nbhrmsmuseum.org

TEXAS STATE RAILROAD
Train ride
Standard gauge

BILL LANGFORD

Description: Established in 1881, the Texas State Railroad now carries visitors on a four-hour, 50-mile round trip across 24 bridges as it travels through the heart of the east Texas rolling pine and hardwood forest. Victorian-style depots are located in Rusk and Palestine.

Schedule: March through November, weekends. June and July, Thursdays through Sundays.

Admission/Fare: Round trip–adults, $15; children, $9. One way–adults, $10; children, $6. Air-conditioned coach: round trip–adults, $20; children, $12. One way–adults, $13, children, $9.

Locomotives/Rolling Stock: No. 201, 1901 Cooke 4-6-0, former Texas & Pacific no. 316; no. 300, 1917 Baldwin 2-8-0, former Texas Southeastern no. 28; no. 400, 1917 Baldwin 2-8-2, former Magma Arizona no. 7; no. 500, 1911 Baldwin 4-6-2, former Santa Fe no. 1316; more.

Special Events: Murder on the Dis-Oriented Express, Special Dogwood Excursion, Civil War and World War II re-enactments, Victoria Christmas train, starlight excursions.

Nearby Attractions: Rusk–nation's longest foot bridge, Jim Hogg State Park. Palestine–National Scientific Balloon Base, "Old Town" Palestine.

Directions: Highway 84, 2 miles west of downtown Rusk, 3 miles east of downtown Palestine.

Site Address: 2503 W. Sixth, Rusk, TX
Mailing Address: PO Box 39, Rusk, TX 78785
Telephone: (800) 442-8951 and (903) 683-2561
Fax: (903) 683-5634
Website: www.tpwd.state.tx.us/park/railroad/

Description: One-third-mile ride behind a Baldwin RS4 switcher with an MP bay window caboose.

Schedule: Thursdays, Saturdays, and Sundays, 9 a.m. to 4 p.m.

Admission/Fare: Adults, $4; children 12 and under, $2.

Locomotives/Rolling Stock: Baldwin 2-6-0 Moscow Camden & St. Augustine Railroad; 0-4-0 saddle tank no. 1 Comal County Power Co.; three cabooses, UP cupola, MP bay window, MP transfer style.

Special Events: Santa's Holiday Depot: Friday, Saturday, Sunday, December 8-10, 15-17, 22-23, 6:30 to 9 p.m.

Nearby Attractions: San Antonio.

Directions: North of airport on Wetmore Rd., 2½ miles north of I-410.

Site Address: 11731 Wetmore Rd., San Antonio, TX
Mailing Address: 11731 Wetmore Rd., San Antonio, TX 78247
Telephone: (210) 490-3554
E-mail: ttm@stic.net
Website: www.txtransportationmuseum.org

Texas, Temple

RAILROAD AND HERITAGE MUSEUM
Museum

MARV IRVING

Description: Housed in the 1910 Gulf, Colorado & Santa Fe depot in down-town Temple, the museum features early Santa Fe and Missouri-Kansas-Texas station equipment and furniture, including a working telegraph for train orders. Observation alcoves with dispatch radios allow visitors to watch and listen to current BNSF operations just outside the museum. Exhibits focus on the effect of railroading on Texas and westward expansion, including a collection of railroad timetables, passes, photographs, and Santa Fe's engineer's tracings for the Southern Division.

Schedule: Year-round. Tuesdays through Saturdays, 10 a.m. to 4 p.m. and Sundays 12 to 4 p.m.

Admission/Fare: Adults, $4; seniors, $3; children 5+, $2.

Locomotives/Rolling Stock: No. 3423, 1921 Baldwin 4-6-2, former Santa Fe; no. 2301, 1937 Alco, the oldest surviving Santa Fe diesel; steel caboose no. 1556, former Gulf, Colorado & Santa Fe; more.

Special Events: Texas Train Festival, third weekend in September; specials.

Nearby Attractions: Lake Belton, camping, fishing.

Directions: I-35 exit Adams/Central Ave. Go east on Central to Seventh St. Turn right and enter parking lot. Enter on trackside.

*Coupon available, see coupon section.

Site Address: 315 W. Ave. "B," Temple, TX
Mailing Address: 315 W. Ave. "B," Temple, TX 76501
Telephone: (254) 298-5172
Fax: (254) 298-5171
E-mail: mirving@ci.temple.tx.us
Website: www.rrdepot.org

WICHITA FALLS RAILROAD MUSEUM
Museum
Standard gauge

DAVID H. GAINES

Description: The museum preserves the railroad history of Wichita Falls and the surrounding area. Artifacts, displays, and the Wichita Falls Model Railroad Club HO gauge layout are housed in some of the museum's rail cars. The museum's yard is located on the site of the Wichita Falls Union Passenger Station and is adjacent to the Burlington Northern & Santa Fe's (former Fort Worth & Denver) Forth Worth to Texline main line.

Schedule: Year-round. Tuesday through Friday, 9 a.m. to 4 p.m.; Saturday, 12 noon to 4 p.m., unless temperature is below 32°F or precipitation is falling.

Admission/Fare: Donations appreciated. Fee for special events.

Locomotives/Rolling Stock: FW&D 2-8-0 no. 304; MKT NW-2 no. 1029; FW&D RPO baggage no. 34; CB&Q power combine no. 7300; more.

Special Events: Zephyr Days Railroad Festival; check museum's website for specific dates and detailed information.

Nearby Attractions: Kell House Museum, Wichita Falls Police and Fire Museum, Texas Tourist Information Center.

Directions: From Holliday or Broad Streets, go toward downtown. At Ohio St. turn toward Ninth St.; at Ninth St. turn toward the BNSF tracks to museum's main gate. (Many downtown streets are one way.)

     M arm

Site Address: 500 Ninth St., Wichita Falls, TX
Mailing Address: PO Box 4242, Wichita Falls, TX 76308-0242
Telephone: (940) 723-2661 and (940) 692-6073
E-mail: wfrrm@wf.quik.com
Website: www.wf.quik.com/wfrrm/wfrrm01.htm

Utah, Heber City

HEBER VALLEY RAILROAD
Train ride, dinner train
Standard gauge

MIKE LEWIS

Description: Historic train excursions from 90 minutes to 3½ hours. Travel across farmland, lake shore, and into a glacier-carved canyon.

Schedule: Year-round. Daily in summer. Call for winter schedule or check website.

Admission/Fare: $14-$21. Discounts for children and senior citizens.

Locomotives/Rolling Stock: 1907 Baldwin steam 2-8-0s nos. 618 and 75; no. 1813 MRS1 (EMD); no. 1218 Davenport 44-ton; nos 270 and 250 Lackawanna coaches; no. 248 Clinchfield; nos. 365, 366, 501, 504 open-air cars; no. 3700 UP caboose; DRGW 7508 and 7510 coaches; more.

Special Events: BBQ train, Polar Express, Murder Mystery Train, "Haunted Canyon" Train, Sunset Special, Pioneer Day Old West Festival, Christmas Train. We also have a Casino Express Gaming Train.

Nearby Attractions: Homestead Resort, Heber Valley Railway Park, golf course, Cascade Springs.

Directions: Forty-five minutes from Salt Lake City. Take Highway 40 to Heber City. Go 6 blocks west of Main St. to the train.

†See ad on page A-17.

Site Address: 450 S. 600 W., Heber City, UT
Mailing Address: PO Box 609, Heber City, UT 84032
Telephone: (435) 654-5601 and (801) 581-9980
Fax: (435) 654-3709
Website: www.hebervalleyrr.org

Description: Ogden Union Station is primarily a railroad museum. Other features include John M. Browning Museum, classic cars, natural history, and an art gallery.

Schedule: Mondays through Saturdays, 10 a.m. to 5 p.m.

Admission/Fare: Adults, $4; seniors 65+, $3; children under age 12, $2.

Nearby Attractions: Historic 25th Street shops and restaurants, Hill Aerospace Museum, Eccles Dinosaur Park.

Directions: I-15 exit 344A, left at Wall Ave., north to Union Station.

*Coupon available, see coupon section.

Site Address: 2501 Wall Ave., Ogden, UT
Mailing Address: 2501 Wall Ave., Ogden, UT 84401
Telephone: (801) 629-8444 and (801) 629-8535
Fax: (801) 629-8555
E-mail: jeannieyoung@ci.ogden.ut.us
Website: www.theunionstation.org

Utah, Promontory Summit

GOLDEN SPIKE NATIONAL
HISTORIC SITE
Standard gauge

Description: This is the spot where the famous Golden Spike ceremony was held on May 10, 1869, completing the nation's first transcontinental railroad. Exact operating replicas of the original locomotives are on display and running, from May 1 through Labor Day. (These are photo runs only; no rides are available.) The locomotives operate between the hours of 10: 30 a.m. and 5 p.m. In the Visitor Center are color movies and many exhibits, with park rangers on hand.

Schedule: Visitor Center hours are 9 a.m. to 5:30 p.m. daily. Closed Mondays and Tuesdays starting late October through April 30. Closed New Year's Day, Thanksgiving, and Christmas. Outside attractions are open during daylight hours.

Admission/Fare: Per car–$5 winter, $7 summer. Adults on motorcycle or bicycle, $4. All prices are for seven days.

Locomotives/Rolling Stock: Full-sized operating replicas of Union Pacific 4-4-0 no. 119; and Central Pacific 4-4-0 no. 60, the "Jupiter."

Special Events: Golden State Anniversary Celebration, May; Annual Railroader's Festival, second Saturday in August.

Directions: 32 miles west of Brigham City, via Highways 13 and 83 through Corinne.

Site Address: Promontory, UT
Mailing Address: PO Box 897, Brigham City, UT 84302
Telephone: (435) 471-2209, ext. 18
Website: www.nps.gov/gosp/

GREEN MOUNTAIN RAILROAD
Train ride
Standard gauge

Description: Green Mountain Railroad offers two scenic rail excursions. The *Green Mountain Flyer* is a two-hour round trip departing from Bellows Falls to Chester Depot, closed Mondays. The excursion travels along the Connecticut and Williams Rivers, past two covered bridges, and the Brockways Mills gorge with a cascading waterfall. The *Vermont Valley Flyer* travels from Manchester to North Bennington with a stop at Arlington, home of the Norman Rockwell Museum. Manchester offers many specialty shops and an old-fashioned diner within walking distance from the station. Public transportation will make a loop to Manchester Center, offering a wide variety of outlet shops, and return to the train station.

Schedule: Late June through mid-October.

Admission/Fare: Varies with location and length of trip.

Locomotives/Rolling Stock: Alco RS-1 no. 405, former Rutland; 3000 EMD no. 302; 3000 EMD no. 304; 1750 EMD no. 803; 1750 EMD no. 804.

Special Events: Easter Bunny Express, Mother's Day, Santa Express.

Nearby Attractions: Basketville, Santa's Land, Vermont Country Store, Bellows Falls fish ladder.

Directions: I-91 exit 5 to Bellows Falls, take Route 5 north 3 miles.

Site Address: 354 Depot St., Bellows Falls, VT
Mailing Address: PO Box 498, Bellows Falls, VT 05101
Telephone: (802) 463-3069 and (800) 707-3530 (toll-free)
Fax: (802) 463-4084
E-mail: railtour@vermontrailway.com
Website: www.rails-vt.com

Virginia, Fairfax Station　　　**FAIRFAX STATION RAILROAD MUSEUM**
Museum, layout

Description: A restored Southern Railway depot rich in Civil War and local history. Clara Barton was a nurse here after the Second Battle of Manassas.

Schedule: Year-round, Sundays, 1 to 4 p.m. Labor Day, 12 to 5 p.m.

Admission/Fare: Adults, $2; children 3-10, $1.

Locomotives/Rolling Stock: Caboose N&W no. 518606.

Special Events: Model train layouts, every third Sunday of the month; annual Model Train Display, first weekend in December; annual Civil War/Community Day; Quilt Show; Art Show.

Nearby Attractions: Washington, D.C., museums, Manassas Museum, Fairfax City Museum.

Directions: Three miles south of Fairfax. We're located ¼ mile from the corner of Route 123 (Ox Rd.) and Fairfax Station Rd.

Site Address: 11200 Fairfax Station Rd., Fairfax Station, VA
Mailing Address: PO Box 7, Fairfax Station, VA 22039
Telephone: (703) 425-9225 and (703) 278-8833
E-mail: fxstn@fairfax-station.org
Website: www.fairfax-station.org/

Virginia, Fort Eustis

U.S. ARMY TRANSPORTATION MUSEUM
Museum, display

Description: This military-history museum displays items of transportation dating from 1776 to the present. Inside the 15,000-square-foot museum are dioramas and exhibits; on five acres outside are rail rolling stock, trucks, jeeps, amphibious marine craft, helicopters, aircraft, and an experimental hovercraft.

Schedule: Year-round, Tuesdays through Sundays, 9:30 a.m. to 4:30 p.m. Closed Mondays and federal holidays.

Admission/Fare: Free.

Locomotives/Rolling Stock: Steam locomotive 2-8-0 no. 607; steam locomotive 0-6-0 no. V-1923; ambulance ward car no. 87568; steam wrecking crane; 40-T and 50T flatcars; cabooses; Berlin duty train cars.

Nearby Attractions: Camping, Colonial Williamsburg, Jamestown, Yorktown.

Directions: I-64 exit 250A. Eleven miles south of Williamsburg.

Site Address: 300 Washington Blvd., Fort Eustis, VA
Mailing Address: 300 Washington Blvd., Fort Eustis, VA 23604
Telephone: (757) 878-1115
Website: www.eustis.army.mil/DPTMSEC/museum.htm

395

MARK MILLIGAN

Description: Thirty-five-minute excursion ride on the Virginia Railway Express.

Schedule: June 7, 2003, 10 a.m. to 4 p.m.

Admission/Fare: Free. $5 per person for excursion train ride.

Locomotives/Rolling Stock: Locomotives and rolling stock provided by Norfolk Southern, Virginia Railway Express, and Amtrak.

Special Events: Railway Festival, June 7; memorabilia, modular exhibits, living history and folklore, rail excursions, children's amusements, and great food.

Nearby Attractions: Manassas Museum, Manassas Battlefield Park, Splashdown Water Park.

Directions: From I-66 in Virginia take Route 234 business south. Follow it for 7 miles. Turn left on Center St. Turn right on Main St. Cross over the railroad tracks, and the festival is off to the right.

Site Address: 9431 West St., Manassas, VA
Mailing Address: 9431 West St., Manassas, VA 20110
Telephone: (703) 361-6599 and (877) 848-3018
Fax: (703) 361-6942
E-mail: hmi@erols.com
Website: www.visitmanassas.org

EASTERN SHORE RAILWAY MUSEUM
Museum

JOHN E. BATES

Description: Home of the Delmarva Chapter of the NRHS, this is a restored 1920s Pennsylvania Railroad station, with the original crossing shanty, a toolshed, artifacts, and a gift shop. An antique auto museum is also located on the grounds.

Schedule: Year-round: Mondays through Saturdays, 10 a.m. to 4 p.m.; and Sundays, 1 to 4 p.m. November through March: closed Wednesdays.

Admission/Fare: $2; children under age 12 are free.

Locomotives/Rolling Stock: 1920s RF&P post office car; 1962 NKP caboose no. 473; 1949 Wabash caboose no. 2783; Seaboard Airline diner car no. 8011; 1950 RF&P Fairfax River; 1927 Pullman "Diplomat" parlor/observation car.

Special Events: Parksley Festival, first Saturday in June.

Nearby Attractions: Chincoteague Island, Kiptopeke State Park, Ocean City.

Directions: Midway between Chesapeake Bay Bridge Tunnel and Salisbury, Maryland. From Route 13, it is 2 miles west on State Route 176.

Site Address: 18468 Dunne Ave., Parksley, VA
Mailing Address: PO Box 135, Parksley, VA 23421
Telephone: (757) 665-RAIL

Description: The Old Dominion Railway Museum tells the story of
  Virginia's railroading heritage through artifacts, videos, static displays,
  and an HO layout. It is located within a few blocks of the 1831 birth-
  place of Virginia railroad operations. Through its affiliate, the Old
  Dominion Chapter, NRHS, seasonal rides are offered on the
  Buckingham Branch Railroad.

Schedule: Year-round: Saturdays, 11 a.m. to 4 p.m.; and Sundays, 1 to 4 p.m.

Admission/Fare: Donations appreciated.

Locomotives/Rolling Stock: RF&P express car 185; David M. Lea & Co.
  0-4-0T no. 2; SCL caboose 21019; Seaboard System boxcar 111935;
  Fairmont motor car.

Special Events: Floodwall Guided Walking Tours, second Sunday of each
  month at 2 p.m. Rides on Buckingham Branch Railroad, May, October,
  and December.

Nearby Attractions: Downtown Richmond tourist area, Triple Crossing,
  Richmond Floodwall Promenade, James River boating, fishing, nature
  walks, downtown canal.

Directions: Take I-95 to exit 73 (Maury St.). Turn right onto Maury St., go
  two blocks. Turn left onto W. Second St., to right on Hull St., to
  museum on right.

      arm

Site Address: 102 Hull St., Richmond, VA
Mailing Address: PO Box 8583, Richmond, VA 23226
Telephone: (804) 233-6237
Fax: (804) 745-4735
Website: www.odcnrhs.org

Virginia, Roanoke

VIRGINIA MUSEUM OF TRANSPORTATION, INC.
Museum, display, layout
Standard gauge

Description: Diesel, steam, and electric locomotives, railcars, trolleys, carriages, automobiles, trucks, aviation, and rockets. Interactive exhibits, an oral history exhibit on African American Heritage on the N&W Railroad, O gauge train layout, resource library and archives, and more.

Schedule: Daily except major holidays and Mondays in January and February. Monday through Friday, 11 a.m. to 4 p.m.; Saturdays, 10 a.m. to 5 p.m.; Sundays, 1 to 5 p.m.

Admission/Fare: Adults, $6; seniors (60 and up), $5; children 3-11, $4; under 3 free, plus Roanoke City admission tax.

Locomotives/Rolling Stock: No. 611, J class 4-8-4, former Norfolk & Western; no. 4, 1910 Baldwin class SA 0-8-0, former Virginian Railway; no. 6, 1897 Baldwin class G-1 2-8-0, former N&W; no. 763, 1994 Lima class S-2 2-8-4, former Nickel Plate; no. 1, Celanese 0400 fireless locomotive; many diesels, City of Roanoke trolley, and D.C. Transit trolley: more.

Special Events: Calendar of events available on website.

Nearby Attractions: Visitor Center, Blue Ridge Parkway, two national forests, two state parks on lakes, museums, zoo, shopping, award-winning downtown Farmer's Market.

Directions: I-81 to I-581, exit 5 to downtown Roanoke, follow signs.

         M arm

Site Address: 303 Norfolk Ave. SW, Roanoke, VA
Mailing Address: 303 Norfolk Ave. SW, Roanoke VA 24016
Telephone: (540) 342-5670
Fax: (540) 342-6898
E-mail: info@vmt.org
Website: www.vmt.org

DAYTON HISTORICAL DEPOT SOCIETY
Museum

Description: This is the oldest train depot in the state of Washington, fully restored and on the National Register of Historic Places. It is used as a repository for train memorabilia and artifacts (mostly photos) from early Columbia County history.

Schedule: Tuesdays through Saturdays, 10 a.m. to 5 p.m. Sundays and Mondays, by appointment.

Admission/Fare: $2 per person.

Locomotives/Rolling Stock: UP caboose 25219 built in 1952.

Special Events: Depot Days, third Saturday in September, celebrating railroad history in the northwest.

Nearby Attractions: Three historic districts nearby.

Directions: Coming through Dayton on Highway 12, turn north on Second St., go one block.

       M arm

Site Address: 222 Commercial St., Dayton, WA
Mailing Address: PO Box 1881, Dayton, WA 99328
Telephone: (509) 382-2026

MOUNT RAINIER SCENIC RAILROAD
Train ride, display
Standard gauge

MARTIN HANSEN

Description: Mount Rainier Scenic Railroad has a collection of five operating steam logging locomotives. We offer 1½-hour excursions.

Schedule: June and September, weekends; July and August, daily; Santa Train, first three weekends of December.

Admission/Fare: Adults, $12.50; seniors, $11; children under 12, $8.50.

Locomotives/Rolling Stock: 2-8-2 71-ton Porter 1924; 70-ton 3-truck Climax 1928; 90-ton 3-truck Shay 1929; 70-ton 3-truck Heisler 1912; Alco 2-8-2 85-ton 1929; all steam locomotives.

Special Events: Tacoma Railfan Days, first weekend in May; Elbe Railfan Days, Tacoma, Thanksgiving weekend.

Nearby Attractions: Thirteen miles from south entrance to Mount Rainier National Park.

Directions: Take Highway 7 from Tacoma or Morton to Elbe.

*Coupon available, see coupon section.

Site Address: Elbe, WA
Mailing Address: PO Box 921, Elbe, WA 98330
Telephone: (888) 783-2611
Fax: (360) 569-2802
Website: www.mrsr.com

Washington, Pasco

WASHINGTON STATE RAILROADS HISTORICAL SOCIETY MUSEUM
Museum

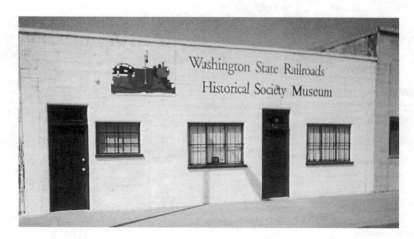

Description: Museum with 1909 and 1910 Northern Pacific & Great Northern cabooses being restored in yard. It also owns a 1900 Great Northern passenger car to be restored.

Schedule: April through December, Saturdays, 9 a.m. to 3 p.m.

Admission/Fare: Free. Donations appreciated.

Locomotives/Rolling Stock: Main rolling stock in Port of Pasco.

Nearby Attractions: BNSF hump yard and refueling facilities nearby; Franklin County History Society Museum.

Directions: Take Fourth Ave. exit south from I-182 in Pasco. Turn east on Clark to Tacoma St. Turn south to 122 N. Tacoma Ave.

Site Address: 122 N. Tacoma Ave., Pasco, WA
Mailing Address: PO Box 552, Pasco, WA 99301
Telephone: (509) 543-4159
E-mail: wsrhs@hotmail.com
Website: www.cbvcp.com/wsrhs

Washington, Snoqualmie

NORTHWEST RAILWAY MUSEUM
Train ride, museum, display
Standard gauge

Description: This is an operating railway museum with exhibits at the restored 1890 Queen Anne-style Snoqualmie Depot. It offers 10-mile round-trip train excursions to Snoqualmie Falls on restored heavyweight passenger coaches pulled by first-generation diesel locomotives.

Schedule: Train–April through October: Saturdays, Sundays, Memorial Day, July 4, Labor Day, some weekdays. Museum and gift shop–10 a.m. to 5 p.m. year-round. Memorial Day through Labor Day, seven days a week; Labor Day through Memorial Day, Thursday through Monday.

Admission/Fare: Train–adults, $8; seniors (62+), $7; children 3-12, $5. Museum–free.

Locomotives/Rolling Stock: Kennecott Copper no. 201, Alco RSD-4; Weyerhaeuser Timber Co. no. 1 Fairbanks-Morse H-12-44; Spokane, Portland & Seattle nos. 272 and 276, Barney and Smith steel coaches; Spokane, Portland & Seattle no. 213, Barney and Smith wood coach; OWRR&NCO no. 1590, Pullman observation car; more.

Special Events: Mothers Ride Free, May 10-11. Pops on Us, June 14-15. Snoqualmie Railroad Days, August 2-3. Santa Train, November 29-30, December 6-7, and December 13-14.

Directions: I-90, eastbound exit 27 or westbound exit 31.

*Coupon available, see coupon section.

Site Address: 38625 SE King St., Snoqualmie, WA
Site Address: 205 McClellan St., North Bend, WA
Mailing Address: PO Box 459, Snoqualmie, WA 98065-0459
Telephone: (425) 888-3030
Fax: (425) 888-9311
E-mail: info@trainmuseum.org
Website: www.trainmuseum.org

HAROLD K. CHANDLER

Description: This museum operates a tourist train on the former Northern Pacific White Swan branch line. Passenger excursions are 20-mile round trips from Harrah to White Swan. The 1911 former NP railroad depot in Toppenish serves as the museum and gift shop. The freight house has been converted to an engine house and the former NP section foreman's house is also adjacent to the depot.

Schedule: Train–September through October: Saturdays, 10:30 a.m. Museum–May through November: Monday through Saturday, 10 a.m. to 5 p.m.; Sunday, 1 to 5 p.m.

Fare/Admission: Train–adults, $10; children, $5. Museum–adults, $2; seniors and children, $1.

Locomotives/Rolling Stock: 1902 NP Baldwin 4-6-0 no. 1364; 1953 150-ton; two 1920s P70 heavyweights, former PRR; 1947 NP coach no. 588; NH combination coach; 1907 NP wooden caboose.

Special Events: Transportation Show, third weekend in August.

Nearby Attractions: Over 50 murals by noted artists.

Directions: Twenty minutes south of Yakima, Washington.

      M arm

Site Address: 10 Asotin Ave., Toppenish, WA
Mailing Address: PO Box 889, Toppenish, WA 98948
Telephone: (509) 865-1911
Website: www.nprymuseum.org/

NEW TYGART FLYER, WEST VIRGINIA CENTRAL RAILROAD
Train ride, dinner train
Standard gauge

LARS O. BYRNE

Description: Choice of 24-, 46-, 62-, or 102-mile excursions through two river valleys, over mountains, through a unique S-curve tunnel, and into two remote canyon areas with many scenic views.

Schedule: May through October. Winter excursions are scheduled. Call for dates.

Admission/Fare: Rates start at $15 and vary according to choice of excursion. Lounge car service is available.

Locomotives/Rolling Stock: FP7A no. 67; FP7B no. 415; FA-2 no. 303; BL-2 no. 82; all in WM speed lettering. Train is climate-controlled with dinette, snack coach, lounge car, and coaches.

Special Events: Civil War re-enactments in Bellington and Beverly, West Virginia, mid-July; Elkins Forest Festival, first week of October.

Nearby Attractions: Monongahela National Forest, Davis and Elkins College, Canaan Valley resort area, Cheat Mountain Salamander railbus ride.

Directions: Belington is located on U.S. Route 250, 5 miles north of U.S. 33. Elkins is located at the intersection of U.S. 33, Route 219, and Route 250 in east central West Virginia.

Site Address: Watkins Ave., Belington, WV
Mailing Address: E. Main St., Durbin, WV 26264
Telephone: (877) MTN-RAIL
Fax: (304) 456-5246
E-mail: jksmith@neumedia.net
Website: www.mountainrail.com

West Virginia, Cass

CASS SCENIC RAILROAD STATE PARK
Train ride, dinner train, museum
Standard gauge

Description: Experience the past with an excursion on a Shay steam locomotive past unparalleled views. Stay in a turn-of-the-century two-story logging house with all the modern conveniences. Enjoy the country store, museum, dinner train series, walking tours, and other special activities.

Schedule: Cass to Whittaker Station–May 24 through August 31, daily; departs Cass 10:50 a.m., 1 and 3 p.m. Cass to Bald Knob–May 24 through October 31, daily except Mondays; departs Cass 12 noon.

Admission/Fare: Prices vary with event, and reservations are recommended. Group rates are available. Call or check our website for details.

Locomotives/Rolling Stock: No. 2 1928 Pacific Coast Shay; no. 4 1922 70-C Shay; no. 5 1905 80-C Shay; no. 6 1945 150-C Shay; no. 11 1923 formerly Pacific Coast Shay no. 3.

Special Events: Special fall schedules are available.

Nearby Attractions: Green Bank National Radio Astronomy Observatory, Snowshoe Resort.

Directions: State Route 28/92 between Dunmore and Green Bank in Pocahontas County, eastern West Virginia.

†See ad on page A-3.

Site Address: Main St., Route 66, Cass, WV
Mailing Address: PO Box 107, Cass, WV 24927
Telephone: (304) 456-4300 and (800) CALL WVA
Fax: (304) 456-4641
E-mail: cassrr@neumedia.net
Website: www.cassrailroad.com

West Virginia, Cheat Bridge/Elkins

CHEAT MOUNTAIN
SALAMANDER RAIL RIDE
Train ride
Standard gauge

LARS O. BYRNE

Description: A 34-, 42-, or 76-mile mountain wilderness ride on top of Cheat Mountain through the spectacular Monongahela National Forest. Self-propelled railroad crosses 4,066-foot mountain pass and stops at inspirational high falls of the Cheat River, where it meets the *New Tygart Flyer* excursion train.

Schedule: April through October, 11 a.m. and 2:30 p.m. Earlier spring departures for campers and fishermen. Call for special winter trips.

Admission/Fare: Adults, $18; seniors, $16; children, $10. Special all-day fare–adults, $32; seniors, $28; children, $16.

Locomotives/Rolling Stock: No. M-3, a self-propelled 50-passenger Edwards Railway Company motor coach.

Special Events: Fall foliage runs.

Nearby Attractions: Monongahela National Forest, Durbin & Greenbrier Valley Scenic Railroad, Cass Scenic Railroad.

Directions: Cheat Bridge is located 28 miles south of Elkins or 7 miles north of Durbin on U.S. Route 250 in east central West Virginia.

*Coupon available, see coupon section.

Site Address: Red Run Rd., Cheat Bridge, WV
Mailing Address: PO Box 44, Durbin, WV, 26264
Telephone: (877) 686-7245
Fax: (304) 456-5246
E-mail: jksmith@neumedia.net
Website: www.mountainrail.com

**DURBIN & GREENBRIER
VALLEY RAILROAD**
Train ride
Standard gauge

LARS O. BYRNE

Description: A 10.5-mile, two-hour round trip on ex-C&ORR Greenbrier Division along the upper Greenbrier River. The *Durbin Rocket* is powered by a rare Climax steam locomotive.

Schedule: May through October, 11 a.m. and 2:30 p.m. Special winter steam operations; call for details.

Admission/Fare: Adults, $10; seniors, $9; children 4-11, $6.

Locomotives/Rolling Stock: Climax no. 3, ex-Middle Fork Railroad, 1910; 55-ton, two-truck Whitcomb no. 1, "Little Leroi"; 20-ton, 1940; 20-ton gas mechanical.

Special Events: Second annual Rails & Trails weekend, May 25; Durbin Days, July 19.

Nearby Attractions: Monongahela National Forest, Gaudineer Scenic Area, National Radio Astronomy Observatory, Cass Scenic Railroad, Cheat Mountain Salamander.

Directions: 35 miles south of Elkins on U.S. Route 250 in east central West Virginia.

*Coupon available, see coupon section.

Site Address: 2 E. Main St., Durbin, WV
Mailing Address: PO Box 44, Durbin, WV 26264
Telephone: (877) MTN-RAIL
Fax: (304) 456-5246
E-mail: jksmith@neumedia.net
Website: www.mountainrail.com

**HARPERS FERRY TOY TRAIN
MUSEUM & JOY LINE RAILROAD**
Train ride, museum, display, layout

Description: One-half mile of 16″ gauge track and a collection of antique toy trains in the museum

Schedule: April through October, weekends and holidays, 9 a.m. to 5 p.m.

Admission/Fare: Adults, $1.50.

Locomotives/Rolling Stock: Two miniature train G-16; S-16; homebuilt 2-4-4T; four M.T. passenger cars; six freight cars; caboose; snowplow; work crane.

Nearby Attractions: Harpers Ferry National Park.

Directions: Take 340 west one mile past Harpers Ferry and turn right onto Bakerton Rd. (Route 27), continue one mile and turn left.

Site Address: Bakerton Rd., Route 27, Harpers Ferry, WV
Mailing Address: Toy Train Museum, Rt. 3 Box 315, Harpers Ferry, WV 25425
Telephone: (304) 535-2521 and (304) 535-2291
E-mail: hfttm@aol.com
Website: mountainrail.com

West Virginia, Kenova

COLLIS P. HUNTINGTON RAILROAD HISTORICAL SOCIETY, INC.

Train ride, museum, display
Standard gauge

JEAN CHAPMAN

Description: Museum and rail excursions.

Schedule: Museum–Memorial Day through late September, Sundays, 2 to 5 p.m. Also by appointment year-round.

Admission/Fare: Museum–donations appreciated. Excursions–from $109.

Locomotives/Rolling Stock: C&O no. 1308 Mallet steam locomotive; C&O and VGN cabooses; operating hand car; boxcar; baggage car; concession car; RS-3 diesel locomotive former Reading engine; lounge car NYC no. 38.

Special Events: Annual New River Train Excursions, October; one-day 300-mile round trips; Tri-State Railroad Days, March, at Greenbo State Resort Park near Ashland, Kentucky.

Nearby Attractions: Radio Museum, Heritage Museum, Highlands Museum and Discovery Center, Huntington Museum of Art, Blenko Glass, CSX, NS main lines, Greenbo Lake State Resort Park.

Directions: Excursions–Seventh Ave. and Eighth St., Huntington. Museum–14th St. West and Ritter Park, Huntington.

Site Address: 1429 Chestnut St., Kenova, WV
Mailing Address: PO Box 451, Kenova, WV 25530
Telephone: (304) 453-1641
Fax: (304) 453-6120
E-mail: railtwo@aol.com
Website: www.newrivertrain.com

West Virginia, Romney

**POTOMAC EAGLE SCENIC
RAIL EXCURSIONS**
Train ride, dinner train
Standard gauge

D. W. CORBITT

Description: A 35-mile, three-hour ride along the South Branch of the Potomac River on the South Branch Valley Railroad. Potomac Eagle passengers see the "trough," a beautiful forested canyon. We also offer some all-day trips.

Schedule: May through October.

Admission/Fare: Three-hour trip: Coach–adults, $22; seniors, $20; children 3-14, $10. First-class club car–$49. All-day trip: Coach–adults, $40; seniors, $38; children 3-14, $20. First-class club car–$99.

Locomotives/Rolling Stock: 1952 EMD F-7 locomotive; mid-20s coaches; 1950 lounge cars.

Special Events: We have various special trains for home tours, Railfan Day, evening trips. Call, write, or check our website.

Nearby Attractions: Western Maryland Scenic Railroad.

Directions: Take Route 50 east or west to Route 28 north.

Site Address: Route 28 North, Romney, WV
Mailing Address: 2306 35th St., Parkersburg, WV 26104
Telephone: (304) 424-0736
Fax: (304) 485-5901
Website: www.wvweb.com/potomaceagle/

West Virginia, Wheeling

Layout

Description: See a 1,400-square-foot O gauge model railroad display. It boasts 14 working tracks with detailed scenery from the 1930s to mid-1950s.

Schedule: Open daily, 11 a.m. to 4 p.m.

Admission/Fare: Included with gate admission to facility. Adults, $5; children, $4.

Locomotives/Rolling Stock: Lionel, MTH, Williams, Weaver.

Special Events: Annual Oglebay Model Railroad Show, January 18-19. January 18, 10 a.m. to 5 p.m.; January 19, 10 a.m. to 3 p.m.

Nearby Attractions: Oglebay Resort, Wheeling Downs Racetrack and Casino, Kruger Street Toy and Train Museum, Marx Toy Museum.

Directions: From I-70 east or west, take Oglebay Park exit, then West Virginia Route 88 north 4 miles to Oglebay Park, and follow the signs.

Site Address: Oglebay Resort, Wheeling, WV
Mailing Address: Oglebay Resort, Route 88 North, Wheeling, WV 26003
Telephone: (304) 243-4034
Fax: (304) 243-4110
E-mail: smitch@oglebay-resort.com
Website: www.oglebay-resort.com

KRUGER STREET TOY AND TRAIN MUSEUM
Museum, layout

THOMAS POLLARD

Description: The museum houses a wide variety of toys, dolls, games, trains of all types, and playthings from all eras. The collections are housed in a restored 24,000-square-foot vintage 1906 Victorian schoolhouse. There are several operating train layouts and a gift shop on site.

Schedule: January through April, Friday through Sunday. May through October, open six days a week (closed Tuesdays). November and December, open seven days a week. Hours: 10 a.m. to 5 p.m.

Admission/Fare: Adults, $8; seniors (65+), $7; students (10-18), $5; under 10 free with adult.

Locomotives/Rolling Stock: Restored B&O caboose C-2019, an I-5 type caboose built in 1926.

Special Events: Host site for the Marx Toy and Train Collectors National Convention each June. Contact us for details.

Nearby Attractions: Oglebay Resort and Conference Center, Wheeling Island Racetrack and Gaming Center, and Jamboree USA, as well as many other smaller tourist sites. The Pennsylvania Trolley Museum is ½ hour away in Washington, Pennsylvania.

Directions: From I-70 or I-470, take exit 5. Turn left at bottom of exit ramp. Go to first traffic signal and turn left again onto Kruger St. Museum is about 100 yards up Kruger St. on the right-hand side.

       M

Site Address: 144 Kruger St., Wheeling, WV
Mailing Address: 144 Kruger St., Wheeling, WV 26003
Telephone: (304) 242-8133
Fax: (304) 242-1925
E-mail: museum@toyandtrain.com
Website: www.toyandtrain.com

Wisconsin, Brodhead

BRODHEAD HISTORICAL SOCIETY DEPOT MUSEUM
Museum

BRODHEAD INDEPENDENT REGISTER

Description: This restored Chicago, Milwaukee & St. Paul depot was built in 1881 and houses a permanent railroading display and other rotating historical displays. Milwaukee Road switch engine no. 760 and caboose no. 1900 stand alongside the depot and are also open to visitors.

Schedule: Memorial Day through September 30: holidays, Wednesdays, and weekends, 1 to 4 p.m. or by appointment.

Admission/Fare: Donations gratefully accepted.

Locomotives/Rolling Stock: Milwaukee Road switch engine no. 760; Milwaukee road caboose no. 1900.

Special Events: Depot Days, April 26-27, 2003, 10 a.m. to 5 p.m.

Nearby Attractions: Veteran's Memorial Park, Sugar River State Trail, Rustic Road, Amish attractions, antique shops, campsites, apple orchards.

Directions: Take Highway 11 to Brodhead. Highway 11 is 1st Center Ave. in Brodhead.

Site Address: 1108 1st Center Ave., Brodhead, WI
Mailing Address: 1108 1st Center Ave., Brodhead, WI 53520
Telephone: (608) 897-2549 or (608) 897-2639

Wisconsin, Colfax

COLFAX RAILROAD MUSEUM, INC.
Museum
Standard and narrow gauge

HERBERT F. SAKALAUCKS JR.

Description: The museum houses a large collection of railroad memorabilia, an extensive reference library, and offers a ride on a railroad speeder.

Schedule: May and September: Saturday, 11 a.m. to 5 p.m.; Sunday, 1 to 5 p.m. June through August: Thursday and Friday, 11 a.m. to 4 p.m.; Saturday, 11 a.m. to 5 p.m.; Sunday, 1 to 5 p.m.

Admission/Fare: Adults, $2; children 7-14, $1; children 6 and under free.

Locomotives/Rolling Stock: Soo Line GP-30 no. 703; Soo Line wooden caboose no. 273; Soo Line outside-braced boxcar no. 33400; Soo Line Barney & Smith coach no. 991; Milwaukee Road flanger no. 000931; two Canadian National speeders; velocipede; two GE 3-foot gauge electric locomotives.

Nearby Attractions: Hoffman Hills State park, Red Cedar River, Altoona Roundhouse.

Directions: Exit 52 off I-94 toward Chippewa Falls approximately ¾ mile, go north 8 miles on Highway 40 to Colfax. Take the first right after the railroad tracks; go one block and it's on the right.

Site Address: 500 Railroad, Colfax, WI
Mailing Address: PO Box 383, Colfax, WI 54730
Telephone: (715) 962-2076 and (715) 233-0434
Fax: (715) 235-3126
E-mail: colfaxrr@wwt.net

EAST TROY ELECTRIC RAILROAD
Train ride, dinner train, museum
Standard gauge

SCOTT PATRICK

Description: Ride restored trolleys or the museum's award-winning dinner train over Wisconsin's landmark railroad.

Schedule: May 24 through October 26, weekends, 11:30 a.m. to 4 p.m.; June 18 through August 22, Wednesdays through Fridays, 10 a.m. and 12 noon. Closed holidays. Call for dinner train schedule.

Admission/Fare: Trolley ride–adults, $9; children 3-11, $5; dinner train–$52.

Locomotives/Rolling Stock: CSS&SB 9, 13, 21, 24, 25, 30, 111; CTA 35, 45, 4420, 4453; Duluth-Superior Streetcar 253; P&W 64; ETER 21; TMER&L 200, D23, L6, L8, and L9; CNS&MRR 228 and 761; SEPTA PCCs 2120 and 2185; TTC PCC 4617; WP&L 26 and TE-1.

Special Events: Call for complete schedule.

Nearby Attractions: Many nearby historic attractions and other family activities.

Directions: One mile off I-43, north on Highway 120. Just 20 minutes north of Lake Geneva and 35 minutes southwest of Milwaukee.

*Coupon available, see coupon section.

Site Address: 2002 Church St., East Troy, WI
Mailing Address: PO Box 943, East Troy, WI 53120-0943
Telephone: (262) 642-3263
Fax: (262) 642-3197
Website: www.easttroyrr.org

NATIONAL RAILROAD MUSEUM
Museum
Standard gauge

Description: Explore America's railroad heritage at one of this country's oldest and largest railroad museums. Sit in the cab of the Union Pacific Big Boy, the world's largest steam locomotive. View General Eisenhower's World War II command train. Examine the future of railroading in the sleek 1955 General Motors Aerotrain. Enjoy a train ride aboard vintage rolling stock with historical narrative provided by the conductor. Admission includes train ride, all exhibits, model railroad layout, theater presentation, and 85-foot observation tower. The museum gift shop offers a wide selection of railroad-related items.

Schedule: Monday through Saturday, 9 a.m. to 5 p.m.; Sunday, 11 a.m. to 5 p.m. Closed New Year's Day, Easter, Thanksgiving, Christmas Eve, and Christmas. Open New Year's Eve, 9 a.m. to 2 p.m.

Admission/Fare: Adults, $7; seniors, $6; children 4-12, $5; 3 and under, free.

Locomotives/Rolling Stock: Union Pacific Big Boy no. 4017; Pennsylvania no. 4890 GG-1; General Motors Aerotrain; Eisenhower's World War II command train.

Special Events: Call for dates and details. Events throughout the year.

Directions: Highway 41 or 172, Ashland Ave. exit, travel north to Cormier Ave. and east three blocks.

Site Address: 2285 S. Broadway, Green Bay, WI
Mailing Address: 2285 S. Broadway, Green Bay, WI 54304
Telephone: (920) 437-7623
Fax: (920) 437-1291
E-mail: staff@nationalrrmuseum.org
Website: www.nationalrrmuseum.org

JOHN BROEKER

Description: Steam locomotive Soo Line 1003 is operated on cooperating railroads for special longer duration trips. Trips are usually in conjunction with local historical or holiday celebrations in the Wisconsin, Illinois, Michigan, and Minnesota areas. When not operating, the locomotive may be viewed at the Wisconsin Automotive Museum in Hartford.

Schedule: Approximately two or three excursions are operated each year at varied locations and on various dates. Events will be noted by message at (847) 438-6133 and through other advertising.

Locomotives/Rolling Stock: Soo Line 1003, 2-8-2, Class L1, built in 1913 and modernized by the Soo Line railroad in 1941. Its last regular operation was in 1955. The locomotive was restored and first operated again in November of 1996. Trains are assembled with vintage passenger cars as needed or requested.

Special Events: Call for dates and details. Events throughout the year.

Nearby Attractions: Our trips are chosen to be in conjunction with a fair, festival, or other celebration that includes activities such as art fairs, unique food concessions, historic town tours, amusement rides, etc.

Directions: Directions/map to special trip departure points are provided with ticket.

Mailing Address: Box 3466 RFD, Long Grove, IL 60047
Telephone: (847) 438-6133 and (651) 484-4843
Website: www.sooline1003.com

**CAMP FIVE MUSEUM
FOUNDATION, INC.**
Train ride, museum

Description: Camp Five offers visitors a unique mix of history, steam railroading, and ecology. Visitors ride the *Lumberjack Special* steam train (2.5 miles one way) to the museum complex; once there, they take a guided surrey tour through beautiful forests managed on a perpetual-cycle basis. A hayrack/pontoon ride on the Rat River is also an optional offer. The logging museum features an early-transportation wing and an active blacksmith shop; half-hour steam engine video; nature center with northern Wisconsin wildlife diorama; petting corral; and a large outdoor display of logging artifacts.

Schedule: June 18 through August 30, Mondays through Saturdays. Train leaves at 11 a.m., 12 noon, 1 and 2 p.m. Closed Sundays.

Admission/Fare: Adults, $15; students 13-17, $10; children 4-12, $5; 3 and under, free.

Locomotives/Rolling Stock: 1916 Vulcan 2-6-2; three cupola cabooses.

Special Events: Horse Pull, July 5; Heritage Festival, August 1-2; Fall Festival, September 20, 27, and October 4.

Directions: West of Laona on Highway 8.

*Coupon available, see coupon section.

Site Address: 5480 Connor Farm Rd., Laona, WI
Mailing Address: 5480 Connor Farm Rd., Laona, WI 54541
Telephone: (800) 774-3414 and (715) 674-3414
Fax: (715) 674-7400
E-mail: info@camp5museum.org
Website: www.camp5museum.org

PINECREST HISTORICAL VILLAGE
Museum

Description: An outdoor interpretive museum with 25 restored historic buildings and exhibit areas. Caboose 99006 has been recently restored and is open for public viewing.

Schedule: Daily, May 1 through third Sunday in October; also, second weekend in December.

Admission/Fare: Adults, $6; children 6-17, $4; 5 and under, free

Locomotives/Rolling Stock: Soo Line 0-6-0 no. 321 steam locomotive, built in 1887; Wisconsin Central caboose no. 99006, built in 1886; Soo Line depot from Collins, Wisconsin, built in 1896.

Special Events: German Fest, July; Fall Harvest Festival, October; Christmas at Pinecrest, December.

Nearby Attractions: Other attractions can be found in nearby Manitowoc and Two Rivers.

Directions: Seven miles west of Manitowoc. From I-43 follow JJ 3 miles west to Pine Crest Ln.

     M

Site Address: 924 Pine Crest Ln., Town of Manitowoc Rapids, WI
Mailing Address: MCHS, PO Box 574, Manitowoc, WI 54221-0574
Telephone: (920) 684-5110 (seasonal) and (920) 684-4445 (year-round)
Fax: (920) 684-0573
Website: www.mchistsoc.org

WHISKEY RIVER RAILWAY
Train ride
16" gauge

D. KLOMPMAKER COLLECTION

Description: A 2-mile scenic ride over the Wisconsin countryside, featuring many animals, including llamas, sheep, cattle, emu, longhorn steer, and zebra.

Schedule: Memorial Day through Labor Day: daily. October: weekends. December: daily.

Admission/Fare: $4.50. Unlimited rides: under 42″ tall, $10; 42″ and up, $13.

Locomotives/Rolling Stock: Gene Autry's Daylight Melody Ranch Special; Oakland Acorn Pacific; Gracy's Atlantic 1919 8½-ton Pacific (built in house); McCallister collection, including Atlantic, Shay, and 2-8-8-4 Mallet.

Nearby Attractions: Amusement park, miniature golf.

Directions: Located ¼ mile east of Highway 73 on Highway 19 in Marshall.

Site Address: 700 E. Main St., Marshall, WI
Mailing Address: 700 E. Main St., Marshall, WI 53559
Telephone: (888) 607-7735
Fax: (608) 655-4767
E-mail: gardyloo@jvlnet.com

MIKE NEPPER

Description: This railroad has operated at the Milwaukee County Zoo since 1958, carrying over 13 million riders. The 1.25-mile trip across zoo property lasts about eight minutes.

Schedule: May through September: daily, 10 a.m. to 4 p.m. March, April, October: weekends, 10 a.m. to 4 p.m.

Admission/Fare: Zoo admission required–adults, $9; children 3-12, $6; parking, $6. Train–adults, $2; children, $1.

Locomotives/Rolling Stock: Sandley light locomotive and rolling stock–coal-fired steam locomotive 4-6-2 no. 1924; coal-fired steam locomotive 4-4-2 no. 1916; diesel hydraulic switcher no. 1958; F2 diesel hydraulic no. 1996; 12-passenger day coaches nos. 1080-1096.

Nearby Attractions: Wisconsin State Fair Park, Summerfest Grounds, Miller Park baseball, Milwaukee Public Museum, Mitchell Park Domes, Wehr Nature Center, Whitnall Boerner Botanical Gardens, Cool Waters Water Park, many other area attractions.

Directions: The zoo is located 8 miles west of downtown Milwaukee at the intersection of I-94, I-894, and Highway 45.

Site Address: 10001 W. Bluemound Rd., Milwaukee, WI
Mailing Address: 10001 W. Bluemound Rd., Milwaukee, WI 53226
Telephone: (414) 771-3040
Fax: (414) 256-5410
Website: www.milwaukeezoo.org

**GREEN COUNTY
WELCOME CENTER**
Museum

DALTON PHOTOGRAPHY

Description: This beautifully restored Milwaukee Road Depot is home to the Historic Cheesemaking Center, serving as a shrine to the dairy and cheese industries. It also houses railroading memorabilia and serves as a regional Welcome Center and trailhead for the Cheese County Recreational Trail. Have lunch in our Rolling Ribsider Caboose!

Schedule: March through November, daily, 8:30 a.m. to 3 p.m.; December through February, Thursday through Saturday, 11 a.m. to 3 p.m., or by appointment.

Admission/Fare: Adults and children over 12, $1.

Locomotives/Rolling Stock: Milwaukee Road caboose no. 2094.

Special Events: Depot Days, third weekend in April–April 25-27, 2003; 8:30 a.m. to 5 p.m.

Nearby Attractions: Cheese factories, brewery, Green County Historical Museum, Cheese Country Trail, hockey rink, Cadiz Springs State Park, antique shops, historic town square.

Directions: Take Highway 69 to Monroe. The Welcome Center is located at the intersection of Highway 69 South and 21st St.

        M

Site Address: 2108 Seventh Ave., Monroe, WI
Mailing Address: PO Box 516, Monroe, WI 53566
Telephone: (608) 325-4636
Fax: (608) 325-4647
E-mail: info@greencountywelcomecenter.org
Website: http://cheese.htm

Description: A restored CNW depot, complete with railroad artifacts.

Schedule: June through August: first and third Sundays, 1 to 4 p.m. or by appointment.

Admission/Fare: Donations appreciated.

Locomotives/Rolling Stock: U.S. Army no. 4555 renumbered U.S. Army no. 7436, built by Vulcan Iron Works 1941, sold to Laona & Northern Railway October 1948 to become engine 3101; Soo Line caboose no. 138; CNW caboose no. 11153; Laona & Northern engine 101.

Special Events: Rail Fest Days, second Sunday in August.

Nearby Attractions: Mosquito Hill Nature Center, Memorial Park.

Directions: Route 45 north to Business 45, High St. east to railroad tracks, north to the depot.

      M

Site Address: 900 Montgomery St., New London, WI
Mailing Address: 101 Beckert Rd., Apt. 204, New London, WI 54961-2500
Telephone: (920) 982-5186 and (920) 982-8557

Wisconsin, North Freedom

MID-CONTINENT RAILWAY HISTORICAL SOCIETY
Train ride, dinner train, museum
Standard gauge

PAUL SWANSON

Description: Seven-mile, 50-minute diesel-powered ride in rural setting. Trains depart from a restored 1894 C&NW depot. On display is an extensive collection of early 1900s-era vintage freight, passenger, and company-service equipment. Caboose and cab rides are offered. Dinner and first-class service operate on select dates. Call or visit website for details.

Schedule: Mid-May through Labor Day: daily, 10:30 a.m., 12:30, 2, and 3:30 p.m. Weekends through mid-October.

Admission/Fare: Adults, $11; seniors, $10; children 3-12, $6; under 3, free. Cab ride–$27. Caboose–adult, $13; child, $7. First class–$21. Dinner train–$69. Extra fare for Snow Train. Reservations required for dinner.

Locomotives/Rolling Stock: MCRY no. 7, ALCO S-1 (1944); C&NW no. 1385, ALCO 4-6-0 (1907); Polson Logging Co. no. 2, Baldwin 2-8-2 (1912); WC&C no. 1, MLW 4-6-0 (1913); Dardanelle & Russellville no. 9, Baldwin 2-6-0 (1884); DL&W combine and coaches; C&NW combine no. 7409; more.

Special Events: Snow Train, mid-February; Civil War Encampment, July; Autumn Color Weekends, early October; Santa Express, late November. Call or visit website for dates and times.

Directions: Seven miles west of Baraboo. State Highway 136 west to County Highway PF to North Freedom. Follow signs.

*Coupon available, see coupon section.

Site Address: E8948 Museum Rd., North Freedom, WI
Mailing Address: PO Box 358, North Freedom, WI 53951-0358
Telephone: (608) 522-4261
Fax: (608) 522-4490
E-mail: inquiries@midcontinent.org
Website: www.midcontinent.org

Wisconsin, Osceola

OSCEOLA & ST. CROIX VALLEY RAILWAY
MINNESOTA TRANSPORTATION MUSEUM

Train ride, museum
Standard gauge

JAKE LUECKEL

Description: Enjoy the scenic St. Croix River Valley on a 90-minute round trip between Osceola and Marine-on-St. Croix, Minnesota, or a 45-minute round trip through rural Wisconsin between Osceola and Dresser. See the restored Osceola Historical Depot, featuring exhibits about railroading and the Osceola area, and the U.S. Railway Post Office exhibits aboard Northern Pacific triple combine no. 1102.

Schedule: Memorial Day through October, weekends. Charters available during the week.

Admission/Fare: Marine trip–$7 to $13; Dresser trip–$5 to $10.

Locomotives/Rolling Stock: Northern Pacific no. 328 4-6-0 steam locomotive; NP no. 105 LST&T switcher engine; nos. 2604 and 2608 cars, former Rock Island; NP triple combine car no. 1102; DL&W no. 2232 commuter coach; Soo Line 559 1951 Electromotive GP7; three streamline coaches.

Special Events: Mother's Day Brunch, Dinner and Pizza Train, Fireworks Express, Park Naturalist Trips, and Fall Color Trips.

Nearby Attractions: Cascade Falls, St. Croix River, St. Croix Art Barn, Interstate Park, and campgrounds.

Directions: I-35W to Forest Lake, Highway 97 east to Highway 95, north to I-243 across the St. Croix River to Highway 35S, to Depot Rd.

*Coupon available, see coupon section.

Radio frequency: 161.355

Site Address: 114 Depot Rd., Osceola, WI
Mailing Address: PO Box 176, Osceola, WI 54020
Telephone: (715) 755-3570, (800) 711-2591, and (651) 228-0263
Fax: (715) 294-3330
E-mail: oscvrlwy@centurytel.net
Website: www.mtmuseum.org or www.trainride.org

Wisconsin, Platteville

THE MINING MUSEUM AND ROLLO JAMISON MUSEUM
Train ride, museum
24" gauge

Description: Tour an 1845 lead mine, and ride a 1931 mine locomotive above ground. Tour home and farm exhibits in Rollo Jamison Museum. (The train ride is part of the mine tour and takes three to five minutes.)

Schedule: May through October, daily, 9 a.m. to 5 p.m. Self-guided exhibits, November through April, Monday through Friday, 9 a.m. to 4 p.m. Group tours available year-round.

Admission/Fare: Adults, $7; seniors, $6.30; children 5-15, $3.

Locomotives/Rolling Stock: Whitcomb Co., Rochelle, Illinois, 1931 locomotive.

Nearby Attractions: First Capital Historic Site, University of Wisconsin-Platteville.

Directions: Corner of Main St. and Virgin Ave., three blocks north of Highway 151.

*Coupon available, see coupon section.

Site Address: 405 E. Main St., Platteville, WI
Mailing Address: PO Box 780, Platteville, WI 53818-0780
Telephone: (608) 348-3301
Fax: (608) 348-4640
E-mail: kleefiss@uwplatt.edu

LITTLE FALLS RAILROAD & DOLL MUSEUM
Train ride, museum
24" gauge

JIM BROWN

Description: A three-acre campus with a doll museum building and a train museum building. We have a picnic area, swings, and a 12″ gauge train with 300 feet of track (being expanded to 2,000 feet).

Schedule: April 1 through November 1, daily except Wednesdays, 12 to 5 p.m.

Admission/Fare: Each museum, $3; admission to both, $5. Children's train ride, $1.50.

Locomotives/Rolling Stock: Milwaukee bay window caboose 992175.

Special Events: Operating garden railroad daily, weather permitting.

Nearby Attractions: Wegner Grotto, Majestic Pines Casino.

Directions: Halfway between Sparta and Black River Falls, 1.8 miles east of Cataract on County Highway II.

        M

Site Address: 9208 County Highway II, Sparta, WI
Mailing Address: 9208 County Highway II, Sparta, WI 54656-6485
Telephone: (608) 272-3266
Fax: (608) 272-3266
E-mail: raildoll@centurytel.net
Website: http://raildoll.com

RAILROAD MEMORIES MUSEUM
Museum, display, layout

CARL SCHULT

Description: Historical, educational museum covering all aspects of railroading. Tools, equipment, track vehicles, memorabilia, and history from the 1800s. Many station signs, books, art, and rare uniforms. Guided tours, videos, models, eleven large rooms full and an 8 x 12-foot scale diorama of the Spooner yard and complex from the years when Spooner was a big, busy terminal.

Schedule: Memorial weekend through Labor Day weekend, daily, 10 a.m. to 5 p.m. Groups by appointment.

Admission/Fare: Adults, $3; children 6-12, $.50; under age 6 are free.

Nearby Attractions: Namekagon Scenic River System, Bulik's Amusement Park, Museum of Wood Carving, Heart O' North Rodeo, State Fish Hatchery.

Directions: Two blocks from Highways 70 and 63; in old CNW depot at Walnut and Front Streets.

*Coupon available, see coupon section.

       arm

Site Address: 424 Front St., Spooner, WI
Mailing Address: N8425 Island Lake Rd., Spooner, WI 54801
Telephone: (715) 635-3325; when closed, (715) 635-2752, 635-3833
Website: www.spoonerwi.com/rail_museum.htm

Wisconsin, Wisconsin Dells

RIVERSIDE & GREAT NORTHERN RAILWAY
Train ride, museum, display
15" gauge

MARSHALL L. "PETE" DEETS

Description: A scenic 3-mile ride on a railroad dating back to the 1850s, through rock cuts and thick forest just north of Wisconsin Dells. The R&GN is a living museum preserving miniature steam equipment and the facilities of the Sandley Light Railway Equipment Works, manufacturers of narrow gauge railroads for over 30 years.

Schedule: Memorial Day through Labor Day: daily, 10 a.m. to 5:30 p.m.; trains run every 45 minutes. Friday and Saturday, Sunset Specials run to dusk. May, October, November, and December: weekends, 10 a.m. to 4 p.m.; trains run on the hour. Weather permitting, call ahead to check operation schedule.

Admission/Fare: Adults, $6.50; seniors, $5; children 4-15, $4.50; under age four are free; family pass, $20.

Locomotives/Rolling Stock: No. 82 1957 4-4-0 steam engine former Milwaukee County Zoo; vertical boiler "Tom Thumb" steam engine; no. 98 1953 4-4-0 steam engine; no. 95 SW-style diesel engine.

Nearby Attractions: Wisconsin Dells-Lake Delton area.

Directions: West of Kilbourne Bridge in Wisconsin Dells. Go north on Stand Rock Rd. for about one mile to a stop sign at the railroad viaduct, turn right under the viaduct, then left into the driveway.

Site Address: N115 Highway N, Wisconsin Dells, WI
Mailing Address: N115 Highway N, Wisconsin Dells, WI 53965
Telephone: (608) 254-6367
E-mail: simstrains@compuserve.com
Website: www.randgn.com

Wyoming, Evanston

ROUNDHOUSE RESTORATION, INC.
Display

RICHARD COLLIER

Description: Not a museum but a historic depot with a 28-stall roundhouse and working turntable. Tours are available. The Joss House is a Chinese museum.

Schedule: Winter–Mondays through Fridays, 8 a.m. to 5 p.m.
Summer–Mondays through Fridays, 9 a.m. to 9 p.m.; Saturdays, 9 a.m. to 7 p.m.; and Sundays, 12 noon to 6 p.m.

Admission/Fare: Free.

Special Events: Roundhouse Festival, second weekend in August (model train show, arts and crafts, book fair, tours).

Nearby Attractions: Wyoming Downs horseracing, summer months. Very close to Park City and Salt Lake City, Utah. South of Jackson Hole and Yellowstone Park Uinta Mountains.

Directions: Main St., on I-80, 85 miles east of Salt Lake City.

Site Address: 1500 Main St., Evanston, WY
Mailing Address: 1200 Main St., Evanston, WY 82930
Telephone: (307) 783-6320
Fax: (307) 783-6390
E-mail: urevan@allwest.net
Website: www.roundhouserestoration.org

Alberta, Calgary

HERITAGE PARK HISTORICAL VILLAGE
Train ride
Standard gauge

Description: Heritage Park is Canada's largest living historical village, where the past comes to life right in front of your eyes. We are a first-class summer tourist attraction and a year-round catering and convention facility.

Schedule: May through Labor Day, daily, 9 a.m. to 5 p.m. Weekends until Thanksgiving.

Admission/Fare: Call or write for information.

Locomotives/Rolling Stock: Two port steam 0-4-0T 1909 compressed air; 1902 no. 3 Vul Steam 0-4-0T; 1905 no. 4 CP CPR steam 0-6-0; 1942 no. 2023 USA Alco steam 0-6-0; 1944 no. 2024 Lima Steam 0-6-0; 1949 no. 5931 CPR MLW steam 2-10-4; 1944 no. 7019 CPR 1 MLW S2 1000.

Special Events: Opening weekend in May; Festival of Quilts, May; Railway Days and Father's Day, June; Canada Day, July; Hayshaker Days and Heritage Family Festival, August; Old Time Fall Fair and Fall Harvest Sale, September; October West, October. Call for information.

Nearby Attractions: Calgary Zoo, Olympic Park, Glenbow Museum, Fort Calgary, Alberta Science Centre.

Directions: Follow Heritage Dr. west.

Site Address: 1900 Heritage Dr. SW, Calgary, AB
Mailing Address: 1900 Heritage Dr. SW, Calgary, AB Canada T2V 2X3
Telephone: (403) 268-8500
Fax: (403) 268-8501
E-mail: info@heritagepark.ab.ca
Website: www.heritagepark.ab.ca

Alberta, Edmonton

EDMONTON RADIAL RAILWAY SOCIETY
Train ride
Standard gauge

ARTHUR HAMILTON

Description: We offer two trolley rides: The Park Division operates a 1.1-mile streetcar ride within Fort Edmonton Park. The Bridge Division trolley operates across a high-level bridge and continues south to the carbarn. The ride is about 1.5 miles.

Schedule: Park Division–third weekend in May to Labor Day, daily; 10 a.m. to 4 p.m. July and August: until 6 p.m. September: Sundays only. Bridge Division–third weekend in May to Labor Day, daily; 11 a.m. to 4 p.m. September: weekends.

Admission/Fare: $3 round trip; $10 family round trip. One-way and group rates are available.

Locomotives/Rolling Stock: Park Division–five trolleys are in operation. Bridge Division–Hankai (Osaka, Japan) no. 247 (1921).

Special Events: Park Division–Harvest Fair last weekend in August; trolley charters are available. Bridge Division–ten-day fringe theater festival, mid-August; we run 11 a.m. to 10 p.m. then.

Directions: Park Division–Whitemud Freeway to south end of Quesnel Bridge; east on Fox Dr. 100 meters to Park Drive. Bridge Division–Grandin subway station is one block west of the north terminal. The south terminal is at 85th Ave. and 103rd St.

         M
arm VIA Bridge Division is

Site Address: Park Division–Fort Edmonton Park, Fox Dr., Edmonton, AB
Bridge Division–Strathcona Barn, 84th Ave. and 103rd St., Edmonton, AB
Mailing Address: PO Box 45040, Edmonton, AB Canada T6H 5Y1
E-mail: info@edmonton-radial-railway.ab.ca
Website: www.edmonton-radial-railway.ab.ca

433

Alberta, Edmonton

FORT EDMONTON PARK
Train ride
Standard gauge

Description: Nestled in Edmonton's river valley, Fort Edmonton Park is brought to life by costumed staff reenacting life as it was in Edmonton at the 1846 fur trading fort, and on the streets of 1885, 1905, and 1920. The train transports visitors through the park.

Schedule: May 18 through September 1, daily; Sundays in September.

Admission/Fare: Adults, $8; seniors and youth 13-17, $6; children 2-12, $4.25; families, $24.50. Price includes train ride.

Locomotives/Rolling Stock: 1919 Baldwin 2-6-2 no. 107, former Oakdale & Gulf Railway (restored to its 1905 appearance).

Special Events: Call, write, or check website for information.

Nearby Attractions: Downtown Edmonton and West Edmonton Mall.

Directions: Edmonton, Alberta.

          VIA

Site Address: Fox Dr. and Whitemud Dr., Edmonton, Alberta
Mailing Address: PO Box 2359, Edmonton, AB Canada T5J 2R7
Telephone: (780) 496-8787
Fax: (780) 496-8797
Website: www.edmonton.ca/fort

Alberta, Stettler

ALBERTA PRAIRIE RAILWAY
EXCURSIONS
Train ride, dinner train
Standard gauge

Description: Round-trip tours of several different types are featured from Stettler to a combination of rural lineside communities such as Big Valley, Castor, Halkirk, and Coronation. Excursions are operated on a former Canadian National branch line through picturesque parkland and prairies in central Alberta and on a former Canadian Pacific branch line past Stettler to Coronation. All excursions include full-course roast beef dinner and onboard entertainment and commentary. Fine dining excursions to Big Valley include a five-course meal and entertainment.

Schedule: Late May through August: weekends and selected weekdays. September through mid-October: weekends. Fine dining–November through April, select dates.

Admission/Fare: Varies; call for complete schedule and fare information.

Locomotives/Rolling Stock: No. 41 1920 Baldwin 2-8-0, former Jonesboro Lake City & Eastern; no. 41, former Frisco; no. 77, former Mississippi; more.

Special Events: Murder Mysteries, Canada Day, Red Coat, Train Robberies.

Nearby Attractions: Ol' MacDonald's Resort, museum, golf, Rochon Sands Provincial Park.

Directions: A two-hour drive from Edmonton or Calgary; one hour east of Red Deer in central Alberta.

Site Address: 4611 47 Ave., Stettler, AB
Mailing Address: PO Box 1600, Stettler, AB Canada T0C 2L0
Telephone: (403) 742-2811
Fax: (403) 742-2844
E-mail: info@absteamtrain.com
Website: www.absteamtrain.com

British Columbia, Cranbrook

WALTER LANZ

Description: The museum collects and restores vintage CPR passenger train sets. It is scheduled to move to its new location in September 2002, which integrates the Royal Alexandra Hall Cafe (1906), Freight Shed (1898), and other facilities.

Schedule: Year-round. Canadian Thanksgiving (U.S. Columbus Day) until Easter: Tuesday through Saturday, 10 a.m. to 5 p.m.; tours, noon until 5 p.m. Easter until Canadian Thanksgiving: daily, 10 a.m. to 6 p.m.

Admission/Fare: Please check website for 2003 prices.

Locomotives/Rolling Stock: The museum will eventually have displays from the following train sets: 1880s *Pacific Express;* 1907 *Soo-Spokane Train Deluxe;* 1929 *Trans-Canada Limited;* 1936 *Chinook;* 1955 *Canadian.*

Special Events: Sam Steele Day, mid-June; Rockin in the Rockies Vintage Car Show, June; Gala Christmas dinner, late November and early December.

Nearby Attractions: Fort Steele Heritage Town, Kimberley Bavarian Town, local campgrounds, restaurants, shops, golf courses, ski hills in winter.

Directions: On Van Horne St. go north on Hwy. 3/95 in downtown Cranbrook. Parking is at King St. intersection. The new museum, at 57 Van Horne St. S, is 1½ blocks south of the old site across the parking lot.

*Coupon available, see coupon section.

         M arm

Site Address: 57 Van Horne St. S, Cranbrook, BC
Mailing Address: Box 400, Cranbrook, BC Canada V1C 4H9
Telephone: (250) 489-3918
Fax: (250) 489-5744
E-mail: mail@trainsdeluxe.com
Website: www.trainsdeluxe.com

BRITISH COLUMBIA
FOREST DISCOVERY CENTRE
Train ride, museum
Narrow gauge

Description: A 1910 steam train ride (1½ miles long), forest discovery walks, historical collection, picnic and playground area, much more. We are on a 100-hundred-acre site with a figure-eight track.

Schedule: Train from Easter to Labor Day.

Admission/Fare: Adults, $9; seniors and students 13-18, $8; children 5-12, $5; under age 5 are free. Group rates available.

Locomotives/Rolling Stock: Bloedel Stewart & Welch no. 1; Hillcrest Lumber Co. no. 1; Shawnigan Lake Lumber Co. no. 2; Mayo Lumber Co. no. 3; Hillcrest Lumber Co. no. 9; locomotive no. 25; locomotive no. 24; no. 27 speeder; White Pass no. 1; Plymouth no. 26; Whitcomb no. 9; more.

Special Events: National Forestry Week, Mother's Day, Father's Day, Classic Tractors, Celebration of Steam, Labor Day Picnic, Terry Fox Run, Thanksgiving Family Harvest Celebration.

Nearby Attractions: Duncan Totem Tours, Native Heritage Centre, Chemainus Murals.

Directions: Located five minutes north of Duncan off Trans Canada Highway.

*Coupon available, see coupon section.

Site Address: 2892 Drinkwater Rd., Duncan, BC
Mailing Address: 2892 Drinkwater Rd., Duncan, BC Canada V9L 6C2
Telephone: (250) 715-1113
Fax: (250) 715-1170
E-mail: bcfm@islandnet.com

British Columbia, Fort Steele

FORT STEELE RAILWAY
Train ride
Standard gauge

MARTIN ROSS

Description: Currently a Montreal Locomotive Works 2-6-2 Prairie-type locomotive pulls passengers around a 2.5-mile loop of track with a stop at a lookout point to explain the view and local railroad history.

Schedule: Daily, end of June to Labor Day, 12:30 p.m. to 5:30 p.m.

Admission/Fare: Adults, $6; seniors (65+), $5; youth 13-18, $3; children 6-12, $2. Children under 6 are free.

Locomotives/Rolling Stock: Montreal Locomotive Works 2-6-2 Prairie-type no. 1077, built in 1923; Shay class 90 Pacific Coast no. 115, built in 1934; Dunrobin, Sharp & Stewart 2-4-0 side tank engine, built in 1895.

Nearby Attractions: Fort Steele Heritage Town, Fairmont and Radium Hot Springs, Wasa Provincial Park.

Directions: Southeast corner of British Columbia, 16 kilometers northeast of Cranbrook, B.C., on Highway 93/95.

Site Address: Fort Steele Heritage Town, Fort Steele, BC
Mailing Address: 9851 Highway 93/95, fort Steele, BC Canada V0B 1N0
Telephone: (250) 417-6000 and (250) 426-7352 (24-hour information line)
Fax: (250) 489-2624
E-mail: info@fortsteele.bc.ca
Website: www.fortsteele.bc.ca

British Columbia, Kelowna

**OKANAGAN VALLEY
WINE TRAIN**
Train ride, dinner train
Standard gauge

Description: A five-hour scenic family rail excursion featuring a round trip from Kelowna to Vernon on restored railcars from the the Super Continental cross-country passenger train.

Schedule: July to October, Saturdays. Trains depart at 5 p.m.

Admission/Fare: Theme car–$79.95 (Canadian) per person plus GST. Day coach–$29.95 (Canadian) per person plus GST.

Locomotives/Rolling Stock: 1954 CN Super Continental train cars.

Directions: From the Grand Okanagan (Water St.) go to the Skyreach Centre (Clement), turn left on Ellis at the CNR station and right onto Recreation Ave., where you will see the flags for the Okanagan Valley Wine Train by the train station.

Site Address: 600 Recreation Ave., Kelowna, BC
Mailing Address: Suite 903, East Tower, Edmonton Inn/Ramada North, 11830 Kingsway Ave., Edmonton, AB Canada T5G 0X5
Telephone: (250) 712-9888 and (888) 674-TRAK. **Fax:** (780) 482-7666
E-mail: funtrain@telusplanet.net
Website: www.okanaganvalleywinetrain.com

ALBERNI PACIFIC RAILWAY
Train ride, museum
Standard gauge

BERT SIMPSON

Description: A train ride from downtown Port Alberni to McLean Mill National Historic Site steam sawmill, 35 minutes each way.

Schedule: June 19 to September 1, 2003. Thursday to Monday, three trips per day.

Admission/Fare: Adults, $22 (Canadian); seniors and youth, $16; family, $45.

Locomotives/Rolling Stock: 1929 Baldwin 2-8-2T; Alco RS-3; five renovated CN transfer cabooses.

Special Events: Train robberies, long weekends in summer; Dixieland band concert, Labor Day weekend.

Nearby Attractions: Alberni Valley Museum, Maritime Discovery Centre.

Directions: On Vancouver Island, take Highway 9 to Port Alberni and follow the signs.

*Coupon available, see coupon section.

    M

Site Address: 5633 Smith Rd., Port Alberni, BC, Canada
Mailing Address: Site 125, C14 Port Alberni, BC V9Y 7L5
Telephone: (250) 723-1376
Fax: (250) 723-5910
E-mail: info@alberniheritage.com
Website: www.alberniheritage.com

British Columbia, Revelstoke

REVELSTOKE RAILWAY MUSEUM
Museum
Standard gauge

Description: History of the Canadian Pacific Railway from construction to present day, focusing on western Canada.

Schedule: Year-round. July and August, 9 a.m. to 8 p.m. December through March, 1 to 5 p.m. April through June and September through November, 9 a.m. to 5 p.m.

Admission/Fare: Adults, $6; seniors, $5; youth, $3; children 6 and under, free; family, $13. Group rates available.

Locomotives/Rolling Stock: CP steam locomotive 5468; business car no. 4; caboose no. 437477; road repair car no. 404116; 40-foot flatcar no. 421237; service flanger no. 400573; Jordan spreader no. 402811; wedge plow no. 401027; baggage car no. 404944.

Special Events: Revelstoke Railway Days, third weekend in August.

Nearby Attractions: Revelstoke Hydroelectric Dam, Mt. Revelstoke and Glacier National Parks, British Columbia Interior Forestry Museum, City Museum, Canyon Hot Springs.

Directions: In downtown Revelstoke, at Victoria Rd. along the tracks.

Site Address: 719 Track St. W., Revelstoke, BC
Mailing Address: PO Box 3018, Revelstoke, BC Canada V0E 2S0
Telephone: (250) 837-6060 and (877) 837-6060 (toll free in North America)
Fax: (250) 837-3732
E-mail: railway@telus.net
Website: www.railwaymuseum.com

**WEST COAST RAILWAY
HERITAGE PARK**
Train ride, museum
Standard and 7½" gauge

Description: Western Canada's largest heritage railway collection, located in a 12-acre beautiful mountain valley setting. A mini rail (7½" gauge) ride circles the park.

Schedule: Year-round, daily, 10 a.m. to 5 p.m. Closed Christmas and New Year's Day.

Admission/Fare: Adults, $8 (Canadian); seniors, $7; children, $5.

Locomotives/Rolling Stock: Canadian Pacific Royal Hudson no. 2860; Canadian Pacific FP7A no. 4069; Pacific Great Eastern 2-6-2 no. 2; 1890 business car British Columbia, RPO, plus 65 other pieces of heritage rolling stock from five major railways that served western Canada.

Special Events: Canada Day, July 1; Christmas Lights at the Park, December.

Nearby Attractions: 40 miles north of Vancouver, B.C., on the way to Whistler resort area.

Directions: Follow Highway 99 north from Vancouver to Squamish, and follow signs from highway to the Heritage Park.

*Coupon available, see coupon section.

Site Address: 39645 Government Rd., Squamish, BC
Mailing Address: PO Box 2790 Stn Main, Vancouver, BC Canada V6B 3X2
Telephone: (604) 898-9336
Fax: (604) 898-9349
E-mail: manager@wcra.org
Website: www.wcra.org

**KETTLE VALLEY STEAM
RAILWAY SOCIETY**
Train ride
Standard gauge

DAVID WEST, WEST PHOTOGRAPHIC ARTS

Description: Enjoy a 90-minute journey traveling along cliffsides overlooking beautiful orchards and vineyards of the scenic Okanagan Valley, while enjoying a historical commentary.

Schedule: May, June, September, and October: weekends and Mondays, 10:30 a.m. and 1:30 p.m. July and August: Thursdays through Mondays, 10:30 a.m. and 1:30 p.m.

Admission/Fare: Adults, $15; seniors/students, $14; children 3-12, $10; age 2 and under are free. Group rates available with reservation for 20 or more.

Locomotives/Rolling Stock: 1924 Shay no. 3 locomotive; two vintage coaches, and two open-air cars.

Special Events: The Great Train Robberies and barbecues, Teddy Bear Picnic, Historic Tales on Rails, Carnival Train.

Nearby Attractions: Summerland is an old English theme town with many local festivals. Giants Head Park, Summerland Ornamental Gardens, Summerland Museum, many campgrounds, and beautiful beaches.

Directions: Six kilometers off Highway 97, 45 kilometers south of Kelowna, 16 kilometers north of Penticton.

Site Address: 18404 Bathville Rd., Summerland, BC
Mailing Address: PO Box 1288, Summerland, BC Canada V0H 1Z0
Telephone: (250) 494-8422 and (877) 494-8424
Fax: (250) 494-8452
E-mail: kvr@telus.net
Website: www.kettlevalleyrail.org

British Columbia, Surrey

BEAR CREEK PARK TRAIN

Train ride
15" gauge

Description: A ⅝-mile, eight-minute ride into Bear Creek Park's forest and gardens, through a tunnel with displays that change every two months, and over a trestle.

Schedule: January through November 29, daily, 10 a.m. to sunset. November 29 through January 2, 10 a.m. to 10 p.m. for Christmas lights.

Admission/Fare: Adults, $2.50; seniors, $2; children, $1.75. Group discounts available.

Locomotives/Rolling Stock: 1967 Dutch-built steam engine based on Welsh mining design; 1988 Alan Keef diesel locomotive; covered British antique coaches, open touring coaches in summer.

Special Events: Easter Egg Treasure Hunt; Canada Day Exhibit; Halloween Festival, October 10-31, night rides 6 to 10 p.m.; Christmas Enchanted Forest, 10 a.m. to 10 p.m.

Nearby Attractions: Bear Creek Park is a 160-acre park with picnic facilities, art center, playground, water park, skate bowl, five-acre landscaped garden, walking trails, and sports fields.

Directions: Twelve miles from U.S. border via King George Highway (99A); 20 miles from downtown Vancouver via Highway 1.

Site Address: 13750 88th Ave., Surrey, BC
Mailing Address: 13750 88th Ave., Surrey, BC Canada V3W 3L1
Telephone: (604) 501-1658
Fax: (604) 507-2620
Website: www.bctrains.com

**GRANVILLE ISLAND MODEL
TRAIN MUSEUM**
Museum, layout

Description: A three-dimensional operational layout. The museum has thousands of model and toy trains by Lionel, Marx, Hornby, Dorfan, and American Flyer.

Schedule: Year-round, daily, 10 a.m. to 5:30 p.m.

Admission/Fare: (In Canadian) Adults, $6.50; seniors, $5; children, $3.50; family, $16.50.

Nearby Attractions: The museum is part of Granville Island Museums–Model Trains, Model Ships, and Sport Fishing. Granville Island is a tourist attraction with markets, crafts, plays, restaurants, etc.

Directions: Below the Granville Street Bridge in Vancouver.

Site Address: 1502 Duranleau St., Vancouver, BC
Mailing Address: 1502 Duranleau St., Granville Island, Vancouver, BC
Canada V6H 3S4
Telephone: (604) 683-1939
E-mail: staff@granvilleislandmuseums.com
Website: www.granvilleislandmuseums.com

British Columbia, Vancouver

PAUL PHIBBS

Description: A 3-kilometer ride along the south side of False Creek.

Schedule: Mid-May through mid-October, weekends and holidays, 12 to 5 p.m.

Admission/Fare: Adults, $2; seniors and children, $1. Charters, $150 per hour.

Locomotives/Rolling Stock: BCER interurban no. 1207 1905 all-wood passenger car; BCER interurban no. 1213 1913 steelside passenger car.

Nearby Attractions: Granville Island Public Market at west end of line. Science World (Omnimax theatre) at east end of line. VIA Rail/Amtrak station at east end of line, walking distance to Chinatown.

Directions: First Ave. and Ontario St., two blocks southwest of Skytrain's Main St. Station.

*Coupon available, see coupon section.

P 🚌 ✳ ✉ **M** 🚂 **VIA**

Site Address: 1601 Ontario St., Vancouver, BC
Mailing Address: TRAMS, 949 W. 41st Ave., Vancouver, BC Canada V52 2N5
Telephone: (604) 665-3903
E-mail: buses@telus.net
Website: www.trams.bc.ca

Manitoba, Winnipeg

WINNIPEG RAILWAY MUSEUM
Museum
Standard gauge

RON EINARSON

Description: A railway museum with a display of artifacts and rolling stock.

Schedule: Winter hours: Saturdays and Sundays, 12 to 4 p.m. Summer hours: Thursdays through Sundays, 11 a.m. to 5 p.m.

Admission/Fare: Adults 16 and over, $2; under 16 free when accompanied by adult.

Locomotives/Rolling Stock: CP Rail no. 1 steam engine "Countess of Dufferin"; CN 1900; CN steel caboose; Jordan spreader; baggage cars; combine car; CP wooden reefer cars; maintenance-of-way equipment; handcars; railbus; Packard inspection car; railway firetrucks, both CN and CP.

Special Events: Railway Days, September 7-8.

Nearby Attractions: The Forks National Historic Site, Goldeyes Baseball Diamond.

Directions: Inside the VIA Rail station, 123 Main St.

     M VIA

Site Address: 123 Main St., Winnipeg, MB
Mailing Address: 123 Main St., Winnipeg, MB Canada R3C 1H3
Telephone: (204) 942-4632
Fax: (204) 942-4632
Website: www.icentre.net/~prs

Newfoundland, Corner Brook

Description: One-hundred-year-old freight shed converted to a museum, containing historic artifacts and a display of locomotives and rail cars.

Schedule: June through August, 9 a.m. to 9 p.m.

Admission/Fare: $2 membership fee. Children under 17, free. Group rate, $20.

Locomotives/Rolling Stock: Baldwin steam locomotive no. 593 built in 1920; NF box baggage car no. 1598 built in 1954; steel baggage car no. 1900 built in 1943; steel passenger coach no. 758 built in 1949; steel diner coach no. 10 built in 1943; diesel locomotive no. 931 built in 1956; caboose no. 6072 built in 1956.

Nearby Attractions: Marbe Mountain Ski Lodge, Corner Brook Museum, Captain Cook site.

Directions: Intersection of Riverside Dr. and Station Rd.

      M

Site Address: Station Rd., Corner Brook, NF
Mailing Address: PO Box 673, Corner Brook, NF Canada A2H 6G1
Telephone: (709) 634-5658
Fax: (709) 686-2081

Description: The Northern Ontario Railroad Museum and Heritage Centre emphasizes railroading history in northern Ontario and the impact railroads had on mining and lumbering; also, early settlements in the area and how they came about because of the railroads.

Schedule: June 1 through August 31, 11 a.m. to 4 p.m., Tuesday through Sunday. From September to May, by appointment only.

Admission/Fare: Donation.

Locomotives/Rolling Stock: CN no. 6077 Mountain-type steam locomotive (4-8-2) built by MLC; velocipede; four-man handcar; gas car; wooden caboose no. 77562; rules instruction car no. 15019. A newly acquired exhibit includes two INCO electric locomotives (not yet on display); a wooden CN snowplow car; and a metal caboose.

Special Events: Garden tour with blueberry tea, July; Capreol Daze, August; Remembrance displays in November. Call or write for dates.

Nearby Attractions: Numerous lakes in area for fishing, camping, boating. Contact the City of Greater Sudbury Regional Development Corporation for information on tourism: (705) 671-CITY.

Directions: Located 40 kilometers (25 miles) northeast of Sudbury. Take Regional Road 80 from Sudbury, then Regional Road 84 to Capreol.

      M VIA

Site Address: 26 Bloor St., Capreol, ON, Canada
Mailing Address: PO Box 370, Capreol, ON Canada P0M 1H0
Telephone: (705) 858-5050
Fax: (705) 858-4539
E-mail: normhc@sympatico.ca
Website: www.3.sympatico.ca/normhc/

Ontario, Chatham

CHATHAM RAILROAD MUSEUM
Museum

GARY SHURGOLD

Description: The Chatham Railroad Museum is a retired Canadian National baggage car built in 1955 in Hamilton, Ontario.

Schedule: Mondays through Fridays, 9 a.m. to 4 p.m.; Saturdays, 11 a.m. to 4 p.m.

Admission/Fare: Free. Donations accepted.

Special Events: Annual Railway Fun Day with special presentations.

Nearby Attractions: Chathem-Kent Museum.

Directions: Located across from the Chatham Train Station.

     M

Site Address: 2 McLean St., Chatham, ON
Mailing Address: PO Box 434, Chatham, ON Canada N7M 5K5
Telephone: (519) 352-3097

CNR SCHOOL ON WHEELS 15089
Museum, display

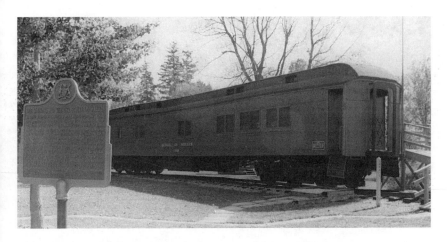

Description: This museum allows modern children and nostalgic seniors to visit one of the seven schools on wheels that taught children along the northern Ontario railways.

Schedule: May Victoria Day through Labor Day: Thursdays and Fridays, 2 to 5 p.m.; weekends and holidays, 1 to 5 p.m.

Admission/Fare: Free. Donations.

Locomotives/Rolling Stock: Canadian National 15089.

Nearby Attractions: Campgrounds, state parks, 10 minutes from Lake Huron.

Directions: Off Highway 4 near London, Ontario.

     VIA

Site Address: Victoria Terrace, Clinton, ON
Mailing Address: Box 488, Clinton, ON Canada N0M 1L0
Telephone: (519) 482-9583 (7 to 9 p.m.)

Ontario, Cochrane

COCHRANE RAILWAY AND PIONEER MUSEUM
Museum

Description: This museum preserves a three-dimensional picture of the pioneer railway and homesteading days as a tribute to men and women who opened northern Ontario, an empire bigger than the territories of many United Nations members. A model train display aboard a former Canadian National coach introduces the main railway exhibits, which include a telegraph operator's corner, a ticket office, a document display, an insulator collection and uniforms. There is also a large varied display of photographs. Many of the pictures are from the large collection assembled by the Rev. W. L. Lawrence around 1912, for which the museum is now trustee. Also, in Train "Tim" Horton Memorial Museum is a display of hockey artifacts.

Schedule: June 23 through September 3, daily, 8:30 a.m. to 8 p.m.

Admission/Fare: Adults, $2; seniors, $1; students/children, $1.50; families, $5. Group rates available.

Locomotives/Rolling Stock: No. 137 2-8-0, former Temiskaming & Northern Ontario.

Special Events: Museum Days, August.

Site Address: 210 Railway St., Cochrane, ON
Mailing Address: PO Box 490, Cochrane, ON Canada P0L 1C0
Telephone: (705) 272-4361
Fax: (705) 272-6068
E-mail: towncoch@puc.net
Website: www.town.cochrane.on.ca

ONTARIO NORTHLAND

Description: Summer excursion train to the edge of the Arctic, a 186-mile train ride operating between Cochrane and Moosonee, Ontario.

Schedule: Late June through Labor Day, daily except Fridays. Depart Cochrane 8:30 a.m., arrive Moosonee 12:50 p.m. Depart Moosonee 6:00 p.m., arrive Cochrane 10:05 p.m.

Admission/Fare: Adults, $58; seniors (60+), $53; students, $50; children 2-11, $29; under age 2 are free. Family plan available. All fares include GST.

Nearby Attractions: Gold Mine Tour, Hunta Museum, Shania Twain Centre.

Directions: Take Highway 11 north through North Bay past New Liskeard to Cochrane.

Site Address: 200 Railway St., Cochrane, ON
Mailing Address: 555 Oak St. E., North Bay, ON Canada P1B 8L3
Telephone: (800) 268-9281
Fax: (705) 495-4745
E-mail: choochoo@polarbearexpress.ca
Website: www.polarbearexpress.ca

Ontario, Fort Erie

FORT ERIE RAILROAD MUSEUM
Museum, display

Description: This museum displays railroad-related exhibits in two train stations, one built in 1910 and another built in 1873; also on display are maintenance-of-way equipment, a steam engine, a caboose, and a fireless engine.

Schedule: Victoria Day (May 19, 2003) through Labor Day: daily, 9 a.m. to 5 p.m. Labor Day through Thanksgiving (October 8, 2003): weekends, 9 a.m. to 5 p.m.

Admission/Fare: Adults, $2; children under age 13, $.50.

Locomotives/Rolling Stock: No. 6218, former Canadian National 4-8-4; Porter fireless locomotive.

Nearby Attractions: Niagara Falls, Fort Erie Historical Museum, Battlefield Museum, Historic Fort Erie, Mahoney Dolls House, Willoughby Museum.

Directions: On Central Ave. between Gilmore Rd. and Wintemute, northwest of the west end of the Peace Bridge.

Site Address: Central Ave. and Oakes Park, Fort Erie, ON
Mailing Address: PO Box 339, Ridgeway, ON Canada L0S 1N0
Telephone: (905) 894-5322
Fax: (905) 894-6851

Ontario, Guelph

CRAIG WEBB

Description: CN and CP passenger and freight trains pass constantly through the countryside, freight switching takes place, locos are turned on turntables. There is a ten-minute night scene with the lights dimmed.

Schedule: First two weekends in May, also three weekends in October following Canadian Thanksgiving (U.S. Columbus Day). Other openings by arrangement for groups (three weeks notice is requested).

Admission/Fare: Adults: $6; seniors and students, $3; children, $2 (all Canadian dollars).

Locomotives/Rolling Stock: Fourteen CN steam models; 16 CN diesel-electric models; 6 CP steam models; 15 CP diesel-electric models; 35 CN passenger cars; 23 CP passenger cars; 253 freight cars.

Nearby Attractions: Nearby flea market on summer Sundays, many attractions in Guelph, a 20-minute drive away.

Directions: Take Highway 401 to exit 299. Drive north on Brock Rd. about 2 miles. We are in a metal building on the east side of Brock Rd.

*Coupon available, see coupon section.

      VIA

Mailing Address: c/o F. Dubery, 53 Rhonda Rd., Guelph, ON Canada N1H 6H1

Ontario, Huntsville

**MUSKOKA HERITAGE PLACE
STEAM TRAIN**
Train ride, museum
42" gauge

Description: A one-kilometer train ride along the Muskoka River behind a fully restored steam locomotive.

Schedule: Mid-May to mid-October, Tuesdays through Saturdays.

Admission/Fare: Adult, $5; children, $3; under 3 free.

Nearby Attractions: Algonquin Park.

Directions: Two hours north of Toronto, just one kilometer from historic downtown Huntsville.

          VIA

Site Address: 88 Brunel Rd., Huntsville, ON
Mailing Address: 88 Brunel Rd., Huntsville, ON Canada P1H 1R1
Telephone: (705) 789-7576
Fax: (705) 789-6169
E-mail: manager@muskokaheritageplace.org
Website: www.muskokaheritageplace.org

Ontario, Komoka

KOMOKA RAILWAY MUSEUM
Museum

PIERRE OZORAK

Description: Relive railroad history at this restored railroad station, letting your imagination run down the tracks as you examine early railway equipment. Take a few minutes to relax in air-conditioned comfort while watching multi-media presentations like "Workin on the Railroad."

Schedule: June through August: Friday, Saturday, Sunday, Monday, 9 a.m. to 5 p.m.

Admission/Fare: Adults, $3; seniors/teens, $2; elementary students, $1. Group tours booked in advance, $2 each.

Locomotives/Rolling Stock: 1913 Shay logging locomotive; 1939 CN baggage car no. 8731; 1972 GTW caboose no. 79198; collection of CN maintenance jiggers (speeders).

Nearby Attractions: Oriole Park Campground, Delaware Speedway, Little Beaver Restaurant, Komoka Provincial Park, Belamere Farm Market and Winery.

Directions: Eight miles west of London on Glendon/Commissioners Rd.

       M arm VIA

Site Address: 133 Queen St., Komoka, ON
Mailing Address: PO Box 22, Komoka, ON Canada N0L 1R0
Telephone: (519) 657-1912
Fax: (519) 657-6791
E-mail: railmus@komokarail.ca
Website: www.komokarail.ca

Ontario, Milton

HALTON COUNTY RADIAL RAILWAY
Museum
4'10⅞" gauge

J.D. KNOWLES

Description: Come and ride a variety of streetcars and radial cars on a 2-mile scenic trip through rural forested right-of-way.

Schedule: May, June, September, and October, weekends and holidays. July and August, daily.

Admission/Fare: Adults, $7.50; seniors, $6.50; youth, $5.50; 3 and under free.

Locomotives/Rolling Stock: Open car no. 327; Peter Witt no. 2424; London & Port Stanley interurban no. 8; Montreal & Southern Counties no. 107; PCC no. 4600; maintenance equipment.

Special Events: Wildflower weekend; Canadian Heritage Streetcar Day, July 1; Ice Cream and Starlight, Saturdays in August; Santa Special, December.

Nearby Attractions: Conservation areas, Mohawk Race Track, Halton Region Museum, golf courses, Canadian Warplane Museum.

Directions: Highway 401 to exit 312 (Guelph Line), north for 9 miles, or Highway 7 to Guelph Line, south for 3 miles.

Site Address: 13629 Guelph Line, Milton, ON
Mailing Address: PO Box 578, Milton, ON Canada L9T 5A2
Telephone: (519) 856-9802
Fax: (519) 856-1399
E-mail: streetcar@hcry.org
Website: www.hcry.org

Description: This museum features all types of transportation, from Canada's earliest days to the present time. On display in the Steam Locomotives Hall are four huge steam locomotives, a CNR narrow gauge passenger car from Newfoundland, and a caboose. The visitors have access to two of the cabs, where sound effects give the feeling of live locomotives. The engines are meticulously restored, with polished rods and lighted number boards and class lights.

Schedule: Museum–May 1 to Labor Day: daily, 9 a.m. to 5 p.m. Labor Day through April: Tuesdays through Sundays, 9 a.m. to 5 p.m. Closed Mondays and Christmas Day. Free train ride with admission–July through August: Wednesdays and Sundays.

Admission/Fare: Adults, $6; seniors and students, $5; children 6-14, $3; children under age 4 are free; family of 2 adults/3 children, $14. Group rates available.

Locomotives/Rolling Stock: 1923 Shay steam locomotive; CN6400 4-8-4 Montreal 1936; CP926 4-6-0 1912; CP2858 4-6-4 Royal Hudson, Montreal 1938; CP3100 4-8-4 Montreal 1928; CNR business car "Terra Nova"; CNR 76109 caboose.

Directions: Located ten minutes from downtown Ottawa. Queensway (Highway 417) exit St. Laurent south for 2.6 kilometers, left at Lancaster Rd. (at the lighthouse).

Site Address: 1867 St. Laurent Blvd., Ottawa, ON
Mailing Address: PO Box 9724, Stn. T, Ottawa, ON Canada K1G 5A3
Telephone: (613) 991-3044
Fax: (613) 993-7923
E-mail: cts@nmstc.ca
Website: www.science-tech.nmstc.ca

AL HOWLETT

Description: From the station in Port Stanley, on the harbor next to the lift bridge. Trains run northward for up to 7 miles through the Kettle Creek Valley. Port Stanley is a commercial fishing village on the north shore of Lake Erie. Equipment includes cabooses, heavyweight coaches, open coaches, baggage cars, boxcars, flatcars, hopper cars, a snowplow, tank cars, and more. Ticket office and displays are in the former London & Port Stanley station. Open excursion cars; cabooses, former Canadian National, modified into enclosed coaches; standard coaches, former VIA. The "Little Red Caboose" can be chartered for birthday parties and other events with advance reservation.

Schedule: April through November, weekends; July through August, daily.

Admission/Fare: Adults, $9.50; children 2-12, $5.

Locomotives/Rolling Stock: GE 25- and 44-ton and converted cabooses.

Special Events: Easter, Santa, and Entertainment Trains.

Nearby Attractions: St. Thomas Elgin Railroad Museum.

Directions: Located on the north side of Lake Erie, 25 miles (50 kilometers) south of London, Ontario, on old Highway 4.

Radio frequency: 160.575

Site Address: 309 Bridge St., Port Stanley, ON
Mailing Address: 309 Bridge St., Port Stanley, ON Canada N5L 1C5
Telephone: (519) 782-3730
Fax: (519) 782-4385
Website: www.pstr.on.ca/

ELGIN COUNTY RAILWAY MUSEUM
Museum, display, layout
Standard gauge

Description: Ongoing restoration and display of engines, rolling stock, and artifacts, and model train layout.

Schedule: All summer, daily, 10 a.m. to 4 p.m. Remainder of year, Mondays, Wednesdays, and Saturdays, if staff is available.

Admission/Fare: By donation.

Locomotives/Rolling Stock: CN no. 5700 4-6-4 Montreal Locomotive Works 1930; Wabash no. 51 "Tillie" 43-ton GE 1939; London & Port Stanley Railway no. 14 electric coach, Jewett, 1917; L&PS electric freight locomotive, GE 1915; CP no. 8921 RSD-17 (the only known RSD-17 ever built) Montreal Locomotive Works 1957; more.

Special Events: Nostalgia Days, first weekend in May; Heritage Days, last weekend in August.

Nearby Attractions: Elgin Pioneer Museum, statue of "Jumbo," elephant killed by a train in St. Thomas; Elgin Military Museum; village of Port Stanley to south; city of London to the north.

Directions: From Highways 401 or 402, south on Highway 4, Wellington Rd. or Highbury Ave.

Site Address: 255 Wellington St., St. Thomas, ON
Mailing Address: PO Box 20062, St. Thomas, ON Canada N5P 4H4
Telephone: (519) 637-6284
Fax: (519) 631-0662
E-mail:thedispatcher@ecrm5700.org or tours@ecrm5700.org (for tours)
Website: www.ecrm5700.org

Ontario, Sault Ste. Marie

ALGOMA CENTRAL RAILWAY INC.
Train ride
Standard gauge

ELMER KARS/ACRI

Description: We operate both tour trains and regular passenger service. Tour trains take you on a one-day wilderness excursion to Agawa Canyon Park. Regular passenger train provides service to Hearst, Ontario, as well as access to a variety of wilderness lodges. Private car and camp car rentals are available.

Schedule: Passenger service train–year-round. Agawa Canyon train–June through mid-October: daily. Snow train–January through mid-March: weekends. Group rentals available.

Admission/Fare: Varies, call for information.

Locomotives/Rolling Stock: CN Rail GP40s; SD50s; refurbished 1950s VIA coaches.

Nearby Attractions: Depot is located downtown close to hotels, restaurants, shopping.

Directions: Located in downtown Sault Ste. Marie, minutes from International Bridge.

Site Address: 129 Bay St., Sault Ste. Marie, ON
Mailing Address: PO Box 130, Sault Ste. Marie, ON Canada P6A 6Y2
Telephone: (705) 946-7300 and (800) 242-9287
Fax: (705) 541-2989
E-mail: kelly.booth@cn.ca
Website: www.agawacanyontourtrain.com and www.algomacentralrailway.com

Ontario, Smiths Falls   **SMITHS FALLS RAILWAY MUSEUM**
Museum

Description: Smiths Falls Railway Museum of Eastern Ontario is a restored Canadian Northern Railway Station/National Historic Site. We offer exhibitions, heritage vehicle rides, special events, and a children's area.

Schedule: July and August, daily, 10 a.m. to 4 p.m. Check website for May, September, and October schedule. Open year-round by appointment for groups.

Admission/Fare: Adults, $4; seniors over 65, $3; students 12 and up, $2.50; children 6-11, $1; children under 6, free.

Locomotives/Rolling Stock: Canadian northern no. 1112, 4-6-0; CPR S-3 no. 6591, railway dental car; CP Cadillac inspection car; two Wickham track inspection vehicles; boxcars; cabooses; velocipede; handcars.

Special Events: Check website for up-to-date schedule.

Nearby Attractions: Heritage House Museum, Rideau Canal and Rideau Canal Museum, Hershey's Canada plant.

Directions: One hour from Ottawa, one hour from Ogdensburg, New York, three hours from Montreal.

      M arm VIA

Site Address: 90 William St. W., Smiths Falls, ON
Mailing Address: PO Box 962, Smiths Falls, ON Canada K7A 5A5
Telephone: (613) 283-5696
Fax: (613) 283-7211
E-mail: sfrm@superaje.com
Website: www.magma.ca/~sfrm/

YORK DURHAM
HERITAGE RAILWAY
Train ride
Standard gauge

JOHN SKINNER, EAGLE VISION PHOTOGRAPHY

Description: Twelve-mile train ride through the beautiful rural area between the towns of Uxbridge and Stouffville.

Schedule: Call or write for information.

Admission/Fare: Adults, $17; seniors, $13; students 12-18, $13; children 4-12, $9; under age 4 and over age 90 are free.

Locomotives/Rolling Stock: No. 3612 Also RS-11; no. 1310 Alco RS-3; nos. 3209 and 3232 cafe cars, former VIA; 1920s heavyweights 4960 and 4977; former rules instruction car; caboose; flatcar.

Special Events: Mother's Day, Christmas in July, Father's Day, Teddy Bear Day, Halloween Spook Trains, Christmas Trip (weather permitting). Call or write for dates.

Nearby Attractions: Sales Barn. Uxbridge–Uxbridge Scott Museum, Lucy Maude Montgomery Home, restaurants, gift shops.

Directions: Thirty minutes northeast of Toronto, Ontario. Take Highway 404 to the Bloomington Sideroad, go east on the Bloomington Sideroad, which becomes Highway 47 into Uxbridge.

Site Address: Railway St., Uxbridge, ON
Mailing Address: PO Box 462, Stouffville, ON Canada L4A 7Z7
Telephone: (905) 852-3696
E-mail: lbhill@interhop.net
Website: www.ydhr.on.ca

Ontario, Tottenham

SOUTH SIMCOE RAILWAY
Train ride
Standard gauge

Description: Enjoy a scenic journey through the Beeton Creek Valley aboard South Simcoe Railway's vintage steam train. Excursions last just under an hour and are highlighted by the friendly and informative commentary of the conductor. It's a unique trip into the past the whole family will enjoy!

Schedule: May 18 through October 13: Sundays and holiday Mondays. Departs 10 and 11:30 a.m., 1, 2:30, and 4 p.m. Other special excursions operate through the year. Call or visit our website for full schedule.

Admission/Fare: Adults, $10; seniors, $9; children, $6.50 (taxes included in fares).

Locomotives/Rolling Stock: Rogers Locomotive Works 4-4-0 no. 136 (built 1883); Montreal Locomotive Works 4-6-0 no. 1057 (built 1912); vintage open-window day coaches dating from the 1920s.

Nearby Attractions: Nearby family attractions include the Falconry Centre, Puck's Farm, Gould's Apple Orchard, and a large Conservation Park with swimming and picnic pavilions. Nearby restaurants and camping.

Directions: From Highway 400, take Highway 9 west 20 kilometers to traffic lights at Tottenham Rd. and turn north. Turn left at first traffic lights in Tottenham, follow signs to free parking. Driving time from Toronto is approximately 50 minutes.

Site Address: Mill St. W., Tottenham, ON
Mailing Address: PO Box 186, Tottenham, ON Canada L0G 1W0
Telephone: (905) 936-5815
Fax: (905) 936-1057
Website: www.steamtrain.com

Quebec, Hull

HULL-CHELSEA-WAKEFIELD STEAM TRAIN
Train ride, dinner train
Standard gauge

G. BURBIDGE

Description: Scenic steam train tour through western Quebec's picturesque Gatineau Hills. The award-winning dinner train features exquisite French cuisine.

Schedule: May 10 to October 26; various departure times.

Admission/Fare: From $19 (children) to $45 (adults). Dinner train is from $89 (regular class) to $129 (first class).

Locomotives/Rolling Stock: 1907 Swedish locomotive class 2-8-0 no. 909; 1962 European GM diesel no. 244; eight passenger cars, 1940; one first-class luxury dinner/parlour car (1940), Swedish built by SJ (Swedish national railway).

Nearby Attractions: Minutes from Canada's capital city, Ottawa. Parliament buildings, Canadian Museum of Civilization, five other major national museums, casino.

Directions: Located at 165 Devreault St., ten minutes from downtown Ottawa, and 1 mile from Casino Lac Leamy.

Site Address: 165 Deveault St., Hull, QC
Mailing Address: 165 Deveault St., Hull, QC Canada J8Z 1S7
Telephone: (800) 871-7246
Fax: (819) 778-5007
E-mail: info@steamtrain.ca
Website: www.steamtrain.ca

Quebec, Saint-Constant

CANADIAN RAILWAY MUSEUM
Train ride, museum
Standard gauge

KEVIN ROBINSON

Description: Canada's finest collection of railway equipment, with more than 152 vehicles. Take a ride on our vintage streetcar and our miniature railway.

Schedule: May 2003, opening of the new pavillion, Exporail. From May to Labor Day: daily, 10 a.m. to 5 p.m. September to March 31: Wednesday to Sunday, 9 a.m. to 5 p.m.

Admission/Fare: $6-$12 (Canadian).

Directions: We are south of Montreal. Take Highway 15 south and Route 132 west in the direction of Chateauguay, then Route 209 south.

Site Address: 1110 St. Pierre St., St. Constant, QC
Mailing Address: 1110 St. Pierre St., St. Constant, QC Canada J5A 1G7
Telephone: (450) 632-2410
Fax: (450) 638-1563
E-mail: mfcd@exporail.org
Website: www.exporail.org

Quebec, Vallee-Jonction

TRAINS TOURISTIQUES DE CHAUDIERE-APPALACHES
Train ride, museum
Standard gauge

MARTIN LAFLAMME

Description: Enjoy French Canadian hospitality on our scenic excursions in the Chaudiere Valley. Bilingual guides and musicians entertain guests on trips lasting 1½ to 5 hours. Our museum on the Quebec Central Railway is in a heritage station built in 1917.

Schedule: April to June 24, weekends. June 24 to Labor Day, six days a week. September to November, weekends, some weekdays. Call for details.

Admission/Fare: Regular adult fares vary, depending on length of trip, from $17.95 to 35.95 (taxes included). Rebates for children; age 5 and under are free. Prices are subject to change.

Locomotives/Rolling Stock: TTCA power car no. 616; TTCA Pullman coach nos. 2722, 2709, 2841. On display–CNR 4-6-4T no. 46; caboose no. 434065 (ex-CPR).

Special Events: All-day excursions to Sherbrooke and Lac-Frontiere, spring and fall; Sugar Bush specials, April; Fall Foliage; Santa Claus Train in November.

Nearby Attractions: Historical Quebec City; Frontenac Provincial Park; Cabanc a Pierre, traditional maple sugar camp; Cache a Maxime winery.

Directions: Thirty minutes south of Quebec Bridge (and junction with Trans Canada Highway 20) on Highway 73 south, exit 81, Vallee-Jonction.

*Coupon available, see coupon section.

       M

Site Address: 399 boul. Rousseau, Vallee-Jonction, QC Canada
Mailing Address: 399 boul. Rousseau, Vallee-Jonction, QC Canada G0S 3J0
Telephone: (877) 642-5580 (toll-free)
Fax: (418) 253-5585
E-mail: francoiscliche@videotron.ca
Website: http://beaucerail.iquebec.com

RUSTY RELICS MUSEUM
Museum

Description: A museum housed in a 1910 CNR station containing early CNR and CPR artifacts. A Canadian Pacific Railway caboose is out front.

Schedule: June through Labor Day, Monday through Saturday, 9 a.m. to 5 p.m.; Sunday, 1 to 5 p.m.

Admission/Fare: Adults, $2; children, $1; preschool children free.

Nearby Attractions: Kenosee Lake Provincial Park Waterslides.

Directions: At the junction of Highways 9 and 13, approximately 40 miles north of the U.S. border and 40 miles west of the Manitoba border.

Site Address: 306 Railway Ave. W., Carlyle, SK
Mailing Address: PO Box 840, Carlyle, SK Canada S0C 0R0
Telephone: (306) 453-2266
Fax: (306) 453-2812
E-mail: mwhume@sk.sympatico.ca

Saskatchewan, Moose Jaw   **WESTERN DEVELOPMENT MUSEUM**
Museum

Description: A museum of transportation with displays in air, water, land, and rail galleries.

Schedule: Daily, 9 a.m. to 6 p.m. Closed Mondays, January through March.

Admission/Fare: Adults, $6; seniors, $5; students, $4; children $2; preschool children are free. Family (two guardians and dependent children under 18), $14.

Locomotives/Rolling Stock: Vulcan 0-4-0 no. 2265; DS-6F no. 6555; G20 no. 2634; combination no. 3321; CPR coach no. 95; CPR caboose no. 6139; 1934 inspector's Buick M-499.

Special Events: May long weekend through Labor Day: weekends and holidays, weather permitting, shortline railway 1914 Vulcan runs on museum grounds.

Nearby Attractions: Museums, historic sites, camping, mineral spa, variety of cultural and sporting events.

Directions: Junction of Highways 1 and 2.

*Coupon available, see coupon section.

Site Address: 50 Diefenbaker Dr., Moose Jaw, SK
Mailing Address: 50 Diefenbaker Dr., Moose Jaw, SK Canada S6J 1L9
Telephone: (306) 693-5989
Fax: (306) 691-0511
E-mail: wdm.mj–wdm@sasktel.net
Website: www.wdm.ca

SASKATCHEWAN RAILWAY MUSEUM
Museum
Standard gauge

CAL SEXSMITH

Description: Museum with static displays and ½-mile motor car rides.

Schedule: Victoria Day weekend (late May) to June 30, Saturdays, Sundays, and holidays. July and August, daily. September, weekends. 1 p.m. to 6 p.m.

Admission/Fare: Adults, $3; children over 6, $2; prices are subject to change.

Locomotives/Rolling Stock: CP S-3 no. 6568; Saskatchewan Power GE 33-ton; 18 pieces rolling stock, ten historic railway buildings.

Nearby Attractions: Western Development Museum, Pike Lake Provincial Park, Meewasin Valley Cenre, Wanuskewin Heritage Park.

Directions: West on 22nd St. to Highway 7. West on Highway 7 to Highway 60, then 2 kilometers south on Highway 60 at CNR crossing.

       M VIA

Site Address: Highway 60 South Saskatoon, SK
Mailing Address: Box 19, Site 302, RR 3, Saskatoon, SK Canada S7K 3J6
Telephone: (306) 382-9855
E-mail: saskrailmuseum@canada.com
Website: www.geocities.com/saskrailmuseum/

Yukon Territory, Dawson City

**DAWSON CITY MUSEUM AND
HISTORICAL SOCIETY**
Display
Narrow gauge

GREG SKUCE

Description: Three Klondike Mines Railway locomotives: no. 1 Brooks
2-6-0, built 1881; no. 2 Baldwin 2-8-0, built 1885; no. 3 Baldwin 2-8-0
Vauclain Compound, built 1899. Also Detroit Yukon Mining Co. Porter
0-4-0T, built 1904.

Schedule: Mid-May to mid-September, weekends, 10 a.m. to 2 p.m.
Otherwise by appointment.

Admission/Fare: Adults, $7; seniors and students, $5; families, $16. Pre-
booked tours, $5 each (includes museum admission).

Nearby Attractions: Old territorial administration building, a National
Historic Site of Canada; also several other National Historic Sites.

Directions: North on Klondike Highway 2. From Whitehorse, turn right on
Fifth Ave. The museum is three blocks north.

Site Address: 595 Fifth Ave., Dawson City, Yukon
Mailing Address: PO Box 303, Dawson City, YT Canada Y0B 1G0
Telephone: (867) 993-5291
Fax: (867) 993-5839
E-mail: dcmuseum@yknet.yk.ca

Other Tourist Trains

These are additional sites that may be of interest to you. We are unable to provide complete information, so be sure to write or call for details.

Alaska, Wasilla
Museum of Alaska Transportation & Industry
PO Box 870646, Wasilla, AK 99687
(907) 376-1211

California, Anaheim
Disneyland Railroad
PO Box 3232, Anaheim, CA 92803
(714) 781-4000

California, Napa
Napa Valley Wine Train
1275 McKinstry St., Napa, CA 94559
(800) 427-4124

California, Toluca Lake
Los Angeles Live Steamers
PO Box 2156, Toluca Lake, CA 91610
(323) 669-9729

California, San Francisco
San Francisco Cable Car Museum
1201 Mason St., San Francisco, CA 94108
(415) 474-1887

California, Fremont
Society for the Preservation of Carter Railroad Resources
PO Box 783, Newark, CA 94560
(510) 797-9557

Colorado, Limon
Limon Heritage Museum & Railroad Park
899 First St, PO Box 341, Limon, CO 80828
(719) 775-2373

D.C., Washington
Smithsonian Institution, National Museum of American History
Room 5004, MRC 628, PO Box 37012, Washington, DC 20013-7012
(202) 357-2700

Florida, Parrish
Florida Gulf Coast Railroad Museum
PO Box 355, Parrish, FL 34219
(941) 776-0906

Florida, Tampa
Tampa Heritage Streetcar System, c/o Tampa Tank, 5205 Adano Dr., Tampa, FL 33619-3251
(813) 623-2675, ext. 49

Georgia, Stone Mountain
Stone Mountain Scenic Railroad
PO Box 778, Stone Mountain, GA 30086
(770) 498-5600 and (770) 498-5616

Idaho, Athol
Silverwood Central Railway/Theme Park
N 26225 Hwy 95, Athol, ID 83801
(208) 683-3400

Ilinois, Mendota
Union Depot Railroad Museum
783 Main St., PO Box 433, Mendota, IL 61353
(815) 627-9027

Indiana, Corydon
Corydon Scenic Railroad
210 W. Walnut St., PO Box 10, Corydon, IN 47112
(812) 738-8000

Kentucky, Covington
Railway Museum of Greater Cincinnati
PO Box 15065, Covington, KY 41015
(859) 491-7245

Maine, Unity
Belfast & Moosehead Lake Railroad
1 Depot Square, PO Box 555., Unity, ME 04988
(800) 392-5500

Maryland, Walkersville
Walkersville Southern Railroad
34 W. Pennsylvania Ave., PO Box 651, Walkersville, MD 21793-0651
(877) 363-WSRR

Michigan, Manistee
Society for Preservation of the SS City of Milwaukee
115 US Highway 31, Beulah, MI 49617
(231) 398-0328

Michigan, Niles
Niles Railroad Historical Association
PO Box 35, Niles, MI 49120
(616) 641-5785

Michigan, White Pigeon
Little River Railroad
13187 State Route 120, Middlebury, IN 46540
(219) 825-9182

Missouri, Springfield
Frisco Railroad Museum Inc.
543 E Commercial St., Springfield, MO 65803-2945
417-866-7573

New Jersey, Flemington
Black River & Western Railroad
PO Box 200, Ringoes, NJ 08551
(908) 782-6622

New York, Cooperstown
Cooperstown & Charlotte Valley Railroad
P.O. Box 681, Oneonta, NY 13820
(607) 432-2429

New York, Brooklyn
New York Transit Museum
130 Livingston St., 9th Floor, Box E, Brooklyn,
NY 11201
(718) 243-8601

New York, Owego
Tioga Scenic Railroad
25 Delphine St., Owego, NY 13827
(607) 687-6786

Ohio, Cuyahoga Falls
Lorain & West Virginia Railway
PO Box 382, Cuyahoga Falls, OH 44222
(800) 334-1673 and (440) 323-9700

Ohio, Chippewa Lake
Northern Ohio Railway Museum
PO Box 458, Chippewa Lake, OH 44215-0109

Oklahoma, Choctaw
Choctaw Caboose Museum
2701 N Triple X Rd., Choctaw, OK 73020
(405) 390-2771

Oklahoma, Walters
Rock Island Depot Railroad Museum
PO Box 364, Walters, OK 73572
(580) 875-2384

Oklahoma, Tulsa
Sunbelt Railroad Museum
PO Box 470311, Tulsa, OK 74147-0311
(918) 584-3777

Pennsylvania, Altoona
Horseshoe Curve National Historic Landmark
1300 Ninth Ave., Altoona, PA 16602
(814) 946-0834 and (888) 425-8666

Pennsylvania, Gallitzin
Tunnels Park Caboose/Museum
411 Convent St, Ste. 20, Gallitzin, PA 16641-1295
(818) 886-8871

South Carolina, Charleston
Best Friend Museum
375 Meeting St., Charleston, SC 29403
(843) 724-7174

Tennessee, Shelbyville
Walking Horse & Eastern Railroad
PO Box 1317, Shelbyville, TN 37160
(800) 695-8995

Texas, Cedar Park
Austin & Texas Central Railroad
PO Box 1632, Austin, TX 78767
(512) 477-8468

Texas, Galveston
Galveston Railroad Museum
123 Rosenberg Ave., Galveston, TX 77550
(409) 765-5700

Texas, Grapevine
Tarantula Excursion Train
831 N. Pontiac Trl., Lot 12., Walled Lake, MI 48390
(817) 625-7245

Texas, Houston
Cherokee County & Rusk Narrow Gauge Railroad
1006 Crossroads Dr, Houston, TX 77079
(713) 467-8197

Vermont, Shelburne
Shelburne Museum
PO Box 10, Shelburne, VT 05482
(802) 985-3346

Vermont, Middlebury
Vermont Rail Excursions
PO Box 243, Middlebury, VT 05753
(802) 388-0193

Washington, Chehalis
Chehalis & Centralia Railroad Association
1945 S Market Blvd., Chehalis, WA 98532
(360) 748-9593

Washington, Wickersham
Lake Whatcom Railway
PO Box 91, Acme, WA 98220
(360) 595-2218

West Virginia, Summersville
Elk River Railroad
PO Box 460, Summersville, WV 26651
(304) 872-2224

Wisconsin, Spooner
Wisconsin Great Northern Railroad
PO Box 46, Spooner, WI 54801
(888) 390-0412 and (715) 635-3200

Wyoming, Cheyenne
Union Pacific Railroad
1800 Westland Rd, Cheyenne, WY 82001-3339
(307) 778-3214

Manitoba, Winnipeg
Prairie Dog Central
RPO Polo Park, PO Box 33021, Winnipeg, MB
Canada R3G 3N4
(204) 832-5259

Index